PRAYING THE SEASONS

A TREASURY OF PRAYERS
for
Corporate Worship
Private Meditation
and
Community Gatherings

Sylvia Casberg

Sunny Fields Publishing

PO Box 546, Solvang, CA 93464-0546

Book design by Sylvia Casberg

First edition

ISBN 978-0-9827781-2-8

DEDICATION

To my parents, Melvin and Olivia (Van Valin) Casberg

and my grandparents,
Samuel and Jessie (Lively) Casberg
William and Ethyl (Barnhart) Van Valin

and
to all the women, men and children
who pray in their homes, churches and communities

~

TABLE OF CONTENTS

Prayers have no shelf life.
Once prayed, they swirl throughout the heavens,
touching and retouching the spheres
with the depths of human honesty,
forever.

ACKNOWLEDGEMENTS

Thank you to everyone who actually listens to prayers, who doesn't tune out and think about Sunday afternoon sports or what to fix for lunch. Thank you to those who pray.

I am deeply grateful to my family for believing prayer is an integral part of daily life. We prayed at meals, at bedtime, before leaving on family vacations and every occasion that warranted checking in with God. Sometimes we prayed just because we felt like it. We didn't need a reason. A sunny day or starry night quickened us to words of thanksgiving.

Thank you to my copy editors, Pauline Nelson and Susan Dempsay. They caught what Spell Check missed.

And to all my parishioners, you encouraged me to pray without ceasing.

Sylvia Casberg

THOUGHTS FROM THE AUTHOR

My early childhood was played in the jungle village of Bihar, India. We Casbergs were a three-generation family, Grandma and Grandpa, Mother and Dad, my brother, Buddy, and I. We were missionaries sent by the Free Methodist Church to serve the bodies and souls of the indigenous people.

Grandpa built the church, the hospital, two bungalows and various outbuildings. Grandma taught literacy and the Bible. My dad staffed the hospital and Mother home schooled Buddy and me.

I don't know when I started talking to God; actually I can't remember when I didn't. I thought everyone did.

When it rained, I'd find a place to sit on the veranda, a place alone and close enough to the screen so I could feel drops splashing on my face. I decided God was touching me, baptizing me, answering me. At night in the dark, I felt especially surrounded by heavenly mystery and sat long periods of time just feeling.

Back in the States, geography and WWII separated our family. I continued to pray, especially when Dad was overseas in the Army. I made a little altar in my bedroom with a beautiful, pink seashell that had a light inside. Here I would pray for Dad.

I began writing poetry and sending it to Grandma. She
corrected my mistakes with red pencil and urged me to do my
very, very best, not just so-so. The red pencil would have
bothered someone with less spirit. But I was high-spirited, made
the corrections, and kept writing.

I began mixing prayers with poetry and searching for the
most descriptive words, the most beautiful phrases for God's
ears. There were many short prayers, prayed with shouts of,
"Help!" But for the most part I wanted to offer God the most
beautiful prayers I could.

Years later, I entered San Francisco Theological Seminary as
a second career student. I graduated and took my first call as
Associate Pastor at Wellshire Presbyterian Church in Denver,
CO. I discovered associate pastors do more praying than
preaching. My nose was a little out of joint because I like
preaching, but I realized praying is what I do.

And I did. I prayed in church worship, in meetings, on
capitol steps, in soup kitchens, with the dying, the retiring, the
marrying and the divorcing. I prayed at baptisms, graduations,
picnics, Rotary and Eagle Scout ceremonies. You name the
occasion; I found words for prayer.

So it has been these last thirty years. Parishioners have asked
me to publish my prayers. I promised I would. And so, for those
people in Colorado, in Moscow, Russia, in California and places
in-between, I keep that promise.

To my readers I offer this. It's impossible to plagiarize
prayers, because once offered to God, they belong to everyone.
Please use these prayers, either as they are, or personalized with
your own words. Feel free. Be my guest. Pray.

Someday I hope to walk into worship somewhere I've never been, and hear a strange voice pray words that sound familiar.

Sylvia Casberg
Solvang, CA
2011

There are still days I wish Grandma were here to help me with her red pencil.

THE SEASONS

WINTER

Light and darkness

We pray for the light of Christ to enter our dark lives,
    for the joy of Christmas love to flood the shadows
        of sleepless nights.
In the ordinary days of work and play and study and rest,
    we yearn for the extraordinary moments that make memories
        for the scrapbooks in our hearts.
Thank you for the gathering of loved ones,
    for faces missed and eagerly kissed,
        for tastes remembered, and music never to be forgotten,
           for smells long in the hunger of our memories,
             and new babes to touch.

We pray for those who remember faces now gone.
    May they know how joyfully Christ welcomes them to his
        birthday party in heaven.
We pray for those who suffer physically and mentally.
    May they feel the comfort of this babe,
        the great physician yet to be.

Thank you for the abundance of your love never withheld,
        always generous,
    for your overflowing grace enfolding us at our worst
        and calling us to our best.
Thank you for lighting up our lives,
    giving us angels to sing and shepherds to rejoice,
        hearts to be filled and friends to stand with us,
           for surprising us with your brilliance
             in the darkest of times. Amen

A little Advent prayer

Come to us in the silent nights of quiet pondering.
Come to us in the busy mornings of hurry up sounds.
Grant us rest of spirit,
Good company among your family,
Good news within your holy word.
May our spirits pause during these next few weeks,
so we might gather at the manger,
refreshed, smiling, full of joy! Amen.

Christmas music

Christmas child, thank you for music filling the air,
for the crescendo of anticipation each Advent,
for favorite carols, favorite faces, favorite memories.
We're deeply grateful for our church family,
those who see us through the worst,
and help us celebrate the best.
Thank you for children's voices blending with their parents',
for the harmony of grandparents and friends,
all joining a chorus singing through the generations
of a manger and a child.

We pray for those who sing in a minor key,
those with lumps in their throats and tears on their cheeks,
who have empty places in their hearts and at their tables.
We pray God's comfort for those who know sorrow, suffer loss,
Who met grief since last they sang of the Christmas child.
Give to them whispers of hope and the echo of alleluias.

We pray the presence of God for those who have lost
    the warmth of intimacy,
        and gained the cold of distance.
           Leave them not alone.

May each of us be sensitive to the silence of some
    when laughter and merriment cause them to pause
        and cast down their eyes.
May we reach out to those who mourn,
    so they may know the touch of Christ through our touch.

We pray for those who sing in a new key,
    rejoicing in new professions,
        new relationships,
           new challenges.
Give us patience with ourselves when we meet something strange
    and different and uncomfortable.
Grant us curiosity when challenged by the new and unexpected.

We pray for those who sing the strains of a familiar melody,
    who have met less change this year,
        who feel a gratitude for the sameness of their lives,
           and praise God for the gift of the ordinary.

We praise you for the richness of your repertoire:
    good health, beloved friends, warm homes, kindly smiles,
        gifts of forgiveness, and pardon, and welcome home.

We thank you for sacramental songs,
    sung here at the baptismal font,
        for the blend of parents and friends,
           promising to tell your story to each generation.

We are grateful for the song of commitment
celebrated here through promise and pledge,
for those willing to serve you as servant-leaders,
promising time and energy, talent and vision,
serving you through an institution
both human and divine.

Thank you for bringing joy to the world.
Amen.

Christmas waiting

God of Advent, you who wait with us through these days
of constant activity,
bring us home for Christmas.
Bring us home to your family, the Church,
to this place, where we worship and wait,
a place where we baptize and celebrate the Eucharist.

Prepare us for the joy of homecoming
through the cleansing of our hearts.
Give us your grace to forgive those who have hurt us,
especially those closest to our hearts
who bruise us by deed and word,
and pretend to ignore our pain.

Make us wise with insight into our own intentions.
Quicken us to ask pardon for our mean and spiteful deeds,
and humble us to confess and ask forgiveness.

Prepare us for the gifts we receive in this place,
the sacraments lifting us beyond ordinary times,

the stories and songs reminding us
   of good memories in the past,
      and hope for years to come.

Make us ready to meet the Word, the Christ present with us,
   approachable in our very human form.
      Groom our spirits to greet the child divine.

Soften our hearts with a smile of deep of joy,
   happiness beyond good health,
      beyond comfortable bank accounts,
         beyond acclaim or popularity.
Give us a joy we know because we know you
   and you know us, and you love us anyway.

Lord Jesus, Son of the living God, wait with us for your coming,
   your entering into our lives,
      softening our hearts
         and quickening our hands
            to serve those born in barns and caves
               and shanty towns. Amen.

Advent days and Christmas nights

In the beauty of these Advent days and silent nights,
   we greet you, Lord, in prayer.

Thank you for the gift of Christmas celebrated in our past,
   for the memory of faces loved and gone,
   for the lingering smell of pine and cinnamon,
      the taste of chocolate,

the feel of velvet,
for the echo of organ with string and voice
encircling the years with carols
long known in our hearts.
May the gifts of our past fill us to overflowing.

Thank you for this Christmas now upon us,
for meals shared with family and neighbor and friend,
for stories of love and hope and good humor
enjoyed through the magic of a beloved voice.

Thank you for kind words when we especially need to hear them,
and a gentle touch when our skin is lonely.
May these wondrous gifts cause us to ponder our privileged lives
and offer you our thanksgiving.

Thank you for the hope of Christmas yet to be,
for a world less threatened by terror,
for children to be born and others to be married,
for gifts of the Spirit yet to come,
undaunted by present troubles,
unhindered by ill health,
for the unseen,
the unknown,
the mystery of our future.

Trusting you to meet the needs of each day even before we ask,
may we celebrate our tomorrows as unopened gifts
held in our expectant hands.
Amen.

Welcome, Jesus

Lord Jesus, come into our home, the home of our hearts,
   the place where we live and breathe and have our being,
      among those who love us for who we are
         even more than for what we do.

Come, that we might thank you for living with us
      in the inner most parts of our souls,
   where we glimpse eternity in brief moments of reverie
      midst the mundane duties of living,
   where we feel everything is just right and we belong.

Come to us in the routine of rising and resting,
   of bathing and brushing,
      of dressing and dreaming,
   where simple movements remind us
      of the glory in our human frame,
         the exquisite balance of body and health,
   where all those things we take for granted
      regain their created majesty
         and we are humbled in gratitude.

Come into our home, where our heart is nourished by familiarity.
Come and quicken our celebration for the comforts we enjoy:
   tables filled with foods from every corner of the earth,
   chairs of conversation, of reading and watching,
   beds waiting upon our weariness each evening,

Come, Lord, share with us your presence
    as we clean our homes,
        prepare for parties,
            work in our yards
                and talk with neighbors.
Be present with us in our everyday tasks.

Come among us, Lord Jesus,
    as we listen to carols,
        wrap gifts and address cards,
    as we plan for guests
        in the setting of tables and the making of beds.
Be present with us.

Lord, we open to you the doors of our hearts
    as we consider the joys and sorrows of this year past.
We wonder about joys
    unexpected and undeserved.
We ponder the sorrows
    unexpected and undeserved.
Thank you for being with us through tears and laughter.

Lord God, in this season when the inns of the world are full,
    grant us the gift of hospitality
        so we might welcome others into kindly space.
May we see you in the eyes of the lonely
    and invite them in.
May we hear you in the voice of the outcast

and hold wide the door.
May we welcome you
by welcoming others in your name.
Amen.

Communion after Christmas

Loving Lord, you sit with us at every meal,
inviting us to your table, unworthy as we are,
coaxing us from the silent corners of our hearts,
into the sunrise of a fresh new morn.

Thank you for being with us during the days of our unknowns,
the emptiness of belonging nowhere in particular,
the loneliness of having no one special,
the fear of terminal news,
the void of direction on each page
of an empty calendar.

You are with us in emptiness and loneliness,
in fear and void.
Your spirit is companion to our anxious wanderings.
And so we kneel at your table and consider your gifts,

We praise you for seeing beyond the eyes of this world,
for seeing us as the persons we really are,
longing to be loved, yearning for direction,
wanting to be good and kind and proud of ourselves.

You see us young and wishing to be grown up.
> You speak forgiveness to our embarrassed confessions.
>> You see us old and wishing we were young again.
>>> You know the things we wish we could do over.

Each time we fear, you speak,
> "Fear not, for I have overcome the world."

Loving God, if our faith were only stronger,
> we could feel hope in the dark nights of December,
> we could hear you whisper
>> of good cheer in tomorrow's morn,
> we might better balance between the holiday highs and lows.

Give us ears to hear bells above sirens,
> singing rather than curses, laughter beyond weeping.

Give us the joy of feeling welcomed by each person at this table.
May our comfort come through compassionate acts,
> feeding the hungry,
>> housing the homeless,
>>> helping the unemployed to again enjoy
>>> the labor of their hands.

Bring comfort to those who feel worthless,
> humor where irritation furrows tired brows.

Send laughter to convert scowls,
> hope to offer quality of life when days are numbered,
> companionship to those who live with empty chairs,
> challenge to the bored, and rest to the overworked.

Thank you for coming to us scrappy, sinful folk,
    for kneeling with us at the table,
        and making us more loving,
            more fun,
                more hopeful.

Thank you for bringing joy to the world.
Amen.

Prayer for a new year

God of calendar and clock,
Lord of precious moments and painful memories,
    we gather as your family to worship you
        at the break of a new year,
            a year full of possibility and wonder.

Give us reverence for the happenings of this last year past,
    the joys,
        the tragedies,
          the challenges,
            and the pain.

Remind us of your presence through it all,
    standing with us mid each moment
        on mountain's brilliant crest,
          and valley's darkest deep.

Our hearts are grateful for the time we are given
>to journey this earth,
>>making memories and dreaming dreams.

Lord, in our collection of facts and fantasies over the past year,
>we grieve our shortcomings
>>and wish we could forget each one,
>>>but we are people with a memory.
We need your help to lay down the leftovers of last year,
>and press ahead to the goal of a higher calling.
We need direction for finding a way
>to face the future
>>without the bondage
>>>of last year's baggage.

And so we bend to your touch.
>We bow to your grace.
>>We begin again.

May our steps into this new year be cautious
>where we fear to tread,
>>and challenged where we see a well known path.
May we greet each day with expectation
>and each night with peace.
Grant us thy blessing, Lord, thy blessing upon our future.
Turn our hearts joyfully
>toward the days and weeks
>>and months ahead.

Make us grateful for new calendars and new possibilities.

May we honor you as we fill in the blank pages

and live in the time you give to each of us.

We pray this in the name of Jesus,

the man of all seasons,

the God of all time.

Hear our prayers, O Lord.

Amen.

Prayer for a new calendar

Lord of each ending and beginning,

Giver of time and life, hear my prayer:

May I walk with you leading me though the days ahead.

May the time spent in your good company

prepare me for whatever lies in my path,

whatever endings, whatever beginnings.

Write hope upon each page on my new calendar.

Hold my hands in dark times.

Lift my eyes to the future.

Leave me not alone or to my own devices.

Let me see your touch in the timing of events.

Give me holy moments beyond calendar time,

moments in the fullness of time,

precious moments of holy transition.

Amen.

Growing old

Lord God, life is such a gift!
I waken each morning glad to be alive;
    glad to stretch a wrinkly arm above my head,
    glad to feel those getting-out-of-bed aches and pains.
But there is a limit to my gladness.

I really hate feeling invisible.
What happens to us when we get old?
Nobody looks at me anymore.
I walk down the street and everyone's
    looking at young people,
        handsome faces,
            tanned bodies.
Forgive me for being self-centered,
    but I just want to be noticed
        now and then.

When I reach out with compliments,
    they look me in the eye.
When I encourage their work,
    they listen intently.
They need me, even seem to trust my judgment.

Lord, perhaps as our generations pass
    my purpose is to mentor the young,

and encourage the faint-hearted
who look so confident on the outside.
If this be so, I pray for the words they yearn to hear.
I ask for my path to cross theirs.

As seasons spin into the future like skidding on ice,
grant me soft eyes to blur wrinkles,
daily exercise for my body, mind and soul,
intimate conversations with the very young,
and gratitude for every breath I have left.
Amen.

Prayer for the year ending and the year beginning

God of every ending, Lord of each beginning,
Forgive our fragile faith
when the past holds us captive
and we cannot escape,
when the future opens before us
and we fear what we cannot see.
Guide us Creator, as you have in the past,
do so in the future.
Bless the babes baptized this year.
May each little one grow strong and in your favor.
Care for those married as they begin sharing their lives.
Comfort those divorcing, as they walk separate paths.
For those suffering the death of a loved one,
help them build again their lives.

Forgive us for remembering the worst of times
> and forgetting some of the best.
Redeem our memories, to celebrate the good times
> and to accept the valley of shadows
> > as part of every journey.
May our doubts evaporate like morning fog
> as we step into the days ahead.

When the nights seem dark and long,
> hold our hands.
Be gentle with our worries,
> and lift us into the future
> > like expectant children entering a kitchen
> > > that smells of chocolate chip cookies.
Thank you for your amazing world. Amen.

Annual church meeting

We gather here as your church, Lord,
> grateful for the year just past,
> > for the gifts you gave to us,
> > > and the gifts we passed to others.

We thank you for our spiritual growth this year,
> growth through worship and education,
> > through stewardship of time and money,
> > > and the sharing of our talents,
> > > > as we volunteered in our church and community.

Bless and multiply the work of our hands.
Nurture the seeds we planted, and bring them to bloom.

As we stand on the brink of this new year,
  watching war clouds rain fire around the world,
    we have no recourse but prayer,
      nowhere to go but our knees.

Stand with those who work and die for peace.
Bring about righteousness in your world.
Help us see beyond national boundaries
  to international good.
May we work for a quick resolution to suffering of all kinds.

Strengthen our faith in these dark times.
Remind us we are called to be the salt of the earth,
  even though we are fearful,
    even though we feel helpless,
      even with deep, agonizing questions.

Remind us we are called to be the light of the world,
  in the darkest of days,
    in the most hopeless of situations.
You challenge us to be of good cheer
  for you have overcome the world. Amen.

SPRING

Beauty of the earth

We praise you for the beauty of this earth,
  for the sky's glory,
    and the love you have given us
      since before our birth.
We cannot escape your glory surrounding us night and day.
To thee, Lord God, we raise our prayers of grateful praise!

How often we drive the busy freeways of our lives,
  missing the delight of everyday sights,
    the horizon,
      the sky,
        the faces we pass.

Thank you for being present in our absentmindedness.
Not dependent upon our praise or acknowledgement,
  you go right on fashioning
    that which is lovely and lasting.

How often we take for granted the lavish carpet of spring color
  so simple to purchase at the farmers' market,
    so easy to plant.
Thank you for creating flowers and seeds,
  then placing in our hands
    the tools and the time
      for planting and nurturing.
You continue blessing us with the beautiful.

Give us grateful hearts growing throughout the seasons
    of rain and storm and drought,
        through gentle afternoons and starry, starry nights.
Give us abundant gratitude for life,
    for the love of persons
        and the gift of things.
For the work of our hands
    and the play along our path,
        we raise our prayers of grateful praise.

How may we serve?
How might our thankful hearts
    find life and form and purpose?
We ask for springtime work,
    the work of faith in slower, warmer times.
Give us a place to serve the needs of others
    who have no down time or extra hope.
May we respond to our blessings
    by giving of ourselves to the needs of others.

Use us to help others
    who see no beauty,
        living with ugliness and pain and despair,
    who feel no hope,
        living without voice or family or faith,
    who have never had the luxury
        of soil to tend or pot to plant.

Use us as instruments of your love in action.
May our cups,
>   running over with your gracious gifts,
>   be poured into their dry lives.
May our cups,
>   spilling over with health and opportunity,
>   be shared with those who thirst.
Now, in the name of the one who loves us
>   and calls us to serve,
>   we lift our hearts.
Amen.

Great God, ruler of all lesser gods

Thank you for the glory of opportunity in our lives,
>   the choices we are offered,
>   the support we feel from family and friends.

May we be good stewards of your gifts,
>   celebrating food and health,
>   money and power,
>   knowing you created our abundance
>   and freedom to choose.

May our hearts and our hands
>   care for those who have less than we have.
May we use our power and money and influence

to serve the least of these.
May we learn generosity from you,
    and practice sharing our bounty.

We lift to you prayers for those who are sick,
    lonely,
        in harms way
            and deeply worried.
Be to them a calming presence in their souls.
    Grant them peaceful spirits and hopeful dreams.
        Leave them not alone.

We pray for our soldiers in far away places.
    Comfort loved ones waiting for their return.
Be present in the dust
    and sand
        and barren wastes of their daily work.
Hold their lives in your keeping.
 In these days of world unrest,
    we turn to you,
        the creator of nations.
In these times of hunger and disease,
    may we celebrate our abundance
        and good health by sharing.
In these nights of worry over investments and bank accounts,
    may we not forget those
        who have no investments or bank accounts.

Lift our concern beyond what we don't have
    to being creative with what remains.
Lift our spirits above the losses in our lives
    to the amazing possibilities
        of new challenge,
            and new hope.
Lift those in grief and pain
    through the smiles and touches we have to share.

Thank you for the days of sunshine and spring colors.
We rejoice in your goodness.
Amen.

Thank you for teachers

We come in praise, Lord God, for your presence in the past
    and your promise in the future,
        for standing with us at graduations and retirements,
            at weddings and in court,
                at baptisms and at funerals.
You are ever present, ever available to whisper your comfort.

Thank you for the end of winter,
    for stretching spring days
        into brilliant dawn and lingering evening,
    for tipping the earth toward a summer of sunny mornings
        and surprising afternoon showers,
    for the ending of school and thoughts of vacation.

We praise you for the knowledge stirred within us
>   by teachers in church and weekday school,
> for months of their creative preparation
>   and kindly patience,
> for ideas planted and gifts nurtured
>   by these servants of the next generation,
>   these caretakers of tomorrow's minds and souls.

May teachers realize the harvest of their service
> perhaps not yet evident.
Assure them the seeds they planted
> will be watered by you through the years ahead.
The gifts sown yesterday
> will sprout and move
>   toward mature growth tomorrow.

May the satisfaction of having given their best
> blossom within each heart,
> becoming bouquets of memories blessed by your words,
>   "Well done, good and faithful servants."

Grant us the desires of our hearts for those we name,
> the hurting,
>   the lonely,
>   those who mourn,
>   those who wait wondering about the future.
Thank you for the joys we celebrate,

happy endings,
    challenging beginnings,
        hopes and dreams.

Lord of yesterday and tomorrow,
    may each of us walk with you leading us in the days ahead.
May the time spent in your good company
    prepare us for
        whatever lies in our paths,
            whatever beginnings,
                whatever endings.

Hold our hands as we journey toward tomorrow.
    Lift our eyes to the future
        as we honor the living of our past.
    Leave us not alone or without hope.
We are your people enfolded in your timeless arms.
Amen.

God of powerful patience

We praise you for calling us to believe in your name,
    but we confess our doubts about so many things,
        our tongues hesitant to speak of faith,
        our hands limp with idleness,
        our averted glances
            fearing you may call us to serve.
Forgive us, Lord Jesus,

for the stupid things we do and say each day,
>
hurting those we love the most.

Our family deserves better.

Those who work with us each day
>
need support, not criticism.

Even strangers warrant our welcome,
>
not caustic remarks.

Grant us courage in the midst of doubt,
>
and words in spite of stumbling speech,
>
> so we might open our mouths at the right moments.

May we remember to retell your mighty deeds.

Help us live out the little courage we do have.

Grant us belief in the midst of trouble, pain and sickness,
>
especially when others have hurt us deeply.

Whisper those promises we forget so quickly.

Remind us of your comfort in times past,
>
when grief held us captive
>
> and you set us free.

Knock on the doors we have closed to others,
>
and give us the grace to receive and forgive.

Open our hearts
>
that we might try again.

Unstop our ears
>
to hear your encouragement.

Close our minds
    to old messages that would damage our spirits.
Speak clearly
    through the confusion of this noisy world.
Remind us
    your presence travels with us
        whether we feel it or not.
We know you can change lives.
    Change ours.
You came to encourage us.
    Grant boldness.
In the worst of times, leave us not alone.
Sing into our hearts.

Through the somber days of this season,
    we share with you our disappointments.
You who knew no sin,
    watch us sin daily.
You who came to love,
    see us turn from you
        without a second thought.
You,
    God's spirit wrapped in human form,
        understand our daily dilemmas.

Forgive us, Lord, son of the living God.
Forgive us.
Amen.

Marshal of every parade

Lord, Jesus Christ, son of the living God,
Thank you for being ever present in our daily lives,
    marshal of every parade,
        messiah of every season.
Hear us as we lift our hearts in gratitude for our safekeeping.

Before we open our eyes in the morning, you are with us,
    spreading your blessings over the day ahead,
        softening the hard edges of difficulties we must face.

When we stop for our noonday meal, you sit at table with us,
    bringing encouragement through timely pause in our day,
        strengthening our body and mind with the gift of food.

We greet the shadows of each evening,
    knowing we are not alone,
    having walked with us through the day,
        you understand our needs better than we do,
    having known weariness and disappointment,
        you whisper rest and hope.

Thank you for becoming one of us, for knowing how we feel,
    for standing with us as we wait for news
        that could change our lives,
    for celebrating with us when that news is good,
        and comforting us when it is not.

Grant us courage to walk with you through this week,
 daring honesty as we contemplate your death and ours,
  risking questions about God's will in your life and ours,
   knowing we pray with more hope than assurance.

Give us eyes to see the beauty of the earth, the glory of the skies
 and the dawning of tomorrow.
Jesus Christ, son of the living God,
 savior of compassionate memory,
  remember us as we too wait and wonder.
Amen.

Crisis as opportunity

Lord of the cross,
God of life and death and resurrection,
 we come to you in prayer
  during these passionate days of Lenten pause.
 We come with thanksgiving and concern,
  with fear and hope.
Hear now our prayers:

Lord of the Church universal,
 of every denomination calling you Christ,
  we pray for strength of ecumenical mission,
   so we might reach out with many hands
    to bring relief to those suffering.

May the tithes and offerings we give
    serve the present needs
        of those who hunger and thirst,
        those naked and in prison,
        those who are sick and have no home.
Hear the cry of the helpless,
    and use us as your hands in the world.

God of all people great and small,
giver of what is right and just,
    we pray for women and men
        across the earth who might influence
            negotiations to bring about peace between enemies.
Give to them the wisdom of gentle persuasion
    modeled for us by Jesus.
Let justice roll down like cooling water
    upon the burning emotions of hatred.

God of creation, we weep for the desecration
    of the land and sea and air.
Come, creating ways to mend the broken beauty of our earth.
May the soiling of your world
    create in us a heart for restoring
        the precious land of your Genesis touch.
May our concern stretch to lands far and near,
    every place you give us to live,
        every creation over which you have given us
            dominion.

As stewards, may we acknowledge
>   the earth as yours to bless,
>   and ours to protect.
May you see again your creation
>   and be able to say,
>   "It is good."

God of the Church,
>   you are acquainted with crisis.
Come to us in the heat of ethical dilemma
>   and theological debate.
May disagreement
>   become opportunity to define who we are
>   and what we believe.
Cast out our suspicion of diversity.
>   Open our stopped ears.
>   Touch our hardened hearts.
>   Rub our stiff necks.
May we greet new thoughts with childlike curiosity
>   and mature scrutiny,
>   willing to engage in study and dialogue
>   as we search for your truth.
Come among us, Lord Jesus.
Amen.

Lord of these forty days

You travel toward the cross. We ponder your journey.
Thank you for those times when life is not fair,
    times we failed and you forgave,
        times we stumbled and you picked us up,
            times we deserved punishment and you smiled.
Thank you for your gracious judgment.

Lord of this world and all that is therein,
    we are surrounded by a host of witnesses.
Your church stretches beyond political systems
    and national boundaries,
        worshipping in every language
          heard in the heart of God,
        praising your name in every country and culture.
Thank you for the Church universal.

Lord of all time and space,
    we met you in the past, and look for you in the future.
Lives of the faithful witness to your unchanging love.
Young lives wrestle with questions in the heat of their days.
Little ones reach to us for examples.
Thank you for generations of believers who have kept the faith.

Great Physician,
    you who know the pain of others even better than we do,
        stand by the needy in hospital, court, bedroom and jail.

Those who suffer physically,
    grant their bodies release.
Those in the depths of emotional illness,
    reach out to them and whisper comfort.
Victims and criminals alike,
    redeem, restore and return them to community.
Thank you for the hope of light after darkness.

Go with us now into the days and nights ahead.
Give us time to ponder the meaning of this somber season.
Make us truly grateful for the journey before us. Amen.

Easter

Creator of divine surprise,
    hear our prayers.
We worship you with light hearts and singing spirits,
    no longer burdened with the fear of death,
        or stooped with the baggage of past sin,
    no longer dragging grievances we held against a distant god.

You have come among us
    living the daily, ordinary human life,
        dying the fleshy pain of nails and sword and suffocation;
            then waking into the surprise of Easter sunrise,
                knowing God's promises to be true.
Dare we believe resurrection might be in our future?
Dare we believe we too shall live again?

Come as close to us as our breath,
   our pulse,
      our very thoughts,
         and dwell therein.
Slip into our doubts,
   daring us to live each day with alleluia's
      on the tips of our tongues.
Challenge us to look our fears in the eye
   and see reflected there an empty tomb.

May we whistle in dark and empty gardens
   and from the distance
      hear your echo.
Quicken us to listen for the morning dove
   and feel the brush of wings,
      to search each sunrise for greater meaning
         than the world believes.
 Then open our hearts to your divine surprise.

Comforter throughout the years,
We thank you for the days gathering into years
   and adding up to decades.
Be to us the risen Lord of all our seasons.

When we pass through the summer of our lives,
   sweating the problems
      of love and work and responsibility,
         breathe cool upon our fevered hearts.

When we gather the harvest of fall,
    and the fruits of our labor
        seem less than our dreams,
            grant us the grace to lift our hearts in praise.
When we greet the snows of winter
    with mixed feelings,
        wondering what lies ahead
         and dreading the unknown,
            bless us with more curiosity than fear.
Then, when again we feel spring rains
    and see daffodils peeking over hillsides,
        remind us of your constant care
         through all the years encircling,
            and gladden each morning with Easter ecstasy.

Resurrected Savior,
Dare we believe the good news?
    For we too would rush from the empty tomb
        wondering if our eyes betray us.
Is it too good to be true? No!
Dare us to believe!
Amen.

Easter skies

Good morning God, as your sun rises into the eastern skies,
    we thank you for morning, for dawn,
        for the moments of hope a new day brings,
           for light, bright ideas and good morning times.

Loving God, as darkness loses its power over our spirits,
     our eyes blink back the night's residue of worry.
We praise you for the end of dusk,
     and the silence of dark whispers
          wandering through our evenings and our dreams.
You are Lord of dusk and dawn,
     dark and light,
          valley and mountain crest.

You are creator of our daily cycles,
     causing night to reign only long enough
          to open its arms to morning's embrace.
Thank you, Lord.
Thank you for the constant promise of morning,
     for we are a people who need dawn.
We are folks who live in all the hours of a day.

We know long hours of fear,
     of waiting,
          of pain and sadness.
We wish we had the power to stop the clock during good times,
     lengthening the hours of joy and play,
          vacation and ecstasy.

We are plain folk come to worship you this morning.
Please receive our simple thanks,
     for your smile of health upon our loved ones,
          the blessed end to suffering,
     for jobs giving us work to do and ideas to share,
     for school and the pursuit of an education,

for family that loves and fusses and hugs,
    and for a future
        calling us to renewed energy and creativity.

Thank you for the quiet ending
    of days filled with stress and frustration,
        for the sun setting upon sickness
            and meanness
            and injustice,
        for bringing nights of nurturing touch and laughter,
Thank you for the end of winter,
    and the beginning of spring,
        the dawn of daffodils, brilliant in yellows,
            for longer days and softer evenings.

Thank you for the arms of love holding us
    beyond the miles
        and beyond the grave,
            for the dawn of recognition
                awaiting us someday on yonder shores,
            for the dusky twilight
                set alive by memory's candlelight.
We praise you for darkness without fear,
    and death without finality,
        for the promise Easter heralds
            of empty cross and empty tomb,
        for the days of our lives spreading out ahead of us,
            days of merry mornings and gracious evenings.

O Lord,
    may we waken each day with hope
        and lie down each evening in peace.

For you alone are with us at all times
    to uphold and care for us wherever we are,
        whatever we do,
            however we are feeling.
You are with us as dawn breaks
    and evening draws nigh,
        and we are glad.

Receive now the gratitude of your Easter people.
Alleluia!
Amen!

I am so happy

Lord, sometimes I am so happy I feel guilty.
Spring dances in all its glory,
    tulips splash brilliance across the fields,
        and I can't stop whistling.
Yet, I look at the world.
    Cries from across the oceans,
        cries from across the street dare me to smile.
Famine, fighting and disease
    would dull the colors of April.
Children born to die,
    lie helpless in the corners of forgotten places,
        and yet, I can't stop my soul from soaring.
How can this be, my Lord?
I am a compassionate person.
How can I feel joy in a sad world?
My heart reaches out to those in need.

I give to the poor and pray for the helpless,
    and yet I can't stop my feet from skipping.
Am I wrong?
Is my joy inappropriate,
    my feathery heart unfitting after evening's news?

When I think of you,
I remember children laughing on your lap
    in the midst of civil unrest.
You dined and drank, even with the rich,
    as poor ones starved.
You broke the bread and fed the crowds,
    while swollen bellies growled around the world.
You healed the sick and raised the dead,
    as others died and families wept over fresh graves.
Is it all right for me to sing?
It's spring, Lord.

Death is kissed by life

Death is kissed by life, and we live.
    Thank God!
Night is swept aside as morning tidies up the day.
    Thank God!
Children begin their play to the echo of a dirge far away
    and almost forgotten.
Alleluia! Amen!

Thank you for the real thing

Praise to you, Lord Jesus! Praise to you for coming back,
> for proclaiming your father's mansion
>> and reserving for us a room,
> for declaring death no longer stings
>> and wounds will not last forever.
Thank you for seeing beyond the grave,
> for translating the words we speak,
>> but rarely understand,
> for laughing at those things we fear,
>> but taking us seriously.
Thank you for loving us in spite of ourselves.

Bending in prayer,
> we gaze into your tomb.
Burial cloths lie neatly folded,
> reminding us of our own dirty linen, now clean.
A shroud discarded,
> witnessing to our sin forgiven and your mantle of grace.
Kneeling in confession,
> we thank you for loving us before we loved ourselves,
>> for coming to us before we knew we needed you,
>> for setting our lives afire with hope
>>> so we need not shuffle along our daily paths,
>>>> making shadows by artificial light.
Thank you for the real thing. Amen.

Good morning, God

Good morning, God!
You win!
Darkness battled light,
    and the sun comes out.
Death killed life,
    and your son empties the tomb.
Blood stained our hands,
    and you wash us clean.
Our lives are worth living again.
Thank you from the depths of last night,
    into the heights of this morning. Amen.

The wonder of resurrection

God of life and breath and all the wonder of resurrection,
    we creep from the shadows of a tomb
        into the dazzling light of Easter,
            covering our eyes
                and wondering what it is we see.
Is it true?
Can your grave be empty?
Has light indeed overcome the darkness?
Yes!
Death is dead.
Life is alive.
Praise God!

Lord of Easter morn

God of resurrection,
    Lord of Easter morn,
We come praying in humble reverence for your gift of life.
We come singing the alleluia of Easter morning,
    wondering what this mystery is all about.
What signs of resurrection do we discover in our own lives?
What difference will this joyful morning make
    tonight?
What wondrous love is this,
    O my Lord?

God of resurrection,
    Lord of Easter morn,
Thank you for shouts of faith
    and songs of praise.
May they linger through the weeks ahead,
    weeks of ordinary living,
        pointing out the gifts of daily resurrection,
           good food to renew our bodies,
                good company to renew our humor,
                    good work to renew our creativity.

May Easter music echo through our moments of despair,
    reminding us that death
        will not win in the end,
           will not separate us for long,

will not injure us permanently,

will never destroy us.

For you have tasted death,

and seasoned it with victory.

For all time,

you laugh out loud at the grave.

God of resurrection,

Lord of Easter morn,

Grant us Easter eyes

to see beyond our momentary afflictions,

to catch the vision of a quiet sunrise coming,

only waiting for darkness to wear out.

Grant us Easter eyes to see the power of Christ's rising

in the small resurrections we encounter each day,

wintery gardens

breaking open with green shoots,

the touch of babies' hands

and the smell of puppy breath,

the scent of blossoms,

and the sound of chimes.

Grant us Easter eyes to celebrate

the small resurrections of weekday living,

births and birthdays,

anniversaries and turning points,

lives connected again,

loves beginning anew,

fears set aside,
decisions to risk once more.

May these small, ordinary,
daily resurrections
remind us of
your grand and glorious Easter surprise,
your return from death,
your greatest act of love power.
You came back!

God of resurrection,
Lord of Easter morn,
As the sun sets upon this day,
let sunrise linger in our hearts.
Write upon each day your encircling benediction. Amen.

Faith, hope and love

Creating God, where does it all begin?
the goodness of this faith
blessing us with hope,
and comforting us with love?
Where does it begin?

Begin with us,
in us.
Nurture the small beginnings of faith.

Suckle the wee ones with your nurturing Spirit.

Sit the young ones upon laps of those who believe.

Whisper tenderly into tiny ears,

"Jesus loves you."

Remind those of many years,

"Jesus loves you still."

Thank you Lord,

for beginning with little lives

and then allowing us to witness the growth of faith,

for beginning with insignificant moments on ordinary days

and transforming them into memories eternal,

for beginning in the coldness of winter,

hidden to our eyes,

the growth that charms our springtime vision.

Gracious God,

where does hope begin?

Begin with us,

in us.

May your Spirit breathe the incredible story of Easter

upon these ordinary days.

May your story swell throughout the years

and join the eternal chorus

"Jesus Christ is risen indeed!"

Thank you, Lord,

for those hopeful echoes come to us

through centuries of sanctuaries,

for the amplification of your living word
> in the ordinary days of our lives,
for the faith of our fathers and mothers,
> grandparents and teachers,
>> bringing us to this place
>> in these times,
for the affirmation of hope
> we witness in deeds of love and kindness
> among your people.

Gentle shepherd, where does love begin,
> love that endures?
Begin with us,
> in us.
Greet us here at the font
> filled with waters of promise.
Lead us to the table
> for your bread and cup of unceasing sustenance.
Here it is, Lord,
> we stumble into your everlasting arms
>> and dare to begin with faltering steps.
We are a simple people,
> knowing not the answers to great mysteries,
>> nor the length of our days.
Yet, Lord, we would greet thee,
> taking a first step toward your loving invitation.
Encourage us, and bless each small gain,
> each tiny act of kindness we attempt.

Touch our small hearts with the magnification
    of your creative love.
When the evil of this world seems too great,
    darkness too pervasive, and death too final,
        sing to us of Bethlehem babes
            turning the world right side up.
Teach us the magnitude of the small. Amen

Lord over death

Lord over death,
    giver of all life,
        we praise you for the empty places of Easter morning,
    for an empty cross
        bloodstained and hammered,
            witnessing to life even on a hill of death,
    for an empty cross,
        ill used and hated,
            pointing from the darkness of our past to a new day.

Thank you for the empty places in our lives,
    solitary occasions
        awaiting opportunity,
    possibilities
        not yet named,
    relationships for which we have prayed,
        but not yet found,

Be our guest,
> abide with us,
>> fill the void.

Thank you for filling the empty places.
The tombs of grief and mourning,
> you fill with angels pointing to better times.
Into the barren wastes of loneliness,
> you breathe the name of a friend.
Even in good-byes,
> you walk with us to the next hello.

Thank you for emptying our lives
> of those things that create our lesser selves.
>> Tombs of guilt and shame,
>>> you sweep clean
>>>> and dust away cobwebs of despair.
>> Tombs of self hate,
>>> you polish and ready for a new reflection.
Tombs that decay our bodies, you enter,
> take our ashes
>> and fashion us into the spiritual creations
>>> we have yearned to be.

We pray for those who still carry crosses up steep hills.
Empty them of loneliness,
> of bearing their burdens alone.

Those with constant physical suffering,
     stand by their pain.
Leave them not alone.

Those with aching hearts,
     whisper hope beyond reason.
Leave them not alone.

Those who have nothing to look forward to,
     sing to them a new song.
Leave them not alone.
Lift their load.
Share their cross.

We pray for those who have yet to empty their tombs.
Help them.
     Dead bodies of hatred,
          carefully wrapped and long preserved,
               exhume.
     Dry bones of anger,
          scraps of envy and shards of denial,
               dig up,
                    wash and lay in the sunshine.
     Decayed hope and rotted dreams,
          purify.

Lord Jesus, son of the living God, have mercy on us.
Amen.

Day of resurrection

You know how it feels to empty yourself.
    Now fill us.
You walk from the tomb into the light.
    From our darkness,
        call us forth.
You love us in spite of ourselves.
    Use us in your service,
        even us.
Hear our prayer, O Lord.

Living Christ,
    loving creator,
        come to us this morning.
Let us see your face.
Move with us beyond the tombs and crosses of yesterday,
    beyond used linens
        and the smell of death.
Lead us to the miraculous discovery of a savior alive.

May this day of resurrection change every day of our lives,
    bringing new energy to the ordinary,
        filling us with joy from dawn to dusk,
    granting us echoes of love from those
        who have died
            and gone before us.

Lift us above our demands of proof,
   to simply welcome the touch of your hand,
      leading us from doubt
         to a place of hope.
Transpose our sighs into song;
   end each dirge with alleluia.
Wipe dirt from our faces;
   change shame to smiles.

Thank you for speaking our names,
   and letting us see you in the face of a gardener,
for placing ordinary saints
   in our everyday paths,
for acquainting us with the needy
   and giving us a cause,
for startling our complacency
   with curiosity about how much more might be.

We pray for those who missed Easter this year,
   who continue to wait upon beds of pain,
      who weep beside empty chairs,
         and linger within tombs yet sealed.
Give us words to comfort,
   and patience with those who suffer so profoundly
      they cannot hear trumpets.

May we never deny the anguish of others
   as we sing of the risen Christ,

> never make light of the shadowed valleys
> through which they pass,
> never question the faith of those
> who suffer the depths of depression,
> or the power of addiction.

Set them free, Lord.
In the name of the risen Christ,
set us all free.
Amen.

You who dance from out the tomb

God of resurrection,
you who dance from out the tomb,
thank you for the promise of Easter,
for hope made real,
for your testimony to life beyond death.
We praise you for the song in out hearts,
for a new and nobler life we claim as a people forgiven.

To you we lift the remains of our shadowy doubts.
Transform those fears that continue to cower
in the corners of our hearts.
Give us Easter hope
even as we see precious relationships die.
Give us Easter hope
even as we wake from dreams we held so dear.

Give us Easter hope
even as we watch the news
and grieve a sin-sick world.

Let not our hearts grow weary with weeping.
Open the graves within our souls;
revive us with power to see beyond dark moments.
Open our eyes to a vision beyond separation,
beyond illness,
beyond despair.
Open our hearts to receive those in pain,
in prison,
in bondage to all manners of evil.

May the overworked know rest,
the guilty find forgiveness
and a lightness of heart,
the hungry
enjoy all manner of food for body and soul.
May those who are rich
find purpose for their abundance,
those who are healthy
rejoice without ceasing,
and those who discover their gifts,
be willing stewards of each talent.

Leap before us, Lord,
that we might follow with a spring in our step.

Sing to us a new song, O God,

>that we might harmonize with the alleluia chorus.

Laugh at death, risen savior,

>so we might hear again the paradox of Easter,

"From the grave comes life!"

Amen.

<u>Victor over death</u>

Lord of life, victor over death,

We praise you for wiping away the tears of darkness,

>for surprising us with a vision of life after death,

>for seeing beyond the facts of this world,

>>and believing beyond the reality of dust.

You are love come from the tomb.

We sing songs of joy,

>alleluias echoing into every shadow,

>>laughing into graves,

>>>humming down hospital corridors,

>>>>and repeating the melody in our hearts.

We are your Easter people,

>euphoric with promise,

>>running through shadowed valleys to mountain crests,

>>>dancing to the rhythm of eternal life,

>>>>stretching into the morning after darkness lifts,

>>>>>and being glad.

We are your people of the resurrection,
>born into the community,
>>believers of your way,
>>>beginning at the font of baptism,
>>>>finding nurture in meditation and prayer,
>>>>practicing confession
>>>>>and receiving forgiveness.

We are your jubilant people,
>living without despair as the years pass us by,
>>inviting the lame to dance,
>>>the silent to sing
>>>>and the blind to see visions,
>>breathing deeply of your spirit,
>>>and waiting in the days to come,
>>>>to catch the scent of lilies.
Amen.

Great and goodly teacher

Thank you,
>goodly teacher,
>>for your tender words and deeds.

Standing tall before the crowds
>you rescued children from those who would dismiss them,
>>and send them away.
You lifted them onto your lap and smiled into their eyes.

Those who lay upon beds of despair,
> you raised to their feet
>> and brought them again into community,
>>> challenging each to fullness of life.

Bless your people gathered here.
Call each of us to be a blessing.
Thank you for your compassionate service
> among the least of these,
>> asking of us no more than you ask of yourself.

Thank you for giving us opportunities to follow your example,
> healing the sick at heart who pass our way,
>> clothing the vulnerable with encouragement,
> visiting those who live lonely in a crowded world,
>> and feeding the hungry who yearn for soul food.

We ask your blessing upon those
> whose names we remember before falling asleep.
Hear our silent prayers as we lift each into your care…

Lord God, give us courageous hearts
> to speak for those who have no voice,
>> to fight what is wrong and work for the right,
>>> to stand with those crippled in body and spirit
>>>> and please remember the twilight people
>>>>> forgotten and alone.

May our hearts be poised and ready to praise in moments of joy,
    for birth
        and marriage
           and baptism,
    for beauty
        and health
           and beloved faces,
    for the sacrament of bread and wine,
        and the healing of our wrongs.

May we be quick to count our blessings and slow to criticize,
    for we are your sisters and brothers blessed by our kinship.
Continue with us now
    through these days in Easter wake.
May we follow in your footsteps,
    remembering your journey of ultimate obedience.
To you we lift our hearts, O Lord.
Amen.

Birthday of the Church Universal

Dear God, thank you for celebrations in the church,
    for birthdays and baptisms,
        for children's songs and parent's prayers.
We praise you today for the birthday of the Church.
We are humbled by the mystery of fire and wind
    filling the streets of Jerusalem on that first Pentecost.

We are amazed by the infant church growing into our own time,
in spite of institutional controversy and theological diversity.

Thank you for those who kept the faith
by telling of your action throughout history.
Thank you for warm laps where we heard stories of Jesus,
stories that guided our faith journey
to this place today.
Thank you for birthdays.

We praise you for those times in our lives we can see
progress and new beginnings,
times of learning,
times of accomplishment,
times to honor the past and celebrate the future.
May we lavish gratitude upon those
who helped us reach this place.

We praise you, for the voices of children leading us in worship,
for their melodic sermon,
singing words they have yet to understand.
May these lyrics linger in the music of their memory,
someday blossoming within their spiritual grasp.

We are deeply grateful for the church
in spite of its earthly imperfections.
Continue with us as we seek to grow more insightful of your will.
Do not leave us in our ignorance. Teach us. Amen.

Pentecost

Lord God, we praise you for the church,
    for birthing an institution made with human hands,
        and invigorated by the power of your spirit.

Thank you for calling women and men
    to fashion worship pleasing in your sight,
        and mission fitting the needs of those we serve.

We celebrate the red of fiery tongues,
    binding strangers with common cause
        and sparking a flame that will not die.

In spite of evil within and evil without, you don't give up on us.
    You lead us to confess.
        You forgive us
            and you charm us to grow beyond human frailties.

We celebrate the life-giving scarlet
    spilled beneath a cross on Calvary,
        reminding us we are forgiven
            and inviting us to begin again.

You will not leave us to our own devices.
You will not turn your back on our backward ways.
You welcome us home, as a father opens his arms to prodigals.

And so Lord God, we celebrate in red.

We sing of the Church,

    the body of Christ.

We sing of beginnings on Jerusalem's streets.

We sing of the Spirit breathing life into a gathering of strangers.

Spirit of God, breathe into us.

Amen.

Living waters

Giver of living waters,

We come as thirsting folk,

    some half empty,

        others half full,

            but few with cups running over.

We come with parched lips,

    living with a dry, empty feeling,

        wondering why such plenty never seems to fill us.

Be to us that whisper,

    like a mountain stream,

        leading us to a quiet pool of reflection,

            a place, to ponder our talents

                and search for direction.

Be to us a watering hole,

    to quench our thirst,

a moment to pause,
giving thanks for peace
like a river overflowing.

Be with those whose tears season their food day and night,
those who fear death of body
and live with emptiness of soul,
those who exist with daily pain and weary spirit.
Give those who yearn your fresh, sweet water.
Let them drink deeply of your cool and calming presence.

Thank you for afternoon storms,
challenging us with things unexpected,
and driving us to take shelter
beneath your everlasting wings.
Thank you for questions and surprises and accidents,
knocking us off balance,
and causing our feet to search
for your firm foundation.

Thank you for the emptiness of a long ago tomb,
for the shock of possibility,
the hope unheard of before,
rushing to fill the darkness of death's last gasp,
for the flood of living water,
the bathing of parched lives,
the cooling of high noon's heat.

We praise you for the waves of hope
    pounding against
        our stumbling stones of disbelief,
    refining them into soft sand
        beneath our bare souls.

Lord Jesus,
    son of the living God,
        pour into our lives
            the delight of laughter,
                the bouncing rhythm of hope,
        and fill our emptiness with the gift of joy.
Amen.

SUMMER

Children of God

Holy Parent, we are your children and you our God.
Thank you for your constant presence in our lives,
>   for calling us your children
>>   no matter what our age,
>   and showing us your love
>>   whether we are lovely or not.
You see us at our worst, and call us to our best.

Your gracious parenting is beyond our understanding,
>   for the world only loves us
>>   when we are lovely,
>   and only supports us
>>   when we obey their rules.

You have called us your children
>   since we came to this font of promise,
>   since we were held, and touched with water,
>>   and promises were made
>>>   to be your children of the church
>>>   to grow in wisdom and stature
>>>>   and in favor with you and our neighbors.

Thank you for nurturing us
>   through the years of infancy and childhood,
>>   and all the trials of growing and schooling.
You looked upon us as we tried to separate from family
>   and try our wings.
You smiled at our confusion
>   as we tried to become our own persons,
>   making decisions independent of our parents.

Thank you for loving each of us as if we were an only child,
    for giving us the freedom to choose and fail,
        then standing close
            to pick us up.

We praise you for being there when we need you,
    to grieve with us when we weep
        and laugh with us when we celebrate,
    to walk with us into each new trial our life unfolds,
    to wait with us when the clock ticks slowly,
        until at last, when our time runs out,
            you hold open the door of your heavenly mansion,
                where there is room for all God's children.
Until that day,
    come live with us in the spending of our time.
Sing with us and play with us.
    Eat at our table
        and dance at our parties.
Smile at our mistakes
    and take our hands in the dark.
We love you. Amen.

Lord of the merry spirit, giver of the happy heart

We praise you for the sense of wonder that floods our lives,
    for the joy of ordinary moments, the cyclic magic of seasons.
We celebrate these days on the brink of summer,
    praising you for the playfulness in park and yard and water,
        for the pleasure of a change in routine,
            for longer days and shorter nights.

Thank you for the wonder of birth and the power of growth.
    for these tiny babes given to our keeping
        who will manage the affairs of tomorrow's world.
Thank you for small plants and trees
    that grasp the earth with rooted determination.

We praise you for memory of winter and the hope of harvest,
    making precious the spring and summer of our lives,
        for the balance of life and death,
            the natural ordering of dusk and dawn,
                for candles in the night.

Grant that we might be blessed with your merry spirit,
    able to smile through lonely days,
        able to see beyond momentary afflictions,
            and envision the good gifts yet to be.

Grant that our merry spirit might be a blessing to others,
    sharing laughter with those who frown,
        sharing hope with those who wait,
            gentle persuasion with stiff-necked intolerance.

May we remember our own birth into your family,
    our own baptism into the church,
        praising you for those who brought us to this font.
We praise you for those who taught us and were patient,
    who wiped our tears and held us close.
We are your grateful people, Lord. Amen.

Lord of the depths and hilltops

Lord of the depths, who whispers to us with a still small voice,
    we call to you from streets and basements
        and tunnels without light at the end.
Lord of the heights, who sings to us with choruses of angels,
    we lift to you our grateful hearts
        from happy homes and hilltops.

We call from the streets of work,
    sad with disappointments.
        So many opportunities fizzle.
        So many days aren't worth the getting up.
        Too many nights feeling useless and helpless.
All these visions keep us awake.

Whisper to us of better days yet to be,
    days of hope and energy and opportunity to try again.

We call from the basements of our hearts,
    where we store our secrets,
        wishing we could erase the hurting words we spoke,
            those deeds diminishing the smiles of others,
            and the desires washing us in guilt.

Forgive the times we used our hurt to strike out,
    trying to bandage our wounds
        by wounding others.

We call from highways without end,
    bored by the repetition of sameness,

praying we might move beyond the tedium of work
and the monotony of boring relationships.

Re-create in us childlike excitement and wonder
about what might be,
what amazing surprise waits just around the corner.

Still small voice,
remind us of dejected prophets under long ago trees,
waiting upon wind and fire
to break through depression.

May we too wait for your whisper,
knowing it will come.
May we too wait for that barely heard comfort,
assured in your promise to be with us always,
even to the ends of the earth.

Give us courage to lean into the harshest of wind,
listening for your voice in the worst of the storm.

From happy homes and hilltops,
we call to you,
thankful for summer days of green and growth,
grateful for rain and sun,
cloud and wind.

You bless us in the summer
watching young bodies running free in suntanned play,
gardening and swimming and travel,
shade and breeze, good books, long days and cool nights.

Praise be to you for these good gifts.

Thank you for your quiet assurance in hard times,
    for holding our hands at death.
Praise be to you for joyful times,
    and dancing with us at weddings.
Blessed be your name
    in the depths and upon the hilltops.
Amen.

Fruits of the Spirit

Creating God, caretaker of the garden we call earth,
Thank you for the harvest of summer
        fruits and vegetables fresh in our hands,
            foods we eat and share and prepare for later seasons
                when we want a taste of summer.

Thank you for flowers that color our lives and scent our homes,
    for children's laughter singing into long summer evenings.
We are truly grateful for the goodness of our lives,
    goodness we have done nothing to deserve,
        goodness calling forth a harvest of gratitude.
Tend the fruit we bear, Lord.
    Grant us abundant crops of love and joy.
From our lives may peace abound,
    dropping its seeds in fertile grounds,
    germinating quickly and spreading among warring souls.

Where impatience taps its foot and frowns,
    may the fruit of endurance
        offer good company and cool water.
In a world of mean competition and hurting souls,
    grant us plentiful fruits of kindness,
        enough wisdom and good will to share with others.

Lord, touch our spirits so the fruits of faithfulness might blossom
    even in a culture where promises are easily broken,
        and one's word is not taken seriously.

Caretaker of our souls, may gentleness and self-control grow
    throughout our lives.
May we tend these fruits in our lifetime,
    sharing them with children and grandchildren
        so someday they may plant their own gardens
            and harvest their own fruits of the spirit.
Kind One, grant these desires of our hearts. Amen.

Amazing Grace

Graceful God,
    how sweet the sound are your loving words of forgiveness,
    how sweet in a world of little grace,
        a world stingy with compassion,
            lacking in kindness and mercy.
In a world like ours,
    you offer the satisfaction of our soul's deep longings.

When culture dictates standards of acceptance,
    you welcome us to the foot of your cross just as we are,
        reminding us you died for all,
            the lazy and driven,
                the hateful and greedy,
                    the abuser and addicted.
All of us are welcome,
    and your amazing grace rescues us from our disgrace.

When we disappoint ourselves
    and family criticizes our poor choices,
        you put your arms around us just as we are.
Like prodigal children returning home to a father and mother,
    you love us into loving ourselves again.
Thank you for your redeeming welcome.

When summer days unwind the spools of our routine,
    your smile lights our days with change,
        making a way for the unexpected,
            giving us choices we had not dreamed.
God of vision, thank you for opportunities we had not foreseen.

When friends break our trust and wander off,
    you call our names and mend together
        the broken pieces of our self esteem,
            giving us the spirit of renewal.
Thank you, friend of the friendless.

When life is good and times are happy,
>   you fill our cups to overflowing,
>   making us instruments of your grace,
>   using our hands to help the needy.
Thank you, Lord God, for opportunities to serve others.

When others give us their paths to follow
>   and dismiss us for choosing our own,
>   you hold a lamp to our feet as we stumble along
>   making our way toward the truth we perceive
>   and the values we deem worthwhile.
Like a shepherd, lead us Lord.

When children break our hearts and remember only our mistakes,
>   you redeem our naive and earnest parenting,
>   transforming mistakes into opportunities
>   for truth and reconciliation,
>   untying our burdens
>   and replacing them with a yoke of love.
We are deeply grateful, Lord Jesus.

When wars and rumors of wars are never far from headline news,
>   you remind us of your lordship in history,
>   lifting the lowly,
>   feeding the hungry,
>   bringing down irresponsible powers
>   and healing the harm they have done.
We praise you mighty God, just and holy are your ways.

When loved ones leave and take with them our dreams,
> you embrace us in your everlasting arms,
>> re-fashioning our hearts so that one day
>> our spiritual cups may again spill over with laughter.

Dear physician,
> thank you for healing the cuts and bruises on our hearts.

When evil seems so close and goodness far away,
> you take our hands and lead us in the paths of righteousness,
>> lighting the future with lanterns of promise,
>>> pledging you will guide us always.

Light up our lives with goodness, O Lord.

In times of sickness and disease
> when questions seem our only companions,
>> your spirit hovers in our midst,
>>> breathing through our very being,
>>> bringing loved ones and friends
>>>> to decorate our days
>>>>> with cards and food and flowers
>>>>> and prayers.

Gracious God, thank you for your kindly family.

In times of challenge and commitment,
> when called by your church to serve,
>> you provide strength and courage to meet each day,
>>> bringing opportunity for healing and creativity,
>>> laughter and vision.

Lord God, bless our leaders as they ponder your will.

When our hearts are weary and our spirits weak,

    your amazing grace finds our tarnished souls,

        sings to us a new song,

            and the echoes of this melody embrace us.

Your spirit dwells with us in the dusty corners of despair,

    whispering of a love that will not let us go.

        If you are lost,

            I will find you.

        If you are blind,

            I will give you sight.

        If you confess,

            you are forgiven. Amen.

<u>Light and water</u>

Lord, Jesus Christ, son of the living God,

You are light for our world,

    light leading us out of dark corners

        and beyond shadowy detours.

You are light,

    shining constantly upon the routine tasks of our daily life,

    bringing focus and future to common moments.

You are light,

    coaxing us toward hope at the end of dreary afternoons,

        waiting through dark nights,

            searching out our souls.

Thank you for being light,
> for being brightness,
>> for being God's sunshine.

May we pass the strength of your torch into trembling hands,
> those groping for your presence along cold hallways
>> and strange, empty rooms.

May we carry your warmth with the excitement of children
> sharing jars of summer's fireflies with friends after dark.

Lord, Jesus Christ, son of the living God,

You are water for our earth,
> water touching babes with baptismal promise,
>> drops gathering one by one
>>> to fill a lake of lifetime blessings.

You are water, cooling hot heads and softening hard words
> like summer rain on dusty paths.

You are heaven's rain, washing summer's blistering sidewalks.

You are incense rising like steam,
> evaporating our gross misdeeds.

Thank you for being water,
> for quenching our soul's deep thirst,
>> for being God's refreshment.

Pour your blessings upon our times,
> letting justice roll down into valleys
>> parched by meanness and greed,

greening dry hearts,

dampening evil spirits,

encouraging last spring's seeds to try again.

We pray for justice to flow across the boundaries of nations,

and for deep reservoirs of mercy and wisdom to be filled.

May we share your cup of cool water with those held hostage

by prison bars,

by memories,

by sickness,

and loneliness.

Lord, Jesus Christ, son of the living God,

thank you for being to us light and water.

May we be to others nothing less,

in a dark and thirsty world.

Amen.

Prayer for the refugee

Lord God, comforter of the homeless,

and all the wandering souls upon this earth,

We pray your blessing on each roaming heart.

Wait with those who cannot go home,

whose hearts reach toward loved ones,

whose hands would touch the past,

whose bags hold only memories.

Give food to those who hunger and thirst
>for the necessities of life.

Grant hope to those who have little reason to hope.

Lord of the refugee, walk with your children.

Lord of wisdom, stay close to those who are students,

We pray together for your blessing.

Give encouragement to those who study in foreign lands,
>whose education comes with great difficulty,
>>whose earnest endeavors seem endless,
>>>whose minds weary from long hours of study.

Give daily bread to each who hunger for knowledge.

Grant hope to those who long for wisdom in unfriendly places.

Lord God, wanderer of mountain crest and lonesome valley,

We pray for your blessing.

Stand with those who work and serve in foreign countries,
>whose daily work takes twice as long,
>whose plans seem always to fall through,
>whose frustrations waken them each morning
>>and night pulls down shades of worry.

Give them the food of patience and a generous portion of humor.

Grant bright colored encouragement
>on the darkest of winter's short days.

Lord, you have walked as a refugee,
>with no place to lay your head.

You have been a student,
>with much to learn and understand.

You, Lord, have faced the politics of institutions
>and been frustrated by people's greed.

The problems of our world are known well to you.

Grant us dreams of someday, someday better.
Hold our hearts open when doors close.

So, come Lord Jesus,
>be present on the streets of our lives.

Remember the desires of our hearts.
Hear our prayers before they are spoken,
>and give us a double portion of your comfort.

Amen.

Summer's heat

Lord of summer's heat and seasonal fires,
>we thank you for your presence in sunshine and smoke,
>>for your whispers strengthening us in times of waiting,
>>for your witness encouraging us to endure,
>>>to hold on just a little longer.

Thank you for examples of strong character
>formed like diamonds through the pressures of time,
>>for the gift of hope we discover
>>>like new growth on summer's roses.

We need not fear the trials of life,
for you are God with us,
the one who will not let us stray from your embrace.

Lord of lightning and fire,
we praise you for never disappointing us,
for molding undeserved suffering
into strength,
for shaping the agony of endurance
into patience,
for building our character through most unlikely times,
and graciously offering new life
after ashes blanket the evening.

Thank you
for giving us encouragement
in the midst of disappointments at work and at home,
for hope in spite of frustrations with family and friends.
We are grateful for endurance growing within our souls,
for lifting us from the depths of sadness
to heights with new vision
of who we are and why we're here.

We praise you, Lord, for those who risk their lives for our safety,
those fighting the demons of wildfire and wind,
water and earthquake,
combating the elements on our behalf.
We praise you for those who fight diseases
threatening our health,
for their wisdom and kindness,
practicing their skills for our well-being.

Thank you, Lord.
>for a new perspective on old problems,
>for summer gardens growing silently within us,
>>sending roots deep into the ground of our very being,
>for securing our spirits for times of wind and drought,
>>illness and suffering,
>for a garden that one morning will surprise us
>>with new buds ready to burst open
>>>and bright blossoms of hope.

God of strength, Lord of summer's heat,
>we thank you for your spirit growing within us,
>>for the unexpected flowers one morning we find.
Amen.

Teach us to pray

You, God, shout each great amen
>and whisper through each silent prayer.
>>Teach us to pray.
Teach us to ask in honesty and simplicity
>those things for which we yearn,
>things for which tears gather
>>in the shadows of our heart's desire,
>things which keep our nights wakeful
>>and our dreams troubled.

Teach us to pray with yearning hearts when words fail us.
>When everyday talk seems too common,
>>remind us every conversation with you is sacred.

When emotions run so high we can no longer reason,
     remind us your spirit groans on our behalf.
When the only appropriate word is profane,
     remind us you hear our every cry.

O, still small voice of every prayer unspoken,
teach us to trust you can gather each fragment of our prayers
     and make from their scattered thoughts
       your one grand answer.
Lift us above the logic of this world
     into the spiritual realm of eternal secrets,
       and lighten our burdens into your care
         so we might walk with strength and purpose
           into the days ahead.

Lord of our heart's true home, teach us to believe the best
     in a skeptical, cynical, worn-out world.
You know what will come to be.
You dream better than we can imagine
     the miracles you have in store.
You control ultimate results,
     while we gaze dimly through a darkened mirror
       trying to find permanent answers in temporary times.

Confound our skepticism
     by fashioning from the honesty of our heart's desire
       even greater things than we can imagine.

Remind us you gaze into our broken hearts
 with everlasting compassion
  and cure our wounds for now and all eternity.

Lord of the answered prayer,
 we are so thankful.
Keep us returning to our knees
 even when the sun shines and the rains end.
When our spirits soar once more,
 may we remember nights of tear-stained pillows
  so we might stop for a moment
   and whisper a prayer of gratitude.
When we feel old scars, let us smile,
 and recall your touch of healing.
Receive our prayers of praise.
Amen.

Changing seasons

Lord of seasons past and seasons yet to come,
 changing greens to gold and heat to cool,
  guide us from summer into autumn.
Be within our plans as we harvest the spiritual fruits of summer
 and preserve them for tomorrow.
Be in our plans as leisure finds more structure on our calendars
 and fills the pages of our day-timers.
As new school supplies fill our back-packs
 and fall bouquets our office vases,
  make us truly grateful for the means to start anew.

Thank you for changes in the seasons of our lives,
    changes with a history of remembered routines,
        beginnings and endings we have lived before,
        holidays and work days.
We are grateful for joyful celebrations
    that balance the somber occasions
        we remember so well.

Thank you for rituals and rites of passage
    comforting and sustaining us in times of transition,
        retirement,
            death,
                marriage,
                    graduation.
You give us words to cope with change.

God of all time, thank you too for challenging us to grow
    beyond the familiar,
        for giving us change that stretches our minds
            and causes us to feel surprise,
                making us feel innocent and expectant again.
Make us young at heart with new ideas, new projects,
    even new problems to solve.

As our spirits tip-toe, oh so tentatively,
    into the next phase of the year,
        be with us.

Be in our homes, our work, our play.

Travel with us along highways,

    on congested city streets,

        in meetings, schools, stores

            and in the longer, cooler evenings of autumn.

May the blessings of our lives overflow

    into the emptiness of others.

As we eat,

    let us remember the hungry.

Before we sleep,

    may we pray for the restless and homeless.

As we store up treasures,

    may we find ways to share our abundance.

Go with us now from summer into fall.

Give us pause to

    thank you for the past.

And give us the heart

    to promise you our future.

Amen.

AUTUMN

Autumn thanks

Bountiful God, you love us more than we can understand,
   giving us more than we dare ask,
      forgiving us more than we deserve.
Thank you for the gifts of life that make our hearts leap
   and our eyes moisten with happiness.
Thank you for the great cloud of beloved ones who have
   gone before us to their reward,
      leaving to our keeping
         their witness to faith and their testimony to joy.

This world is so precious.
Thank you for
   distant plains and majestic mountains,
      tiny petals still blushing with Indian summer,
         babies' hands and four-footed, furry paws,
            grand ideas, sweet smiles, and kindly whispers.

Thank you for moments quickening our generosity,
   when our hearts yearn to give you all we have,
      when we ask, "What would you have me do, Lord?"

As we look back upon our lives
   how grateful we are for your presence,
      for nurturing us as babes
         then youth
            and finally into maturity.

Thank you for preserving the Church
   throughout the centuries,

in spite of sinful decisions
and institutional wrong doings.

We praise you
for calling leaders from within this congregation,
for the presence of your spirit as we fellowship,
for a place to worship in the beauty of holiness,
a spiritual home nurturing us
to serve the least of these,
for one place in the world where giving is filling,
losing is finding, and receiving is pure grace.
Thank you. Amen.

Gracious God, giver of all good gifts

We are a thankful people,
grateful for our heritage of family and faith.
Thank you for our family of origin,
for parents and grandparents who loved us in spite of our
awkward growth through childhood and adolescence,
for brothers, sisters and cousins who grew up with us
laughing and crying,
fighting and forgiving,
for ancestors whose genes have made us
like no other person living on this earth.
We are a people grateful for family.

Thank you for the gifts passed to us through our senses,
seeing skies and seas and toddlers sleeping,
hearing songs and stories and voices calling,

Thank you for feeling soft skin and clean computer keys,
    cool winds, laughing wrinkles
      and comfortable shoes.
For tasting fine wine, peach ice cream and sweet lips,
    we are deeply grateful.
Thank you for the smell of pancakes and babies' necks.
We are a people grateful for the gifts of being human.

We are grateful for growing up in your family of faith,
    for church nurseries where we felt the arms of comfort,
      classrooms filled with good humor, good tastes and fun,
    for retreats and choir parties, laughter and silliness.
Thank you for people who stopped to listen when we needed to
    talk or cry or tell our latest joke,
      for teachers and pastors who told us our first bible
        stories and taught us to sing, "Jesus Loves Me,"
    for folks who found us lost in hallways,
      who helped fill our plates at potlucks,
        held us on their laps
          and told us we were wonderful
            when we didn't think so.

Thank you for this family
    with whom we study, worship and serve;
    those who bring food when we're sick,
      and call when we need a good word
        to pick up our fallen spirits,
    who encourage us to offer our gifts in kindly service

and take time to show us how,
those who serve on council and committees,
who teach and volunteer in our congregation.
May we be quick to thank them as they serve in your name.

We thank you too for these sanctuary walls surrounding us,
for the comfort and beauty we share in this building,
for weddings performed,
funerals shared,
concerts enjoyed,
sacraments celebrated,
for the good news preached in this very place,
supporting us in sorrow
and challenging us in service.
Lord God, giver of every good and perfect gift,
receive our thanks,
our prayers,
our offerings. Amen.

Grant us vision

God of story, dream and vision,
lead us to a fullness of life in your service.
Let us not forget the private cares of our lives either,
but willingly lift to you all those things most personal:
our health,
our loved ones,
the intimate moments feeding our souls.

Receive the work of our hands.

Take it.

Use it.

Bless it to the glory of your kingdom.

Grant us discerning minds and insightful hearts.

Let us not grow weary spinning our wheels

on roads leading nowhere.

Let us find purpose and focus for our hearts and hands.

Give us wisdom to see through false statements

and well meaning advice.

Then guide us with your clear reflection in our souls.

Amen.

Boldness

God of boldness, God of power,

We praise you for calling us to be brave in your name,

to listen, speak, and act:

to listen for your quickening spirit,

to speak of your mighty deeds,

to act for you in our daily lives.

May your spirit whisper of those things we forget:

the times we were comforted in the darkness of night,

in the valley of pain, uncertainty and grief,

the times we were nurtured in the midst of our foolishness,

encouraged in spite of ourselves,

in spite of our guilt and wrongdoing.
the many times we were forgiven of sin,
over and over again,
and then once more... always once more.

Give us ears to hear and hearts to listen.
Grant us power, fueled in gratitude, so we too might be bold.

May your spirit speak to remind us of your mighty deeds,
deeds that changed the lives of simple people,
empowering them to make the world a better place,
commissioning each to serve
using different talents to meet the earth's needs.

Grant us memory of your deeds,
changing the direction of our own lives,
turning us toward what is right
and saving us from wrong.

Quicken memory of baptism promises
that gave our lives purpose
and our feet paths to follow.
Give us minds to think and wisdom to discern.
Grant us power, founded in history
so we too might be bold as those who believed before us.

Lord, may your spirit act through us in our daily lives
giving us words to speak our own stories of your grace.
May we sing of your forgiveness,
tell of your direction when we knew not where to go.

Giver of all good gifts,
    fashion our hands to touch those who weep,
        those who need to feel your spirit
            stirring within their wanderings.
Grant us a heart to look for those in trouble,
    those searching to be healed,
        in need of a friend.
And then let us act with your boldness.
Let us act in your name,
    for you alone have the power to make a difference,
        you alone empower us to serve others.
Amen.

By our love

The world knows who we are by our love, dear God.
The world looks upon us as we worship,
    as we serve the needy,
    as we speak good news,
        but what the world really sees
            is whether or not we love each other.

We can do all things in your name,
    preaching, teaching, praying,
        serving in soup kitchens,
    working for justice,
        evangelizing our neighborhoods,
            but if we don't love each other,
                our witness is worthless.

Forgive us for confusing Christian love
    with a shallow sharing of common conscience.
Grant us wisdom to receive Christian faith in its many forms,
    learning to find truth in countless souls.

God of love, God of grace, bind us with cords of many colors.
May our love for you be greater than our misunderstandings
    of one another.

Meet us at table and font with all who call you Lord.
May we find you among us
    quickening friendships among our differences.

May the taste of grape and bread
    remind us of generations gathered here to share this meal.
Then give us a generous portion of courage
    to look ahead together.
Grant laughter as we look into one another's eyes,
    and openness as we celebrate the uniqueness of each soul.
May we be known as yours, because we love one another. Amen.

Change

Lord of constant change,
You challenge us to think beyond the way things are
    and dream of how life might be.
You blow across the waters of our lives
    bringing ripples and tides we had not foreseen.
We feel swept off-balance and cling to the familiar.

We prize our comfortable habits and friends and opinions,
    building walls around well-worn patterns,
    wanting to preserve each moment
        just as it is
            over and over and over.

Yet from within these confines
    you are able to bring forth new life
      we had not expected.

Be to us comfort in the midst of change.
Breathe upon us when we gasp in surprise.
Blow among us possibility when we dare the impossible.

When change is hard,
    billow our sails with your spirit.
When routine undermines possibility
    startle our hearts.
When "the way it's always been done" threatens
    to win the battle with "what might be,"
      cause us to wonder.
When our friendship with "sameness"
    deafens us to the call of new directions,
      unstop our ears.
Soften our minds with wisdom.
Dare us to risk vulnerability.

Give us patience with each other.
Rub our stiff necks,
    so we might be less rigid.
Give us cause to laugh at ourselves and smile at opportunity.
Nudge us from our seats

with the gift of curiosity,
the presence of creativity,
and the support of a wise community.

Be with those who weep today,
worried about loved ones,
fearful about finances,
anxious over war and rumors of more.
Comfort those apprehensive about tomorrow,
not knowing where to call for help.
Touch those who lie in beds of pain.
Fill those empty and desperate.
Bring hope where there is none.

Set our sails for service, Lord.
Blow us toward a worthy mission.
Whisper to us again,
"Go minister in my name,
touching the hungry,
welcoming the homeless,
speaking to the tearful."

Thank you for the consolation of your spirit,
for so much goodness in our lives,
for courage to meet tomorrow's challenge
and creative ideas giving us energy and excitement.

Dwell with us.
We depend on you.
Amen.

Coming home to who we are meant to be

Lord God, creator of all the places we call home,
    we praise you for always being there when we need you.
Stay close as we wander through our lives drifting here and there,
    chasing after dreams,
        forgetting promises,
    watering down commitments,
        lessening convictions,
    forgetting who we are
        and from where we have come.

In spite of our feeble attempts, you stand firm,
    waiting to bless us even when our ways lead us in circles,
    waiting for the moment we turn our heads
        and look into your face,
    waiting to welcome us back home.

Thank you for standing close to us when the party is over
    and we find ourselves alone and empty.

We praise you for giving us direction
    when we have lived with false reflections
        in a fun house maze,
            and it isn't fun anymore.

Call us to our best selves
    when we have forgotten the person we set out to become.

Stand fast on our behalf.

Remind us who we are when we forget.

Lord of the promise,

> thank you for those who helped us become who we are:
>
> > parents who brought us to the baptismal font,
> >
> > > pledging to teach us about Jesus.

> > for teachers who nurtured us in church school,
> > > reading bible stories
> > > > and sharing cookies,
> > for choir directors who made singing fun,
> > > and youth advisors who lost sleep
> > > > listening to us when we needed to talk.

Thank you for all these people who kept their promises to us,

> and gave us a good example for our own lives.

God of commitment, help us to be trustworthy,

> to keep vows we made to our beloved ones,
>
> to renew those pledges grown old and weak,
>
> to fulfill the promises we made for our own children.

Grant us the power to honor our marriage vows

> when our hearts feel empty,
> > and routine threatens to undo us in a world
> > > that worships excitement.

Help us remember when we forget.

Help us feel loved even when we are lonely.

Tell us again of the family to which we belong.
Hear us now as we pray for those who weep...

Hear our prayers as we thank you for those who celebrate...

Go with us now into the week ahead.
Hold us in the hollow of your hand.
In the name of our brother, Jesus, we pray.
Amen.

<u>Covetousness</u>

O God of generous spirit,
    we are a people who want and want and then want more.
We covet those things stuffing our closets
        and houses and garages,
    yet leave us still wanting, and our souls empty.

Come to us with gifts that satisfy our longing hearts,
    gifts that do not rust or mold or go out of fashion.
Give to us abundant insight
    so we might covet what is right and good,
    so we might hunger for just living,
        and thirst for Christ-like deeds
            to fill our barns for eternal storage.

When we are alone and sad, feeling small,
    come to us as spirit and joy, laughter and hope.

Give us the precious gifts of spiritual faith,
    not faith in things purchased at a check-out stand.
When we feel covetous,
      satisfy our raging consumerism with simple appetites
        and the wisdom to know when enough is enough.

We pray for those who feel isolated,
    cut off from friends and family,
      worried over health,
      praying for children
        and weeping for parents.
We ask you to be present for each one.

May our prayers be heard and hearts assured,
      for you are the giver of good and perfect gifts,
        loving us better than family or friend.
You stand by each sick bed,
    and pray with us for our children.
You kneel before the weary and old,
    and weep with us over our aches and pains.

The desires of our hearts are known by you
    before we speak.
May our requests be the same as your plans for us,
    our yearnings be worthy of your blessing.
May our covetousness be for your kingdom.
May our generosity abound, our hearts overflow,
    indebted to your generosity. Amen.

Diversity

Creating God, from your imagination springs forth
 each unique idea,
  each distinct creature,
   and every color's hue.
You never let us weary of sameness,
You never give us only grey choices or
 day upon day of vanilla living.

Thank you for the variety of faith,
 the individuality of our imaginations,
 the plentiful fruits of the spirit,
  and the abundance of choice, flavor and style.

Grant to us spiritual hospitality as we meet those
 who would contradict our decisions,
 who would challenge our theology,
  or count themselves better Christians.

Give us wisdom to listen, to search, and to smile,
 using conflicting ideas of others as tools
  to challenge the clarity of our own faith,
Redeem denominational mischief.
 May it only strengthen our search for truth.
We trust you to bridge the gap
 between us children
  scrimmaging in your sanctuaries.

Come to us now, Lord, in the diversity of our needs,

    touching those who suffer,

    enfolding those who are lonely,

    dancing with the joyful,

    laughing with the hopeful.

Create a new heart in us so we might

    celebrate the variety of spiritual expression,

        and acknowledge beauty in the assorted seasons

            of Christian maturity.

Harmonize the distinctly separate tones of our traditions

    into one great anthem

        praising your goodness to us,

            your imagination among us

                and your diversity through us.

Amen.

Jesus

Ever surprising,

    constantly loving God,

We praise you for humbling your majesty

    and coming among us as a man.

Thank you for knowing our physical limitations first hand,

    for worrying about the sick enough to touch their illness,

    for hungering on a Galilean hillside

        enough to multiply the loaves and fishes,

for hearing the cries of the outcasts and caring
>enough to join them at table
>>eating and laughing together.

When we forget to care for the sick,
>or feed the hungry
>>or touch the outcasts,
>>>remind us of you.

When we feel distant and confused,
>unable to know you as we would,
>>come to our tables,
>>>and sit with us awhile.

When we are stressed and worried,
>not knowing what to do,
>>whisper to us, "What do you think I would do?"

When we feel weak and helpless,
>as a child crying in the night,
>>remind us, "Of such is the kingdom of heaven."

Give us curious minds and open hearts as we answer,
>"Who do you say I am?"
Take from us fears of daring to imagine you in a new way.
Give us a portion of your imagination,
>so we might think boldly outside theological boxes
>>we have inherited.

May our conversations with you be part of our daily routine,

  using simple words,

  speaking heartfelt concerns.

Hear now our prayers for others:

  the sick,

    the dying, and those who wait beside their beds;

      those in harm's way,

        those beginning new grades in school,

          others facing difficult decisions,

all those who ache inside and out.

Hear our prayers for them and for ourselves.

Thank you, Jesus,

  brother,

    friend,

      guest,

        son of God,

          carpenter,

            and so much more. Amen.

New church year

God of our roots, Lord of our family, your church,

Thank you for the home we find here among your people.

  for teachers and singers,

    preachers and organizers,

      leaders,

        and folks who smile and make us feel welcome.

We look forward to this new beginning of the church year,
    the excitement of seeing old friends,
    the opportunity of studying your word,
       and the joy of praising you together in worship.

Give us the wisdom to establish healthy patterns
      for our Christian lives,
    making time to think and pray and read,
    giving good example for those who watch,
    choosing to serve you by word and deed.

Make us aware of the love that sits next to us,
    known by name, or waiting to be known.
Make us grateful for the journey
    that brings each of us into this place,
for the people who carried us to the font,
    for those who made us curious about you,
      or those who cleaned windows and organized rooms,
       who designed bulletin boards
         and moved furniture into friendly patterns.

Thank you for grandparents, teachers, parents and friends -
    all those who brought us to this sanctuary,
    who prayed for us over the years,
      and did not grow weary of waiting for us to return.
For those in the world who spread good tidings of peace,
    we thank you.

For those who model turning of cheek and the shaking of hands,
> who sign bold political agreements
>> and risk their lives to end war,
> we praise you.

You have called peacemakers your children.
Protect them from harm
> and allow them to fulfill their blessed destiny.

We praise you for the gift of baptism,
> birthing us into your family,
>> for promises made today and kept tomorrow,
>> for a place where we always belong.

When we are sick in body or soul,
> may this church bring comfort.
When we are afraid of the future,
> may your light lead us through the darkness.
When we are facing death,
> may we look toward your kindly welcome without fear,
>> remembering those who have gone before us
>> to make heaven a friendlier place.
When we are troubled, speak to us
> through the lips of our brothers and sisters in faith.
Thank you for Jesus Christ,
> our brother and our savior.
Amen.

People of the church and new members

Lord of mountains, seas and skies,
We lift our eyes unto the hills,
    inviting you to come among us as our strength,
    calling ourselves to honor you through our worship here
        in the beauty of your holiness.
We people of the church, pray for your guidance and direction.

Our hearts are heavy for the sick among us,
    the troubled hearts, the grieving we call by name.....

Enfold them in your comforting embrace.
Whisper of hope and grant them peace.

Forgive us for thoughtless words and careless deeds,
    for energy wasted in worry over things soon forgotten
        and not worth remembering,
    for creativity drained away
        by pouting and pointing fingers,
    for gifts laid aside
        until we have the time that never comes.

Grant us spiritual wisdom
    to count each moment perfect which is filled with joy,
    to spend each day with care as though it were our last,
    to celebrate each person we meet
        so they might be glad to have passed our way.

Grant to us an economy of time well spent,
>   and a sense of gracious stewardship as we use your gifts
>   for the work we do in your name.

Thank you for the new members come to us this morning,
>   for the gifts they bring, fresh ideas
>   and new ways of looking at worship and service.
May we be to them a spiritual family, a listening ear,
>   a ready hand to lead them into our fellowship.
Give us all joy in your presence,
>   and point us toward the needs in your world. Amen.

Prayer for new leaders in the community and nation

Lord of all great moments,
>   from the beginning of time until the end,
>   and through all the small moments in between.
Thank you for the years laid before us,
>   years to quicken our talents
>   and bring forth the best in us and our nation.
Thank you for your presence through the past
>   and your promise to stand with us in the years ahead.

We thank you for the service of those leaders who now pass
>   their responsibilities into the hands of others.
Grant them time to rest.
May the good they have initiated grow,
>   and the poor decisions dissipate.

God of possibility, Lord of this world and universe,
we pray for your presence with the powerful people of our time,
    for those who rule the kingdoms of this world.
May they be quickened by cool heads and caring hearts,
    by wisdom and sage advice,
        rather than a call to podium or pocketbook.

May each dare to be imaginative in a world that fears change.
May each claim a vision of hope,
    and compose plans with purpose and conviction.
We pray for the powerful leaders of this world.

God of nations,
    Lord of history past and history yet to come,
We pray for new leaders coming into office
    near to home, across the continent and around the world.
May their call to service
    quicken in them energy during times of despair.
May constituents uphold them
    when they receive criticism for unpopular
        but right decisions.

May there be quick learning curves in each elective office,
    for our county, state, nation and world need hasty reform.
Leave these servants not alone.
Grant them days of challenge,
    days of comfort and a large helping of comedy
        to carry them through serious issues they encounter.

Touch us all, Lord.

We need your presence through days of illness,
loneliness and worry.

Lift us into a venue of hope,
good nature and mirth in spite of uncertainty,
for in days of shifting sands,
you are the rock beneath our feet.

Amen.

The Bible

Giver of sacred text, guardian of the living word,
turn the pages of our lives, find us eager to know your truth.

We praise you for the many stories throughout scripture,
stories of those who struggled to live as your people,
knowing good times and evil times in their lives,
discovering your discipline,
welcoming your forgiveness,
and coming to the end of their lives,
glad for having lived in the company
of your word.

We praise you for the law we receive through scripture,
giving us guidance for choices we must make,
challenging us to struggle for understanding,
bringing us to our knees when we discern our sin,
and granting us pardon even when we don't deserve it.

Thank you for the greatest story ever told,
    a tale of Jesus, the Christ,
        coming in human vulnerability,
        growing up in this world the same way we grow,
            and dying too soon
                because he loved righteousness.

Thank you for your church,
    the body of Christ,
        born through his death,
        growing with his resurrected spirit,
            living through your grace,
                and serving the world through human hands.

Give to us the gift of wonder,
    great enough to sustain a lifelong study
        into the depth of your word.
Let us not expect our search to be simplistic or effortless,
    but a journey into mores, customs and wisdom of the day.
Grant us minds open wide with childlike enthusiasm,
    asking questions no matter how basic,
        never assuming we know all there is to know,
        never believing ourselves complete,
            or our hearts big enough to stop growing,
                but always eager for more.

May our spirits live young at heart until the day we die.

May we cling to your word

the closer we grow to heaven.

And when the final days appear,

may we rest in the knowledge of your promises

stored securely in our hearts.

Amen.

SEASONS OF CONFESSION

ADVENT AND CHRISTMAS

Loving creator of both great and small,

we are not worthy of your gifts.

We no longer stop to stare at stars,

or watch a child at play.

We worry about what is missing from our lives,

and overlook the abundance of what we have.

Forgive our small hearts for loving things,

and forgetting people.

Forgive our lame excuses,

when called by angels to gather at the manger,

we say we are too busy. Amen.

Holy child, born of a singing mother,

forgive us our monotone lives,

for seeing darkness rather than angels and stars,

for listening to bad news rather than magnificent music,

for living with dread rather than delight.

Redeem us.

Enliven us.

Give us new hope in our hearts and a song on our lips. Amen.

Lord Jesus, son of the living God, have mercy on us.

We demand stars to lead us all year round.

We forget to remember our dreams each morning.

We fear unknown paths that call us into the future.

Forgive our fearful departure from the manger's glow.

Make strong our vision for tomorrow.

Make straight our hesitating steps.

Make plain and simple our love for serving you. Amen.

<u>Small child of God, forgive our feverish ways.</u>

Forgive our rushing feet, running circles around the manger.

Forgive our careless hands,

dropping small and precious moments.

Forgive our angry words,

scolding the weary and overworked.

Blessed babe, wash away our lesser selves.

Turn our steps from stumbling and create in us a dance.

Give our hands a soft touch to soothe the hurting,

and lips to sing good tidings of great joy. Amen.

<u>Child of light, we cannot bear the brightness angels bring.</u>

Like shepherds, we wonder about good news of great joy.

Might it bring change and uncertainty?

Like sheep, we would follow routine and tradition,

hoping we might not need to be transformed.

Like weary travelers in rowdy inns,

we miss the quiet miracles just around the corner.

Child of God, empty us of our couch potato habits,

and fill us with enough curiosity to get up and look. Amen

Forgive us, Christmas child,

for kneeling at your birth wondering what we will get this year,
    for wondering about recipes rather than the needs of others.
May our selfish expectations be transformed by stars,
    our shortsighted vision aged into wisdom,
        and our doors opened to welcome angels. Amen.

Forgive us for thinking only of ourselves,

    when the world cries out for our attention,
for taking offense at the trivial,
    when others suffer the depths of cruelty,
for limiting Christ to a cuddly child,
    when he came to conquer the world.
Forgive us.
Open our eyes to God's great plans. Amen.

God of time and changing seasons,

we confess our sin this year just passing,
    for those good deeds we never made time to do,
        and those things we never should have done.

Forgive the good we left unfinished,
    and the wrong we completed.
Wipe our new calendars clean
    and grant us a new beginning. Amen.

Christmas God, we confess our lives are hurried and distracted.

We can't spare the time to celebrate the heart of Christmas.

We are too busy shopping to appreciate your gift,

> too engaged in entertaining to kneel at your feet.

Our lives worship details,

> and we miss the ultimate act of history.

Forgive us.

Forgive us for engaging in temporary details,

> and missing the eternal. Amen.

Lord of the cradle and the cross,

> we confess we are often unable to move beyond sorrow.

We cannot see the sunrise midst the shadows in our souls.

The promise of joy and life seems empty.

Our spirits drag behind us,

> pulled across cold ground, sounding like dry weeds.

We hear brittle sounds instead of carols,

> and miss the sight of angels.

We have forgotten the reason for hope.

Have mercy upon us, Lord.

Lift us from chaos of the deep.

Guide us from dark valleys onto plains covered with morning.

Point us to paths made straight,

> prepared for those who follow a savior. Amen.

Christmas child, Prince of peace,

We gather in celebration to hear the good news of angels,
>   and the air is filled with our own voices.

We wait with anticipation for the sight of a birth,
>   and peer into windows filled with things to buy.

We pray for peace here and abroad,
>   yet know too well the unrest of our heart and home.

Forgive our foolish ways.

Redeem our feverish days.

Cause us to stop and kneel in silence.

Give us time to truly ponder the wonder of your birth. Amen

LENT AND EASTER

God of power, Lord of compassion,

we will never understand your love so great, so humble.

We can never return enough service, enough thanks.

We can only hang our heads in shame.

Our hearts are small and beat with selfishness.

Our hands are able but unwilling.

Our lips shout "hosanna" but mutter excuses.

Forgive us.

Transform us.

Use us.

Amen.

Loving Christ, patient friend of the impatient,

save us from our restless selves.

Grant us holy moments within this passionate week ahead.

Allow us time to ponder our souls,

to ask forgiveness,

to wait.

Save us from the trivial,

distracting us from the depth of our disappointments.

Forgive us.

May the purple hues of Lent direct our gaze within.

May all lesser gods fade into the darkness

as we prepare for Easter dawn. Amen.

Risen Christ,

we live in the wake of your powerful resurrection.

We find hope through your life after death.

Yet we confess our fear of death,

our doubt and our dread.

Forgive our fear of dying, our doubts in the deep of night.

Set us upon the mountaintops of Easter.

Lift our eyes to the promise of morning.

Show us the light! Amen.

Gentle Savior, you come to us as a suffering servant.

We turn our backs so our eyes will not be offended.

We turn our heads so our minds will not be changed.

We turn our feet in the opposite direction.

Forgive our fear of suffering, our avoidance of grief.

Give us confidence

your hands can soothe our pain.

Give us memory

your footsteps always walk our path.

Give us hope in your promise always kept. Amen.

Lord God, forgive us for worshipping our sins more than you,

for holding onto grudges, for grabbing all we can get,

for believing our sin greater than your forgiving heart.

May we take up our cross and follow you,

finding it rests easy upon our shoulders,

and gently upon our hearts.

Grant us eyes to see those miracles already among us. Amen.

BAPTISM AND EUCHARIST

Creating power, hovering above the waters,

>   we are suspect of new beginnings.

We forget promises made in the waters of baptism.

Forgive our casual commitments.

Lord Jesus, we walk the sands of life,

>   intent on making our own paths, rather than following yours.

Forgive our wayward feet.

Comforting spirit, we look to skies darkened by war

>   and doubt the promise of rainbows.

Forgive our pitiful memories. Amen.

Gracious Host, we gather from near and far.

We come confessing our foolish ways,

>   times of following selfish paths,

>   times of caring little for your direction,

>   times of disobedience in full knowledge of our sin.

Forgive us.

Lead us from death to life,

>   from despair to hope, from doubt to trust.

Let peace fill our hearts to overflowing.

Let unity of spirit unravel misunderstandings.

May the bread we break together knit our voices into prayer.
Amen.

Lord of the table and towel, hear our confession.

You invite everyone;

    our guest list is selective.

You welcome us to the seat of honor;

    we worry about what to wear.

You bathe our feet;

    we try to hide our corns and calluses.

You prepare a menu for royalty;

    we hope our enemies are jealous.

Forgive us.

Renew in us a heart of hospitality.

Clothe us in garments of generosity;

    launder our spirits.

Give us enemies to love. Amen.

PRAYERS OF CONFESSION FOR ORDINARY TIMES

Merciful God, in the quiet, look into our hearts.

We are ashamed to admit those secrets we hide from others.

We even try to conceal them from ourselves

    by staying distracted,

        but they creep into the corners of our minds

            and will not let us forget.

Give us courage to admit our wrongdoing,

    to purge our darkest corners,

        and lay before you our shame.

Forgive us Lord.

Grant us a bountiful harvest of grace. Amen.

Oh, God, we are so judgmental.

Forgive our superiority, our moralistic attitudes,

    for judging others from out of the secrets in our own hearts.

    for criticizing ourselves just as harshly

      as we condemn others,

    for doubting your pardon,

        and clinging to our guilt.

When we give up believing you wash us clean, forgive us.

When we blame and criticize and point fingers, forgive us.

Chasten us when we refuse to forgive others.

Grant us a double portion of kindness to share. Amen.

<u>Great giver of bountiful blessings,</u>

    forgive our constricted hearts,

        our limited understanding,

        our constant flirtation with drama and spotlight.

We stumble along our journey toward wholeness,

    refusing to recognize our need to forgive others,

        or our opportunities to drop the burden of hate.

Lift the numbness of apathy

    and charm us with new possibility,

        new hope, new beginnings in your family of faith.

Amen.

<u>Lord of the dream,</u>

    we resist your purpose if it doesn't fit our plans.

We kill the dreams of others,

    because we dare not risk our own.

Forgive our fear of visions,

    our reluctance to share ourselves fully.

When we play "if only," call us to account.

When we refuse to let go of our grudges,

    remind us why you died.

When we hold onto worn out sorrows,

    empty our hearts, and offer us dreams of something better.

Forgive our foolish ways. Amen.

<u>Loving God, Lord of the family and hope of the future,</u>

    forgive us when we forget to count our blessings.

Forgive us when we blame others for our bad days.

Forgive us when we tear down rather than build up.

Give us happy hearts and willing hands to work in your family.

Give us humor and laughter to enjoy these days of our lives.

Grant us your presence turning darkness into dawn. Amen.

God of the merciful heart, forgive us

for dragging our feet on the path toward right living,

for resisting your gentle company on our journey,

for struggling with the past rather than

loving the present,

dancing with optimism,

and singing a new song.

Have mercy upon us

when we don't grasp the opportunity to forgive,

when we refuse to listen to good advice,

when our senses are dulled by irritation.

Come into our struggle.

Resurrect within us a desire to be free of revenge.

Hear our confession, and forgive our sin. Amen.

God of honor and majesty,

we come to you clothed in ragged garments.

They are torn by rushing here and there,

frayed by stress and worry.

Forgive our agitated ways.

God of earth and sky and sea,

cover us with your mantle,

so we may not be shaken.

For we would sing your praise! Amen.

God of story, dream and vision,

    forgive us for our poor memory.

We don't remember where we came from,

    or who it was that cleared the path.

Forgive us for letting others diminish our desires,

    for listening to their voices above yours,

        and lessening our unique call to serve.

Forgive us for dreading tomorrow,

    thinking the image in our mirror is all we are.

God of yesterday, today and tomorrow,

    give us deep gratitude for our beginnings,

        clarity for our singular talents,

            and childlike anticipation for what's next. Amen.

Generous God, giver of all good and perfect gifts,

    we are a people with sticky fingers and hidden pockets.

We prefer to gather than give, save than share.

We confess hoarding our talents and time,

    and giving as little as we can.

Forgive our stingy hearts and calculating minds.

Forgive us for building barns and storing up treasures.

    May generosity burst into our lives.

        and thanksgiving loosen our tight fists

            quickening our hands to serve you. Amen.

God of each beginning, Lord of every ending,

forgive our fragile faith.

Forgive us when the future opens before us

and we fear what we cannot see.

Have mercy upon us

when the past holds us captive, and we cannot escape;

when we remember the worst, and forget the best.

Be gentle with our constant worries,

and lift us into the future you are preparing for us. Amen.

God of action,

known by your touch in each generation,

forgive us for sitting on our hands.

We meditate and pray.

We indulge our selfish needs, praying for your attention,

but we do not go the second mile.

We sit in reflection, enjoying the luxury of contemplation,

but rarely leave our chairs.

Forgive our faith without works.

Redeem our vegetative state, our works mostly selfish.

Resurrect us into a celebration of action. Amen.

Gracious God, forgiving and energizing spirit,

we are complacent folks,

quick to receive your blessings and slow to pass them on.

We are careless citizens of church and state,

quick to complain and slow to engage.

We are critical of others' work,

quick to find fault

and slow to consider the heart of the matter.

Give us your spirit of insight and surprise so we might

celebrate our blessings by sharing,

support the kindly hearted by word and deed,

see the best in one another by listening with love.

Convict us.

Forgive us.

Enliven us. Amen.

God of reason and understanding,

come into our minds and souls.

Fill us with desire to know your word and your will.

Open our hearts to wisdom and humility.

Empty this sacred time of daily worries,

and direct our wandering attention to things eternal.

Come, Lord Jesus, come. Amen.

God of the nations, we humbly confess our apathy.

We would criticize rather than work for justice.

We would be cynical, rather than exercise our citizenship.

Forgive us.

Grant us a renewed sense of purpose to be your blessing

within our community, our nation and our world. Amen.

Holy and merciful God,

we come bowed down and ashamed of our foolish ways.

We yearn to belong, yet feel separated and alone.

We are born into families, yet feel like orphans.

Give us hearts to discover those ties that bind,

hands to work with common bonds of service,

and family through the bloodline of Christ. Amen

Shepherd of Israel, hear our humble prayer.

You enable us to be partners in mending your broken creation.

You see our world captive to greed and injustice.

Why are we silent?

Why do we not cry out against the spoiling of our earth?

You see our wars, hear our lies,

feel our viciousness and smell our sin.

Forgive us, God, for failure to see ourselves as we are.

Help us to open every corner of our lives

to the light of your presence,

the instruction of your word,

and the willingness born into our hearts.

Then forgive us when we fail, and equip us to try again. Amen.

Lord God, forgive us

> for those times we were tired,
>> and could not forgive our tiredness,
> for those occasions we tried,
>> and failed to meet our expectations,
> for those moments we felt empty,
>> and could not fill our own emptiness,

We come with humility, to receive your heavenly smile,
> and hear the words,

"Well done, good and faithful servants." Amen.

God of abundant generosity

> we are a people who suffer from gathering more than giving.

Our hearts ache from smallness.

Our minds calculate how to keep more than we need.

Forgive us.

Grant us the freedom of generosity,
> so we no longer hoard our talent or our time.

May gratitude swell our hearts.

May thanksgiving open our hands.

May we offer you more than a tip, nothing but our very best.
Amen.

Lord of blessing and promise, we confess our doubts.

We doubt we are a blessed people chosen by you.

We doubt you are the one who keeps your promises.

In the night, we even doubt your presence.

Forgive our fair-weather faith,
> a faith that whistles but cannot pray.

Forgive our lukewarm spirits
>   that no longer dare to take that first step.

Forgive our inability to wait,
>   to ponder, to endure.

We need your touch.

We covet your courage. Amen.

God of yesterday, today and tomorrow,

Lord of every season under the sun,
>   we confess our hesitation with change.

We yearn for comfort more than challenge.

We love the predictable more than surprise,
>   and court what is known rather than what awaits us.

There is little risk in our life.

Forgive our limited vision, unwilling to dream the unseen.

Forgive those ties that bind us to the past.

Grant us enough confidence to say goodbye,
>   and more trust to await your everlasting hello! Amen.

Lord Jesus, we confess how quickly we frown,

>   how easily we bear witness to the negative,
>>   and how joyfully we argue the down side of hope.

Forgive us for expecting bad news,
>   for waiting on the other shoe to drop,
>   for anticipating hurricanes when a breeze begins to blow.

Grant us visions of an upside-down world,
>   where the last shall be first,
>   the weeping rejoice, and boundaries no longer divide. Amen.

Lord God, we humbly confess our divisive spirits,
>
> our holier-than-thou attitudes,
>> our delight in a stiff-necked position.

Forgive us for separating from those who are different,
> from those who see the world in unusual shades,
> those burdened by our judgment and in need of our love.

Grant us a vision beyond our limited sight,
> glimpses of your just kingdom. Amen.

God of holy conscience, we confess blindness
> by turning away from scenes that haunt memory's eye,
>> by trying to heal our sick hearts with distraction.

Forgive us for allowing the evil we see each day
> to go unquestioned,

for getting busy rather than involved,

for waiting on others to do the work of righteousness.

Grant us commitment in healing the world. Amen.

Lord God, we humbly confess our hunger pains,
> our hunger for peace,
>> yet our low profile commitment,
> our hunger for justice,
>> yet the fear of our own voice.

Forgive us for coming to be fed while forgetting,
> those who yearn for the bread of body and spirit,
>> those who starve for your word and our help.

Grant us energy and vision beyond this world's limits,

Lead us with glimpses of your kind kingdom. Amen.

<u>Lord God of family, church, and all good community,</u>

you create for us fellowship,

and we want freedom.

You nurture our souls,

and we try to hide secrets.

You call us to join the chorus,

and we hum our own tune.

Forgive our rugged goals of individualism,

our worship of self satisfaction, and mistrust of others.

Forgive our "know-it-all" isolation in a world created for sharing.

Redeem our hermit hearts. Amen.

<u>Holy One, everlasting comforter,</u>

we come before you with lives full of unnecessary clutter,

too busy to stop and think about the meaning of life;

our barns too full to wonder what we might share.

We fear confronting the truth of death,

and put off end of life decisions.

Forgive us when we ignore our responsibility

to those who will live beyond our days. Amen.

<u>Lord God, our thirsty hearts long for you.</u>

We wake in the night with longing.

Our souls feed upon tears all the day.

Forgive our yearning for the wrong things,

for short term distractions,

for shortsighted happiness,

for short memories of your kindly rescue.

Give us hope

> amid the despair of this world.

Help us

> when we believe no one hears our cries.

Grant us patience to wait upon the lifting of our sorrow. Amen

God of truth and wisdom,

> we try to protect your law by building fences around it.

We forget your power to rule the earth and all therein.

We see your truth in part only,

> and think we know it all.

Forgive us the walls we build

> to keep us from the heart of the matter.

Forgive us the walls we mend

> without considering the damage they might do.

Forgive us the walls we worship

> instead of you. Amen

God who sees within

> receive the secrets of our hearts,
>
> > those for which we are sorry,
> >
> > > and those still burning us to the core.

Take from us the weight of anxiety,

> for those things unworthy of our attention.

Convict us of those things that bind us to wrongdoing.

Shine light into our shadows,

> for we would be better citizens of your kingdom. Amen.

Creator, sustainer, redeemer God,
>   we come before your grace to confess our sin.
We confess our sorry attitudes,
>   our grumbling hearts.
We dare reveal our mean-spirited actions,
>   rejoicing over wrong,
>>   pleased over the faults of others,
>>>   wearing holier-than-thou lifted chins.
We beg your tender mercies.
Give us souls like trusting children,
>   unafraid to try and fail, and then try again.
May we be dead to our sin, and alive to all that is good. Amen.

Lord of the ages, God of all history,
>   forgive our fear of passing years,
>>   our disdain of aging.
Forgive our love of youth,
>   our dread of growing old.
Give us a spirit of wisdom to see beyond wrinkles,
>   to find gifts in the vintage of decades,
>   to see patterns of hope threaded throughout the tapestry
>>   of long lives.
Reawaken castoff dreams.
Recycle the desires of our youth into future possibility,
>   for you alone know the measure of our days. Amen.

Lord of laughter, Christ of joy,

>forgive our long faces,
>>our loss of lighthearted living.

Forgive us for taking ourselves too seriously,
>forgetting our human nature is frail,
>>demanding too much of ourselves
>>>and playing too little.

Give us the grace of humor to lighten our burdens,
>childlike freedom to poke fun at ourselves,
>>and the presence of a laughing Christ.

Save us from our small, grumpy selves. Amen.

Forgive us Lord when we forget to be thankful,

>when we are too busy to count our blessings,
>>and complain more than celebrate.

Give us the insight needed to discover our blessings.

Quicken hope in the darkest of nights,
>and joy in the promise of dawn. Amen.

God of the ages, forgive us our selective memories,

>for not remembering your promises,
>>for not saying thank you for our daily blessings.

Forgive our fear of stepping beyond our comfort zones,
>for leaving your call unanswered,
>>and avoiding new opportunities.

Forgive our fainting hope,
>for counting losses rather than gifts,
>>for blaming others rather than growing up.

Give us wisdom to welcome maturity,

the gift of not taking our wrinkles too seriously,

and grace to live with age spots. Amen.

Lord of life and all that is life giving,

forgive us for blaming others for our mistakes,

for irresponsibility in our personal behavior,

and indignant surprise when we reap our just deserts.

Forgive us for wallowing in sorrows past,

and listening to evil echoes over and over again.

Give us a future beyond our small imaginations,

a hope beyond boring dreams,

a life beyond constant chaos.

Come to us in the mystery of your peace. Amen.

God of good company, forgive us for living lonely in a crowd,

for believing ourselves far from you,

and not stepping up to bridge the distance with prayer.

You are as close as the words we speak,

as the breath we feel upon our lips.

Forgive us for hurting each other,

for mean and ugly words,

for thoughtless deeds.

Touch our hearts and soften them with kindness. Amen.

God of the fallen, you have seen us slip, and picked us up.

You have led us through troubled waters,

and set our feet on dry ground.

Hear us as we confess our wrongdoing.

We praise you for making us one,

 yet suffer from distrusting others.

We are challenged to envision a new tomorrow,

 yet choose blinders and old, accustomed ways.

We put our trust in human systems

 and revere heritage more than insight.

  and familiar folkways rather than fresh paths.

Help us say goodbye to what has been, and greet what might be.

          Amen.

<u>Gracious Lord, here we are again,</u>

 trying to remember the sin we want to forget:

  short tempers, angry words

   and compliments left unspoken.

We want to forget our less than honorable moments:

 thoughtless gossip, fearful silence

  when meanness needs kind words to intervene.

Bend to us, hear our confessions admitted so timidly.

 and fill us with forgiveness overflowing. Amen.

<u>Forgive us, Christ, for not taking the church seriously,</u>

 for doubting your call to greater works even than you.

We mumble our excuses and busy ourselves with small projects.

Forgive our inadequate expectations,

 our small prayers, our unwillingness to try once more.

Remind us of the power you placed within us.

Help us dig up the dreams we buried in the past,

 and discover compelling treasures we had forgotten. Amen.

God, you fashion us by hand and call us by name,

> and we do not listen.

You place before our eyes the needs of the world,

> and we complain of aches and pains.

Cries of the helpless reach our ears,

> and we turn up our iPods so we won't be depressed.

Forgive us.

Open our idle hands.

Give sight to our limited vision.

Quicken our creativity and make us lively servants again. Amen.

Lord of Creation, you give us so much,

> yet we want more.

You lavish upon us a shockingly beautiful world,

> and we take it for granted.

You place us in a time of unmatched privileges,

> and we live as if these gifts are due us.

When illness and hard times steal into our homes,

> we feel singled out for punishment.

Forgive our arrogance, Lord,

> for thinking you owe us beauty, and privilege, and health.

Make us truly grateful for what we have.

Give us humility.

Give us thanksgiving. Amen.

Forgive us, God,

for speaking your name with a dull sense of duty,

> for entering your presence expecting to be bored,

and counting the minutes until we can leave.

Forgive us for seeking entertainment rather than challenge,

for asking rather than giving,

and waiting to be served rather than serving.

Receive our lame expectations,

and transform them into surprising discoveries. Amen.

Lord God, come to us in these moments of confession,

for we yearn to grow beyond our sin.

Lead us to discover the power of your love.

We confess a dullness of spirit

and a distraction of soul.

Renew a right disposition within us.

May we waken to power,

find direction,

and learn to whistle again. Amen.

God of the loving call,

we acknowledge our invitation to be yours.

We boast of our intelligence and power,

forgetting true wisdom comes from an understanding heart.

We take pride in ourselves

forgetting authority needs to be matched by compassion,

and weakness needs to be confessed,

for in doing so we find our strength.

Forgive our reaching only for the standards of this earth,

believing yours too high for our grasp.

Lift us beyond our reach. Amen.

God of presence, so close we breathe your very spirit,

Forgive us for turning away from you,

> for searching in the wrong places for the right answers,
>> for asking ill-advised people for directions,
>>> and ignoring the wisdom within your family.

Forgive us for thinking you are irrelevant in today's world;

> for accepting trivial solutions for universal questions,
>> for asking ultimate questions of the uninformed,
>>> and ignoring your presence in human affairs.

Accept our confession.

Forgive us.

Renew us, and hold us in the hollow of your hand. Amen.

Creator of all life,

you brought into being all that is, and pronounced it good.

> We are careless with your gift.

You invite us to be stewards of your creation.

> We take much and return little.

You want us to live in unity,

> yet build boundaries between people and nations.

Heal our divisive, miserly ways.

Forgive our greed.

Create in us hearts of generosity and humility. Amen.

God of glory, your kingdom comes,

> growing among us day by day.

Yet we still do not fully trust your power.

Forgive our arrogance thinking we know it all.

Forgive us for stopping our ears to others' diversity,
    those who worship you in different ways.
May we build bridges to link our diversity.
May we grow in compassion to silence our criticism,
    and enlarge our hearts to include others. Amen.

Loving God, we are called to be your family,
    and we busy ourselves claiming no time for others.
You offer us a home in your heavenly kingdom,
    and we prefer our real estate on earth.
Forgive us for assuming your gifts are due us,
    for receiving them so casually, so carelessly.
Pardon us for demanding instant gratification,
    then complaining
        when our prodigal ways lead nowhere.
We are sorry.
    Bring us home again. Amen.

Loving lord, forgive our fickle affection
    expressed only when we want something.
Forgive our hurried prayers
    offered after we have tried everything else.
Give us hearts overflowing with gratefulness,
    and prayers of friendly conversation throughout the day.
May our hands reach toward the needs of others
    even as we need to be touched.
Grant our souls peace through meekness and humility. Amen.

Almighty God, you love us in spite of our brittle hearts,

You speak to us, and we do not listen.

Forgive us for walking away from neighbors in need,

    wrapped up in our own concerns.

Forgive us for following paths of prejudice, warfare and greed.

Help us be honest with ourselves so we might confess,

    turn to you, and receive forgiveness. Amen

Merciful God, forgive us for always wanting more,

    when we haven't thanked you for what we have.

Forgive us for comparing ourselves to the rich, and complaining,

    instead of comparing ourselves to the poor, and sharing.

Enrich our hearts. Redeem our greed. Amen.

When in the living of our daily lives

    we forget to stop and celebrate each special moment,

        forgive us, Lord, for being so easily distracted.

When we are bogged down by unimportant details

    and miss opportunities to say, "I love you,"

        forgive us for mixing up our priorities.

When patience is used up and frustration takes over,

    forgive us for losing our identity as your people. Amen

Almighty God, you created us for life in a garden.

We turned from your desires,

    and chose to hate one another.

We have not loved as you commanded,

    and take more than we have given.

Forgive our disobedience.

Cause love to grow like perennials,

   and weeds of disdain to dry up on rocky paths.

Grant us patience to wait upon the seasons of goodly change.

Amen.

<u>Almighty God, you spread good gifts before us,</u>

   more than we deserve, more than we even need.

You feed our bodies and heal our souls.

You teach us truth and save us from our lies,

   and we always want more.

Enough is never enough.

Forgive us for not sharing as freely as you give,

   for resenting what we lack,

      and envying those who have more than they need.

Give us a liberal portion of divine generosity. Amen.

<u>God of light, help us confess.</u>

We hang our heads and mumble,

   rather than coming clean before your forgiveness.

We live in darkness

   rather than open our blinds and smile into the sunshine.

We bury our sin

   rather than planting gardens of perfumed beauty.

Create in us clean hearts and dirty hands

   digging in the soils of rich renewal. Amen.

<u>God of grace,</u>

forgive our mistrust when we hear a language not our own.

Forgive our suspicion when we see a face not our color.

Pardon our superiority

when we look down upon different cultures.

We need your blessing of open mind and open heart. Amen.

<u>Ever present God, forgive our shortsightedness,</u>

for watching our feet drag along well-worn paths,

rather than searching skies for shooting stars,

for worshipping security

rather than risking the search.

Forgive us for small hope and limited faith,

for falling short of our potential,

and thinking our sins too great to be forgiven.

Give us greater conviction in your power. Amen.

<u>Gracious God, you come knocking on the doors of our hearts,</u>

and we refuse to let you in.

Your love searches in the darkest of places for our thirsty souls,

and we resist being found.

You offer living waters

and we choose desert sands.

Find us, Lord, and forgive us.

Allow your Spirit to refresh us,

renew us,

ready us to serve. Amen.

<u>Forgive us, Lord, for living like strangers in your church,</u>

> for not speaking to new faces,
>
> and finding our comfortable seats with familiar friends.

Forgive the alibis we make

> for not speaking a simple welcome.

Open our mouths with smiles,

> and speak through us a kindly hello.

May we share our homes,

> our lives,
>
> > ourselves. Amen.

<u>Loving Lord,</u>

> forgive us for saying we love you
>
> > only when we want something.

Forgive us for praying only when we need help.

Give us thankful hearts to praise you all the days of our lives.

Grant us kind words to speak

> in a world that needs kindness,
>
> > and give focus to our lives
>
> > > in the midst of chaos. Amen.

<u>Forgive us, comforting Lord,</u>

> when in the midst of sadness we choose to suffer alone,
>
> > refusing to name our pain among your family,
>
> > > trying to go it alone.

Forgive us, dancing savior, when in the midst of gladness

> we are unaware of other people's sorrow.

Recapture for us memories.

In times of loss, may we trust your promise to carry our burdens.

In the midst of gifts, make us aware of others' loss,

> others' loneliness, others' separation.

Take from us those things that blind us

> from seeing you face to face,

>> our self-pity, our splintered and shrunken lives.

Unstop our ears so we might hear the cries of others,

> not just our own sniffling.

Give us a taste of tears upon the cheeks of others,

> so we might stay with them in their sorrow.

May our hands reach out in service,

> even during seasons of our own need.

Be to us a companion in the midst of our sighs. Amen.

<u>Lord of hearth and home and family, hear our confession:</u>

We have given advice rather than listened,

> pushed too hard when we could have held hands,

> humiliated others when affirmation was needed.

Forgive us when we didn't trust another with our truth,

> when we were absent to their need,

>> and too serious when laughter would have healed.

We have lived to get our own way:

> forgetting duties, fussing over food and clothes,

>> doubting the sincerity of others,

>>> unaware of friendship being offered.

Forgive our feverish ways.   Amen.

Forgive our fear when life turns upside down.

We are anxious and slow to follow your lead,

    remaining settled rather than risk the unknown,

        living contentedly among our insecurities.

Forgive us when we feel shy,

    and refuse to talk of your blessings to others.

Forgive us when we confuse

    what we need with what we want,

    when we allow our souls to grow shallow,

        our vision to become clouded,

            and our service to end before completed.

Come to us with unexpected challenges.

Give us strength to brave the insecurity of new ideas.

Teach us a new dance step for our tired feet.

Remind us we are to be a blessing to this world.   Amen.

Lord God, you shower us with good gifts,

    and we worship them more than you.

We praise you for blessing us, but hide from your testing.

When trials come, we deny your sovereignty.

When troubles arise,

    we question your power, testing your patience.

Forgive us, Lord.   Amen.

SEASONS OF TROUBLE AND SORROW

In times of trouble

September 11, 2001

You are with us, Creator.

In times of terror, you hear our screams.

In times of weeping, you wipe away our tears.

 Come to us in these times,

  for we are confused and afraid.

We are confused by hate

 that premeditates the destruction of the innocent.

We cannot understand the distant ploys

 of those who care so little for life.

We wonder about evil plans waiting upon tomorrow.

Come to us in these troubled times,

 for we cannot live without you.

We are afraid for our country

 and know not what our leaders will do.

We are afraid for our cities

 and wonder how they will protect themselves.

We are afraid for our loved ones and ourselves.

We want a future.

Come to us in these times,

 for we are humbled by our fears.

Come, Creating God.

Give us strength and wisdom:

strength to endure the present
      and create a future;
   wisdom to find where evil lurks,
      and to deal justly for the innocent.

Give us humility and resolve:
   humility to acknowledge
      our wrong doing at home and abroad;
   resolve to pursue
      a more equitable position in the world community.
Give us a chance to begin again.

May the genesis of these days
   bring forth a country gathered together for good.
May the promises and prayers of these days
   come to reality in your hands.

Give ear to those who have no words.
Record in your eternal memory those voices calling for help.

Walk among the glass and cement and body parts
   lying on shadowed streets.
Listen to the loved ones cry.
Touch them.
Stand near to those who dig,
   who bind,
      who carry.

Walk amid grief and heaviness and down turned eyes.

Whisper comfort.

    Hold the empty.

        Renew the broken.

Blow among us the seeds of peace.

    Scatter them in fertile places;

        water them with tears.

Give us tomorrow. Amen.

For all the saints

Creating God,

    you bend to us at our beginning,

        breathing into our nostrils the breath of life.

    You bend to us at our endings,

        whispering of spirit and promise.

Remind us death is but the graduation

    of promises made at our baptism.

Death invites us to sit at your heavenly banquet.

Death births life,

    where we shall see you face to face.

When tears fill our eyes,

    blurring the vision of your empty tomb,

        comfort us.

When crying fills our ears,

    dulling the alleluias yet to come,

        comfort us.

Be patient with our grief.

> Hold us in your arms.

Comforter in sorrow,

> thank you for the saints who have touched our lives,
>> for their examples of godly living.

May we keep their spirits alive

> by living their ethics,
>> and passing on their morals
>>> to the next generation.

Everlasting arms,

> you alone can turn death's shadow
>> into morning's song.

Abide with us.

> Smile hope upon us,
>> and dry our tears with the breath of your spirit.

Amen.

And then I remember the empty tomb

O God, I look at the world and grieve.

There is no peace.

I mourn those who hunger and hate,

> those diseased and in pain,

> those crying for justice.

And I despair.

I despair until I remember the empty tomb.

Something good came from the darkness,
    something very, very good.

But in the waiting time,
    between the fullness sealed by rock
        and the emptiness guarded by angels,
            there was weeping.

Where is the Prince of Peace?
Where have the peacemakers gone with Middle Eastern names,
    African names, Korean names?
Where are they?

I despair.
And then I remember the empty tomb.

O God, I look at the church and grieve.
There is no peace,
    fighting over social issues, theology and money.
I can't find Christ.
Have we converted the Church to our liking?
Is the work of the saints for nothing?

I despair.
And then I remember the empty tomb.

Something good came from the darkness,
    Something very, very good.

O God, I look at my life and grieve.

There is no peace.

    I trouble over many people,

        many decisions,

            many words.

I fight the demons within me called by a legion of names,

    Loneliness,

        Greed,

            Depression,

                Envy.

And I despair.

Then I remember the empty tomb.

Something died.

Then something stirred in the deepness of emptiness.

Something woke.

Something good came from the darkness,

    something very, very good.

Peace.

God of shadow and sunlight

God of all times,
>   whose face is hidden to our limited sight,
>>   thank you for turning things around.
From evil,
>   you clear a path of forgiveness moving us toward good.
From loss,
>   you create a yearning in our hearts to be well-filled.
Even the victims of this world recover their sight,
>   their voice,
>>   their anticipation.

We yearn for you as we stumble through the valleys of death,
>   and hear your whisper,
>>   "Fear no evil."
We cover ourselves with shame,
>   disgraced before the world,
>>   and you lean toward us,
>>>   longing to forgive our confession.
At our worst,
>   you love us best,
>>   covering us with a mantle of your love.

May we see beyond the gloom of our human failings
>   into the possibilities you bring into being.
We can never give up on ourselves,
>   for you don't.

We can never give in to despair,

    for you are not dismayed.

Thank you for always welcoming us home

    with a feast.

Amen.

Prayer for unity in the Church

Ever-loving and ever-creating God,

    we bow before you in prayer–

    we who are your people,

        your Church,

            your son's body,

                commissioned to serve you

                    in this place and at this time.

We pray for unity within the Church,

    not to believe alike,

        but to believe the same savior,

    not to serve alike,

        but to serve the same master,

    not to worship alike,

        but to worship the same lord.

We pray that from the labor of conflict

    there might be born

        greater energy for spreading good news,

    that from the pain and dis-ease of argument

    there might blossom renewed spiritual health,

that this human institution we call the Church
might claim the other side of it's nature
and become more divine.

Forgive our inability to love one another
when we discover how diverse each of us is,
how unique you have fashioned each mind and heart.
Forgive our need for sameness,
and our fear of differing ideas.
Reform our lack of theological growth,
our refusal to listen,
our spiritual childishness.

Grant wisdom to our leaders.
Be ever present as they discern your will for the future.
Touch each with loving interpretation.

Lord God,
we wonder at your eternal patience,
for our human patience is so short-lived.
May we speak truth in such a kindly way
we win friends for Christ,
rather than an argument for ourselves.

As we debate issues,
give us deep concern for unity of spirit.
May we be bonded in our search for what is right,
not simply agreeing with each other to keep the peace.

Give us grace to serve you with integrity,

    taking our task sincerely

        without taking ourselves too seriously.

We are a people with limited knowledge and partial truth,

    a people who trust you to speak

        in many ways

            and in many places.

May we listen carefully amid the noises that seek to distract us.

Smile kindly upon us

    with your amazing patience.

Amen.

I never thought it would come to this.

I knew we yelled and made each other cry.

But, Lord, I always thought we could make it up.

I had faith in our promises.

So much for promises.

The walls of my house are no longer a home.

They lie to me with smiling faces of a bride and groom.

    Babies and pets and campers picture the perfect family.

My ring finger has a circle of white the sun never tanned.

Everything is changed, Lord.

I can't even talk the same.

I used to say *we* and *us* and *ours*.

    Now I choke on *I* and *me* and *mine*.

My bed is too big.

What do I do with Christmas cards sent to Mr. and Mrs.?

I'm so afraid for our children.

How do we divide our money, our house, our dog?

Friends have stopped calling.

They don't know which one of us to invite to their parties.

They can't decide who to blame.

We threaten them.

If it could happen to us, they fear it could happen to them.

How can things change so quickly, so completely,

    so terribly and permanently?

I'm lost, Lord.

How do I find my way into tomorrow?

There's no one I can trust.

At least it feels that way.

I trusted my marriage.

Now I can only depend upon my tears.

Lord, help me.

Please...

Lord God, hear our prayers

We lift to you the yearnings of our hearts
        for the tears of the world,
    those who hunger and thirst for food and water,
    those who have no homes in which to lay their babes,
    those who have no will to live any longer.

We lift to you those who fight on foreign soils,
    so tired they cannot remember why they kill,
    so traumatized they will never be the same,
    so lonely in spirit they dream empty dreams.

We lift to you those who fight within our nation,
    fighting for equal rights in a country struggling to be fair,
    fighting for jobs and homes in a place of plenty,
    fighting to renew worthy commitments to their ideals.

We lift to you those who fight in their living rooms,
    discouraged by years of humdrum relationships,
    praying for their children who think different thoughts
        and walk unusual paths,
    wishing others would agree with their values
        and support their decisions.

Lord God, hears our prayers.
    for those who mourn the loss of beloved ones,
    those who pray and find no answers,

those who wish they could return to the past
>   and do things differently.

Give wisdom to all who struggle to do the right thing,
>   to parents and children who can no longer communicate,
>   to teachers who wish they could improve
>   the lives of their students,
>   to leaders who truly care for their constituents.

Be to us hope.
Bring to us energy.
Be our God of strength.   Amen.

Everything is gone

From the darkness of nothing,
>   you created the earth and all that eyes can see
>   and hands can touch.
Now the world of my making is gone.
I planted the gardens, drew the first plans, chose colors and
    fabrics and door handles.
It's gone.

It was there and beautiful,
>   the house of our dreams.
I had just finished dusting.
We left for a couple hours that stretched into forever.

How can I ever trust again?

I turn my back for an instant and it's gone.
I know nothing lasts forever,
>   but usually a few things remain to remind me of who I am.

O God, I can no longer touch grandmother's sewing machine
>   and remember her stitching leather gloves.
I can't slip grandfather's baby ring on my own finger
>   and feel the generations encircle me.
I can't finger Dad's military medals
>   or smooth the flag we were given at his funeral.
Mother's silver is a tarnished memory.
A candy dish passed through the family is gone.
>   Were the flowers lavender or blue?

Are the pictures framed in my mind enough
>   to recapture their faces?
What if my memory wanders?
I wanted to pass on the pictures of our family,
>   but their faces are only in our memories now
>   and will fade with our passing.

I wake each morning and sigh,
>   "Thank God, it was only a dream."

But it isn't.
It's surreal,
>   but real.

How can we complete the endless paperwork?
I can't concentrate.
Paragraphs I read three times don't make sense.

My friends try to console, but their try-to-fix-it words don't help.
You can't fix something that no longer exists.
The best they can say is,
    "I'm so sorry for your troubles."

Months have passed
    and I'm stuck in a sinkhole of anger.
I'm so full of fury and grief.
I bounce back and forth between compulsive activity
    and overwhelming fatigue.

Please lift the smoke
    and show me blue skies.
Grant me bouquets from my own garden again.
Dust the ashes from my soul
    and blow the scent of lavender into my heart.
Give me a home once more,
    not just a house.
Can you?

God who does not hide from us

Loving Lord,
    thank you for being a God who does not hide from us
        or wear masks to hide your face,

for being a God who faces us openly
with the fullness of creation-
allowing us to see your power in the small,
unexpected moments
of deep and touching insight-
for smiling at us through the eyes of babes,
and touching us with wrinkled hands, gentle and wise,
for looking at us through the eyes of those who need us,
then toasting at our weddings
and laughing at our parties.
You are not far.
Yet, we often don't expect to see you
and don't know where to look.

Give us hearts to search for you in unexpected places.
In the midst of quarrels and hateful words,
may we know you listen and understand and weep.
In the hospital rooms of birth and death,
may we feel you hovering as close
as the first cry and the last breath.
In daily struggle with street and school and business place,
may we be reminded you are here with us,
in spite of our disbelief.
You are with us, always with us, even in the strangest of places.

May we find the delight of your presence
in party and laughter and sport.
Remind us your first miracle was at a wedding celebration.
Forgive us for thinking you are hidden and proper and distant,
for you are as close as our hands and cheeks.
It is you who breathed into us and caused us to live.

Waken us now to the divine possibility we might be your
     servants, your chosen people,
          your very hands and feet and voice in this place,
             and in this time.
Lead us to be your agents of change for good.
Excite us! Inspire us!
Remind us
     we can actually change things,
          make a difference,
             bring good news into a bad news world.

Help us love those who hurt us.
Teach us to confront with kindhearted honesty
     those who tear our hearts apart.
Correct those who need new direction.

Get our arms dirty up to the elbows
     in service you would
          do if you were here.
Comfort those who are afflicted by every kind of doubt.
Give each of us the hope we need
     to make it through another day.

Celebrate with those who feel like laughing and dancing.
Teach us to look for miracles in simple,
     everyday occurrences.
Lord God,
     cup our faces in your hands,
          and breathe again into each of our lives
             challenge and curiosity
                 and a saving sense of humor. Amen.

Decision making

Loving God, we lift our hearts in joyful praise.

    Our lives are full of loved ones.

    Our homes are filled with comfort.

    And our world is full of dilemmas.

Come to us through scripture,

    the life of Christ and the testimony of the church.

May we search for wisdom,

    and honor our life experience in the search for truth.

We pray for the church struggling to minister in a hostile world.

    May our leaders be blessed with prophecy

        and our congregations eager to follow.

When headlines report the worst of crimes,

    and hatred seems to rule the day,

        give us hope and direction to work for a better world.

When sickness and death threaten to overcome us,

    grant your holy comforter presence among our grief.

Hear now our silent prayers

    for those we hold so dearly in our hearts…

(silent prayer)

We pray for this congregation,

    those who have been raised in this sanctuary

        and those who have come to worship in recent months.

May each find this a place to serve and be served.

May our witness be seen by those beyond these walls,
> as a testimony of kindness,
>> as a community filled with the spirit of forgiveness,
>>> and genuine warmth expressed in our welcome.

Go with us into the week.
May we be a blessing to those who cross our paths,
> and bring us again into your presence
>> in the cycle of Sabbaths ahead.
Amen.

Her collar hangs above my desk

I held her head as she died.
Her eyes closed.
Her breathing stopped.
Everything was quiet.

I'm sad, Lord.
You created the beasts for our keeping,
> to name and feed and love.
I did my part, but she did more.

When I was glad, she danced.
When I cried, she lay by my feet.
When I was lonely,
> she stood close and looked me right in the eye.

Her toys are scattered around the yard and house.
I don't want to move them.
That is so final.
But her collar hangs above my desk.

I can still see her chasing a tennis ball,
    jumping for her Frisbee,
        racing to welcome my grandson.
I hear her bark,
    an addendum to the doorbell.
Her smell is still on my bedspread.
But she's dead.

Dear God,
    please let her visit my dreams.
Let me smell her bad breath now and then.
May I find her black hair on my clothes in the closet,
    and please take her for a walk now and then.

She likes her rump scratched too.

Financial insecurity

Loving Lord, we come concerned about those we love,
    the tired and old,
        the hurting and humbled,
            all the aching souls.

Give us the time to encourage the tired,
    the wisdom to appreciate the old.
Give us the hands to touch the hurting
    and the strength to lift the humbled.
And those aching souls,
    allow us to soothe their pain
        and sit with them in silence.

So often, we don't know what to do or say
    in the midst of grief and shock.
Give us the wisdom to simply sit with the hurting
        and abide in silence with those who need support.

In these days of financial insecurity,
    may we trust in that which is everlasting.
As the market goes up and down
    and economic strategists throw up their hands,
        may we declare allegiance to your firm foundation.

When we worry about the price of groceries,
    may we remember those who don't have the luxury
        of simply choosing a cheaper brand.
When the price of gas shocks us,
    may we care about those who have no bus fare.
When we downsize to pay our mortgages,
    let us remember those who have no homes.

Lord, kindly lift our eyes in gratitude to hope's horizon.
May we find strength beyond our difficulties,
    strength to share with those who hurt more than we do.
May we know your presence in our lives with such assurance,
    we might assure others.
And when we don't,
    when we are weak and wondering,
        give us a helping hand.

We can only be strong for so long
    until we need your support.
We can only believe so long
    until we need your extra portion of assurance.
Life is hard, Lord.
Without you it seems impossible.

We call for your confidence in our lives,
    your guidance for our steps,
        your strength in our attempts to hang on,
            your direction for our heart's delight.

Hear our prayers now, O Lord.
Amen.

Leaders of the world and the least of these

God of glory, Lord of this earth,
  we pray your presence with the powerful people of our time,
    for those who rule the kingdoms of this world.
May they be quickened by cool heads and caring hearts,
  rather than the seduction of podium and pocketbook.
May they dare to be creative in a world suspicious of change.
May they claim hope,
  and plan with wisdom.
We pray for the powerful leaders of this world.

God of glory, lord of the world to come,
  we pray for your presence
    among the religious leaders of our time,
      for those who proclaim your kingdom.
May they confront us with vision and prophetic imagination,
  not just comfortable eloquence.
May we hear rustlings of your spirit,
  disquieting the passive.
May prophecy again give fair warning.
We pray for your leaders in the church.

God of glory, lord of the least of these,
  we pray for your presence with the powerless,
    for those without choice,
      stripped of options.

We lift into your powerful care:
>the refugee,
>>grieving the loss of roots and home,
>the captive,
>>shackled in body and spirit,
>the victim,
>>living behind the bars of memory,
>the lonely,
>>washing only one place setting after each meal.

May we who claim your name, claim also your spirit
>so we might find resourceful ways of bringing
>>nourishment to the hungry,
>>home to the aimless,
>>dignity to the naked,
>>>and a future to those at the end of their ropes.
We pray for the small ones in this world.

God of glory, our lord and savior,
>we pray for your presence with the church, your family,
>>for those of us claiming your sacrificial bloodline.
May our hearts not faint in discouragement,
>our call not fade in the embers of burnout.
Surprise us with your power of divine comedy,
>your laughter that turns this world upside down,
>>the pleasure of knowing you have the last word,
>>>the lyrics that begin at a cross
>>>>and end with an alleluia. Amen.

Low self esteem

Beloved parent,
    kindly father, who quickens our beginnings,
        sheltering mother, who nurtures our birth,
            hear our prayers of thanksgiving.

We, who feel unfinished and undone,
    need to be held by your amazing love
        and feel you smooth the rough edges
            of our splintered self esteem.

We do not love ourselves
    as you love us.
We do not feel our self worth
    as you have given us to be.
We scarcely believe we are loved at all
    or deserving of your personal interest
        by the time we finish our own denigration.
Come and hold us.
Stroke our bruised egos.

Rock us in the infancy
    of our desire to begin again.
Fill our doubting hearts with the unshakeable truth
        that we are precious.
    We are beloved.
    We are useful, and can become a mature child of the holy.

Bring us into your presence,

    a place where we can hear your affirmation

      and hurtful voices are silenced,

    a place where your voice shouts good news

      that rings out in the deepest black hole of our despair.

Call us to you where morning breaks through dark doubts

    of age and illness, sadness and broken dreams.

May the warmth of your arms around us

    mend our aching hearts

      so we are not broken beyond repair.

Son of the living God, heal us,

    so that our gifts may be shared

      as long as we are here to share them.

And when this life is finished,

    and our new life begins where mirrors are no longer dark,

      may we see you face to face.

May we see the love in your eyes

    and know all things have been made right.

Give us a heartfelt rhythm to our faith,

    a mantra of grace

      that hums throughout our days,

        and sings in the night,

          repeating over and over again:

            "You are loved, beloved.

              You are loved, beloved.

                You are loved." Amen.

Peaceable kingdom

Lord God, ruler of the peaceable kingdom, creator of Eden,
We are far from the likeness of that child
  who would play near the hole of an asp
    or reach out to the adder's den.

We have lost our childlike trust,
  lost the promise of your garden,
    lost our way to your holy mountain.

Come to us with your vision of hope.
  Our sight is clouded by the smoke of bombs
    and silenced by sirens.
  We have nowhere to go but to our knees.

Hear now the yearning of our souls as we pray silently for peace.
  We pray for our loved ones, who fight in the air,
    on the waters, across the sand...
  We pray for world leaders who direct war and negotiate
    peace...
  We pray for ourselves, caught in a dilemma as
    peacemakers who hate evil and support justice,
      yet resist the option of war...
  And because Jesus commands us to – even though it is
    difficult – we pray for our enemies...

Lord, hear our prayer for the vision of a peaceable kingdom.
May that old stump of Jessie's tree bring forth a new shoot,

young enough to trust the wolf and lion,

innocent enough to pet the lamb

and hope in your promise,

willing enough to court your spirit

to rest upon this weary earth,

bringing wisdom and understanding,

counsel and righteous might.

Mighty and everlasting God, bring justice to your world,

and hope to your people.

Amen.

Anger, rage, frustration and fear

Creator of all human feelings,

We thank you for your power and control

over any emotion we feel,

all anger, rage, all frustration and fear.

We know you were acquainted with these emotions.

You felt what we feel.

You grieve for us,

seeing the results of our unleashed anger,

feeling the intensity of rage within our human hearts,

knowing personally the frustration that dwells among us,

for you died at the hands of anger, rage and frustration.

We haven't changed much since then, Lord.

We still need your touch to calm the earthquake within us,

that rolling and pulsing chaos when control disappears,

when we would strike out at anything

and anyone who steps into the arena of our rage,
when our mind's eye is blinded
and we cannot reason.

May the breath of your spirit blow
stronger than the winds whipping us into a frenzy,
stronger than gales toppling things
we have worked so hard to build,
stronger than the hurt caused by our hurricane fury.

Pour cool waters on the fires that destroy so quickly,
flames of passion,
spreading sorrow from home to home,
flames of greed,
leaving too little for too many,
consuming flames that leave only ashes.

Lord of earthquake, wind and fire,
We call upon your power to bring recovery,
your ability to bring light into darkness,
to turn evil to good,
to empty tombs,
and to laugh away the things we fear.
Touch us with reason,
remind us of your law,
grant us a recovered sense of responsibility
to make things right in the world.

You who still the earthquake,
help us steady the shaking beneath our feet,
to walk valleys of slippery ethics
protected by thy rod and staff,

to remember you are the rock,
    the firm foundation.
Though mountains tremble and oceans rage, you are God.

You who quiet the wind,
    blow with gentleness upon the flushed and contorted
        faces of our stress,
    rub the stiffness in our necks,
    massage the tension of our souls.
Breathe hope where there seems none.

You who quench the fires of evil,
    stoke flames of justice and mercy in our hearts.
Put a right spirit within us,
    so that righteous indignation might energize us to action,
    rage might find focus in productive labor,
    frustration might be given helpful words,
        and fear become bold,
            through the powerful intimacy of your spirit. Amen.

Save the children

Lord Jesus, son of the living God,
You knew early years of playfulness,
    you laughed and ran through the springtime seasons
        of your childhood.
Hear our prayers of thanksgiving.
We praise you for the children of every land,
    Somalia, Sudan, South Africa, and South Carolina,
    Children of Afghanistan, Alabama, Brazil and Louisiana,
    Children of Iran and Cairo, Haiti and Hawaii.

Lift them into your lap.
Run your fingers through their hair.
Whisper hope into their small ears
    and wipe away their big tears.

Lift them into our laps.
    Teach us to care for them.
Give us your wisdom as we seek to protect and nurture
    children of prodigy and prostitute,
        of rapture and rape,
        the runaway, throwaway little ones
            who struggle every day
                without parent or place, friend or future.

Give us wisdom to protect those who have,
    and those who have not.
We pray for those who can skip in Nikes and chatter on iPhones,
    who watch videos and chat on Twitter,
    who sing spontaneously and slightly off key,
    who dance and jump and tumble.
And we pray for those who wish they could,
    but can't.

We pray for children who are loved and unloved,
    wanted and unwanted,
        well fed and starving.

Lord Jesus, son of the living God,

    use our hands to reach out to the beggar,

        the beaten, the abused and neglected,

        those who are emotionally fragile,

           and those who rebel and ridicule,

                who torment and taunt.

Use our hearts to care for those suffering,

    from a mother's drug abuse,

        from famine, and bellies filled with air.

Use our power to minister unto these children of destiny

        and of despair,

    children of war and peace,

    children disfigured, diseased, and dying,

    children without hope,

        and other children with hope to spare.

Lord Jesus, son of the loving God,

    Let the little ones come unto you.

        Forbid them not.

Lord Jesus,

    Let the little ones come unto us

        to find love and protection

           through the power and compassion you give us.

We would serve you, Lord,

    by serving the wee ones.

Amen.

<u>Save the earth</u>

Creating God,
    holy one who rescues us from flood and fear,
    redeeming one who would save us from killing the earth,
      and turn us from our thoughtless greed:
thank you for people who dare to say,
    "Yes, I can.
      Yes, I will work to save the beasts,
        the babes and the flowers.
      I will help rescue the land,
        the sea and the sky."

May we be those who follow Noah's steps,
    bringing safety to endangered creatures
      disappearing from land and sea.
Give us eyes to see beyond consumerism,
    so we might save the forests.
May we live beyond convenience,
    caring enough about creation to recycle, re-use, re-purpose.
May we recognize our dependence upon all creatures
    both great and small.

Thank you for those animals that feed us,
    bringing strength to our bodies.
Thank you for animals that clothe us,
    keeping us warm in the cold and cool in the heat.
Thank you for creatures that work and play upon the earth,

turning the soil,
    spreading the seeds,
        pleasing our eyes,
            balancing the natural order.

We especially remember those animals we have given names,
    ones that live with us
        and love us when no one else seems to care.
We praise you for their licks and purrs,
    their barks and squeaks,
        for swimming beauties and singing beaks,
        for the good companionship of feather and fur.

Grant us purpose to be conscientious gardeners upon the earth,
    gentle caregivers of all you have made,
        for this is the only place we are given to live.
Grant us courage to be outspoken stewards
    of all your beasts, that creep and swim and fly.

We have known your care, Lord.
May we pass it on to those who depend upon us.

We celebrate your great love for us
    and for all that lives and has its being
        on this blue planet we call home.
Thank you God, for life in this lovely place.
Amen.

In the shelter of your wings

Sheltering Lord, in the shadow of your wings,
　　we gather as a family.
Here in gratitude,
　　we find the gifts of your presence,
　　　　comfort, warmth and rest.
Cover those who have been stripped by sorrow,
　　those who grieve the direction their lives have taken,
　　those who lie awake, anxious about decisions made,
　　　　and over which they now have no control.

In the security of your shadow,
　　　　we lift our prayers of intercession,
　　naming those most familiar and most beloved:
　　　　mothers, fathers, brothers and sisters,
　　　　　　children and grandchildren,
　　　　　　　　our dear ones, our neighbors, our friends.
Be to each what we cannot be.
Give to each what we cannot give.
Care for each in ways we cannot even know.

In the warmth of your wingspread,
　　we lift our prayers of thanksgiving:
　　　　for the good times when life was perfect
　　　　　　and joy gave dance to our step.
　　　　for romance grown into commitment,
　　　　　　and the promise of new life,

for health returned

and the hope of a few more good years.

Be with us as we laugh and enjoy the touch of winter,

as we taste the goodness of a simple meal,

and look upon kindly faces,

as we wrap scarves around our necks,

and know the gift of warmth,

as we watch children play

and listen to the sounds of youth.

We want you to know it is good to be alive

and living in your world.

Thank you for life.

Be with us in the rush of traffic,

the pressure of work, the tension of unknowing.

Bring us that needed assurance of calm and peace and rest.

You know our need to reflect,

to fill our souls with a deep breath of fresh air.

You know our need to just stop.

Engage us in the movement of spiritual time,

time not calculated by clocks,

but counted in memories.

Grant us time for holy reverie and soul growth.

God of shadow and shelter,

    lighten our shadows and

        shelter us beneath your wings.

Amen.

Times of instability

Lord in work and play, war and peace,

Come among us in these times of unknowing.

Be present in our future, as you journeyed with us in the past.

Come into our daily living as we read the papers, watch the news,

    open our bank statements and worry about our investments.

Enter our daily living as we wonder about

    our homes and mortgages,

        our jobs and unemployment,

            our health care, and the health care of the earth,

                the poor and hungry, the homeless and sick.

May we lift to you all these problems,

    those that waken us at night after we finally fall asleep,

    those that hang around the back of our minds

        and distract us from following a conversation,

    those that keep us tense

        and our blood pressure high.

Give us a memory,

    a memory of your presence amid overwhelming tribulations.

Let us not forget the great escape you choreographed in Egypt,
    dry land parting the sea,
        manna falling each night to provide daily bread,
            rocks cracking with streams of fresh water.
Let us not forget, lest we despair.

Remind us again:
    wars end, wounds heal, enemies even become friends.
Remind us again
    of history's diseases prevented today,
        of human wisdom capable of amazing solutions.
And give us a heart to celebrate gifts
    that cannot be diminished by recessions,
        will not melt in global warming,
            and do not detour our purpose in your kingdom.
Amen.

Living in two worlds

Lord of street and sanctuary, creator of justice and mercy,
    we are a people who live in two worlds.
We seek to be obedient, law abiding citizens
    in the kingdom of this world,
        while desiring citizenship in that kingdom yet to come.
We balance between the sacred and the secular,
    wanting to be your righteous family,
        yet torn between the laws of this world,
            and those of our heart.

Come among us.

Lead us as we witness to Christ in our everyday lives.

Come among us.

Quicken your wisdom to dwell with us in street, office,
    classroom and home,
        that we might witness to the law of love.

May Sunday inform our Monday living.

Bless our comings and goings
    among the naughty issues of our world.

May the same faithful wisdom affirming resurrection,
    affirm the reforming of our lives
        in this everyday sort of world.

We pray for those who are in prison,
    separated from family and choice,
        shackled by boredom and depression.

We ask you to be present in their cells,
    breathing opportunity for confession,
        pardon and newness of life.

We ask you to be with families who wait
    and hope for release of their loved ones.

Be with others who wait in fear of those to be released.

Stand with victims on both sides of prison bars.

Thank you for the many times you have forgiven us,
    times we deserved to be punished
        and you softened the blow,

times you turned us aside onto different paths,
and gave purposeful direction to our wandering.

Thank you for protecting our children
from the dangers inherent in simply growing up,
for giving support to those who suffer from deep
and lasting sorrow,
for promising your presence in the living of our lives,
through the right and wrong choices we have made.

We need you, Lord.
We need you every hour of our lives.
Come to us.
Hear our petitions and receive our prayers of thanksgiving.
Amen.

I'll never choose his name

He was only eleven weeks when he stopped growing.
I hardly knew I was pregnant.
The doctor said it was probably a boy,
because more boys are conceived.

It wasn't a good time for me.
I didn't need a baby,
but I didn't know what to do.
Is choosing termination killing?
Is choosing another time wise?

Lord, I am so deeply conflicted.
You give us free will,
    and I fear making the wrong decision.
You forgive us when we confess,
    but I want to do the right thing,
        something that doesn't need to be confessed.

Perhaps there isn't a right or wrong answer,
    a good or bad choice.
Perhaps there are times we must choose
    the best among only imperfect choices.
Life is so terribly hard at times like this.

I will wonder all my life.
What might he have been?
Would he have looked like me?
I'll never choose his name.

Is there a special heaven for these small ones?
Is there a special place for me to rest my burden?
Is there a better time in the future?
Support me, Lord.
I need you.

<u>Authority and wisdom</u>

God of all wisdom and authority,
We pray for your guidance.

In a world where institutions make promises they rarely keep,
    we feel forsaken and foolish.
In a world where people make promises they rarely honor,
    we fear commitment and can no longer trust.
In a world where too many authorities have too many answers,
    we wonder what is right and what to do.
In a world where knowledge comes and goes
    and changes before our very eyes,
        we pray for your wisdom to linger throughout the ages.

God of all authority,
We wonder how to answer questions,
    questions never asked before in history,
        with so many possible answers,
    questions which seem easy for others
        and absolutely imponderable to us.
We fear making wrong decisions,
    pain we might cause others,
        the chain reactions of unwelcome consequences
            we might begin,
                and the fear of punishment.
Yet, who is there to turn to who speaks your truth?
    Who shall we trust?

Who can we believe?

How do we discern godly authority?

Give us ears tuned to the frequency of compassion,

for you are compassion.

Give us minds to discover what is just and right,

for you are justice and righteousness.

Give us more than the facts,

for knowledge is not enough.

We need the wisdom of your authority,

for you are the author of all wisdom.

And, Lord, when we ponder the puzzles of everyday morality

and miss the mark,

convict us.

Hear our confession,

and forgive us.

Show us a better way.

When we make wrong decisions,

heal our mistakes.

When we weigh the options and make the wrong choice,

protect us from evil.

for we are your people who would serve you in holiness.

We are your chosen, your blessed,

your beloved sinners,

who would seek to become more saintly.

Thank you for your still, small voice calling us to struggle
>with the ethical dilemmas of our time.

Thank you for our struggles
>and the search for answers to more clearly satisfy our souls.

Thank you for wisdom that dwells in the presence of your
>authority and power.

Amen.

I can no longer write

Creating spirit,
>giver of language and phrase and just the right word,
>>my page is blank.

I remember the days my pen couldn't keep up with my mind.

Ideas tumbled onto the paper in front of me.

All I had to do was sort and arrange and slip pieces
>into the right places.

I had more than I needed.

I had to cut.

Now, my page is blank.

I feel empty,
>an ink hole folding in upon myself.

I am a terrible void,
>once filled with voices and ideas
>>and the rhythm of inspiration.

Come to me.

I yearn to be filled,
    to be overflowing with the power of words,
        to feel the wonder of thoughts churning.

I want to know again the amazement of what's inside me,
    the surprise of an idea I did not know I had,
        shaped with words I did not plan.

I want to find again that hypnotic place of creation
    where my mind is so busy, I never hear the phone,
        a place so compelling, I skip meals
            and never notice my stomach's complaints.

I want to feel compulsive, unable to let go of an idea
    until it curls comfortably upon the page
        and begs for company.

These are the days for which I yearn.

I pray to open again the gifts you have given me.
Blow your spirit of creativity into my soul.
Touch me anew.

               Please...

Prayers from the pit

Lord, I don't know why you'd listen to me.
You, who knew no sin.
How can you abide the likes of me?
    Not only am I a sinner,
        but I'm a sinner many times over.

Time and again,
    I promise myself I will get straightened out.
Time and again,
    I'm right back where I started,
        or worse.

Sometimes I see people who are bigger sinners than I am,
    and I feel a lot better about myself.
But most of the time I don't measure up to the people around me.
Oh, I pretend to be holier than they are
    and I hold my head up,
        but I can't fool myself,
           and I just feel sick inside.

I've broken all the commandments,
    well not murder,
        but nine out of ten isn't good enough.
I drink too much,
    smoke too much, swear pretty bad.

I'm mean to my family,
>   and blame it on being tired.
I cheat when no one is looking,
>   and feel slightly clever.

Some days I sort of give up on myself,
>   and that's when I think about you.

Did you really mean it when you said you loved us sinners?
For the life of me I don't know why you would.
>   But they say you ate with tax collectors.
>> I cheat mine.
You talked with prostitutes.
>   That's not what I do.
If you love me, you must know something about me I don't.
Because, I don't even like myself.

In the middle of the night,
>   I wake and depression suffocates me.
Even my bad dreams are happier than daylight.
Darkness is shaped like fear.
Sounds of the night groan with profound emptiness,
>   and I have no name to call but yours.

Why must life be so deadly?
Why can't I feel useful?
>   There is nothing in this hole for me.
>> No one cares.

They pass me by,
  busy with purpose,
    fulfilling their dreams.

Who can I turn to
  if not you, O Lord?
Who gives a damn
  but you, O Lord?
Whether you answer me or not,
  there is no one else listening.
    I call to you.
      Help me...

No Words

I've no words,
  only tears.
Tears fill my mouth and sobs rack my soul.
Tears wash my day,
  filling the corners of my eyes,
    blurring my vision.
I cannot blink for fear they will spill into the street like a flood
  washing away the people around me.

When I look into the mirror each morning,
  I wonder how long I can keep from screaming.
Will they take me away,
  lock me up, put me in solitary?

I'm already there,
  so painfully alone,
    my body aches.
Maybe I should just give up, Lord.
  You seem so far away.

Yet, who else can I turn to?
  Only you.
    That's all.
      Only you.

Another Day

And so another day is here.
Time lays a crushing weight upon on my soul.
Light overexposes my sorrow.
I feel naked.
Hopeless.

They can see it in my face
  and turn theirs away from mine.
They hear it in my voice
  and pretend they don't hear.
Even the smell of me
  is like the dead.
Who cares?
No one.

Where can I turn for a life?
Who would understand the way I feel?
I'd rather be dead.

Suicide?

I don't have the energy.

I'll get up.
Try not to look in the mirror as I brush my teeth.
I'm not hungry for food.
O, Lord, I hunger only for the sound of my laughter.

SEASONS OF CELEBRATION AND THANKSGIVING

Table grace

God of abundance,
> thank you for good food,
>> for family and friends,
>>> for stimulating ideas,
>>>> and all our blessings.

In the midst of plenty,
> we remember the empty,
>> the hungry,
>>> the friendless,
>>>> the homeless,
>>>>> the dying,
and those who don't have the luxury
> of choice.
Amen.

Blessing the animals

Creating God,
You have touched our lives with joy
> by fashioning animals for our companions.
Thank you for the delight of furry feet and stretching wing,
> of scale and tail
>> and all that makes our days complete
>>> with such engaging company.

We pray for those in our care,
>   for their long and healthy lives,
>   for our wisdom in training and handling.

May we look into their eyes
>   and see your kindly affection for us.

May we rise each morning glad to be loved,
>   and rest each evening
>   more whole through their devotion.

Make us always worthy of their trust.
Amen.

Prayer for a new baby

God, help us be good parents.
Give us patience, strength, wisdom and a sense of humor.
>   Oh, especially the last!

Help us enjoy our baby,
>   not to worry unduly,
>   not to expect too much,
>   and not to strain over details,
>   important today,
>   forgotten tomorrow.

May we give *her/him* what is right,
>   not just what will make *her/him* happiest.

May we teach *her/him* what is good,
>   rather than that which will only make *her/him* popular.

May we discipline correctly,

    not being so insecure we fear

        the momentary loss of *her/his* young love.

May we love *her/him* when *s/he* is unlovely.

And most of all, dear God,

    when the time comes,

        may we have the faith to turn *her/him* over to your care

          and to your plan for *her/his* life,

Amen.

Thanksgiving for twins

Loving God, you who create families, and bond them in love,

    hear our prayer.

We praise you for the safe birth of _____ and _____,

    for the double blessing of twins,

    for our two-fold celebration of their tiny lives.

We ask your constant support of their parents,

        _____ and _____,

Give rest to their weariness,

    and humor when the demands of babies

        seem overpowering.

Give all those who minister to the infancy of their new lives
    twice as much patience,
        bountiful energy,
            and double delight in all the changes lying ahead.

May these two babes be yoked in your love as they grow,
    knowing your constant and abiding care,
        and your vigilance day and night
            at their rising and their sleeping.

Grant now the comfort of routine in the home of
    _____ and _____.

May they discover the unexpected gift of physical strength,
    and the overflowing of their hearts
        with twice as much love.

You, Lord, love each of us as though we were an only child,
    give to this family the joy of hearing a happy duet
        as _____ and _____
            grow in beauty and wisdom.
Amen.

<u>Hopes and fears</u>

Lord God, to you we bring our fears of death,
    weapons of mass destruction we can no longer control,
        diseases without cures,
            growing old
                counting far more years behind than ahead.
We fear what we cannot see.

We fear a life without meaning or direction,
    a life of loneliness and pain.
We tremble to make decisions,
    for we cannot control the outcome,
        finding jobs,
        moving from home,
        an unexpected pregnancy,
        finances.

To you we unburden our hearts
    filled with worry
        about children and parents,
            friends and enemies.
Accept our questions.
Comfort our trembling souls.

Lord God, to you we bring our hopes and joys.
    Rainbows of autumn colors greet us on every street.
        Hearts leap at the sight of loved ones.

Souls smile at kind words,
favorite songs, home cooking and pets.
Thank you for people who love us
and come when we need them
even before we ask.

We praise you for the Church,
not always right
or smart
or relevant,
but always lifting the promise
of your spirit with us.
Celebrate with us in times of joy.
Keep us hoping.

Lord God, you guarantee us nothing in life,
but your loving presence.
Health comes and goes.
Happiness is fleeting.
Wealth and power seem fickle as to whom they visit.

Hear us Lord: we are people who fail,
who sin,
who fear punishment,
who are slow to drop to our knees.
But we also sing and serve and hope,
anticipating your surprising grace.
Hold us in your care. Amen.

Lord of life and dream and vision,

thank you for tears washing us clean with your forgiveness,
  for a fellowship of dreamers supporting us
    when our nights are empty,
      and for new dreams when old ones have ended.
Thank you for your patient reassurance,
  when gifts of forgiveness seem undeserved.
We are a people who plod through life without a dream,
  yet leap with joy when you give us vision.
May we follow you with light-hearted step,
  knowing we are forgiven
    and invited to the table to sit with
      the saints of yesterday, and today,
        and those yet to be born. Amen

Hope beyond despair

Eternal God, so high above us, we cannot comprehend,
  so deep within us we cannot escape.
Our thoughts touch only the outskirts of your kingdom.
Our imaginations are but sound bites of your truth.
Make yourself real to us in this time of prayer.

Come to us Lord God. Come as power.
We pray for smooth sailing,
  yet when waves crash over us,
    we discover you in the midst of the tempest.

You are faithful in our nights of doubt.

You are near in good times and bad.

Help us to recognize,

>   times of challenge are but times for growth.

Times of sadness

>   are but valleys between mountain peaks.

Gracious and loving God,

>   we lift into your care all who are stumbling in despair
>
>>   caused by loss of health,
>>
>>>   loss of financial security,
>>>
>>>   loss of self-esteem,
>>>
>>>   loss of a relationship through love turned sour,
>>>
>>>   loss of a loved one through
>>>
>>>>   the valleys of the shadows of death.

In quiet, heal the hurting.

Grant reassurance.

Remind us of the hope that follows despair,

>   of resurrection morning following the night of the cross.

Come to each of us through the ministry of faithful people.

Grant spirit and strength of heart for our life journey.

Spirit of the living God,

>   come and minister to our intimate, most personal needs.

Walk with your people; be our help and comfort.

Be the inspiration and sustainer of our daily lives,

>   through Jesus' help. Amen.

A prayer for parents and graduating high school seniors

Parents

Lord God, giver of children, support of parents,

Thank you for the incredible gift of life shared in families.

Thank you for the joy of a child given into our care

to nurture,

to share laughter and tears,

to enjoy as friend.

Thank you for the vision we are given through their eyes,

for the memories we have collected together,

like rare gems and painted rocks.

Thank you for the promises made and kept,

for the years we held them in our arms,

and for the assurance that you now hold them in yours.

Graduating Seniors

Lord God, giver of parents, maker of families,

Thank you for placing us in homes,

where we grow and gather values,

where we learn how to leave in the fullness of time,

where we meet you.

Thank you for the patience of our parents who watched us

learn to tie our shoe laces,

struggle with big questions,

and separate into unique individuals.

Thank you for those things they gave up on our behalf:

time and sleep, quiet and orderliness, money and phone.

Parents and Graduates

Lord of child and parent,

We praise you for your steadfast love,

    your pattern of companionship throughout our past,

        the comfort we feel at this moment,

            and the promise of your presence

                in the future of our family.

Amen.

Graduation

Lord God, thank you for celebrations great and small,

    for birthdays and graduations,

        for children's voices and teachers' well-earned rest.

We praise you for the Church of Jesus Christ

        in spite of its faults and failures,

    for the guidance of your spirit through the centuries,

        for raising up those who lead us through

            institutional controversy,

                bonding us in spite of theological diversity.

We praise you for those times in our lives

    we can see progress and new beginnings,

        times of graduation

            and personal accomplishment,

        times to honor the past

            and celebrate the future.

May we lavish gratitude upon those
    who helped us reach this place.
Thank you for others who kept the faith
    by telling us your story,
        directing choirs,
            leading youth groups
                and not asking too many questions.

We praise you for church schoolteachers, Lord,
    trying time and again to explain something confusing,
        getting up early on weekends to prepare,
            coming on Sundays
                when the weather was forbidding
            and other Sundays
                too beautiful to stay inside.
They came.
Thank you for their commitment.

For teachers who taught us to read, count and reason,
    we thank you.
We celebrate coaches, counselors and administrators,
    janitors, cooks and drivers –
        all those who became part of our educational journey.

As these young people begin new journeys,
    we lift to you those who are graduating into their eternal life.
Be with those who mourn their passing.

Comfort those in pain,

> those who suffer alone and feel no one cares.

Be to them a presence real and warm.

> Whisper into their hearts.

>> Sing into their souls.

>>> Leave them not alone.

Amen.

Host of the banquet

Gracious host, you invite us to your joyful banquet.
Thank you.
For gifts of food, kindly company

> and stories of forgiveness seeming too good to be true,

Thank you.

We praise you for calling us to join your people of the feast,

> for our nourishment within your sacrament,

>> for warmth of fellowship and a place to worship.

May we be good guests,

> willing to stay and work after the party is over,

>> to serve after the last guest has left,

>>> to get down on our knees and do the work

>>>> of polishing our souls with prayer.

We lift to you those who wait and don't know what to expect,

> who grieve and despair, who feel numbness and shock.

May our hands be your hands touching them with compassion.
May our feet walk with them through their valleys.

Hear our grateful prayers for your presence in our uncertain days.
Let us never take your companionship carelessly,
>   or starve our faith of your attention.
Through your urging, may our devotion create good works,
From our delight at your banquet,
>   may we be strengthened for service.

Savior of the open invitation,
>   do not let us become complacent guests,
>>   taking your hospitality for granted.
Do not allow your party to end with dessert
>   and cordial leave-taking.
Give us the power of commitment to do your will,
>   serving your beloved needy ones,
>>   long after the table is cleared.
In the name of Jesus Christ, who invites us to pray. Amen.

Loving parent

Loving God, creating and comforting parent,
You suckle us through our spiritual infancy,
>   lift us upon your lap during the dangers of childhood,
>>   encourage our youthful curiosity,
>>>   and bring us into maturity as your faithful people.

Thank you for our families who loved us as babes,
  through sickness in the wee small hours of early morning,
    through stages of growth
      and baffling personality development,
        through accidents, injuries and fear.
To this font they carried us for baptism promising
  to raise us in the knowledge of Jesus Christ,
    to raise us in the church among God's larger family.

Thank you for the love of parents during our childhood,
  days of school and lessons, carpools and discipline,
    for reading our favorite story over and over,
    for watching us struggle to button our coats
      or sew or build or hit,
        and telling us,
          "You can do it. You can do it."
    for knowing we had lied or stolen
      or covered up a trail of misdeeds,
        and taking time to talk with us,
          forgive us,
            and help us start over.

Thank you for the patience of our families
  as we grew through the days of our youth,
    for the delicate balance of their letting go
      and letting us grow,
    for being there when we came running back
      feeling small again,

for trusting us with car keys,
and for those gracious times they listened
and didn't give advice.

Loving Parent, giver of all good gifts,
Thank you for those blessings our parents gave us,
clothing and medical care,
lessons and vacations,
favorite foods, surprises, and Christmas memories,
for doing the best they could in the innocence
of their own ardent parenting.
Give to us a kindly memory as we recall their failures,
a gentle heart acknowledging their mistakes.
Give us the ability to honor that which is honorable and
forgive that which needs your grace.

Loving God, father of our Lord, Jesus Christ,
Thank you for your parenting,
for the love that never lets go of us.
You hold us in your arms
long after our earthly parents are gone,
tying us with everlasting bonds of love
to those who have gone before us
to your eternal mansion.
Amen.

<u>Sanctuary mortgage paid</u>

O God our help in ages past, our hope in years to come,
We, your people, gather to praise you for this day.
We celebrate the end of a financial commitment,
    acknowledging those who dreamed of this sanctuary,
      and committed their money to make that dream come true.

We celebrate the beginning of new dreams,
    grateful for the freedom to serve you now more generously
      through mission and outreach in a needy world.

Thank you for your presence in this place,
    for light and color within these walls,
      reminding us you are the light of the world,
        coloring every day of our lives with love unending.

Thank you for the baptismal font where we brought our children,
    adding another generation to your family.
Here, we are born into the Church.
Here, we learn that wherever we go,
    whatever we do,
      we belong to you.
Here, we will always have a home.

Your family table invites us to gather and celebrate the Eucharist,
    remembering Christ's life,
      death, and resurrection,

binding us to him and to one another,
>> even those who have died and gone before us,
>> even those yet to be born.

For the pulpit, where your word is preached each Lord's Day,
> we give you thanks.
In good times and bad,
>> at marriage and memorial,
>>> your news is always good

For choir loft, where voice and instrument
> remind us through music of your beautiful tidings,
>> lingering in heart and mind
>>> through melody and rhyme.

Thank you for your presence in this place,
> through the ever-circling seasons of Advent and Christmas,
>> of Lent and Easter.
> through your symbols of grace –
>> cross, chalice and font;
> through your smile in the faces of those who greet us,
>> your touch in their hands,
>>> your comfort in their presence.

May this place remain your space for all people,
> those who are great and those who are small,
>> those who come with joy or sadness,
>>> those who come with strong faith or weak.

May we welcome
    all who are at home here
        and those who have no home,
    those who celebrate
        and those who wish they could,
    those who are saintly sinners
        and those who are sinning saints.
May those who seek you here
    never be disappointed.
Amen.

Creator of music and light

Creator of music, Lord of rhyme and melody,
You bring rhythm to life and light to each day,
You are maker of each voice and instrument.
We praise you for music singing through the seasons of our lives.
    In winter's white cold,
        you warm us with memories lingering
            like a favorite melody that will not leave us.
    In spring's teasing days,
        you sing through sunny morns and afternoon storms.
    In summer we are lifted by whistling in our souls.
    And autumn brings a time to reflect
        upon the tunes echoing through a lifetime.
May we hear your promises in the harmonies
    of every season's symphony.

Creator of light,

Lord of bright moments and twinkling darkness,

   May your daylight lift and warm our spirits for work;

      the gleam of a distant star guide us toward adventure;

         the gentle glow of evening turn us to

            reflection and renewal.

May your evening light warm the long nights of darkness,

   waking us with lyrics yearning to join your melody.

In seasons of celebration,

   we praise you for the energy of anticipation

      bubbling up in our souls,

      making merry the drabbest of duties,

      renewing childlike laughter in the midst of solitude.

      curving smiles upon our faces for no apparent reason,

We praise you when we can't help smiling;

   for the irresistible joy of your music in our lives.

May we sing of your goodness

   to those who have forgotten the melody of hope.

May we set the rhythm of renewal at a gentle pace

   so the sad and weary, the old and heavyhearted

      might feel again the possibility of a slow dance.

In dark times, when kingdoms fall and nations kill their own,

   we pause to pray for peace.

We praise you for the refrain of justice
    playing throughout history,
        never to be forgotten,
    echoing your word across land and sea,
    breathing warmth across frozen faces,
    hovering creatively above tables of negotiations.

Gather us in symphony to serve as your instruments of peace.
May the music of your faithful people
    drift through the warring streets of this earth,
        making curb-side play safe again for little ones.

God of eternal music,
May the refrain of good news be a constant melody
    for those who are weary and heavy-laden,
    for those who begin to pack for their heavenly journey,
    for the lonely,
        the lost,
            the guilty,
                the depressed.

May our hands work in the rhythm of your inspiration.
May our lives move in harmony with your direction.
Amen.

<u>Ordination and installation of a new pastor</u>

Loving Lord, we are called into your family through baptism,
   given deep roots in centuries of faith.
You invite us to serve the church as your brothers and sisters.
Thank you for the bonds of commitment we celebrate this day,
   for your call, and _____'s answer,
      for the gifts this church family needs,
         and the talents offered through _____.

Thank you for the joy we know as your adopted ones,
   for nursing us through the infancy of our faith,
      for your patience with our adolescence,
         your challenge to develop our talents,
            and your blessing as we mature.

Thank you for calling _____to serve here in this place,
   and in this time.
Be with her/him as s/he shares your holy sacraments,
   the breaking of the bread at your family table,
      and lifting the cup at your sacred feast.
Be with her/him as s/he pours the waters of baptism,
   acting as midwife at each birth into your family,
      hearing the promises made,
         and nurturing the growth of these promises.

We praise you for a heritage traced
 from our family tree at Calvary,
 for a blood line we can boast,
  sealed in crucifixion.

Be with this pastor when joy is not so evident,
 when pressures mount and waters muddy,
 when the congregation fusses
  and everyone seems to be going different directions.

Give her/him your Holy Spirit
 when confusion and conflict seem to be ruling the day
  and peace slips into the shadows.
Stand firmly with her/him when s/he is tempted
 to avoid discipline that strengthens every family's growth.

Catch her/him off guard with unexpected humor
 when s/he most needs a good laugh.
Surround her/him with the joyful knowledge
 of deep resources to love and be loved,
 of tender opportunities to nurture and be nurtured,
 and of how well you have equipped her/him to serve here.

Give to the members of this congregation a vision,
 not forgetting the past,
 nor disowning their history,
  but celebrating the hope that is great
   in the future of this household.

Grant this family the miracle of birth that keeps
    families growing beyond themselves,
        welcoming new and unique personalities,
        welcoming new ideas,
        forgiving over and over and over again.

Thank you for the work of those who have labored for this day.
May their work reap years of rich benefits
    as pastor and congregation serve together.

May each of us remember the promises of our own baptism
    as we help one another grow in Christian faith,
        and serve Christ by serving the needs of others.

Lord God, in our fellowship and study,
    in our worship and service,
        strengthen the family ties we share
            with your universal household.

We are blessed this day.
Thank you from the depths of our hearts.
Smile upon us.
Amen.

The gift of heritage

O God, our hope through ages past,
    we thank you for those ties binding us to our heritage.
Remembering the support of family and friends,
    we thank you for roots deeply grown
        from the bedrock of our ancestors.
Remembering their example of strength,
    we thank you for courage
        to stretch our wings and take flight.

From distant lands and seas afar,
    we celebrate our lives in this place.
Never let us forget the gifts given to us by others,
    health, strength, encouragement, money, confidence.
May we pass our memories to the young,
    giving them a sense of place and people
        discovered through the telling of family stories.
May we point toward the future,
    giving today's youth strength
        for adulthood tomorrow.

Equip us, Lord, to be bridges from the past into the future,
    so our young will grow their own strong roots.
Stir within us pride for the people of our past,
    and excitement for the future
        as our children live into tomorrow.
In the name of Jesus Christ, son of the timeless God, Amen.

Litany of thanksgiving between pastor and congregation and sending forth the pastor

Pastor   Lord Jesus, son of the living God,

I thank you for the years you have given me to serve the people in this church,

for your hand upon our past and your promise for the future.

People   Living God, we, the people of your family,

celebrate your presence through the ministry of_____.

We thank you for her/his touch upon our lives,

for weddings s/he performed in this sanctuary,

for baptisms at this font,

reminding us wherever we go

and whatever we do, we belong to you.

Thank you for her/him standing with us at hospital beds,

offering prayers for healing,

for wise words when we were confused.

for her/his presence at graveside,

reminding us of resurrection,

for teaching and preaching with insight and ardor.

Hear our prayers of gratitude, Lord God.

Send her/him with your blessing

into the next sphere of service.

Pastor   I give thanks to you, Lord God,

for these people I have served,

for their spiritual gifts offered in your service,

for their many talents well spent over the years
to build up the church in peace and unity,
for their witness to me in my times of crisis
and their support in my times of sorrow,
for the joy we have known together serving you.
I give you thanks, Lord God.

People   Lord God, Father of our Lord, Jesus Christ,
Send forth your servant, _____, with our blessing.
Send her/him into the future with our deep gratitude.
May s/he find rest and re-creation.
May s/he discover renewal and new opportunity.
to serve you with energy,
intelligence,
imagination
and love.

Pastor   Receive now this benediction:
Gracious Lord,
bless the people of this congregation with a future
founded in service to you,
energized by the presence of your spirit,
enlivened by your message and mission,
creative to the needs of tomorrow,
and full of the joy in Christian living.

In the name of the Father and the Son and the Holy Spirit.
Amen.

<u>Gratitude</u>

Living God, as your sun stretches to waken the eastern sky,
>   we open our eyes with sleepy gratitude,
>>   for the return of morning,
>>>   for moments of hope each dawn quickens,
>>>>   for bright ideas and good morning occasions.

Living Lord, as darkness loses its power over our spirits,
>   we blink back the night's residue of worry and praise you
>>   for the end of gloom,
>>   for silencing whispers of fear from the shadows,
>>   for lifting the shades of night to welcome sunbeams
>>>   into last night's dark dreams.

You are Lord of dusk and dawn,
>   dark and light,
>>   valley and mountain crest.
You are creator of our daily cycles,
>   causing night to reign only long enough
>>   to yearn again for the dawn's embrace.

Thank you, for the persistent promise of morning,
>   for we are a people who need light,
>>   who need to believe daybreak will always come.
Our days are a series of great heights and depths:
>   we endure long hours of anxiety and waiting,
>>   pain and sadness,

we celebrate good times of work and play,

> glad surprises and hard-won victories.

We yearn to lengthen the good times and shorten the bad.

Be with us through it all.

Lord, we are plain folks,

> ready to worship in spite of our questions.

Today, we are here to praise you.

> Tomorrow, we return to Monday living.

Receive our simple thanks,

> for jobs that give us work to do and ideas to share,
>
> for families that take us back,
>
> for a future, always quickening our curiosity
>
> > and challenging our energy.

Thank you for quiet endings to stressful days,

> for the setting of the sun upon sickness and meanness,
>
> for laughter at evening meals,
>
> > and nights of nurturing touch.

Thank you for seasons cycling from winter to spring,

> for the dawn of daffodils in shocking yellows,
>
> for longer days blending into softer evenings.

We praise you for the arms of love holding us beyond the miles

> and beyond the grave,

for the hope of recognition someday on yonder shores,

for dusky twilight set alive by memory's candlelight,

for darkness without fear,

and death without finality.

Praise be yours for the time we are given to live our lives,

each gracious morning and gentle evening spread before us.

Let us lie down each evening in peace,

and waken us again with joy.

Lord of yesterday, today and tomorrow,

it is you alone who is with us at all these times.

Uphold us and care for us wherever we are,

whatever we do,

however we may feel in body and spirit.

And we will be glad.

Amen.

SEASONS OF COMMITMENT

A wedding blessing

May you be a woman and a man for all seasons.
Wear each season well, experience each fully.
Together, know the fullness of married life,
    for each season has its own time,
        and a time to move to the next.

Move now from the winter winds of loneliness,
    from the frozen wastelands of solitude,
        from the single stillness of waiting for your love,
           from the coldness of separate paths,
             from snow-covered fields
               of independent decisions
                  into the springtime of marriage.

May spring winds be warm,
    rains gentle, newness lively.
May the title "Mrs." write sweetly on envelopes,
May conversations be peppered proudly with
    "my husband" said this
        and "my wife" did that.
May responsibility be joy,
    and the reality of your commitment
        cause you to ponder
           the beauty of trust,
             to catch your breath,
               and smile knowingly.

In your spring days, you are sowing your future.
You are creating patterns for the seasons of many years.
    Consider well the tapestry of friends, family and stranger
        as you weave them into your own marriage.

Consider well the threads of time as you design
    your work, your service, your play.
May they blend well, giving glorious contrast
    to the colors of your exclusively
        personal moments

Be a man and a woman of summer,
    always growing.
        As you share in conversation,
           support each other;
      as you discover parenting,
          remind each other to laugh;
      as you know disappointment,
          wipe each other's tears;
      as you mature in spirituality,
          share the mystery.

Just grow,
    fear not the weariness of summer heat.
Let not the sweat of reality dampen
    the childlike joy of playing together.
For your play will send you dancing into autumn,
    where laughing wrinkles are quite lovely.

And now those seeds planted together in spring,
    watered in summer,
        bear fruit in the fall.
The mellow richness of years well spent
    will warm you at the hearth of cooling days
        and longer nights.
Colors blaze;
    senses renew the blessings of each dawn.
The harvest is gathered.

It still feels good to hold hands
    as you watch your grandchildren
        and great grandchildren
            leave their separate winters
                and enter their own spring times.

You are beginning a heritage now
    for those who come after you.
God bless you in your marriage!

<u>Indian summer wedding</u>

When in the fullness of autumn,
    warm winds blow into the stillness of hearts
        grown weary of grieving,
            sometimes miracles quicken the pulse.

When during the lean months of filling time with busyness,
    a conversation catches your attention,
        a smile across the room stirs your lips to respond,
        a question enters your heart.

Is it possible to love again?

When nights are filled with restlessness and tossing
    on a bed of cold sheets and damp pillows,
        dreams are heavy
            and mornings can't come soon enough.

Yet, pondering the voice that caught your attention,
    and remembering the smile that lifted your spirits,
        autumn turns warm
            and whispers of an Indian summer.

It is possible to love again!

When leaves have turned color and fallen,
    and weather is sunny and clear,

the season of grace appears and
grants an Indian summer.

Within the cycle of seasons,
this is a venue for late blooming love.
This is a time of unexpected harvest,
a time to rejoice!

Action

God, you act in history creating all that is and ever shall be,
hear our prayer.
You stepped upon the earth as a man,
walking the hills and feeling the rain,
tasting the sweetness of honey and smelling fresh bread,
hearing words of love and hate,
doubt and trust,
seeing the loneliness in the hearts of folks like us.
You acted to heal us.

You came among us to live as we live, to be one of us,
to learn what our life is really like,
to live the length of our days.
But you died before your hair turned gray.

Thank you for your gracious model of strength,
strength in your convictions and strength in your obedience,
strength in weakness even unto death.

Thank you for your action,

    acting as God to rescue the helpless,

        speaking words of hope,

    sending disciples among the nations,

        telling us of your kingdom

           where neither hunger nor thirst exist.

Send us now as your disciples into this wanting world,

    to teach your commandment to love one another,

        to welcome the downhearted,

    to gather regularly as your family

        and praise your name.

Give us the means and the generosity

    to feed the hungry, clothe the cold,

    seek justice for the weak,

        and look with reverent eyes upon the irreverent.

Equip us to stand up to evil where we find it,

    and to love fellow sinners who need to be forgiven.

Send us into the world in which we live

    and help us meet the needs we find.

Lord God, stir our hearts into action;

    don't let us sit out our salvation.

Give us a heart to risk the talents we have,

    to increase your gifts.

Commission us to share our faith.

    And stimulate us with the energy of your spirit. Amen.

<u>Baptism</u>

God of the ages, and all generations,
Thank you for dividing time into years and seasons and moments,
    for giving us endings and beginnings,
        gifts of order and routine in classroom, home and office.

Thank you for the evening of summer and the dawn of autumn,
    for the climax and brilliance of flowers in parks and fields,
        honoring seeds planted long ago.

Thank you for the lives of these children baptized this morning
    into your church family,
        for urging their parents to surrender their little ones
            to your life-time of care.
We celebrate the beginning of their faith journey.

May the promises made by parents and church members
    be like seeds planted for a harvest yet to be,
        so that one day each child may claim you personally
            as friend and mentor.

Lord, we are grateful for our own family roots,
    for the people we claim as kin.
May each of us grow in wisdom
    so that we too might claim the good we have inherited,
        and ask your touch to brush away the seeds
            we would not wish to pass on.

May we recognize responsibility for our own behavior.
> Still the voice within us that would blame others.
>> Help us grow up into our own accountability.

Confront us with our poor excuses
> blamed on sour grapes of another generation.

Give us abundant grace,
> enough to claim your spirit as your agent of change.

We pray for life-giving power to overcome bitter memories,
> to break unhealthy cycles
>> and move toward Christ-like forgiveness.

We pray for those who suffer.
> Give them courage to wait on better days.

We pray for those who wait.
> Give them patience.

And for those who are embarrassed,
> anoint them with understanding words.

For all of us who confess our guilt,
> grant forgiveness, and once more a lightness in our step.

We pray for those who weep.
> Wipe their tears.

And for those who wish to begin anew:
> give them power to look with gladness
>> toward tomorrow.

In the name of the one who makes all things new, Jesus Christ.
Amen.

God of the waters

God of the waters,
  you bring us together in worship around the font of promise
    to celebrate your love for the great and for the small.
Thank you for the music of young voices,
  for the message of faith passed down
    through generations of believers,
  for young hearts and fresh new souls
    beginning their journey of faith.

We praise you for the sacrament of Baptism,
  our Christian rite of passage,
    marking our birth into your family, the Church.
Keep us true to our words so we might fulfill our commitment.
Bless the promises made today by parents and sponsors,
  so that one day _____ might come to know you
    as friend and savior.

Thank you for _____and _____ and all parents
  who care about their children's spiritual growth,
  who encourage them to love those things eternal.
Thank you for teachers who share the stories of our faith,
  and train our young ones to sing your truth.

We ask you to receive our thanks for young ones in our care.
Go before us, God.
Make a path.

Call us to follow you
    to that place where we might drop our burdens
        and begin to feel the lightness of our being forgiven.
Lord of our faith,
    draw near to us now.
Grant to our children wisdom and stature and favor in your sight.
In the name of your son, Jesus Christ, we pray.
Amen.

Bring us home

Merciful redeemer, your love keeps reaching out for us,
    keeps bringing us home.
In spite of wandering souls, you bring us back
    from dangers threatening us physically,
        and from trials which might have crippled us
           emotionally.
You reach out to us with healing for our body and spirit,
    winning us back to safety,
        comforting us in the shelter of your wings.

Thank you for the people who act out your mercy,
    those who listen while we speak of pain,
    who touch us when we feel untouchable,
        and remind us of your all-consuming love,
           when we have forgotten you love each of us
              as though we were your only child.

Thank you for rescuing us from our own blunders,
  mistakes of stupidity, of selfishness,
    of premeditated meanness.
We know your mercy.
We feel your grace in the beautiful gift of forgiveness,
  and welcome your love in simple ways we don't expect,
    the grace of waking one morning and feeling lighter,
      hearing again a melody in our hearts.

We discover your forgiveness when fear,
  like a dark mantle, drops from our shoulders.
We find new songs whistling through our souls
  as you sweep out the dark corners of our shame,
    our naughty secrets and thoughts of revenge.
Thank you for the lightness of being forgiven,
  for your spirit-energy breathing fresh air
    into our musty memories.

Redeemer, thank you for bringing us back to ourselves,
  to the person we want to be,
    the kind of person we admire,
      the Christ-like servant we set out to become.

Thank you for bringing us back to old promises,
  to magnificent and holy dreams,
    to the hopeful child in each of us.

Remembering earlier times when we set our sails
    to grow up in wisdom and stature
        and in your favor,
            we know we have fallen short.
Return us to our commitment
    so we might live in the respect of those whom we love.
Thank you for bringing us back home,
    back to our best selves,
        confessing,
            forgiven
                and learning to forgive others. Amen.

Prayer to open a committee meeting

Gracious and loving God,
    you create from the chaos of our lives
        an orderly time.
Bring forth from dullness
    the ardor of faithful work.
Give us your blessing as we seek to speak your word
    and continue your business
        in the kingdom of our Lord.
May our minds be quickened,
    our hearts be warmed,
        and may the good humor of your people
            be evident as we gather here this evening.
Amen.

Care of God's creatures

Creating God, you touch our lives with joy
    by fashioning animals for our companionship.
Thank you for the delight of furry feet and stretching wing,
    of scale and tail and all that makes our days complete
        with such engaging company.

We pray for those in our care,
    for their long and healthy lives,
        for wisdom in training and handling.
May we look into their eyes and see your kindly affection for us.
May we rise each morning glad to be loved,
    and rest each evening more whole through their devotion.
Make us truly deserving.

Thank you for trusting us with the care of this earth,
    for calling us to be mindful of all that grows
        and drops its seed to grow again,
    for all creatures that hatch and birth
        and move upon the dust from which we all came.
Make us truly grateful.

May we learn kindness from your creatures,
    and respond with kindness.
May we end cruelty and give animals their due respect.

Thank you for the loving attention animals lavish upon us,
     for their instinctive memory of being created
          so we will have their company and not be alone,
     for their innocent trust in us as caretakers of their lives.
Make us truly worthy.

May we remember our calling to be God's image in this world,
     God's partners in caring for creation,
          God's voice to speak and God's hands to act.
May we stretch our hearts to care for the least of these creatures,
     and kindle our imaginations to bring justice for them.
Amen.

Commitment

Keeper of promise, creator of commitment,
     we praise you for keeping your word
          and calling us to do the same.
As we wander through these days,
     drifting with the seasons of cultural change
          and situational choice,
     chasing rainbows that no longer remind us of heavenly
          promise,
               we forget our own vows.

We forget our own vows,
     yet demand others remember theirs.

We break promises,
>	rationalizing they are out-dated, insignificant.
We water down our commitments,
>	weakening them to accommodate our demands
>>		for personal freedom and self expression.
Yet in spite of our wishy-washy convictions,
>	you stand firm in your promise to be our God.
You stand ready to welcome us
>	when our ways lead us in circles
>>		and we need to come home.
You stand close when the party is over
>	and we find ourselves alone and empty.
You rescue us when we live too long with false reflections
>	in a fun house maze,
>>		and it isn't fun anymore.
Thank you.

Keeper of promise, creator of commitment,
>	call us to our best selves
>>		when we have forgotten the person
>>>			we set out to become.
Stand fast on our behalf
>	when we need to remember what we promised.

Thank you for those people who made promises on our behalf,
>	parents who brought us for baptism,
>>		promising to tell us about Jesus,

parents who held us safely upon warm laps,

who woke at night to meet our needs,

and left us knowing we were safe.

Thank you for teachers and choir directors and youth directors,

who encouraged us to be our best,

who endured us at our worst

and demonstrated their love through patience.

For all those who kept their promises to us,

we are truly grateful.

God of promise, help us to be trustworthy,

to keep pledges we made to our beloved ones,

to renew vows grown old,

and strengthen those grown weak.

When our hearts feel empty,

grant us power to honor our marriage vows,

to wait through the worst and pray for the best.

When routine threatens us with boredom

in a world that worships excitement,

grant us renewal, creativity, laughter and joy.

When we grow discouraged with the church,

grant us wisdom and energy

to speak the truth you have placed

in our hearts and minds.

Help us remember who we are,

your children, your chosen, your own.

Amen.

<u>Communion</u>

Jesus Christ, son of the living God,
We gather at your table with thankful hearts,
    grateful for parents and grandparents
        who first brought us to this joyful feast,
    grateful for your grace continuing to bring us back
        over and over again.

Give us spiritual food to sustain our souls
    long after the taste of bread and wine is gone.
Give us leaven within our hearts,
    so we may rise to touch the lonely and forgotten ones
        you loved so dearly when you walked the earth.

Let this table be for us a place of remembrance and celebration,
    remembering your life and death and resurrection,
        celebrating your great love in spite of our great sin.

We remember those who mourn,
    who are heavy laden, who have lost hope.
Give them comfort, lift their yokes upon your shoulders.
Grant them a glimmer of hope.

Let us not forget our joy of prayers answered,
    quietly, often unexpected, after times of waiting.
Even when we give up, you never forget.

Grant us strength to finish the work we have begun at home,
>   in school and office.
And as we look ahead,
>   provide the vision for our first step into the future.

Now Lord God, creator of life and bread and wine,
>   bless us with a common voice to praise you for this meal.
Feed us with the bread that passes from generation to generation,
>   yet never grows stale.
Quench our thirst from the cup that spills into our lives,
>   yet never runs dry.
In the name of our host we pray. Amen.

Holy teacher

Holy teacher, thank you for the opportunity
>   of passing your message to our children.
Grant their young souls the desire to know you and love you.
May they grow in wisdom and stature
>   until that day they will share the faith
>>   with their own small ones.

O God our help in ages past,
Thank you for our own baptism.
Grant us hearts still desiring to know you and love you.
May we continue to grow into the promises made by those
>   who carried us to the font for our own baptism long ago.
In the name of the one we worship, Jesus Christ, our Lord. Amen.

Hands

Lord, whose hands create all for which we are thankful,
    who touches earth daily with a harvest of beauty,
        and reaches into our lives to bandage our bruises,
      we come to you in prayer.

Thank you for your gracious hands,
    shaping the contours of our lives,
        enabling decisions, pointing into our future.
Hold us in the hollow of your hands,
    as we suffer the pangs of being human,
        and cry through our loneliness and worry.

You know us with greater intimacy than anyone else,
    harboring us tenderly in the warmth of your palms,
        forgiving our sin, wiping our tears.
Thank you for taking on our human form,
    for touching the earth and letting the earth touch you,
        for tousling the hair of little ones,
            anointing blind eyes and leprous sores.

Come to us who bear your name.
Touch our hands,
    so we too might hold and comfort and tousle the hair
        of those who need you now,
    so your kindness might be met through us,
        and your warmth felt through our presence.

Thank you for the hands that have molded our lives:
    grandparents and grown-up friends
        who helped us bake cookies
            and play cards on kitchen tables,
        read us stories on warm laps,
        laughed over old photograph albums,
            and played ball with us in the back yard.
For these precious memories, we are deeply grateful.

Thank you for the hands of parents
    cooling feverish heads in early morning hours,
        signing report cards,
            handing us the car keys,
                and waving to us as we grew toward maturity.
For these parents, we are deeply grateful.

Thank you for the hands of teachers,
    who believed in us and told us so,
    who helped us into our coats when we were little,
        and out of our shells when it was time to grow up,
            and for writing red-letter notes of encouragement.

Thank you for hungry hands reaching to us for help,
    hungering for a chance, a meal, an education,
        challenging our patience when they persist,
        and rewarding us with the knowledge
            that our second mile has been your work
            among the least of these.

For small hands reaching for our care,
    too young to tie shoes or understand big ideas,
        we thank you.
For big hands reaching for our support,
    having temporarily lost their grip, we thank you.
For wrinkled hands reaching for our company,
    wanting to share their past,
        and dream of tomorrow,
            no matter how short tomorrow may be,
            we thank you.
May we honor the goodness of their lives
    until their days are full spent.

Thank you for healing hands,
    touching sickness and disease,
        bringing health and comfort.

Thank you for our own hands,
    soothing friends, wrapping gifts, carving turkeys,
        baking pies, lying peacefully in our laps.

To you we lift our hands, Lord Jesus.
    dedicating them to goodness and kindness, in your name.
We open them to generosity,
    to praise,
        to play.
Bless our hands, for we are your hands in a needy world. Amen.

<u>Knowledge comes, but wisdom lingers</u>

Wise and wonderful creator,
> We are but little children on the paths of eternal wisdom,
>> yet we know who to ask when we need help.
> We pray humbly for wisdom to infuse our world.

Grant wisdom to the leaders of all nations,
> May enemies discover the power of reason
>> and come together to protect those they govern.
> May anger burn itself out,
>> and finding relief in exhausted sleep,
>>> waken to learn the ways of peace.

May the leaders of our churches be wise and strong.
> Give them insight into the needs of their people
>> and patience to teach the naïve
>>> and innocent spirits in their care.
> Give to the foolish and selfish new opportunity to grow
>> in wisdom and generosity and faithfulness to the church.

In a time when knowledge is used to make money
> and control people,
>> may wisdom use money to help others
>>> with basic needs to stay alive.
>> May knowledge evolve into wisdom
>>> and give freedom to those
>>>> who would stretch their spirits.

In our local parish, we pray for wisdom,
>   wisdom to forgive,
>>   wisdom to let the past be in the past,
>>>   wisdom to laugh rather than argue,
>>>>   and sing rather than complain.

Lord of all knowledge, creator of wisdom,
>   grant our prayers. Amen.

Responsibility for creation

In the beauty of your holiness,
>   we worship you, Creator, Redeemer, Sustainer God.

Thank you for discerning minds that wonder about the unknown
>   beyond the earth we walk,
>>   and the mountains to which we lift our eyes.
We honor your commands to care for the earth
>   and the skies we touch,
>>   to walk lightly upon the ground and the heavens,
>>>   leaving your footprints, not ours.

As our constantly birthing universe
>   groans in travail toward cosmic growth,
>>   may we be your instruments of care,
>>>   your willing stewards.

Confessing our pollutant greed,
  forgive us so that trees might clap their hands
      and tomorrow's children breathe the rain forest
          and celebrate the whale.

Lord God, may we be quickened to proclaim the mysteries
  of your emerging universe,
      not afraid, but curious,
          curious to see beyond this present day.

May science celebrate your creativity
  and religion wrap its arms around the mystery
      of test tube and telescope.
Give us that day again
  when you look upon the work of your hands
      and see that it is good,
          when the firmament might declare anew
              your glorious handiwork.

In the meantime, may we respond appropriately,
  rendering unto you the work of our hands,
      discovering in sacrifice our spirituality,
          the fragrant harvest of a generous heart.

In the midst of our wonder,
  we consider the needs of those who hunger,
      those who lie on beds of pain, who fear for their future
          and feel they have nothing to look forward to.

Give to them food, relief, hope
> and something to hang on to,
>> something worth living for.

We yearn for peace,
> for enemies to weary of hate,
>> for skies without missiles
>>> and earth unstained with the blood of innocents.

Help us live together without killing each other.

And now, may we go forth without our sandals,
> expectant before each burning bush,
>> each lily of the field,
> intimate with the precious
>> and lavish in our awe.

Amen.

Litany for commissioning volunteers

Leader: You are those God has called for the opportunity of hospitality.

> You are volunteering for

> _____

Someone spoke your name and added,
> "She'd be great! He's the one!"

You were called, and you answered "Yes."

Thank you!

Volunteers: We heard God's call to serve and said,
> **"Here am I. Send me."**

Leader: Therefore, know you are chosen.

Know you are needed.

Know you are loved.

Know you will never be alone.

Volunteers: Lord God,

for the times we are exhausted,

and wonder why we volunteered,

for the unexpected problems we are asked to solve,

for the things we have given up to serve you,

may we hear your whisper,

"Well done, good and faithful servant."

Leader: Christ goes before you and opens the door of hospitality.

You continue to hold it open.

You are the doorkeepers of the Lord.

Volunteers: Lord, Jesus Christ, son of the living God,

take the gifts you have given us

through birth and baptism.

Use them to welcome the first timers,

the old timers, and those filled with awe.

May we stretch forth our hands

and touch them with your welcome.

Leader: The Holy Spirit works quietly,

behind the scenes of our lives.

You too will serve with the low profile of a servant.
You may not always be thanked,
>but the one you serve is eternally grateful.

Volunteers: Spirit of the living God,
>**give us good humor when we minister**
>**to the tired and grumpy.**
>**Give us energy when our smiles feel all worn out.**
>**And when our task is finished,**
>>**give us good memories**
>>**and grateful hearts for this opportunity.**

Leader: I send you forth in the name of Christ.
>Thanks be to God!

Litany for commissioning the choir

Leader: You are those who have come to offer your gift of voice.
>You will help lead worship at_____.
>God has given you the opportunity to practice
>hospitality through the warmth of your
>voices and the power of music.
>You will fill God's house of prayer for all people
>with your harmony.
>Thank you!

Choirs: **God of the alleluia song,**

   thank you for singing through us,

    for allowing each of us to sing the good news,

    for blending our talents in worship and praise.

Leader: May you be responsible in practice,

   patient with untrained voices,

   gentle with the irritable,

   lavish with good humor,

    and may you know a foretaste of

     God's heavenly choir.

Choirs: **May we respect our God-given talent.**

   May we offer our best, and sing to God's glory.

Leader: God dances before you,

   leading the chorus.

  God breathes through you,

   singing throughout history.

  In God's name, continue that melody.

Choirs: **O God of rhyme and rhythm, of words and melody,**

   for the times we are exhausted,

    and wonder why we sing,

   for the unexpected problems we must solve,

    for the things we have given up to serve,

   may we hear,

    "Well done, good and faithful servants."

Leader: Know you are chosen.

Know you are needed, loved and supported.

Know you will never sing alone.

Choirs: Thank you, God,

for the harmony that makes our spirits soar,

for the transformation of heavy hearts

through music,

for the gift of song that feeds our souls.

Leader: Therefore, I send you forth to sing in the name of Jesus..

ALL: Thanks be to God! Alleluia! Amen!

Litany for commissioning ushers and Communion servers

Leader: You are those who come to offer your gifts of service.

You will help lead worship.

God has given you the opportunity to practice

hospitality through the warmth of your voices

and the touch of your hands.

You will fill God's house of prayer for all people

with your friendliness.

Thank you!

Ushers

and Servers: God of gracious invitation,

thank you for this opportunity

to serve your people in worship.

Leader: May you be responsible to your task,

      patient with the tired and confused,

      gentle with the irritable,

      lavish with good humor,

        and may you know

          a foretaste of God's heavenly gathering.

**Ushers
and Servers:**   **May we respect our work as ushers**

      and servers.

May we offer our best,

      and mirror God's love.

Leader: God dances before you, leading the crowd.

      God breathes through you,

        creating unforgettable moments of worship.

    In God's name

      lead this congregation with the warmth

      of welcome.

**Ushers
and Servers:**   **God of praise and prayer and holy worship,**

      for the times we are exhausted,

      for the times we wonder why we

        volunteered,

      for unexpected problems we must solve,

      for the things we have given up to serve,

may we hear your whisper,

      "Well done, good and faithful servants."

Leader: Know you are chosen.

Know you are needed, loved and supported.

Know you will never serve alone.

Ushers

and Servers: **Thank you, for worship moments**

that make our spirits soar,

for the transformation of heavy hearts,

for the gift of the Lord's Supper.

May we serve you well

by serving those who come to worship.

Leader: Therefore, I commission you.

I send you forth to serve in the name of Jesus Christ.

ALL: **Thanks be to God! Alleluia! Amen!**

SEASONS OF
ILLNESS AND DEATH

Knock on the door of our hearts

Lord Jesus, knock on the door of every heart.
Enable us to be open, inviting your power to come among us.
May we share the dream of your forgiveness
    with those who lie awake and stare and wonder.

We pray for those who are battling sickness and sorrow,
    those who are dying, whose days are numbered.
Give to each the hope of life yet to come,
    the promise of love eternal.

We pray for those who feel hopeless,
    those who pray and pray, and hear no answers.
Give to each your presence as they wait,
    the touch of your hand.

May we share our hospitality with the lonely,
    those whose lives are growing smaller.
Give us the words to warm them
    and the good company of smiles.

In our warring world,
    may we bring a peaceful presence.
In our divided nation,
    may we celebrate our common joys.
In the shadows of our hearts,
    open a window and light up of our lives. Amen.

<u>Upon entering the hospital</u>

Kindly Physician,
      you are with us at every critical moment of our lives;
          be with us now. Be with _____.
Thank you for body and breath,
      for medicine and those who touch us with tender hands
        and encouraging words.

Be with _____ through the tests of these days.
As *s/he* begins *her/his* search for answers,
      may *s/he* feel *s/he* is entering your arm's strong embrace.
May s/he know your quiet presence surrounding *her/him*
      and be assured you stand close enough
         to hear the slightest of whispers.

Let your spirit breathe through *her/him* with comforting sighs.
Give *her/him* peace to relax in the promise of hope.
Take confusion and fear into your hands and create trust.
Be as calming as the blankets that cover _____,
      and as near as the sounds of monitors in the room.

Give the hours a friendly quality,
      and pass this time standing at *her/his* side.
Great God, our loving parent, hear our prayer.
Heal _____   Amen.

Card for flowers taken to the sick and shut-ins

Grace and peace from God our creator
    and our Lord, Jesus Christ!
This gift of color and blossom comes to you from your church.

These flowers brightened our sanctuary during worship.
In their presence, worshippers heard
    the glory of music through organ and voice,
        the reading of God's holy word,
            the sermon and prayers of thanksgiving.

Each time you gaze at this little bouquet,
    we pray you will know God's healing touch
        and be comforted by the presence of our Lord,
        the Great Physician.
Amen.

A prayer for patients

Loving physician, comforting God,
You have known our comings and goings
    since before we were born.
Be with _____ in the weeks ahead
    as s/he discovers her/ his path to health.
Bring comfort in the waiting times.
Bless her/ him with the love of family and friends
    who care so deeply.

In times of stress,
    quiet the beating of her/his heart.
In times of fear,
    reach for her/him in the dark.
In times of frustration,
    calm the storm.

We are your people and the sheep of your pasture.
We need your staff,
    your guidance,
        your direction.
When all things seem equal,
    we don't know what options to take.

Speak to us with your still, small voice.
Grant us the answers we yearn for.

In the days ahead,
    walk with_____ through every door.
In the weeks ahead,
    sit with her/him as s/he waits.
In the months ahead,
    lift her/him to her/his feet in a dance of recovery.

Loving Savior, be near. Amen.

A prayer for the sick

Creator of moments –
    those simple occasions
        that measure out my hours
            and give meaning to my life –
grant me a generous portion of time,
an Indian summer,
    a lengthening of my days.
I have more work to do and more stories to tell.

In the small moments of the morning,
    as dawn stretches her arms across the sky,
        before night releases his grasp
            on the last shadows of a dream,
I pray for time.

As the breath of dew evaporates
    and darts of light shoot through the waiting skies,
        before the birds' song is quiet,
I pray for strength.

As this day opens to the living of my dream,
    may my talents be quickened,
        and my purpose focused.
I pray for creativity.

Then as the shadows are rounded up,

and the intimacy of song and star warm the evening,

just before the sunset,

I offer you the fullness of my days. Amen.

Acquainted with grief

Lord, Jesus Christ, son of the living God, have mercy on us.

You are acquainted with grief. We grieve.

You are a man of sorrows. We are deep in sorrow.

Walk with us on our journey through these days

of sorrow and grief.

Hold our hands in the valleys.

Bring your embrace into days that dawn with tears,

and hold a lamp to warm our hearts

with the setting of the sun.

Compassionate God, creator of our human image,

you bless us through the lives of loved ones.

Then – in timing we do not understand –

you gather them into your arms before we would let them go.

Hear our prayers of gratitude for the life of _____.

Make us truly grateful for the years we were given together.

Be ever present in the years ahead.

Thank you for her/his touch upon our lives,

for the strength s/he passed to each of us,

for her/his truth spoken through a life well lived,
for the faith s/he lived
strong to the end,
and now celebrates with you face to face.
Hear our prayer of gratitude for the life of _____.
May s/he live on though our deeds of kindness and compassion.
May we hear her/his whispers of encouragement from heaven
and her/his laughter through the silence left on earth.

O, God our help in ages past, our hope for years to come,
Take kindly to us and comfort us,
for we are stricken with deep sadness.
As time passes,
empower us to live on with the joy we received from
_____.
Direct our eyes toward a new light in one of the windows
of your mansion with many rooms.
Heaven is a friendlier place; knowing s/he is there. Amen.

He smells like blood

O, God, he's dead.

I held him in my arms not so many years ago,
and heard him suckle at my breast.
My first-born.
Now he is silent, lifeless.
It's not right for a son to die before his mother.
It's unnatural.

Waiting outside the emergency room
> I couldn't say, "Your will be done."

I couldn't let go of my prayers for his life.

You bring us to life, not death.

You wouldn't let him die.

I prayed so hard for your help.

I prayed for the doctors and nurses,
> and everyone who worked on him.

But, now he's dead and smells like blood.

His hand curled around my little finger
> the first time I held him.

Now it lies limp and cold.

His eyes smiled into mine as he asked for the car keys.

Now they are closed forever.

Time has stopped.

My heart doesn't want to beat.

I can't imagine the clock moving or the world turning.

Everything has stopped.

Dead.

I don't want to live with this pain.

O, God, help me.

You know what it's like to lose a son.

Waiting for a transplant

Dear God, our Great Physician,

Thank you for the gifts of life:
>for body and breath,
>>for medicine and those who touch with gentle hands,
>>>for words of encouragement.

Thank you for the gift of family,
>for those who came before us and cared for us,
>>for the company of good friends and loved ones,
>>>for home and warmth and kindness.

May these days of waiting bring
>gratitude for all who offer their gifts of healing,
>>confession for those things done thoughtlessly,
>>>forgiveness
>>>>and newness
>>>>>and hope for tomorrow.

May your son, who cured the sick,
>stand close to this bed night and day.
Breathe life through the wisdom of medicine,
>and bring _____a (name organ) for a new lease on life.

We pray that these times of tested patience might become a
>benchmark of trust in the future for _____'s life,
>>grant her/him renewed encouragement each day,
>>>and give purposeful direction to her/his future.

Thank you for loving _____ as if s/he were your only child,
    for being as close as the blankets that cover her/him,
        as deeply nourishing as the food s/he eats,
            as life-giving as the oxygen s/he breathes.

Lord of all the earth and all creation,
    hear our prayer.
Lord of every hospital corridor, waiting room and patient bed,
    hear our prayer.
We call to you for help.
Amen.

Funeral

Loving God, eternal Lord,
    you are acquainted with sorrow throughout the ages.
Come among us gathered here to praise you for the life
    of your beloved servant, _____.

Thank you for the lives of people such as _____,
    who live what they believe,
        who claim the church as family
            and meet their death ready to go home.

We come to you in worship.
Many of us not so sure, not so ready.
    Speak to us.
        Comfort us.
How well you know our daily routine of rising and resting.
You dwell within our very souls,

knowing each thought,
> discerning every word before it forms upon our lips.

If we should run from your presence,
> there is no place to go.

You are in the heights and the depths,
> upon mountain crest,
>> and waiting in each lonesome valley.

Your spirit breathes upon us each morning.
Your hand takes ours in the dusk.

Thank you, even from the depths of sorrow
> we know we do not live alone.

You are always with us,
> wiping tears, forgiving sin,
>> calling us again into the dance of grace.

We thank you from the trials of doubt,
> we do not die alone.

You travel with us the misty unknown,
> lifting a lamp into every tomb,
>> scattering burial cloths
>>> and bringing us forth in laughter.

Thank you for our savior, Jesus Christ,
> who died and lives again,
>> and for his lordship in our living and our dying.

May we live what we believe.
> May we speak aloud what we pray in private.

May the spirit of Christ cause us to live kindly,
 love mercy,
  and walk with humility.

Grant to each of us the joy of faith,
 and the opportunity to serve,
  so we might stand before you in our own time,
   giving account of ourselves without fear,
    knowing we have lived our lives with the Lord.

Give us untroubled hearts,
 believing in God, the beginning and the end,
  the one who stands holding open the door to a mansion
   where each of us will find a room,
  not a room with mirrors where we see dimly,
   but a room filled with morning's sunshine
    where we will meet with gladness
     face to face.

And now, Lord,
 with the blessed assurance of Easter's promise,
  we walk the purple days of sorrow,
   knowing this is not the end,
    only the waiting time for a new beginning.
In the name of Jesus,
 the resurrected Christ of God,
  we lift our hearts in grateful prayer. Amen.

Memorial prayer

Lord of the ages, you gather the saints into your arms.

We praise you for the lives of loved ones born before us,
    those who touched our lives
        and made us feel loved no matter what,
    who gave us powerful ideas
        and created colorful memories,
    who lived and died in your family of faith.

We praise you for the lives of loved ones here among us now,
    those who sustain us in sorrow,
        reminding us of family memories,
            cherished as well as challenging,
                stories bringing laughter midst our tears.

Thank you for hope reaching beyond today into tomorrow
    and toward the days ahead
        when joy and birth and laughter return once again.
We thank you for walking with us
    as we travel the shadowed valleys,
        where we greet the dawn with tears
        and drag our feet toward sunset.

Take our hands.
You know our spiritual frame and emotional frailty.
You are acquainted with our sorrow and understand our
    limitations.
Lead us gently out of the depths when the time is right,
    when we have cleansed our souls with mourning tears.

Thank you for your family,
    great and small,
        for your church through the ages
            bonded by sacraments at table and font,
        for promises once made on our behalf
            by parents and congregation,
                and for promises we have made
                    and have yet to make in the future.

For the gift of bread and cup calling us to the table,
    we give you thanks.
For knowing we sit among the saints of the past
    and those yet to be born,
        we praise you.
Remind us that loved ones departed
    join us in the Eucharist,
        and meet us in reunion at the family feast.
Your table is full.
We are not alone.

Come among us now, Lord Jesus
    Gather the sorrowful into your keeping.
        Dry the tears of grief.
            Keep memories alive of a life well lived.

Sit with us in sorrow,
    and in the fullness of time,
        grant us again a life worth living.
Amen

Dedication of a memorial garden

Words of Dedication:

When God created Paradise, he chose to make a garden,
  a garden where he might walk
    with those created in his own image.
  In a garden we can never be alone.
    For God joins us in a garden.
      Here it is, God walks with us.
        God talks with us.
          God tells us we are his own.

Let the people say, "Amen."

In a garden we can never be without hope.
  For the seasons remind us: spring always follows winter.
    God causes the sun to rise and the sun to set
      with an order we can count on
        in the midst of any season.

Let the people say, "Amen."

In a garden we can never be bored.
  For God's growing things are always changing.
    They are getting ready for the next phase of life.
    They trust change in God's plan.
      They trust cycles in God's presence.
        Growing things love their creator.

Let the people say, "Amen."

In a garden we discover divine mystery.
    For God chose a garden to celebrate resurrection.
        Here it is Jesus Christ calls our name.
            We are known for who we are.
                We are forgiven for who we have been.
              We are challenged to begin again,
              as God's perennials.

Let the people say, "Amen."

Hymn of Dedication   "For The Beauty of the Earth"

Personal words about the garden and the giver

Prayer of Dedication:

Creator of all things seen and unseen,
Lord of sky and sea and earth,
    Thank you for gardens,
        for your good company amid the beauty of growth,
           for your life giving hope in the midst of cold days,
             for your steady assurance
                in unpredictable weather,
             for your promise of life after death.

Lord of life and death,

    Create in our souls a garden,

        where we might find leisure with you,

            where you might touch us with eternal beauty,

                where seasons might come and go in steady
                    rhythm,

                    and we might know your peace.

Amen.

Benediction:

Go into the world blessed by God.

    Go into the day celebrating gardens.

        Go into the moment blessed by the God we know as

            Creator,

                Redeemer,

                    and Holy Spirit.

And may the beauty of every garden

    whose paths you walk,

        remind you of God's love!

Amen.

<u>Pondering Death</u>

When did the ending begin?
Was there warning earlier,
      or did the ending and beginning
          blend into one hazy time?
Even now, it seems to hang between day and dream.

Endings are but seedlings for new beginnings,
      hidden, sheltered, pausing,
      grieving in the dark,
      wondering what color will be spring's bloom.

Beginnings end.
      And endings are mostly sad.
      What is born dies.
      Seen or unseen,
          dew dries.
          Symphonies become echoes.
          Dance stumbles
              and rhythm loses beat.
          Baby skin wrinkles.

Yet,
Hear the good news of the gospel:
      I am with you always,
          even to the ends of the earth.
      I am the beginning and the end.
You are never, never alone!

All I heard was cancer

and I stopped listening, Lord.
I stopped thinking;
stopped seeing,
sat numb.

Where can I go to get away from the reality of that word?
I can't breathe.
I can't move.

This is how it started.

I'm still in shock, but I can think again; a little.
I'm still numb, but I'm beginning to feel my skin again.
I watch the world turning as it always has.
Hours become days.
Days become weeks.
One month is fast passing and moving to the next.
Everything looks the same, but of course it isn't,
and never will be.

Come comforter. Come into the emptiness of my being.

In good faith I can't ask, "Why me?"
Cancer is fickle.
It visits whom it will.

Cancer doesn't care who is good and who is bad.
It draws the bow and lets the arrow fly.
It closes its eyes and pirouettes among the crowd of
    unsuspecting, busy people – people with plans.

I don't know what kind of treatment I should choose.
I can't figure out all the twists and turns in the path ahead.
I don't want to die.

That's all I know: I don't want to die, Lord!
    I want to live to see my children grow old,
        my grandchildren graduate and marry and birth.
I wish I could make a deal with you.
If I could just have my prayer answered with a heavenly, "Yes."
I would do anything.

But the reality is, I still have cancer.

Come to me.
Comfort me.
Give me strength to meet whatever lies ahead,
    to greet, shake hands and get acquainted with my new life.
May I find support through my family and friends,
    encouraging honesty, welcoming help and getting on with it.

Dear God, let me live fully the life I have.
    Give me precious days with quivering senses.
        May I see things I've never noticed,

and ponder over faces I love.

May I hear the call of newborn babes,

    and cry listening to my favorite symphonies.

When I have the strength to bake cookies again,

    don't let me feel guilty for downing a dozen.

May I hold the hands of beloved friends,

    and not hesitate to kiss them.

And if it be your will, may I have many springs

    to breathe the scent of hyacinths. Amen.

Beginnings and endings

We are a people born with beginnings.

Beginnings are potential, future, hope,

    somewhere to go.

We are a people created with endings.

Endings ask of potential,

    "Where did you go?"

Endings make us look back over our shoulders.

    Difficult for stiff-necked people.

        Did we leave the earth a better place?

        What was the testimony of our life?

        Did we share the precious?

    And our journey,

        did it make a difference?

"It's never too late" is a lie.

    We can't go back, only forward.

Therefore, take heart, friends. In Christ we are forgiven.

Coming home

God bends over us in our beginning,
    breathing into our nostrils the breath of life.
God bends to us in our ending,
    whispering spirit into promise.
Death is the fulfillment of
    promises made at our baptism.
Death invites us to
    sit at the heavenly banquet.
Death births life
    where we see face to face,
    where we are beheld as we would be known,
    where we are not lost,
        only gone before.
Death is coming home.
Death is God's family reunion.

The blessed

Blessed are those who die in the Lord,
    who have journeyed with the saints
        in the household of God.
Blessed are those whose feet have trod
    the paths of righteousness,
        walking not in the counsel of wickedness.
Blessed are those who spoke hope to the empty hearted,
    good will to the irritable,
        forgiveness to the mean spirited.

Blessed are those who die all used up,
    having given all they had,
        having shared all they were given.
Blessed are those who enter the mansion traveling light,
    who filled earthly barns with kindly deeds,
        who stored recipes for the heavenly banquet.
Blessed are those who need not cry,
    "If I could only go back and do it over again."
        for they have met forgiveness.

Rejoice and be exceedingly glad!
    We worship a God who gives songs in the night,
        and joy in the morning.
Come and see what God has done!
    We worship a God who
        brings us home at the end of our journey,
        rescues us from fear and pain,
            guilt and shame,
        gives the security of law, and spirit of love,
        builds a family around his dearly beloved,
        births us in baptism,
        sustains us at table,
        and prepares for us a place to come home.
Praise the Lord!

PRAYERS FOR
GOD'S PEOPLE

For those who teach literacy

Lord Jesus, living Word, come to us through human words,
    touching those who do not read,
        creating new opportunity for those who yearn,
            granting insight to those who teach in your name.
Guide those living in darkness
    to find the knowledge for which they hunger.

Give to those of us who enjoy the light of literacy
    time to share,
        time to listen,
           time to care.

Grant us joy and loving curiosity
    for the heart of each person we touch,
        for the home of each one's spirit.
May we be wise and kind as we try to
    heal loneliness and separation,
        end the poverty of illiteracy,
           and serve as your mind and heart in our world.

When frustration and failures unravel our patience,
    give us peace and determination.
When weariness and lack of progress cloud our vision,
    grant us good humor.
When misunderstanding and hurt feelings sap our energy,
    restore us with warm smiles.

We are your people offering our time and talents.

Accept us as we are,

willing to learn as we share,

wanting to grow,

and eager to begin.

Amen.

A Prayer for Rotary

Gracious and generous God,

Thank you for the gifts of time and talent

you give to us in Rotary,

for enriching our hearts with a deep desire

to serve the needs of others.

Thank you for opportunities to touch the lives

of young and old through work we do.

May the scholarships we give grow into the future,

blossoming, and dropping seeds in lives we may never see.

May children in faraway places grow into adulthood

with education equipping them to live abundant lives.

Thank you for giving us a love of country,

for quickening our hands

to reach out as responsible citizens.

Continue to use us to make this world

a better place for all.

Amen.

Eagle Scout blessing

Blessings on you Eagle Scout.
May the winds of life never harm you.
May they rise beneath your wings and always lift you up.

Blessings on you Eagle Scout.
May your memories give you a grateful heart,
for those who nurtured, taught and challenged you.

Blessings on you Eagle Scout.
May your wings stretch out to shelter others.
May they give you flight toward your dreams.
May they carry you in safety across many skies,
with strength enough for any storm,
and always return you to the embrace of home.
Blessings on you Eagle Scout.

A prayer for small children

Dear God,
Thank you for loving small kids with your big heart.
Thank you for small hands to put on
warm clothes in winter,
and shorts in spring.
Thank you for small mouths to pray for
Food when hungry, and help when things get too big.

Thank you for small ears to hear
> how much you love each one.
Please, hold these little ones safe in your arms by day,
> and tuck each one into bed at night,
Amen.

A prayer for boys and girls

Dear God,
> Thank you for laughter,
>> and all the things that make us smile:
>>> tumbling pets and funny cartoons,
>>>> playful parents and friends with jokes.
> Thank you for secret places,
>> and all the special times alone:
>>> reading stories and dreaming ideas,
>>>> watching clouds and birds, and nibbling snacks.
> Thank you for the church family,
>> and all the activities for kids:
>>> potluck dinners and church school,
>>>> choirs and worship and parties.
> Thank you for teachers and parents and all
>> grown-up friends who make kids feel important
>> and loved.
Give "thank you" smiles all day long.
> Amen.

A prayer for youth

God of youth and life and hope,
Thank you for trusting young people with your truth,
for calling them to worship and to serve you.
Thank you for taking each seriously,
and never laughing at their mistakes.
When they are worn out, give them a lift.
When tomorrow seems too far away,
and yesterday too near, bridge their troubled times.
May each be quick to serve when they see others hurting,
slow to pass hurtful stories, gentle with friends,
extravagant with compliments,
and forgiving of those who are mean.
We all ask for this in Jesus' name. Amen.

A prayer for women

Lord God, you touch the ordinary and make it sacred.
Touch us. Make our hands your hands.
In the midst of everyday hours and duties called routine,
we lift to you our hands and pray your blessing.
Take every touch we offer to another,
and make it your blessing.
Grace each needle, pen, brush and key,
to create beauty through our talents.
Slip into our calendar, office, kitchen and carpool,
and feed our souls with laughter and joy.

Grant us,
>   strong hands to knead dough and build bridges,
>>   soft hands to nurture the weak and hold the needy,
>   generous hands to pass on our inheritance of love,
>>   gentle hands to wipe tears and soothe broken hearts,
>   compassionate hands to charm others into righteousness,
>>   quick hands to offer unto others simple gifts
>>>   made sacred by our savior's touch. Amen.

A prayer for men

Mighty, yet ever gentle God,
>   you are the giver of faith and family,
>>   the builder of fraternity and future.
>   You bond us in life with cords of laughter and tears.
>   You court us with challenge through vision and dream.
>   Hear our prayer of thanksgiving
>>   for understanding friends when days feel empty.
>>   for the grasp of caring hands,
>>>   for tastes and smells quickening our memories,
>>>   for eyes to view the spacious skies,
>   Create in us clean hearts, O Lord,
>>   willing to break for the needs of others.
>   Give to us generous hands,
>>   working to build a better world for you.
>   Travel with us in this life, loving brother,
>>   giving us direction, leading the way. Amen.

A prayer for the choir

God of the alleluia song, thank you for singing through us,
    for allowing each voice precious opportunity
        to sing the good news
            and blend our talents in worship and praise.
    May we be responsible to practice,
        patient with untrained voices, gentle with the irritable.
    May we respect your gift of voice,
        offer our best, and sing to your glory.
    We pray for those who cannot sing for lack of food,
        who cannot afford the luxury of time to practice,
            who cannot remember your sing in the darkness.
    Thank you for harmony making our spirits soar,
        for melody transforming our heavy hearts,
            for music to feed our souls.
    May we always sing in praise of Jesus Christ. Amen.

A prayer for teachers

Loving God,
        thank you for the privilege of serving a savior with
            children on his lap,
        for the sacred opportunity of teaching young ones
            in your family.
Give us time to prepare,
        ideas to share,
            patience to repeat and repeat and repeat.

Grant us the wisdom to teach
    with more love than rules,
        with more smiles than frowns.

Bring forth the child in us,
    to lead the young with laughter,
        charming them toward a saving faith.
May we teach stewardship by example,
    living with a precious sense of life,
        sharing with spontaneous generosity.
May we always remind our students of those in need,
    those who suffer for lack of food and shelter,
        those deprived of health and opportunities
            we take for granted.

And when our students leave this classroom,
    may they leave with gladness,
        with anticipation for what happens next,
            feeling strong and ready,
                and remembering they were loved.
In Jesus name,
    we pray for our children
        and for us.
Amen.

A prayer for church leaders

Holy God, head of the church, giver of life,
Thank you for the diversity of our sacred opportunity,
    for different gifts, quickened by your Spirit.
        for different ways to minister within your family.
Bond us with your spirit,
    so we might bring reconciliation to conflict.
Bend to us as we serve those in need.

Thank you for the voice of this family calling us to
    leadership in the name of Jesus Christ.
May we live by his authority,
    listening to scripture, and learning from one another
        what it means to be the church in our world today.

Thank you for our denomination,
    offering justice, kindness and order.
Grant to us duties encouraging our energy
    and intelligence, our imagination and love.

Anoint us with wisdom as we provide for
    worship and instruction in this congregation.
May worship bring you praise.
    May instruction be for your glory.
In all our meetings, on all the levels of your church
    may we serve with honesty, humility and good humor.
        showing tender mercy in the living of our lives.

Grant us faithfulness to your call
　　as we teach charity among your family,
　　　　as we urge Christian concern among your people,
　　　　　　as we direct efforts on behalf of those in need.

Give us strength when we are weary, smiles when doors open,
　　a sense of humor when they close,
　　　　and comfort when our service is misunderstood.
Bless us, Lord Jesus. We only serve because of you.
Amen.

An ordination / installation prayer for ministers

Loving Lord, you call us into your family through baptism,
　　giving us roots in centuries of faith.
You call us to serve the church as brothers and sisters.
Thank you for the bonds of commitment we celebrate this day,
　　for your call, and our answer,
　　　　for the needs of this family,
　　　　　　and the talents offered by _____ .

Thank you for the joy of adoption into your family,
　　for nursing us through our infancy in the faith,
　　　　for patience with our adolescence,
　　　　　　for your challenge to our talents,
　　　　　　and your blessing to the increase of our service.

We praise you for calling (pastor) to serve here in this place,
    and in this time.
Be with her/him as s/he administers your holy sacraments,
    acting as host in the breaking of bread at your family table,
        and lifting the cup at your family's sacred feast.

Be with her/him as s/he pours the waters of baptism,
    acting as midwife at each birth into your family,
        hearing the promises made,
            nurturing growth.

We praise you for our heritage traced to
    your family tree at Calvary,
        for a blood line we can boast,
            bonded by crucifixion.

Be with (pastor) when joy is not so evident,
    when pressures mount and waters muddy,
        when your family fusses,
            wondering about direction.

Give her/him your gracious spirit
    when confusion and conflict seem to be ruling the day,
        when peace evades our grasp.

Stand firmly with her/him when s/he is tempted to avoid
> the discipline needed to strengthen members of this family.
Catch her/him off guard with good humor
> when s/he most needs to laugh.

Surround her/him with the joyful knowledge
> of deep resources available to love and be loved,
>> of tender opportunities to nurture and be nurtured,
> knowing how well the Lord has equipped her/him to serve.

Give to the members of this congregation a vision,
> not forgetting the past,
>> nor disowning their history,
>>> but celebrating the hope for this household's future.

Grant this congregation the miracle of birth,
> blessing this family with growth,
May we be ready to welcome unique personalities,
> adjust to change, court challenge,
>> and forgiving one another over and over again.

Thank you for the work of those who labored to bring this day.
> May each of us remember the promises of our own baptism.
>> May we help each other grow in Christian faith,
>>> working to serve Christ
>>>> by serving the needs of others.

Lord God, strengthen our family ties with your church universal.

Quicken our prayers for your children around the world.

In the name of Jesus Christ,

the head of the Church, we pray.

Amen.

Committee meeting

Loving God, creator of this world and the next,

we gather as your people to praise you

through the work of

council,

committee,

and report.

We come in expectation of the business given us to do.

Give us curiosity to see your spirit in unexpected places:

to feel your friendliness in the faces of others,

to know your warmth through discussion,

and find your creativity

touching the order of our agenda.

Thank you for the responsibility we are given to serve you,

sharing talents of different hues,

speaking for generations with different memories,

voting with different perspectives,

but loving the same savior.

Thank you for each new season,
>for a fresh start in the cycling of time,
>>for flowers and seeds,
>>>rains and snow,
>>>>harvest and heat.

Thank you for the host of Christians living before us,
>who worshipped and worked
>>and died, passing their faith to us.
We praise you for calling us to live in the seasons of hope,
>where darkness cannot overcome,
>>where disappointment can only challenge,
>>>and where we can always
>>>>dance to the rhythm of your amazing grace.
Amen.

A new church directory

Creating God, you love every face in this directory,
>every family,
>>every committee,
>>>every organization found upon these pages.

May each of our smiles radiate your love upon others.
May each of our mouths lift hymns of thanksgiving.
May our eyes discover signs of your work in the world,
>and our ears hear your spirit's whispers.
May the taste of bread and wine draw us into your embrace.

As we turn from page to page,

    quicken our hearts to offer prayers for those who smile as us.

As we remember each person and the challenges facing them,

    enable us to reach out with kindly words.

As we watch our children mature beyond these pictures,

    grant them wisdom, stature, and favor in your sight.

As age, accident or illness invites some

    to join you at a heavenly banquet,

        sustain us at the altar rail.

Create in us clean hearts, O God,

    so we might be your people

        in this place and in this time.

Grant us a yearning to praise your name

    and seek your gracious counsel.

In the name of Jesus, the Christ of God.

Amen.

SEASONS OF
BENEDICTION

<u>Advent</u>

Christians, go into the world.

May the God who breathes upon the waters of creation

saving you for himself,

be with you.

May the God who walks the sands of time

turning you from shadows toward the dawn,

be with you.

May the God who remembers and comforts,

setting rainbows in the skies and stars in the darkness,

be with you always.

Amen.

<u>Fear not, you who are heavy laden</u>

We are waiting on God,

and God will lift your countenance.

Allow God to use your tears for watering the dry soil

of your lives.

Remember the child Jesus, who was born to all,

was also raised for all.

Fear not,

for behold you have received good tidings of great joy,

come to us in the dark of night.

And remember these parting words of your savior,

"Lo, I am with your always, even to the ends of the earth."

Amen.

Epiphany

Remember stars when they vanish from sight.
Revisit dreams and wonder where they might lead you.
Consider the possibility of God's direction through detours.
For the God we know as Creator, Redeemer, and Spirit
is with you this day, and every day.
Amen.

Ash Wednesday

And now as the purple days of faith descend upon you,
may you honor the tears within your hearts,
and weep.
May you honor the tears within your world,
and serve.
May you honor the tears of God,
and know divine grief.
Then, may this God, creator, brother, source of life and hope,
may this God remain near to you
until you catch the scent of lilies.
Amen.

Holy Week

Christians, go into this next week following Jesus.

Walk with him.

Ride with him.

Pray with him.

Wait with him.

And may the God we know as Creator, Redeemer, Spirit,

be with you.

Amen.

Weep with those who weep

Sisters and brothers,

go now into the world to ponder the passion of our Lord.

Be patient.

Weep with those who weep.

Pause to feel the pain in your world.

Be comforted knowing Jesus Christ, son of the living God,

is with you always.

Amen.

Give us power

May the God in whose image you were fashioned,
grant you power.
May Christ untie small-mindedness
with which you are bound.
May the Spirit free all
bringing life into a discouraged world.
Amen.

Be blessings

May the God who calls you to serve
go with you on your journey.
May the Christ you meet in your brother, Jesus,
show you ways to bring justice and make peace.
May the Spirit of God energize you to act creatively
for your moment in time.
Friends, you are called to be blessings.
Go and begin.

Come home

Come home.

God is not dead.

Come home.

God waits at the end of the path,

arms open, eyes tender with tears.

There is gracious welcome waiting,

not needing your explanations.

There is lavish homecoming, freed from a past enslaved.

There is the fitting of weary feet with dancing shoes.

Come home.

It is time to end shame.

It is time to sit again at the father's table.

Here at home, you are truly yourselves.

Come home.

Pentecost

Listen to God speak between the lines and in the pauses.

Listen to Christ tell stories of the kingdom.

Listen to the Spirit breathe the translation of love.

Amen.

The story

God of story who gives you freedom to write the finale,
God of Calvary who reminds you there is no dead end,
God of Spirit who whispers the promise,
excite you with divine mystery. Amen.

As stewards of God's family

Go into the world forgiven.
Having eaten together,
go into the world to serve.
Having heard the whisper of hope,
go skipping toward tomorrow.
The Lord bless you and caress you.
The Lord be gracious and sit at table with you.
The Lord look upon you with delight,
and give you peace. Amen.

Sisters and brothers of Christ

As you leave this place,
know wherever you go, whatever you do, you belong to the Lord.

Comfort the fearful. Touch the lonely.
Sing. Pray. Laugh.
May God create in you a bountiful soul.
May Christ walk beside you.
And may the Holy Spirit add a lightness to your step. Amen.

Christians, the night is cold and dark.

Be warmed in the arms of God.
Be guided by the light of Christ.
Be comforted by the breath of the Spirit.
Amen.

Go into the world with God's blessing.

Know wisdom beyond knowledge.
Practice compassion.
Find joy in service.
And may this God we know as Creator, Redeemer, Spirit
Be with you always.
Amen.

Good night, God.

You wakened us to the music of the spheres.
And now evening bids lullaby to comfort our sleep.
Thank you for inviting us into the rhythm of today's beauty,
for calling us to sing and make melody in the dance of life.
May your spirit breathe upon us in our sleep.
Amen.

<u>With a song in your heart</u>

Christians, go into the world with a song in your heart.

Listen for lyrics of encouragement.

Share hope.

And may the God we know as

Creator

Christ

and Comforter

sing through you always.

Amen.

"Praying the Seasons."

These prayers have been prayed in this country and abroad, with refugees and ambassadors, inmates and victims, at denominational assemblies and in congregations of only a handful. I have prayed them at memorial services and weddings, with dogs rescued from Katrina, and families in the hospital after September 11th.

They are arranged by seasons. From the Season of Spring to the Season of Commitment, from the Season of Sorrow to the Season of Winter, there are prayers for patients, parishioners, choirs, Eagle Scouts, graduates, volunteers, Rotarians and pet owners.

These prayers may be used for personal meditation, community gatherings and congregational worship.

My writing style is poetic; the format is psalmic and the theology is universal.

Once prayed, I believe prayers are for everyone to use. God isn't impressed with copyrights. I want you to feel free to pray these prayers whenever and wherever they are needed. If you feel inclined to mention my name, I'd be pleased.

This is my gift to you.

Sylvia Casberg

Sunny Fields Publishing

P.O. Box 546

Solvang, CA 93464-0546

www.SunnyFieldsPublishing.com

SCasberg@mac.com

CPSIA information can be obtained at www.ICGtesting.com
Printed in the USA
BVOW031259051011

272878BV00001B/1/P

that, by all established rule—and, as regarded some of them, weighed by their own lack of efficiency for business—they ought to have given place to younger men, more orthodox in politics, and altogether fitter than themselves to serve our common Uncle. I knew it, too, but could never quite find in my heart to act upon the knowledge. Much and deservedly to my own discredit, therefore, and considerably to the detriment of my official conscience, they continued, during my incumbency, to creep about the wharves, and loiter up and down the Custom-House steps. They spent a good deal of time, also, asleep in their accustomed corners, with their chairs tilted back against the walls; awaking, however, once or twice in the forenoon, to bore one another with the several thousandth repetition of old sea-stories and mouldy jokes, that had grown to be passwords and countersigns among them.

The discovery was soon made, I imagine, that the new Surveyor had no great harm in him. So, with lightsome hearts and the happy consciousness of being usefully employed—in their own behalf at least, if not for our beloved country—these good old gentlemen went through the various formalities of office. Sagaciously under their spectacles, did they peep into the holds of vessels Mighty was their fuss about little matters, and marvellous, sometimes, the obtuseness that allowed greater ones to slip between their fingers Whenever such a mischance occurred—when a wagon-load of valuable merchandise had been smuggled ashore, at noonday, perhaps, and directly beneath their unsuspicious noses—nothing could exceed the vigilance and alacrity with which they proceeded to lock, and double-lock, and secure with tape and sealing—wax, all the avenues of the delinquent vessel. Instead of a reprimand for their previous negligence, the case seemed rather to require an eulogium on their praiseworthy caution after the mischief had happened; a grateful recognition of the promptitude of their zeal the moment that there was no longer any remedy.

Unless people are more than commonly disagreeable, it is my foolish habit to contract a kindness for them. The better part of my companion's character, if it have a better part, is that which usually comes uppermost in my regard, and forms the type whereby I recognise the man. As most of these old Custom-House officers had good traits, and as my position in reference to them, being paternal and protective, was favourable to the growth of friendly sentiments, I soon grew to like them all. It was pleasant in the summer forenoons—when the fervent heat, that almost liquefied the rest of the human family, merely communicated a genial warmth to their half torpid systems—it was pleasant to hear them chatting in the back entry, a row of them all tipped against the wall, as usual; while the frozen witticisms of past generations were thawed out, and came bubbling with laughter from their lips. Externally, the jollity of aged men has much in common with the mirth of children; the intellect, any more than a deep sense of humour, has little to do with the matter; it is, with both, a gleam that plays upon the surface, and imparts a sunny and cheery aspect alike to the green branch and grey, mouldering trunk. In one case, however, it is real sunshine; in the other, it more resembles the phosphorescent glow of decaying wood. It would be sad injustice, the reader must understand, to represent all my excellent old friends as in their dotage. In the first place, my coadjutors were not invariably old; there were men among them in their strength and prime, of marked ability and energy, and altogether superior to the sluggish and dependent mode of life on which their evil stars had cast them. Then, moreover, the white locks of age were sometimes found to be the thatch of an intellectual tenement in good repair. But, as respects the majority of my corps of veterans, there will be no wrong done if I characterize them generally as a set of wearisome old souls, who had gathered nothing worth preservation from their varied experience of life. They seemed to have flung away all the golden grain of practical wisdom, which they had enjoyed so many opportunities of harvesting, and most carefully to have stored their memory with the husks. They spoke with far more interest and unction of their morning's breakfast, or yesterday's, to-day's, or tomorrow's dinner, than of the shipwreck of forty or fifty years ago, and all the world's wonders which they had witnessed with their youthful eyes.

The father of the Custom-House—the patriarch, not only of this little squad of officials, but, I am bold to say, of the respectable body of tide-waiters all over the United States—was a certain permanent Inspector. He might truly be termed a legitimate son of the revenue system, dyed in the wool, or rather born in the purple; since his sire, a Revolutionary colonel, and formerly collector of the port, had created an office for him, and appointed him to fill it, at a period of the early ages which few living men can now remember. This Inspector, when I first knew him, was a man of fourscore years, or thereabouts, and certainly one of the most wonderful specimens of winter-green that you would be likely to discover in a lifetime's search. With his florid cheek, his compact figure smartly arrayed in a bright-buttoned blue coat, his brisk and vigorous step, and his hale and hearty aspect, altogether he seemed—not young, indeed—but a kind of new contrivance of Mother Nature in the shape of man, whom age and infirmity had no business to touch. His voice and laugh, which perpetually re-echoed through the Custom-House, had nothing of the tremulous quaver and cackle of an old man's utterance; they came strutting out of his lungs, like the crow of a cock, or the blast of a clarion. Looking at him merely as an animal—and there was very little else to look at—he was a most satisfactory object, from the thorough healthfulness and wholesomeness of his system, and his capacity, at that extreme age, to enjoy all, or nearly all, the delights which he had ever aimed at or conceived of. The careless security of his life in the Custom-House, on a regular income, and with but slight and infrequent apprehensions of removal, had no doubt contributed to make time pass lightly over him. The original and more potent causes, however, lay in the rare perfection of his animal nature, the moderate proportion of intellect, and the very trifling admixture of moral and spiritual ingredients; these latter qualities, indeed, being in barely enough measure to keep the old gentleman from walking on all-fours. He possessed no power of thought no depth of feeling, no troublesome sensibilities: nothing, in short, but a few commonplace instincts, which, aided by the cheerful temper which grew inevitably out of his physical well-being, did duty very respectably, and to general acceptance, in lieu of a heart. He had been the husband of three wives, all long since dead; the father of twenty children, most of whom, at every age of childhood or maturity, had likewise returned to dust. Here, one would suppose, might have been sorrow enough to imbue the sunniest disposition through and through with a sable tinge. Not so with our old Inspector One brief sigh sufficed to carry off the entire burden of these dismal reminiscences. The next moment he was as ready for sport as any unbreeched infant: far readier than the Collector's junior clerk, who at nineteen years was much the elder and graver man of the two.

I used to watch and study this patriarchal personage with, I think, livelier curiosity than any other form of humanity there presented to my notice. He was, in truth, a rare phenomenon; so perfect, in one point of view; so shallow, so delusive, so impalpable such an absolute nonentity, in every other. My conclusion was that he had no soul, no heart, no mind; nothing, as I have already said, but instincts; and yet, withal, so cunningly had the few materials of his character been put together that there was no painful perception of deficiency, but, on my part, an entire contentment with what I found in him.

It might be difficult—and it was so—to conceive how he should exist hereafter, so earthly and sensuous did he seem; but surely his existence here, admitting that it was to terminate with his last breath, had been not unkindly given; with no higher moral responsibilities than the beasts of the field, but with a larger scope of enjoyment than theirs, and with all their blessed immunity from the dreariness and duskiness of age.

One point in which he had vastly the advantage over his four-footed brethren was his ability to recollect the good dinners which it had made no small portion of the happiness of his life to eat. His gourmandism was a highly agreeable trait; and to hear him talk of roast meat was as appetizing as a pickle or an oyster. As he possessed no higher attribute, and neither sacrificed nor vitiated any spiritual endowment by devoting all his energies and ingenuities to subserve the delight and profit of his maw, it always pleased and satisfied me to hear him expatiate on fish, poultry, and butcher's meat, and the most eligible methods of preparing them for the table. His reminiscences of good cheer, however ancient the date of the actual banquet, seemed to bring the savour of pig or turkey under one's very nostrils. There were flavours on his palate that had lingered there not less than sixty or seventy years, and were still apparently as fresh as that of the mutton chop which he had just devoured for his breakfast. I have heard him smack his lips over dinners, every guest at which, except himself, had long been food for worms. It was marvellous to observe how the ghosts of bygone meals were continually rising up before him—not in anger or retribution, but as if grateful for his former appreciation, and seeking to repudiate an endless series of enjoyment. at once shadowy and sensual, A tender loin of beef, a hind-quarter of veal, a spare-rib of pork, a particular chicken, or a remarkably praiseworthy turkey, which had perhaps adorned his board in the days of the elder Adams, would be remembered; while all the subsequent experience of our race, and all the events that brightened or darkened his individual career, had gone over him with as little permanent effect as the passing breeze. The chief tragic event of the old man's life, so far as I could judge, was his mishap with a certain goose, which lived and died some twenty or forty years ago: a goose of most promising figure, but which, at table, proved so inveterately tough, that the carving-knife would make no impression on its carcass, and it could only be divided with an axe and handsaw.

But it is time to quit this sketch; on which, however, I should be glad to dwell at considerably more length, because of all men whom I have ever known, this individual was fittest to be a Custom-House officer. Most persons, owing to causes which I may not have space to hint at, suffer moral detriment from this peculiar mode of life. The old Inspector was incapable of it; and, were he to continue in office to tile end of time, would be just as good as he was then, and sit down to dinner with just as good an appetite.

There is one likeness, without which my gallery of Custom-House portraits would be strangely incomplete, but which my comparatively few opportunities for observation enable me to sketch only in the merest outline. It is that of the Collector, our gallant old General, who, after his brilliant military service, subsequently to which he had ruled over a wild Western territory, had come hither, twenty years before, to spend the decline of his varied and honourable life.

The brave soldier had already numbered, nearly or quite, his three-score years and ten, and was pursuing the remainder of his earthly march, burdened with infirmities which even the martial music of his own spirit-stirring recollections could do little towards lightening. The step was palsied now, that had been foremost in the charge. It was only with the assistance of a servant, and by leaning his hand heavily on the iron balustrade, that he could slowly and painfully ascend the Custom-House steps, and, with a toilsome progress across the floor, attain his customary chair beside the fireplace. There he used to sit, gazing with a somewhat dim serenity of aspect at the figures that came and went, amid the rustle of papers, the administering of oaths, the discussion of business, and the casual talk of the office; all which sounds and circumstances seemed but indistinctly to impress his senses, and hardly to make their way into his inner sphere of contemplation. His countenance, in this repose, was mild and kindly. If his notice was sought, an expression of courtesy and interest gleamed out upon his features, proving that there was light within him, and that it was only the outward medium of the intellectual lamp that obstructed the rays in their passage. The closer you penetrated to the substance of his mind, the sounder it appeared. When no longer called upon to speak or listen— either of which operations cost him an evident effort—his face would briefly subside into its former not uncheerful quietude. It was not painful to behold this look; for, though dim, it had not the imbecility of decaying age. The framework of his nature, originally strong and massive, was not yet crumpled into ruin.

To observe and define his character, however, under such disadvantages, was as difficult a task as to trace out and build up anew, in imagination, an old fortress, like Ticonderoga, from a view of its grey and broken ruins. Here and there, perchance, the walls may remain almost complete; but elsewhere may be only a shapeless mound, cumbrous with its very strength, and overgrown, through long years of peace and neglect, with grass and alien weeds.

Nevertheless, looking at the old warrior with affection—for, slight as was the communication between us, my feeling towards him, like that of all bipeds and quadrupeds who knew him, might not improperly be termed so,—I could discern the main points of his portrait. It was marked with the noble and heroic qualities which showed it to be not a mere accident, but of good right, that he had won a distinguished name. His spirit could never, I conceive, have been characterized by an uneasy activity; it must, at any period of his life, have required an impulse to set him in motion; but once stirred up, with obstacles to overcome, and an adequate object to be attained, it was not in the man to give out or fail. The heat that had formerly pervaded his nature, and which was not yet extinct, was never of the kind that flashes and flickers in a blaze; but rather a deep red glow, as of iron in a furnace. Weight, solidity, firmness—this was the expression of his repose, even in such decay as had crept untimely over him at the period of which I speak. But I could imagine, even then, that, under some excitement which should go deeply into his consciousness—roused by a trumpets real, loud enough to awaken all of his energies that were not dead, but only slumbering—he was yet capable of flinging off his infirmities like a sick man's gown, dropping the staff of age to seize a battle-sword, and starting up once more a warrior. And, in so intense a moment his demeanour would have still been calm. Such an exhibition, however, was but to be pictured in fancy; not to be anticipated, nor desired. What I saw in him—as evidently as the indestructible ramparts of Old Ticonderoga, already cited as the most appropriate simile—was the features of stubborn and ponderous endurance, which might well have amounted to obstinacy in his earlier days; of integrity, that, like most of his other endowments, lay in a somewhat heavy mass, and was just as unmalleable or unmanageable as a ton of iron ore; and of benevolence which, fiercely as he led the bayonets on at Chippewa or Fort Erie, I take to be of quite as genuine a stamp as what actuates any or all the polemical philanthropists of the age. He had slain men with his own hand, for aught I know—certainly, they had fallen like blades of grass at the sweep of the scythe before the charge to which his spirit imparted its triumphant energy—but, be that as it might, there was never in his heart so much cruelty as would have brushed the down off a butterfly's wing. I have not known the man to whose innate kindliness I would more confidently make an appeal.

Many characteristics—and those, too, which contribute not the least forcibly to impart resemblance in a sketch—must have vanished, or been obscured, before I met the General. All merely graceful attributes are usually the most evanescent; nor does nature adorn the human ruin with blossoms of new beauty, that have their roots and proper nutriment only in the chinks and crevices of decay, as she sows wall-flowers over the ruined fortress of Ticonderoga. Still, even in respect of grace and beauty, there were points well worth noting. A ray of humour, now and then, would make its way through the veil of dim obstruction, and glimmer pleasantly upon our faces. A trait of native elegance, seldom seen in the masculine character after childhood or early youth, was shown in the General's fondness for the sight and fragrance of flowers. An old soldier might be supposed to prize only the bloody laurel on his brow; but here was one who seemed to have a young girl's appreciation of the floral tribe.

There, beside the fireplace, the brave old General used to sit; while the Surveyor—though seldom, when it could be avoided, taking upon himself the difficult task of engaging him in conversation—was fond of standing at a distance, and watching his quiet and almost slumberous countenance. He seemed away from us, although we saw him but a few yards off; remote, though we passed close beside his chair; unattainable, though we might have stretched forth our hands and touched his own. It might be that he lived a more real life within his thoughts than amid the inappropriate environment of the Collector's office. The evolutions of the parade; the tumult of the battle; the flourish of old heroic music, heard thirty years before—such scenes and sounds, perhaps, were all alive before his intellectual sense. Meanwhile, the merchants and ship-masters, the spruce clerks and uncouth sailors, entered and departed; the bustle of his commercial and Custom-House life kept up its little murmur round about him; and neither with the men nor their affairs did the General appear to sustain the most distant relation. He was as much out of place as an old sword—now rusty, but which had flashed once in the battle's front, and showed still a bright gleam along its blade—would have been among the inkstands, paper-folders, and mahogany rulers on the Deputy Collector's desk.

There was one thing that much aided me in renewing and re-creating the stalwart soldier of the Niagara frontier—the man of true and simple energy. It was the recollection of those memorable words of his—"I'll try, Sir"—spoken on the very verge of a desperate and heroic enterprise, and breathing the soul and spirit of New England hardihood, comprehending all perils, and encountering all. If, in our country, valour were rewarded by heraldic honour, this phrase—which it seems so easy to speak, but which only he, with such a task of danger and glory before him, has ever spoken—would be the best and fittest of all mottoes for the General's shield of arms. It contributes greatly towards a man's moral and intellectual health to be brought into habits of companionship with individuals unlike himself, who care little for his pursuits, and whose sphere and abilities he must go out of himself to appreciate. The accidents of my life have often afforded me this advantage, but never with more fullness and variety than during my continuance in office. There was one man, especially, the observation of whose character gave me a new idea of talent. His gifts were emphatically those of a man of business; prompt, acute, clear-minded; with an eye that saw through all perplexities, and a faculty of arrangement that made them vanish as by the waving of an enchanter's wand. Bred up from boyhood in the Custom-House, it was his proper field of activity; and the many intricacies of business, so harassing to the interloper, presented themselves before him with the regularity of a perfectly comprehended system. In my contemplation, he stood as the ideal of his class. He was, indeed, the Custom-House in himself; or, at all events, the mainspring that kept its variously revolving wheels in motion; for, in an institution like this, where its officers are appointed to subserve their own profit and convenience, and seldom with a leading reference to their fitness for the duty to be performed, they must perforce seek elsewhere the dexterity which is not in them. Thus, by an inevitable necessity, as a magnet attracts steel-filings, so did our man of business draw to himself the difficulties which everybody met with. With an easy condescension, and kind forbearance towards our stupidity—which, to his order of mind, must have seemed little short of crime—would he forth-with, by the merest touch of his finger, make the incomprehensible as clear as daylight. The merchants valued him not less than we, his esoteric friends. His integrity was perfect; it was a law of nature with him, rather than a choice or a principle; nor can it be otherwise than the main condition of an intellect so remarkably clear and accurate as his to be honest and regular in the administration of affairs. A stain on his conscience, as to anything that came within the range of his vocation, would trouble such a man very much in the same way, though to a far greater degree, than an error in the balance of an account, or an ink-blot on the fair page of a book of record. Here, in a word—and it is a rare instance in my life—I had met with a person thoroughly adapted to the situation which he held.

Such were some of the people with whom I now found myself connected. I took it in good part, at the hands of Providence, that I was thrown into a position so little akin to my past habits; and set myself seriously to gather from it whatever profit was to be had. After my fellowship of toil and impracticable schemes with the dreamy brethren of Brook Farm; after living for three years within the subtle influence of an intellect like Emerson's; after those wild, free days on the Assabeth, indulging fantastic speculations, beside our fire of fallen boughs, with Ellery Channing; after talking with Thoreau about pine-trees and Indian relics in his hermitage at Walden; after growing fastidious by sympathy with the classic refinement of Hillard's culture; after becoming imbued with poetic sentiment at Longfellow's hearthstone—it was time, at length, that I should exercise other faculties of my nature, and nourish myself with food for which I had hitherto had little appetite. Even the old Inspector was desirable, as a change of diet, to a man who had known Alcott. I looked upon it as an evidence, in some measure, of a system naturally well balanced, and lacking no essential part of a thorough organization, that, with such associates to remember, I could mingle at once with men of altogether different qualities, and never murmur at the change.

Literature, its exertions and objects, were now of little moment in my regard. I cared not at this period for books; they were apart from me. Nature—except it were human nature—the nature that is developed in earth and sky, was, in one sense, hidden from me; and all the imaginative delight wherewith it had been spiritualized passed away out of my mind. A gift, a faculty, if it had not been departed, was suspended and inanimate within me. There would have been something sad, unutterably dreary, in all this, had I not been conscious that it lay at my own option to recall whatever was valuable in the past. It might be true, indeed, that this was a life which could not, with impunity, be lived too long; else, it might make me permanently other than I had been, without transforming me into any shape which it would be worth my while to take. But I never considered it as other than a transitory life. There was always a prophetic instinct, a low whisper in my ear, that within no long period, and whenever a new change of custom should be essential to my good, change would come.

Meanwhile, there I was, a Surveyor of the Revenue and, so far as I have been able to understand, as good a Surveyor as need be. A man of thought, fancy, and sensibility (had he ten times the Surveyor's proportion of those qualities), may, at any time, be a man of affairs, if he will only choose to give himself the trouble. My fellow-officers, and the merchants and sea-captains with whom my official duties brought me into any manner of connection, viewed me in no other light, and probably knew me in no other character. None of them, I presume, had ever read a page of my inditing, or would have cared a fig the more for me if they had read them all; nor would it have mended the matter, in the least, had those same unprofitable pages been written with a pen like that of Burns or of Chaucer, each of whom was a Custom-House officer in his day, as well as I. It is a good lesson—though it may often be a hard one—for a man who has dreamed of literary fame, and of making for himself a rank among the world's dignitaries by such means, to step aside out of the narrow circle in which his claims are recognized and to find how utterly devoid of significance, beyond that circle, is all that he achieves, and all he aims at. I know not that I especially needed the lesson, either in the way of warning or rebuke; but at any rate, I learned it thoroughly: nor, it gives me pleasure to reflect, did the truth, as it came home to my perception, ever cost me a pang, or require to be thrown off in a sigh. In the way of literary talk, it is true, the Naval Officer—an excellent fellow, who came into the office with me, and went out only a little later—would often engage me in a discussion about one or the other of his favourite topics, Napoleon or Shakespeare. The Collector's junior clerk, too a young gentleman who, it was whispered occasionally covered a sheet of Uncle Sam's letter paper with what (at the distance of a few yards) looked very much like poetry—used now and then to speak to me of books, as matters with which I might possibly be conversant. This was my all of lettered intercourse; and it was quite sufficient for my necessities.

No longer seeking or caring that my name should be blazoned abroad on title-pages, I smiled to think that it had now another kind of vogue. The Custom-House marker imprinted it, with a stencil and black paint, on pepper-bags, and baskets of anatto, and cigar-boxes, and bales of all kinds of dutiable merchandise, in testimony that these commodities had paid the impost, and gone regularly through the office. Borne on such queer vehicle of fame, a knowledge of my existence, so far as a name conveys it, was carried where it had never been before, and, I hope, will never go again.

But the past was not dead. Once in a great while, the thoughts that had seemed so vital and so active, yet had been put to rest so quietly, revived again. One of the most remarkable occasions, when the habit of bygone days awoke in me, was that which brings it within the law of literary propriety to offer the public the sketch which I am now writing.

In the second story of the Custom-House there is a large room, in which the brick-work and naked rafters have never been covered with panelling and plaster. The edifice—originally projected on a scale adapted to the old commercial enterprise of the port, and with an idea of subsequent prosperity destined never to be realized—contains far more space than its occupants know what to do with. This airy hall, therefore, over the Collector's apartments, remains unfinished to this day, and, in spite of the aged cobwebs that festoon its dusky beams, appears still to await the labour of the carpenter and mason. At one end of the room, in a recess, were a number of barrels piled one upon another, containing bundles of official documents. Large quantities of similar rubbish lay lumbering the floor. It was sorrowful to think how many days, and weeks, and months, and years of toil had been wasted on these musty papers, which were now only an encumbrance on earth, and were hidden away in this forgotten corner, never more to be glanced at by human eyes. But then, what reams of other manuscripts—filled, not with the dullness of official formalities, but with the thought of inventive brains and the rich effusion of deep hearts—had gone equally to oblivion; and that, moreover, without serving a purpose in their day, as these heaped-up papers had, and—saddest of all— without purchasing for their writers the comfortable livelihood which the clerks of the Custom-House had gained by these worthless scratchings of the pen. Yet not altogether worthless, perhaps, as materials of local history. Here, no doubt, statistics of the former commerce of Salem might be discovered, and memorials of her princely merchants—old King Derby—old Billy Gray—old Simon Forrester—and many another magnate in his day, whose powdered head, however, was scarcely in the tomb before his mountain pile of wealth began to dwindle. The founders of the greater part of the families which now compose the aristocracy of Salem might here be traced, from the petty and obscure beginnings of their traffic, at periods generally much posterior to the Revolution, upward to what their children look upon as long-established rank,

Prior to the Revolution there is a dearth of records; the earlier documents and archives of the Custom-House having, probably, been carried off to Halifax, when all the king's officials accompanied the British army in its flight from Boston. It has often been a matter of regret with me; for, going back, perhaps, to the days of the Protectorate, those papers must have contained many references to forgotten or remembered men, and to antique customs, which would have affected me with the same pleasure as when I used to pick up Indian arrow-heads in the field near the Old Manse.

But, one idle and rainy day, it was my fortune to make a discovery of some little interest. Poking and burrowing into the heaped-up rubbish in the corner, unfolding one and another document, and reading the names of vessels that had long ago foundered at sea or rotted at the wharves, and those of merchants never heard of now on 'Change, nor very readily decipherable on their mossy tombstones; glancing at such matters with the saddened, weary, half-reluctant interest which we bestow on the corpse of dead activity— and exerting my fancy, sluggish with little use, to raise up from these dry bones an image of the old towns brighter aspect, when India was a new region, and only Salem knew the way thither—I chanced to lay my hand on a small package, carefully done up in a piece of ancient yellow parchment. This envelope had the air of an official record of some period long past, when clerks engrossed their stiff and formal chirography on more substantial materials than at present. There was something about it that quickened an instinctive curiosity, and made me undo the faded red tape that tied up the package, with the sense that a treasure would here be brought to light. Unbending the rigid folds of the parchment cover, I found it to be a commission, under the hand and seal of Governor Shirley, in favour of one Jonathan Pine, as Surveyor of His Majesty's Customs for the Port of Salem, in the Province of Massachusetts Bay. I remembered to have read (probably in Felt's "Annals") a notice of the decease of Mr. Surveyor Pue, about fourscore years ago; and likewise, in a newspaper of recent times, an account of the digging up of his remains in the little graveyard of St. Peter's Church, during the renewal of that edifice. Nothing, if I rightly call to mind, was left of my respected predecessor, save an imperfect skeleton, and some fragments of apparel, and a wig of majestic frizzle, which, unlike the head that it once adorned, was in very satisfactory preservation. But, on examining the papers which the parchment commission served to envelop, I found more traces of Mr. Pue's mental part, and the internal operations of his head, than the frizzled wig had contained of the venerable skull itself.

They were documents, in short, not official, but of a private nature, or, at least, written in his private capacity, and apparently with his own hand. I could account for their being included in the heap of Custom-House lumber only by the fact that Mr. Pine's death had happened suddenly, and that these papers, which he probably kept in his official desk, had never come to the knowledge of his heirs, or were supposed to relate to the business of the revenue. On the transfer of the archives to Halifax, this package, proving to be of no public concern, was left behind, and had remained ever since unopened.

The ancient Surveyor—being little molested, suppose, at that early day with business pertaining to his office—seems to have devoted some of his many leisure hours to researches as a local antiquarian, and other inquisitions of a similar nature. These supplied material for petty activity to a mind that would otherwise have been eaten up with rust.

A portion of his facts, by-the-by, did me good service in the preparation of the article entitled "*Main Street*," included in the present volume. The remainder may perhaps be applied to purposes equally valuable hereafter, or not impossibly may be worked up, so far as they go, into a regular history of Salem, should my veneration for the natal soil ever impel me to so pious a task. Meanwhile, they shall be at the command of any gentleman, inclined and competent, to take the unprofitable labour off my hands. As a final disposition I contemplate depositing them with the Essex Historical Society. But the object that most drew my attention to the mysterious package was a certain affair of fine red cloth, much worn and faded, There were traces about it of gold embroidery, which, however, was greatly frayed and defaced, so that none, or very little, of the glitter was left. It had been wrought, as was easy to perceive, with wonderful skill of needlework; and the stitch (as I am assured by ladies conversant with such mysteries) gives evidence of a now forgotten art, not to be discovered even by the process of picking out the threads. This rag of scarlet cloth—for time, and wear, and a sacrilegious moth had reduced it to little other than a rag—on careful examination, assumed the shape of a letter.

It was the capital letter A. By an accurate measurement, each limb proved to be precisely three inches and a quarter in length. It had been intended, there could be no doubt, as an ornamental article of dress; but how it was to be worn, or what rank, honour, and dignity, in by-past times, were signified by it, was a riddle which (so evanescent are the fashions of the world in these particulars) I saw little hope of solving. And yet it strangely interested me. My eyes fastened themselves upon the old scarlet letter, and would not be turned aside. Certainly there was some deep meaning in it most worthy of interpretation, and which, as it were, streamed forth from the mystic symbol, subtly communicating itself to my sensibilities, but evading the analysis of my mind.

When thus perplexed—and cogitating, among other hypotheses, whether the letter might not have been one of those decorations which the white men used to contrive in order to take the eyes of Indians—I happened to place it on my breast. It seemed to me— the reader may smile, but must not doubt my word—it seemed to me, then, that I experienced a sensation not altogether physical, yet almost so, as of burning heat, and as if the letter were not of red cloth, but red-hot iron. I shuddered, and involuntarily let it fall upon the floor.

In the absorbing contemplation of the scarlet letter, I had hitherto neglected to examine a small roll of dingy paper, around which it had been twisted. This I now opened, and had the satisfaction to find recorded by the old Surveyor's pen, a reasonably complete explanation of the whole affair. There were several foolscap sheets, containing many particulars respecting the life and conversation of one Hester Prynne, who appeared to have been rather a noteworthy personage in the view of our ancestors. She had flourished during the period between the early days of Massachusetts and the close of the seventeenth century. Aged persons, alive in the time of Mr. Surveyor Pue, and from whose oral testimony he had made up his narrative, remembered her, in their youth, as a very old, but not decrepit woman, of a stately and solemn aspect. It had been her habit, from an almost immemorial date, to go about the country as a kind of voluntary nurse, and doing whatever miscellaneous good she might; taking upon herself, likewise, to give advice in all matters, especially those of the heart, by which means—as a person of such propensities inevitably must—she gained from many people the reverence due to an angel, but, I should imagine, was looked upon by others as an intruder and a nuisance. Prying further into the manuscript, I found the record of other doings and sufferings of this singular woman, for most of which the reader is referred to the story entitled *"The Scarlet Letter"*; and it should be borne carefully in mind that the main facts of that story are authorized and authenticated by the document of Mr. Surveyor Pue. The original papers, together with the scarlet letter itself—a most curious relic—are still in my possession, and shall be freely exhibited to whomsoever, induced by the great interest of the narrative, may desire a sight of them I must not be understood affirming that, in the dressing up of the tale, and imagining the motives and modes of passion that influenced the characters who figure in it, I have invariably confined myself within the limits of the old Surveyor's half-a-dozen sheets of foolscap. On the contrary, I have allowed myself, as to such points, nearly, or altogether, as much license as if the facts had been entirely of my own invention. What I contend for is the authenticity of the outline.

This incident recalled my mind, in some degree, to its old track. There seemed to be here the groundwork of a tale. It impressed me as if the ancient Surveyor, in his garb of a hundred years gone by, and wearing his immortal wig—which was buried with him, but did not perish in the grave—had bet me in the deserted chamber of the Custom-House. In his port was the dignity of one who had borne His Majesty's commission, and who was therefore illuminated by a ray of the splendour that shone so dazzlingly about the throne. How unlike alas the hangdog look of a republican official, who, as the servant of the people, feels himself less than the least, and below the lowest of his masters. With his own ghostly hand, the obscurely seen, but majestic, figure had imparted to me the scarlet symbol and the little roll of explanatory manuscript. With his own ghostly voice he had exhorted me, on the sacred consideration of my filial duty and reverence towards him— who might reasonably regard himself as my official ancestor—to bring his mouldy and moth-eaten lucubrations before the public. "Do this," said the ghost of Mr. Surveyor Pue, emphatically nodding the head that looked so imposing within its memorable wig; "do this, and the profit shall be all your own. You will shortly need it; for it is not in your days as it was in mine, when a man's office was a life-lease, and oftentimes an heirloom. But I charge you, in this matter of old Mistress Prynne, give to your predecessor's memory the credit which will be rightfully due" And I said to the ghost of Mr. Surveyor Pue—"I will".

On Hester Prynne's story, therefore, I bestowed much thought. It was the subject of my meditations for many an hour, while pacing to and fro across my room, or traversing, with a hundredfold repetition, the long extent from the front door of the Custom-House to the side entrance, and back again. Great were the weariness and annoyance of the old

Inspector and the Weighers and Gaugers, whose slumbers were disturbed by the unmercifully lengthened tramp of my passing and returning footsteps. Remembering their own former habits, they used to say that the Surveyor was walking the quarter-deck. They probably fancied that my sole object—and, indeed, the sole object for which a sane man could ever put himself into voluntary motion—was to get an appetite for dinner. And, to say the truth, an appetite, sharpened by the east wind that generally blew along the passage, was the only valuable result of so much indefatigable exercise. So little adapted is the atmosphere of a Custom-house to the delicate harvest of fancy and sensibility, that, had I remained there through ten Presidencies yet to come, I doubt whether the tale of "The Scarlet Letter" would ever have been brought before the public eye. My imagination was a tarnished mirror. It would not reflect, or only with miserable dimness, the figures with which I did my best to people it. The characters of the narrative would not be warmed and rendered malleable by any heat that I could kindle at my intellectual forge. They would take neither the glow of passion nor the tenderness of sentiment, but retained all the rigidity of dead corpses, and stared me in the face with a fixed and ghastly grin of contemptuous defiance. "What have you to do with us?" that expression seemed to say. "The little power you might have once possessed over the tribe of unrealities is gone You have bartered it for a pittance of the public gold. Go then, and earn your wages" In short, the almost torpid creatures of my own fancy twitted me with imbecility, and not without fair occasion.

It was not merely during the three hours and a half which Uncle Sam claimed as his share of my daily life that this wretched numbness held possession of me. It went with me on my sea-shore walks and rambles into the country, whenever—which was seldom and reluctantly—I bestirred myself to seek that invigorating charm of Nature which used to give me such freshness and activity of thought, the moment that I stepped across the threshold of the Old Manse. The same torpor, as regarded the capacity for intellectual effort, accompanied me home, and weighed upon me in the chamber which I most absurdly termed my study. Nor did it quit me when, late at night, I sat in the deserted parlour, lighted only by the glimmering coal-fire and the moon, striving to picture forth imaginary scenes, which, the next day, might flow out on the brightening page in many-hued description.

If the imaginative faculty refused to act at such an hour, it might well be deemed a hopeless case. Moonlight, in a familiar room, falling so white upon the carpet, and showing all its figures so distinctly—making every object so minutely visible, yet so unlike a morning or noontide visibility—is a medium the most suitable for a romance-writer to get acquainted with his illusive guests. There is the little domestic scenery of the well-known apartment; the chairs, with each its separate individuality; the centre-table, sustaining a work-basket, a volume or two, and an extinguished lamp; the sofa; the book-case; the picture on the wall—all these details, so completely seen, are so spiritualised by the unusual light, that they seem to lose their actual substance, and become things of intellect. Nothing is too small or too trifling to undergo this change, and acquire dignity thereby. A child's shoe; the doll, seated in her little wicker carriage; the hobby-horse—whatever, in a word, has been used or played with during the day is now invested with a quality of strangeness and remoteness, though still almost as vividly present as by daylight. Thus, therefore, the floor of our familiar room has become a neutral territory, somewhere between the real world and fairy-land, where the Actual and the Imaginary may meet, and each imbue itself with the nature of the other. Ghosts might enter here without affrighting us. It would be too much in keeping with the scene to excite surprise, were we to look about us and discover a form, beloved, but gone hence, now sitting quietly in a streak of this magic moonshine, with an aspect that would make us doubt whether it had returned from afar, or had never once stirred from our fireside.

The somewhat dim coal fire has an essential Influence in producing the effect which I would describe. It throws its unobtrusive tinge throughout the room, with a faint ruddiness upon the walls and ceiling, and a reflected gleam upon the polish of the furniture. This warmer light mingles itself with the cold spirituality of the moon-beams, and communicates, as it were, a heart and sensibilities of human tenderness to the forms which fancy summons tip. It converts them from snow-images into men and women. Glancing at the looking-glass, we behold—deep within its haunted verge—the smouldering glow of the half-extinguished anthracite, the white moon-beams on the floor, and a repetition of all the gleam and shadow of the picture, with one remove further from the actual, and nearer to the imaginative. Then, at such an hour, and with this scene before him, if a man, sitting all alone, cannot dream strange things, and make them look like truth, he need never try to write romances.

But, for myself, during the whole of my Custom-House experience, moonlight and sunshine, and the glow of firelight, were just alike in my regard; and neither of them was of one whit more avail than the twinkle of a tallow-candle. An entire class of susceptibilities, and a gift connected with them—of no great richness or value, but the best I had—was gone from me.

It is my belief, however, that had I attempted a different order of composition, my faculties would not have been found so pointless and inefficacious. I might, for instance, have contented myself with writing out the narratives of a veteran shipmaster, one of the Inspectors, whom I should be most ungrateful not to mention, since scarcely a day passed that he did not stir me to laughter and admiration by his marvelous gifts as a story-teller. Could I have preserved the picturesque force of his style, and the humourous colouring which nature taught him how to throw over his descriptions, the result, I honestly believe, would have been something new in literature. Or I might readily have found a more serious task. It was a folly, with the materiality of this daily life pressing so intrusively upon me, to attempt to fling myself back into another age, or to insist on creating the semblance of a world out of airy matter, when, at every moment, the impalpable beauty of my soap-bubble was broken by the rude contact of some actual circumstance. The wiser effort would have been to diffuse thought and imagination through the opaque substance of to-day, and thus to make it a bright transparency; to spiritualise the burden that began to weigh so heavily; to seek, resolutely, the true and indestructible value that lay hidden in the petty and wearisome incidents, and ordinary characters with which I was now conversant. The fault was mine. The page of life that was spread out before me seemed dull and commonplace only because I had not fathomed its deeper import. A better book than I shall ever write was there; leaf after leaf presenting itself to me, just as it was written out by the reality of the flitting hour, and vanishing as fast as written, only because my brain wanted the insight, and my hand the cunning, to transcribe it. At some future day, it may be, I shall remember a few scattered fragments and broken paragraphs, and write them down, and find the letters turn to gold upon the page.

These perceptions had come too late. At the Instant, I was only conscious that what would have been a pleasure once was now a hopeless toil. There was no occasion to make much moan about this state of affairs. I had ceased to be a writer of tolerably poor tales and essays, and had become a tolerably good Surveyor of the Customs. That was all. But, nevertheless, it is anything but agreeable to be haunted by a suspicion that one's intellect is dwindling away, or exhaling, without your consciousness, like ether out of a phial; so that, at every glance, you find a smaller and less volatile residuum. Of the fact there could be no doubt and, examining myself and others, I was led to conclusions, in reference to the effect of public office on the character, not very favourable to the mode of life in question. In some other form, perhaps, I may hereafter develop these effects. Suffice it here to say that a Custom-House officer of long continuance can hardly be a very praiseworthy or respectable personage, for many reasons; one of them, the tenure by which he holds his situation, and another, the very nature of his business, which—though, I trust, an honest one—is of such a sort that he does not share in the united effort of mankind.

An effect—which I believe to be observable, more or less, in every individual who has occupied the position—is, that while he leans on the mighty arm of the Republic, his own proper strength, departs from him. He loses, in an extent proportioned to the weakness or force of his original nature, the capability of self-support. If he possesses an unusual share of native energy, or the enervating magic of place do not operate too long upon him, his forfeited powers may be redeemable. The ejected officer—fortunate in the unkindly shove that sends him forth betimes, to struggle amid a struggling world—may return to himself, and become all that he has ever been. But this seldom happens. He usually keeps his ground just long enough for his own ruin, and is then thrust out, with sinews all unstrung, to totter along the difficult footpath of life as he best may. Conscious of his own infirmity—that his tempered steel and elasticity are lost—he for ever afterwards looks wistfully about him in quest of support external to himself. His pervading and continual hope—a hallucination, which, in the face of all discouragement, and making light of impossibilities, haunts him while he lives, and, I fancy, like the convulsive throes of the cholera, torments him for a brief space after death—is, that finally, and in no long time, by some happy coincidence of circumstances, he shall be restored to office. This faith, more than anything else, steals the pith and availability out of whatever enterprise he may dream of undertaking. Why should he toil and moil, and be at so much trouble to pick himself up out of the mud, when, in a little while hence, the strong arm of his Uncle will raise and support him? Why should he work for his living here, or go to dig gold in California, when he is so soon to be made happy, at monthly intervals, with a little pile of glittering coin out of his Uncle's pocket? It is sadly curious to observe how slight a taste of office suffices to infect a poor fellow with this singular disease. Uncle Sam's gold—meaning no disrespect to the worthy old gentleman—has, in this respect, a quality of enchantment like that of the devil's wages. Whoever touches it should look well to himself, or he may find the bargain to go hard against him, involving, if not his soul, yet many of its better attributes; its sturdy force, its courage and constancy, its truth, its self-reliance, and all that gives the emphasis to manly character.

Here was a fine prospect in the distance. Not that the Surveyor brought the lesson home to himself, or admitted that he could be so utterly undone, either by continuance in office or ejectment. Yet my reflections were not the most comfortable. I began to grow melancholy and restless; continually prying into my mind, to discover which of its poor properties were gone, and what degree of detriment had already accrued to the remainder. I endeavoured to calculate how much longer I could stay in the Custom-House, and yet go forth a man. To confess the truth, it was my greatest apprehension—as it would never be a measure of policy to turn out so quiet an individual as myself; and it being hardly in the nature of a public officer to resign—it was my chief trouble, therefore, that I was likely to grow grey and decrepit in the Surveyorship, and become much such another animal as the old Inspector. Might it not, in the tedious lapse of official life that lay before me, finally be with me as it was with this venerable friend—to make the dinner-hour the nucleus of the day, and to spend the rest of it, as an old dog spends it, asleep in the sunshine or in the shade? A dreary look-forward, this, for a man who felt it to be the best definition of happiness to live throughout the whole range of his faculties and sensibilities But, all this while, I was giving myself very unnecessary alarm. Providence had meditated better things for me than I could possibly imagine for myself.

A remarkable event of the third year of my Surveyorship—to adopt the tone of "P. P."—was the election of General Taylor to the Presidency. It is essential, in order to a complete estimate of the advantages of official life, to view the incumbent at the in-coming of a hostile administration. His position is then one of the most singularly irksome, and, in every contingency, disagreeable, that a wretched mortal can possibly occupy; with seldom an alternative of good on either hand, although what presents itself to him as the worst event may very probably be the best. But it is a strange experience, to a man of pride and sensibility, to know that his interests are within the control of individuals who neither love nor understand him, and by whom, since one or the other must needs happen, he would rather be injured than obliged. Strange, too, for one who has kept his calmness throughout the contest, to observe the bloodthirstiness that is developed in the hour of triumph, and to be conscious that he is himself among its objects! There are few uglier traits of human nature than this tendency—which I now witnessed in men no worse than their neighbours—to grow cruel, merely because they possessed the power of inflicting harm. If the guillotine, as applied to office-holders, were a literal fact, instead of one of the most apt of metaphors, it is my sincere belief that the active members of the victorious party were sufficiently excited to have chopped off all our heads, and have thanked Heaven for the opportunity! It appears to me—who have been a calm and curious observer, as well in victory as defeat—that this fierce and bitter spirit of malice and revenge has never distinguished the many triumphs of my own party as it now did that of the Whigs. The Democrats take the offices, as a general rule, because they need them, and because the practice of many years has made it the law of political warfare, which unless a different system be proclaimed, it was weakness and cowardice to murmur at. But the long habit of victory has made them generous. They know how to spare when they see occasion; and when they strike, the axe may be sharp indeed, but its edge is seldom poisoned with ill-will; nor is it their custom ignominiously to kick the head which they have just struck off.

In short, unpleasant as was my predicament, at best, I saw much reason to congratulate myself that I was on the losing side rather than the triumphant one. If, heretofore, 1 had been none of the warmest of partisans I began now, at this season of peril and adversity, to be pretty acutely sensible with which party my predilections lay; nor was it without something like regret and shame that, according to a reasonable calculation of chances, I saw my own prospect of retaining office to be better than those of my democratic brethren. But who can see an inch into futurity beyond his nose? My own head was the first that fell

The moment when a man's head drops off is seldom or never, I am inclined to think, precisely the most agreeable of his life. Nevertheless, like the greater part of our misfortunes, even so serious a contingency brings its remedy and consolation with it, if the sufferer will but make the best rather than the worst, of the accident which has befallen him. In my particular case the consolatory topics were close at hand, and, indeed, had suggested themselves to my meditations a considerable time before it was requisite to use them. In view of my previous weariness of office, and vague thoughts of resignation, my fortune somewhat resembled that of a person who should entertain an idea of committing suicide, and although beyond his hopes, meet with the good hap to be murdered. In the Custom-House, as before in the Old Manse, I had spent three years—a term long enough to rest a weary brain: long enough to break off old intellectual habits, and make room for new ones: long enough, and too long, to have lived in an unnatural state, doing what was really of no advantage nor delight to any human being, and withholding myself from toil that would, at least, have stilled an unquiet impulse in me. Then, moreover, as regarded his unceremonious ejectment, the late Surveyor was not altogether ill-pleased to be recognised by the Whigs as an enemy; since his inactivity in political affairs—his tendency to roam, at will, in that broad and quiet field where all mankind may meet, rather than confine himself to those narrow paths where brethren of the same household must diverge from one another—had sometimes made it questionable with his brother Democrats whether he was a friend. Now, after he had won the crown of martyrdom (though with no longer a head to wear it on), the point might be looked upon as settled. Finally, little heroic as he was, it seemed more decorous to be overthrown in the downfall of the party with which he had been content to stand than to remain a forlorn survivor, when so many worthier men were falling: and at last, after subsisting for four years on the mercy of a hostile administration, to be compelled then to define his position anew, and claim the yet more humiliating mercy of a friendly one.

Meanwhile, the press had taken up my affair, and kept me for a week or two careering through the public prints, in my decapitated state, like Irving's Headless Horseman, ghastly and grim, and longing to be buried, as a political dead man ought. So much for my figurative self. The real human being all this time, with his head safely on his shoulders, had brought himself to the comfortable conclusion that everything was for the best; and making an investment in ink, paper, and steel pens, had opened his long-disused writing desk, and was again a literary man. Now it was that the lucubrations of my ancient predecessor, Mr. Surveyor Pue, came into play. Rusty through long idleness, some little space was requisite before my intellectual machinery could be brought to work upon the tale with an effect in any degree satisfactory. Even yet, though my thoughts were ultimately much absorbed in the task, it wears, to my eye, a stern and sombre aspect: too much ungladdened by genial sunshine; too little relieved by the tender and familiar influences which soften almost every scene of nature and real life, and undoubtedly should soften every picture of them. This uncaptivating effect is perhaps due to the period of hardly accomplished revolution, and still seething turmoil, in which the story shaped itself. It is no indication, however, of a lack of cheerfulness in the writer's mind: for he was happier while straying through the gloom of these sunless fantasies than at any time since he had quitted the Old Manse. Some of the briefer articles, which contribute to make up the volume, have likewise been written since my involuntary withdrawal from the toils and honours of public life, and the remainder are gleaned from annuals and magazines, of such antique date, that they have gone round the circle, and come back to novelty again. Keeping up the metaphor of the political guillotine, the whole may be considered as the *posthumous papers of a decapitated surveyor*: and the sketch which I am now bringing to a close, if too autobiographical for a modest person to publish in his lifetime, will readily be excused in a gentleman who writes from beyond the grave. Peace be with all the world My blessing on my friends My forgiveness to my enemies For I am in the realm of quiet

The life of the Custom—House lies like a dream behind me. The old Inspector—

who, by-the-bye, l regret to say, was overthrown and killed by a horse some time ago, else he would certainly have lived for ever—he, and all those other venerable personages who sat with him at the receipt of custom, are but shadows in my view: white-headed and wrinkled images, which my fancy used to sport with, and has now flung aside for ever. The merchants—Pingree, Phillips, Shepard, Upton, Kimball, Bertram, Hunt—these and many other names, which had such classic familiarity for my ear six months ago,—these men of traffic, who seemed to occupy so important a position in the world—how little time has it required to disconnect me from them all, not merely in act, but recollection It is with an effort that

I recall the figures and appellations of these few. Soon, likewise, my old native town will loom upon me through the haze of memory, a mist brooding over and around it; as if it were no portion of the real earth, but an overgrown village in cloud-land, with only imaginary inhabitants to people its wooden houses and walk its homely lanes, and the unpicturesque prolixity of its main street. Henceforth it ceases to be a reality of my life; I am a citizen of somewhere else. My good townspeople will not much regret me, for—though it has been as dear an object as any, in my literary efforts, to be of some importance in their eyes, and to win myself a pleasant memory in this abode and burial-place of so many of my forefathers—there has never been, for me, the genial atmosphere which a literary man requires in order to ripen the best harvest of his mind. I shall do better amongst other faces; and these familiar ones, it need hardly be said, will do just as well without me.

It may be, however—oh, transporting and triumphant thought I—that the great-grandchildren of the present race may sometimes think kindly of the scribbler of bygone days, when the antiquary of days to come, among the sites memorable in the town's history, shall point out the locality of *the town pump*.

THE SCARLET LETTER

I. The Prison Door

A throng of bearded men, in sad-coloured garments and grey steeple-crowned hats, inter-mixed with women, some wearing hoods, and others bareheaded, was assembled in front of a wooden edifice, the door of which was heavily timbered with oak, and studded with iron spikes.

The founders of a new colony, whatever Utopia of human virtue and happiness they might originally project, have invariably recognised it among their earliest practical necessities to allot a portion of the virgin soil as a cemetery, and another portion as the site of a prison. In accordance with this rule it may safely be assumed that the forefathers of Boston had built the first prison-house somewhere in the Vicinity of Cornhill, almost as seasonably as they marked out the first burial-ground, on Isaac Johnson's lot, and round about his grave, which subsequently became the nucleus of all the congregated sepulchres in the old churchyard of King's Chapel. Certain it is that, some fifteen or twenty years after the settlement of the town, the wooden jail was already marked with weather-stains and other indications of age, which gave a yet darker aspect to its beetle-browed and gloomy front. The rust on the ponderous iron-work of its oaken door looked more antique than anything else in the New World. Like all that pertains to crime, it seemed never to have known a youthful era. Before this ugly edifice, and between it and the wheel-track of the street, was a grass-plot, much overgrown with burdock, pig-weed, apple-pern, and such unsightly vegetation, which evidently found something congenial in the soil that had so early borne the black flower of civilised society, a prison. But on one side of the portal, and rooted almost at the threshold, was a wild rose-bush, covered, in this month of June, with its delicate gems, which might be imagined to offer their fragrance and fragile beauty to the prisoner as he went in, and to the condemned criminal as he came forth to his doom, in token that the deep heart of Nature could pity and be kind to him.

This rose-bush, by a strange chance, has been kept alive in history; but whether it had merely survived out of the stern old wilderness, so long after the fall of the gigantic pines and oaks that originally overshadowed it, or whether, as there is far authority for believing, it had sprung up under the footsteps of the sainted Ann Hutchinson as she entered the prison-door, we shall not take upon us to determine. Finding it so directly on the threshold of our narrative, which is now about to issue from that inauspicious portal, we could hardly do otherwise than pluck one of its flowers, and present it to the reader. It may serve, let us hope, to symbolise some sweet moral blossom that may be found along the track, or relieve the darkening close of a tale of human frailty and sorrow

II. The Market-Place

The grass-plot before the jail, in Prison Lane, on a certain summer morning, not less than two centuries ago, was occupied by a pretty large number of the inhabitants of Boston, all with their eyes intently fastened on the iron-clamped oaken door. Amongst any other population, or at a later period in the history of New England, the grim rigidity that petrified the bearded physiognomies of these good people would have augured some awful business in hand. It could have betokened nothing short of the anticipated execution of some rioted culprit, on whom the sentence of a legal tribunal had but confirmed the verdict of public sentiment. But, in that early severity of the Puritan character, an inference of this kind could not so indubitably be drawn. It might be that a sluggish bond-servant, or an undutiful child, whom his parents had given over to the civil authority, was to be corrected at the whipping-post. It might be that an Antinomian, a Quaker, or other heterodox religionist, was to be scourged out of the town, or an idle or vagrant Indian, whom the white man's firewater had made riotous about the streets, was to be driven with stripes into the shadow of the forest. It might be, too, that a witch, like old Mistress Hibbins, the bitter-tempered widow of the magistrate, was to die upon the gallows. In either case, there was very much the same solemnity of demeanour on the part of the spectators, as befitted a people among whom religion and law were almost identical, and in whose character both were so thoroughly interfused, that the mildest and severest acts of public discipline were alike made venerable and awful. Meagre, indeed, and cold, was the sympathy that a transgressor might look for, from such bystanders, at the scaffold. On the other hand, a penalty which, in our days, would infer a degree of mocking infamy and ridicule, might then be invested with almost as stern a dignity as the punishment of death itself.

It was a circumstance to be noted on the summer morning when our story begins its course, that the women, of whom there were several in the crowd, appeared to take a peculiar interest in whatever penal infliction might be expected to ensue. The age had not so much refinement, that any sense of impropriety restrained the wearers of petticoat and farthingale from stepping forth into the public ways, and wedging their not unsubstantial persons, if occasion were, into the throng nearest to the scaffold at an execution. Morally, as well as materially, there was a coarser fibre in those wives and maidens of old English birth and breeding than in their fair descendants, separated from them by a series of six or seven generations; for, throughout that chain of ancestry, every successive mother had transmitted to her child a fainter bloom, a more delicate and briefer beauty, and a slighter physical frame, if not character of less force and solidity than her own. The women who were now standing about the prison-door stood within less than half a century of the period when the man-like Elizabeth had been the not altogether unsuitable representative of the sex. They were her countrywomen: and the beef and ale of their native land, with a moral diet not a whit more refined, entered largely into their composition. The bright morning sun, therefore, shone on broad shoulders and well-developed busts, and on round and ruddy cheeks, that had ripened in the far-off island, and had hardly yet grown paler or thinner in the atmosphere of New England. There was, moreover, a boldness and rotundity of speech among these matrons, as most of them seemed to be, that would startle us at the present day, whether in respect to its purport or its volume of tone.

"Goodwives," said a hard-featured dame of fifty, "I'll tell ye a piece of my mind. It would be greatly for the public behoof if we women, being of mature age and church-members in good repute, should have the handling of such malefactresses as this Hester Prynne. What think ye, gossips? If the hussy stood up for judgment before us five, that are now here in a knot together, would she come off with such a sentence as the worshipful magistrates have awarded? Marry, I trow not"

"People say," said another, "that the Reverend Master Dimmesdale, her godly pastor, takes it very grievously to heart that such a scandal should have come upon his congregation."

"The magistrates are God-fearing gentlemen, but merciful overmuch—that is a truth," added a third autumnal matron. "At the very least, they should have put the brand of a hot iron on Hester Prynne's forehead. Madame Hester would have winced at that, I warrant me. But she—the naughty baggage—little will she care what they put upon the bodice of her gown Why, look you, she may cover it with a brooch, or such like. heathenish adornment, and so walk the streets as brave as ever"

"Ah, but," interposed, more softly, a young wife, holding a child by the hand, "let her cover the mark as she will, the pang of it will be always in her heart."

"What do we talk of marks and brands, whether on the bodice of her gown or the flesh of her forehead?" cried another female, the ugliest as well as the most pitiless of these self-constituted judges. "This woman has brought shame upon us all, and ought to die; Is there not law for it? Truly there is, both in the Scripture and the statute-book. Then let the magistrates, who have made it of no effect, thank themselves if their own wives and daughters go astray"

"Mercy on us, goodwife" exclaimed a man in the crowd, "is there no virtue in woman, save what springs from a wholesome fear of the gallows? That is the hardest word yet! Hush now, gossips for the lock is turning in the prison-door, and here comes Mistress Prynne herself."

The door of the jail being flung open from within there appeared, in the first place, like a black shadow emerging into sunshine, the grim and gristly presence of the town-beadle, with a sword by his side, and his staff of office in his hand. This personage prefigured and represented in his aspect the whole dismal severity of the Puritanic code of law, which it was his business to administer in its final and closest application to the offender. Stretching forth the official staff in his left hand, he laid his right upon the shoulder of a young woman, whom he thus drew forward, until, on the threshold of the prison-door, she repelled him, by an action marked with natural dignity and force of character, and stepped into the open air as if by her own free will. She bore in her arms a child, a baby of some three months old, who winked and turned aside its little face from the too vivid light of day; because its existence, heretofore, had brought it acquaintance only with the grey twilight of a dungeon, or other darksome apartment of the prison.

When the young woman—the mother of this child—stood fully revealed before the crowd, it seemed to be her first impulse to clasp the infant closely to her bosom; not so much by an impulse of motherly affection, as that she might thereby conceal a certain token, which was wrought or fastened into her dress. In a moment, however, wisely judging that one token of her shame would but poorly serve to hide another, she took the baby on her arm, and with a burning blush, and yet a haughty smile, and a glance that would not be abashed, looked around at her townspeople and neighbours. On the breast of her gown, in fine red cloth, surrounded with an elaborate embroidery and fantastic flourishes of gold thread, appeared the letter A. It was so artistically done, and with so much fertility and gorgeous luxuriance of fancy, that it had all the effect of a last and fitting decoration to the apparel which she wore, and which was of a splendour in accordance with the taste of the age, but greatly beyond what was allowed by the sumptuary regulations of the colony.

The young woman was tall, with a figure of perfect elegance on a large scale. She had dark and abundant hair, so glossy that it threw off the sunshine with a gleam; and a face which, besides being beautiful from regularity of feature and richness of complexion, had the impressiveness belonging to a marked brow and deep black eyes. She was ladylike, too, after the manner of the feminine gentility of those days; characterised by a certain state and dignity, rather than by the delicate, evanescent, and indescribable grace which is now recognised as its indication. And never had Hester Prynne appeared more ladylike, in the antique interpretation of the term, than as she issued from the prison. Those who had before known her, and had expected to behold her dimmed and obscured by a disastrous cloud, were astonished, and even startled, to perceive how her beauty shone out, and made a halo of the misfortune and ignominy in which she was enveloped. It may be true that, to a sensitive observer, there was something exquisitely painful in it. Her attire, which indeed, she had wrought for the occasion in prison, and had modelled much after her own fancy, seemed to express the attitude of her spirit, the desperate recklessness of her mood, by its wild and picturesque peculiarity. But the point which drew all eyes, and, as it were, transfigured the wearer—so that both men and women who had been familiarly acquainted with Hester Prynne were now impressed as if they beheld her for the first time—was that SCARLET LETTER, so fantastically embroidered and illuminated upon her bosom. It had the effect of a spell, taking her out of the ordinary relations with humanity, and enclosing her in a sphere by herself.

"She hath good skill at her needle, that's certain," remarked one of her female spectators; "but did ever a woman, before this brazen hussy, contrive such a way of showing it? Why, gossips, what is it but to laugh in the faces of our godly magistrates, and make a pride out of what they, worthy gentlemen, meant for a punishment?"

"It were well," muttered the most iron-visaged of the old dames, "if we stripped Madame Hester's rich gown off her dainty shoulders; and as for the red letter which she hath stitched so curiously, I'll bestow a rag of mine own rheumatic flannel to make a fitter one!"

"Oh, peace, neighbours—peace!" whispered their youngest companion; "do not let her hear you! Not a stitch in that embroidered letter but she has felt it in her heart."

The grim beadle now made a gesture with his staff. "Make way, good people—make way, in the King's name!" cried he. "Open a passage; and I promise ye, Mistress Prynne shall be set where man, woman, and child may have a fair sight of her brave apparel from this time till an hour past meridian. A blessing on the righteous colony of the Massachusetts, where iniquity is dragged out into the sunshine! Come along, Madame Hester, and show your scarlet letter in the market-place!"

A lane was forthwith opened through the crowd of spectators. Preceded by the beadle, and attended by an irregular procession of stern-browed men and unkindly visaged women, Hester Prynne set forth towards the place appointed for her punishment. A crowd of eager and curious schoolboys, understanding little of the matter in hand, except that it gave them a half-holiday, ran before her progress, turning their heads continually to stare into her face and at the winking baby in her arms, and at the ignominious letter on her breast. It was no great distance, in those days, from the prison door to the market-place. Measured by the prisoner's experience, however, it might be reckoned a journey of some length; for haughty as her demeanour was, she perchance underwent an agony from every footstep of those that thronged to see her, as if her heart had been flung into the street for them all to spurn and trample upon. In our nature, however, there is a provision, alike marvellous and merciful, that the sufferer should never know the intensity of what he endures by its present torture, but chiefly by the pang that rankles after it. With almost a serene deportment, therefore, Hester Prynne passed through this portion of her ordeal, and came to a sort of scaffold, at the western extremity of the market-place. It stood nearly beneath the eaves of Boston's earliest church, and appeared to be a fixture there.

In fact, this scaffold constituted a portion of a penal machine, which now, for two or three generations past, has been merely historical and traditionary among us, but was held, in the old time, to be as effectual an agent, in the promotion of good citizenship, as ever was the guillotine among the terrorists of France. It was, in short, the platform of the pillory; and above it rose the framework of that instrument of discipline, so fashioned as to confine the human head in its tight grasp, and thus hold it up to the public gaze. The very ideal of ignominy was embodied and made manifest in this contrivance of wood and iron. There can be no outrage, methinks, against our common nature—whatever be the delinquencies of the individual—no outrage more flagrant than to forbid the culprit to hide his face for shame; as it was the essence of this punishment to do. In Hester Prynne's instance, however, as not unfrequently in other cases, her sentence bore that she should stand a certain time upon the platform, but without undergoing that gripe about the neck and confinement of the head, the proneness to which was the most devilish characteristic of this ugly engine. Knowing well her part, she ascended a flight of wooden steps, and was thus displayed to the surrounding multitude, at about the height of a man's shoulders above the street.

Had there been a Papist among the crowd of Puritans, he might have seen in this beautiful woman, so picturesque in her attire and mien, and with the infant at her bosom, an object to remind him of the image of Divine Maternity, which so many illustrious painters have vied with one another to represent; something which should remind him, indeed, but only by contrast, of that sacred image of sinless motherhood, whose infant was to redeem the world. Here, there was the taint of deepest sin in the most sacred quality of human life, working such effect, that the world was only the darker for this woman's beauty, and the more lost for the infant that she had borne.

The scene was not without a mixture of awe, such as must always invest the spectacle of guilt and shame in a fellow-creature, before society shall have grown corrupt enough to smile, instead of shuddering at it. The witnesses of Hester Prynne's disgrace had not yet passed beyond their simplicity. They were stern enough to look upon her death, had that been the sentence, without a murmur at its severity, but had none of the heartlessness of another social state, which would find only a theme for jest in an exhibition like the present. Even had there been a disposition to turn the matter into ridicule, it must have been repressed and overpowered by the solemn presence of men no less dignified than the governor, and several of his counsellors, a judge, a general, and the ministers of the town, all of whom sat or stood in a balcony of the meeting-house, looking down upon the platform. When such personages could constitute a part of the spectacle, without risking the majesty, or reverence of rank and office, it was safely to be inferred that the infliction of a legal sentence would have an earnest and effectual meaning. Accordingly, the crowd was sombre and grave. The unhappy culprit sustained herself as best a woman might, under the heavy weight of a thousand unrelenting eyes, all fastened upon her, and concentrated at her bosom. It was almost intolerable to be borne. Of an impulsive and passionate nature, she had fortified herself to encounter the stings and venomous stabs of public contumely, wreaking itself in every variety of insult; but there was a quality so much more terrible in the solemn mood of the popular mind, that she longed rather to behold all those rigid countenances contorted with scornful merriment, and herself the object. Had a roar of laughter burst from the multitude—each man, each woman, each little shrill-voiced child, contributing their individual parts— Hester Prynne might have repaid them all with a bitter and disdainful smile. But, under the leaden infliction which it was her doom to endure, she felt, at moments, as if she must needs shriek out with the full power of her lungs, and cast herself from the scaffold down upon the ground, or else go mad at once.

Yet there were intervals when the whole scene, in which she was the most conspicuous object, seemed to vanish from her eyes, or, at least, glimmered indistinctly before them, like a mass of imperfectly shaped and spectral images. Her mind, and especially her memory, was preternaturally active, and kept bringing up other scenes than this roughly hewn street of a little town, on the edge of the western wilderness: other faces than were lowering upon her from beneath the brims of those steeple-crowned hats. Reminiscences, the most trifling and immaterial, passages of infancy and school-days, sports, childish quarrels, and the little domestic traits of her maiden years, came swarming back upon her, intermingled with recollections of whatever was gravest in her subsequent life; one picture precisely as vivid as another; as if all were of similar importance, or all alike a play. Possibly, it was an instinctive device of her spirit to relieve itself by the exhibition of these phantasmagoric forms, from the cruel weight and hardness of the reality.

Be that as it might, the scaffold of the pillory was a point of view that revealed to Hester Prynne the entire track along which she had been treading, since her happy infancy. Standing on that miserable eminence, she saw again her native village, in Old England, and her paternal home: a decayed house of grey stone, with a poverty-stricken aspect, but retaining a half obliterated shield of arms over the portal, in token of antique gentility. She saw her father's face, with its bold brow, and reverend white beard that flowed over the old-fashioned Elizabethan ruff; her mother's, too, with the look of heedful and anxious love which it always wore in her remembrance, and which, even since her death, had so often laid the impediment of a gentle remonstrance in her daughter's pathway. She saw her own face, glowing with girlish beauty, and illuminating all the interior of the dusky mirror in which she had been wont to gaze at it. There she beheld another countenance, of a man well stricken in years, a pale, thin, scholar-like visage, with eyes dim and bleared by the lamp-light that had served them to pore over many ponderous books. Yet those same bleared optics had a strange, penetrating power, when it was their owner's purpose to read the human soul. This figure of the study and the cloister, as Hester Prynne's womanly fancy failed not to recall, was slightly deformed, with the left shoulder a trifle higher than the right. Next rose before her in memory's picture-gallery, the intricate and narrow thoroughfares, the tall, grey houses, the huge cathedrals, and the public edifices, ancient in date and quaint in architecture, of a continental city; where new life had awaited her, still in connection with the misshapen scholar: a new life, but feeding itself on time-worn materials, like a tuft of green moss on a crumbling wall. Lastly, in lieu of these shifting scenes, came back the rude market-place of the Puritan, settlement, with all the townspeople assembled, and levelling their stern regards at Hester Prynne—yes, at herself—who stood on the scaffold of the pillory, an infant on her arm, and the letter A, in scarlet, fantastically embroidered with gold thread, upon her bosom.

Could it be true? She clutched the child so fiercely to her breast that it sent forth a cry; she turned her eyes downward at the scarlet letter, and even touched it with her finger, to assure herself that the infant and the shame were real. Yes these were her realities—all else had vanished!

III. The Recognition

From this intense consciousness of being the object of severe and universal observation, the wearer of the scarlet letter was at length relieved, by discerning, on the outskirts of the crowd, a figure which irresistibly took possession of her thoughts. An Indian in his native garb was standing there; but the red men were not so infrequent visitors of the English settlements that one of them would have attracted any notice from Hester Prynne at such a time; much less would he have excluded all other objects and ideas from her mind. By the Indian's side, and evidently sustaining a companionship with him, stood a white man, clad in a strange disarray of civilized and savage costume.

He was small in stature, with a furrowed visage, which as yet could hardly be termed aged. There was a remarkable intelligence in his features, as of a person who had so cultivated his mental part that it could not fail to mould the physical to itself and become manifest by unmistakable tokens. Although, by a seemingly careless arrangement of his heterogeneous garb, he had endeavoured to conceal or abate the peculiarity, it was sufficiently evident to Hester Prynne that one of this man's shoulders rose higher than the other. Again, at the first instant of perceiving that thin visage, and the slight deformity of the figure, she pressed her infant to her bosom with so convulsive a force that the poor babe uttered another cry of pain. But the mother did not seem to hear it,

At his arrival in the market-place, and some time before she saw him, the stranger had bent his eyes on Hester Prynne. It was carelessly at first, like a man chiefly accustomed to look inward, and to whom external matters are of little value and import, unless they bear relation to something within his mind. Very soon, however, his look became keen and penetrative. A writhing horror twisted itself across his features, like a snake gliding swiftly over them, and making one little pause, with all its wreathed intervolutions in open sight. His face darkened with some powerful emotion, which, nevertheless, he so instantaneously controlled by an effort of his will, that, save at a single moment, its expression might have passed for calmness. After a brief space, the convulsion grew almost imperceptible, and finally subsided into the depths of his nature. When he found the eyes of Hester Prynne fastened on his own, and saw that she appeared to recognize him, he slowly and calmly raised his finger, made a gesture with it in the air, and laid it on his lips.

Then touching the shoulder of a townsman who stood near to him, he addressed him in a formal and courteous manner:

"I pray you, good Sir," said he, "who is this woman?—and wherefore is she here set up to public shame?"

"You must needs be a stranger in this region, friend," answered the townsman, looking curiously at the questioner and his savage companion, "else you would surely have heard of Mistress Hester Prynne and her evil doings. She hath raised a great scandal, I promise you, in godly Master Dimmesdale's church."

"You say truly," replied the other; "I am a stranger, and have been a wanderer, sorely against my will. I have met with grievous mishaps by sea and land, and have been long held in bonds among the heathen-folk to the southward; and am now brought hither by this Indian to be redeemed out of my captivity. Will it please you, therefore, to tell me of Hester Prynne's—have I her name rightly?—of this woman's offences, and what has brought her to yonder scaffold?"

"Truly, friend; and methinks it must gladden your heart, after your troubles and sojourn in the wilderness," said the townsman, "to find yourself at length in a land where iniquity is searched out and punished in the sight of rulers and people, as here in our godly New England. Yonder woman, Sir, you must know, was the wife of a certain learned man, English by birth, but who had long ago dwelt in Amsterdam, whence some good time agone he was minded to cross over and cast in his lot with us of the Massachusetts. To this purpose he sent his wife before him, remaining himself to look after some necessary affairs. Marry, good Sir, in some two years, or less, that the woman has been a dweller here in Boston, no tidings have come of this learned gentleman, Master Prynne; and his young wife, look you, being left to her own misguidance—"

"Ah!—aha!—I conceive you," said the stranger with a bitter smile. "So learned a man as you speak of should have learned this too in his books. And who, by your favour, Sir, may be the father of yonder babe—it is some three or four months old, I should judge—which Mistress Prynne is holding in her arms?"

"Of a truth, friend, that matter remaineth a riddle; and the Daniel who shall expound it is yet a-wanting," answered the townsman. "Madame Hester absolutely refuseth to speak, and the magistrates have laid their heads together in vain. Peradventure the guilty one stands looking on at this sad spectacle, unknown of man, and forgetting that God sees him."

"The learned man," observed the stranger with another smile, "should come himself to look into the mystery."

"It behooves him well if he be still in life," responded the townsman. "Now, good Sir, our Massachusetts magistracy, bethinking themselves that this woman is youthful and fair, and doubtless was strongly tempted to her fall, and that, moreover, as is most likely, her husband may be at the bottom of the sea, they have not been bold to put in force the extremity of our righteous law against her. The penalty thereof is death. But in their great mercy and tenderness of heart they have doomed Mistress Prynne to stand only a space of three hours on the platform of the pillory, and then and thereafter, for the remainder of her natural life to wear a mark of shame upon her bosom."

"A wise sentence," remarked the stranger, gravely, bowing his head. "Thus she will be a living sermon against sin, until the ignominious letter be engraved upon her tombstone. It irks me, nevertheless, that the partner of her iniquity should not at least, stand on the scaffold by her side. But he will be known—he will be known!—he will be known!"

He bowed courteously to the communicative townsman, and whispering a few words to his Indian attendant, they both made their way through the crowd.

While this passed, Hester Prynne had been standing on her pedestal, still with a fixed gaze towards the stranger—so fixed a gaze that, at moments of intense absorption, all other objects in the visible world seemed to vanish, leaving only him and her. Such an interview, perhaps, would have been more terrible than even to meet him as she now did, with the hot mid-day sun burning down upon her face, and lighting up its shame; with the scarlet token of infamy on her breast; with the sin-born infant in her arms; with a whole people, drawn forth as to a festival, staring at the features that should have been seen only in the quiet gleam of the fireside, in the happy shadow of a home, or beneath a matronly veil at church. Dreadful as it was, she was conscious of a shelter in the presence of these thousand witnesses. It was better to stand thus, with so many betwixt him and her, than to greet him face to face—they two alone. She fled for refuge, as it were, to the public exposure, and dreaded the moment when its protection should be withdrawn from her. Involved in these thoughts, she scarcely heard a voice behind her until it had repeated her name more than once, in a loud and solemn tone, audible to the whole multitude.

"Hearken unto me, Hester Prynne!" said the voice.

It has already been noticed that directly over the platform on which Hester Prynne stood was a kind of balcony, or open gallery, appended to the meeting-house. It was the place whence proclamations were wont to be made, amidst an assemblage of the magistracy, with all the ceremonial that attended such public observances in those days. Here, to witness the scene which we are describing, sat Governor Bellingham himself with four sergeants about his chair, bearing halberds, as a guard of honour. He wore a dark feather in his hat, a border of embroidery on his cloak, and a black velvet tunic beneath—a gentleman advanced in years, with a hard experience written in his wrinkles. He was not ill-fitted to be the head and representative of a community which owed its origin and progress, and its present state of development, not to the impulses of youth, but to the stern and tempered energies of manhood and the sombre sagacity of age; accomplishing so much, precisely because it imagined and hoped so little. The other eminent characters by whom the chief ruler was surrounded were distinguished by a dignity of mien, belonging to a period when the forms of authority were felt to possess the sacredness of Divine institutions. They were, doubtless, good men, just and sage. But, out of the whole human family, it would not have been easy to select the same number of wise and virtuous persons, who should he less capable of sitting in judgment on an erring woman's heart, and disentangling its mesh of good and evil, than the sages of rigid aspect towards whom Hester Prynne now turned her face. She seemed conscious, indeed, that whatever sympathy she might expect lay in the larger and warmer heart of the multitude; for, as she lifted her eyes towards the balcony, the unhappy woman grew pale, and trembled.

The voice which had called her attention was that of the reverend and famous John Wilson, the eldest clergyman of Boston, a great scholar, like most of his contemporaries in the profession, and withal a man of kind and genial spirit. This last attribute, however, had been less carefully developed than his intellectual gifts, and was, in truth, rather a matter of shame than self-congratulation with him. There he stood, with a border of grizzled locks beneath his skull-cap, while his grey eyes, accustomed to the shaded light of his study, were winking, like those of Hester's infant, in the unadulterated sunshine. He looked like the darkly engraved portraits which we see prefixed to old volumes of sermons, and had no more right than one of those portraits would have to step forth, as he now did, and meddle with a question of human guilt, passion, and anguish.

"Hester Prynne," said the clergyman, "I have striven with my young brother here, under whose preaching of the Word you have been privileged to sit"—here Mr. Wilson laid his hand on the shoulder of a pale young man beside him—"I have sought, I say, to persuade this godly youth, that he should deal with you, here in the face of Heaven, and before these wise and upright rulers, and in hearing of all the people, as touching the vileness and blackness of your sin. Knowing your natural temper better than I, he could the better judge what arguments to use, whether of tenderness or terror, such as might prevail over your hardness and obstinacy, insomuch that you should no longer hide the name of him who tempted you to this grievous fall. But he opposes to me—with a young man's over-softness, albeit wise beyond his years—that it were wronging the very nature of woman to force her to lay open her heart's secrets in such broad daylight, and in presence of so great a multitude. Truly, as I sought to convince him, the shame lay in the commission of the sin, and not in the showing of it forth. What say you to it, once again, brother Dimmesdale? Must it be thou, or I, that shall deal with this poor sinner's soul?"

There was a murmur among the dignified and reverend occupants of the balcony; and Governor Bellingham gave expression to its purport, speaking in an authoritative voice, although tempered with respect towards the youthful clergyman whom he addressed:

"Good Master Dimmesdale," said he, "the responsibility of this woman's soul lies greatly with you. It behooves you; therefore, to exhort her to repentance and to confession, as a proof and consequence thereof."

The directness of this appeal drew the eyes of the whole crowd upon the Reverend Mr. Dimmesdale—young clergyman, who had come from one of the great English universities, bringing all the learning of the age into our wild forest land. His eloquence and religious fervour had already given the earnest of high eminence in his profession. He was a person of very striking aspect, with a white, lofty, and impending brow; large, brown, melancholy eyes, and a mouth which, unless when he forcibly compressed it, was apt to be tremulous, expressing both nervous sensibility and a vast power of self restraint. Notwithstanding his high native gifts and scholar-like attainments, there was an air about this young minister—an apprehensive, a startled, a half-frightened look—as of a being who felt himself quite astray, and at a loss in the pathway of human existence, and could only be at ease in some seclusion of his own. Therefore, so far as his duties would permit, he trod in the shadowy by-paths, and thus kept himself simple and childlike, coming forth, when occasion was, with a freshness, and fragrance, and dewy purity of thought, which, as many people said, affected them like tile speech of an angel.

Such was the young man whom the Reverend Mr. Wilson and the Governor had introduced so openly to the public notice, bidding him speak, in the hearing of all men, to that mystery of a woman's soul, so sacred even in its pollution. The trying nature of his position drove the blood from his cheek, and made his lips tremulous.

"Speak to the woman, my brother," said Mr. Wilson. "It is of moment to her soul, and, therefore, as the worshipful Governor says, momentous to thine own, ill whose charge hers is. Exhort her to confess the truth!"

The Reverend Mr. Dimmesdale bent his head, silent prayer, as it seemed, and then came forward.

"Hester Prynne," said he, leaning over the balcony and looking down steadfastly into her eyes, "thou hearest what this good man says, and seest the accountability under which I labour. If thou feelest it to be for thy soul's peace, and that thy earthly punishment will thereby be made more effectual to salvation, I charge thee to speak out the name of thy fellow-sinner and fellow-sufferer! Be not silent from any mistaken pity and tenderness for him; for, believe me, Hester, though he were to step down from a high place, and stand there beside thee, on thy pedestal of shame, yet better were it so than to hide a guilty heart through life. What can thy silence do for him, except it tempt him—yea, compel him, as it were—to add hypocrisy to sin? Heaven hath granted thee an open ignominy, that thereby thou mayest work out an open triumph over the evil within thee and the sorrow without. Take heed how thou deniest to him—who, perchance, hath not the courage to grasp it for himself—the bitter, but wholesome, cup that is now presented to thy lips!"

The young pastor's voice was tremulously sweet, rich, deep, and broken. The feeling that it so evidently manifested, rather than the direct purport of the words, caused it to vibrate within all hearts, and brought the listeners into one accord of sympathy. Even the poor baby at Hester's bosom was affected by the same influence, for it directed its hitherto vacant gaze towards Mr. Dimmesdale, and held up its little arms with a half-pleased, half-plaintive murmur. So powerful seemed the minister's appeal that the people could not believe but that Hester Prynne would speak out the guilty name, or else that the guilty one himself in whatever high or lowly place he stood, would be drawn forth by an inward and inevitable necessity, and compelled to ascend the scaffold.

Hester shook her head.

"Woman, transgress not beyond the limits of Heaven's mercy!" cried the Reverend Mr. Wilson, more harshly than before. "That little babe hath been gifted with a voice, to second and confirm the counsel which thou hast heard. Speak out the name! That, and thy repentance, may avail to take the scarlet letter off thy breast."

"Never," replied Hester Prynne, looking, not at Mr. Wilson, but into the deep and troubled eyes of the younger clergyman. "It is too deeply branded. Ye cannot take it off. And would that I might endure his agony as well as mine!"

"Speak, woman!" said another voice, coldly and sternly, proceeding from the crowd about the scaffold, "Speak; and give your child a father!"

"I will not speak!" answered Hester, turning pale as death, but responding to this voice, which she too surely recognised. "And my child must seek a heavenly father; she shall never know an earthly one!"

"She will not speak!" murmured Mr. Dimmesdale, who, leaning over the balcony, with his hand upon his heart, had awaited the result of his appeal. He now drew back with a long respiration. "Wondrous strength arid generosity of a woman's heart! She will not speak!"

Discerning the impracticable state of the poor culprit's mind, the elder clergyman, who had carefully prepared himself for the occasion, addressed to the multitude a discourse on sin, in all its branches, but with continual reference to the ignominious letter. So forcibly did he dwell upon this symbol, for the hour or more during which is periods were rolling over the people's heads, that it assumed new terrors in their imagination, and seemed to derive its scarlet hue from the flames of the infernal pit.

Hester Prynne, meanwhile, kept her place upon the pedestal of shame, with glazed eyes, and an air of weary indifference. She had borne that morning all that nature could endure; and as her temperament was not of the order that escapes from too intense suffering by a swoon, her spirit could only shelter itself beneath a stony crust of insensibility, while the faculties of animal life remained entire. In this state, the voice of the preacher thundered remorselessly, but unavailingly, upon her ears. The infant, during the latter portion of her ordeal, pierced the air with its wailings and screams; she strove to hush it mechanically, but seemed scarcely to sympathise with its trouble. With the same hard demeanour, she was led back to prison, and vanished from the public gaze within its iron-clamped portal. It was whispered by those who peered after her that the scarlet letter threw a lurid gleam along the dark passage-way of the interior.

IV. The Interview

After her return to the prison, Hester Prynne was found to be in a state of nervous excitement, that demanded constant watchfulness, lest she should perpetrate violence on herself, or do some half-frenzied mischief to the poor babe. As night approached, it proving impossible to quell her insubordination by rebuke or threats of punishment, Master Brackett, the jailer, thought fit to introduce a physician. He described him as a man of skill in all Christian modes of physical science, and likewise familiar with whatever the savage people could teach in respect to medicinal herbs and roots that grew in the forest. To say the truth, there was much need of professional assistance, not merely for Hester herself, but still more urgently for the child—who, drawing its sustenance from the maternal bosom, seemed to have drank in with it all the turmoil, the anguish and despair, which pervaded the mother's system. It now writhed in convulsions of pain, and was a forcible type, in its little frame, of the moral agony which Hester Prynne had borne throughout the day.

Closely following the jailer into the dismal apartment, appeared that individual, of singular aspect whose presence in the crowd had been of such deep interest to the wearer of the scarlet letter. He was lodged in the prison, not as suspected of any offence, but as the most convenient and suitable mode of disposing of him, until the magistrates should have conferred with the Indian sagamores respecting his ransom. His name was announced as Roger Chillingworth. The jailer, after ushering him into the room, remained a moment, marvelling at the comparative quiet that followed his entrance; for Hester Prynne had immediately become as still as death, although the child continued to moan.

"Prithee, friend, leave me alone with my patient," said the practitioner. "Trust me, good jailer, you shall briefly have peace in your house; and, I promise you, Mistress Prynne shall hereafter be more amenable to just authority than you may have found her heretofore."

"Nay, if your worship can accomplish that," answered Master Brackett, "I shall own you for a man of skill, indeed! Verily, the woman hath been like a possessed one; and there lacks little that I should take in hand, to drive Satan out of her with stripes."

The stranger had entered the room with the characteristic quietude of the profession to which he announced himself as belonging. Nor did his demeanour change when the withdrawal of the prison keeper left him face to face with the woman, whose absorbed notice of him, in the crowd, had intimated so close a relation between himself and her. His first care was given to the child, whose cries, indeed, as she lay writhing on the trundle-bed, made it of peremptory necessity to postpone all other business to the task of soothing her. He examined the infant carefully, and then proceeded to unclasp a leathern case, which he took from beneath his dress. It appeared to contain medical preparations, one of which he mingled with a cup of water.

"My old studies in alchemy," observed he, "and my sojourn, for above a year past, among a people well versed in the kindly properties of simples, have made a better physician of me than many that claim the medical degree. Here, woman! The child is yours—she is none of mine—neither will she recognise my voice or aspect as a father's. Administer this draught, therefore, with thine own hand."

Hester repelled the offered medicine, at the same time gazing with strongly marked apprehension into his face. "Wouldst thou avenge thyself on the innocent babe?" whispered she.

"Foolish woman!" responded the physician, half coldly, half soothingly. "What should ail me to harm this misbegotten and miserable babe? The medicine is potent for good, and were it my child—yea, mine own, as well as thine! I could do no better for it."

As she still hesitated, being, in fact, in no reasonable state of mind, he took the infant in his arms, and himself administered the draught. It soon proved its efficacy, and redeemed the leech's pledge. The moans of the little patient subsided; its convulsive tossings gradually ceased; and in a few moments, as is the custom of young children after relief from pain, it sank into a profound and dewy slumber. The physician, as he had a fair right to be termed, next bestowed his attention on the mother. With calm and intent scrutiny, he felt her pulse, looked into her eyes—a gaze that made her heart shrink and shudder, because so familiar, and yet so strange and cold—and, finally, satisfied with his investigation, proceeded to mingle another draught.

"I know not Lethe nor Nepenthe," remarked he; "but I have learned many new secrets in the wilderness, and here is one of them—a recipe that an Indian taught me, in requital of some lessons of my own, that were as old as Paracelsus. Drink it! It may be less soothing than a sinless conscience. That I cannot give thee. But it will calm the swell and heaving of thy passion, like oil thrown on the waves of a tempestuous sea."

He presented the cup to Hester, who received it with a slow, earnest look into his face; not precisely a look of fear, yet full of doubt and questioning as to what his purposes might be. She looked also at her slumbering child.

"I have thought of death," said she—"have wished for it—would even have prayed for it, were it fit that such as I should pray for anything. Yet, if death be in this cup, I bid thee think again, ere thou beholdest me quaff it. See! it is even now at my lips."

"Drink, then," replied he, still with the same cold composure. "Dost thou know me so little, Hester Prynne? Are my purposes wont to be so shallow? Even if I imagine a scheme of vengeance, what could I do better for my object than to let thee live—than to give thee medicines against all harm and peril of life—so that this burning shame may still blaze upon thy bosom?" As he spoke, he laid his long fore-finger on the scarlet letter, which forthwith seemed to scorch into Hester's breast, as if it ad been red hot. He noticed her involuntary gesture, and smiled. "Live, therefore, and bear about thy doom with thee, in the eyes of men and women—in the eyes of him whom thou didst call thy husband—in the eyes of yonder child! And, that thou mayest live, take off this draught."

Without further expostulation or delay, Hester Prynne drained the cup, and, at the motion of the man of skill, seated herself on the bed, where the child was sleeping; while he drew the only chair which the room afforded, and took his own seat beside her. She could not but tremble at these preparations; for she felt that—having now done all that humanity, or principle, or, if so it were, a refined cruelty, impelled him to do for the relief of physical suffering—he was next to treat with her as the man whom she had most deeply and irreparably injured.

"Hester," said he, "I ask not wherefore, nor how thou hast fallen into the pit, or say, rather, thou hast ascended to the pedestal of infamy on which I found thee. The reason is not far to seek. It was my folly, and thy weakness. I—a man of thought—the book-worm of great libraries—a man already in decay, having given my best years to feed the hungry dream of knowledge—what had I to do with youth and beauty like thine own? Misshapen from my birth-hour, how could I delude myself with the idea that intellectual gifts might veil physical deformity in a young girl's fantasy? Men call me wise. If sages were ever wise in their own behoof, I might have foreseen all this. I might have known that, as I came out of the vast and dismal forest, and entered this settlement of Christian men, the very first object to meet my eyes would be thyself, Hester Prynne, standing up, a statue of ignominy, before the people. Nay, from the moment when we came down the old church-steps together, a married pair, I might have beheld the bale-fire of that scarlet letter blazing at the end of our path!"

"Thou knowest," said Hester—for, depressed as she was, she could not endure this last quiet stab at the token of her shame—"thou knowest that I was frank with thee. I felt no love, nor feigned any."

"True," replied he. "It was my folly! I have said it. But, up to that epoch of my life, I had lived in vain. The world had been so cheerless! My heart was a habitation large enough for many guests, but lonely and chill, and without a household fire. I longed to kindle one! It seemed not so wild a dream—old as I was, and sombre as I was, and misshapen as I was—that the simple bliss, which is scattered far and wide, for all mankind to gather up, might yet be mine. And so, Hester, I drew thee into my heart, into its innermost chamber, and sought to warm thee by the warmth which thy presence made there!"

"I have greatly wronged thee," murmured Hester.

"We have wronged each other," answered he. "Mine was the first wrong, when I betrayed thy budding youth into a false and unnatural relation with my decay. Therefore, as a man who has not thought and philosophised in vain, I seek no vengeance, plot no evil against thee. Between thee and me, the scale hangs fairly balanced. But, Hester, the man lives who has wronged us both! Who is he?"

"Ask me not?" replied Hester Prynne, looking firmly into his face. "That thou shalt never know!"

"Never, sayest thou?" rejoined he, with a smile of dark and self-relying intelligence. "Never know him! Believe me, Hester, there are few things whether in the outward world, or, to a certain depth, in the invisible sphere of thought—few things hidden from the man who devotes himself earnestly and unreservedly to the solution of a mystery. Thou mayest cover up thy secret from the prying multitude. Thou mayest conceal it, too, from the ministers and magistrates, even as thou didst this day, when they sought to wrench the name out of thy heart, and give thee a partner on thy pedestal. But, as for me, I come to the inquest with other senses than they possess. I shall seek this man, as I have sought truth in books: as I have sought gold in alchemy. There is a sympathy that will make me conscious of him. I shall see him tremble. I shall feel myself shudder, suddenly and unawares. Sooner or later, he must needs be mine."

The eyes of the wrinkled scholar glowed so intensely upon her, that Hester Prynne clasped her hand over her heart, dreading lest he should read the secret there at once.

"Thou wilt not reveal his name? Not the less he is mine," resumed he, with a look of confidence, as if destiny were at one with him. "He bears no letter of infamy wrought into his garment, as thou dost, but I shall read it on his heart . Yet fear not for him! Think not that I shall interfere with Heaven's own method of retribution, or, to my own loss, betray him to the gripe of human law. Neither do thou imagine that I shall contrive aught against his life; no, nor against his fame, if as I judge, he be a man of fair repute. Let him live! Let him hide himself in outward honour, if he may! Not the less he shall be mine!"

"Thy acts are like mercy," said Hester, bewildered and appalled; "but thy words interpret thee as a terror!"

"One thing, thou that wast my wife, I would enjoin upon thee," continued the scholar. "Thou hast kept the secret of thy paramour. Keep, likewise, mine! There are none in this land that know me. Breathe not to any human soul that thou didst ever call me husband! Here, on this wild outskirt of the earth, I shall pitch my tent; for, elsewhere a wanderer, and isolated from human interests, I find here a woman, a man, a child, amongst whom and myself there exist the closest ligaments. No matter whether of love or hate: no matter whether of right or wrong! Thou and thine, Hester Prynne, belong to me. My home is where thou art and where he is. But betray me not!"

"Wherefore dost thou desire it?" inquired Hester, shrinking, she hardly knew why, from this secret bond. "Why not announce thyself openly, and cast me off at once?"

"It may be," he replied, "because I will not encounter the dishonour that besmirches the husband of a faithless woman. It may be for other reasons. Enough, it is my purpose to live and die unknown. Let, therefore, thy husband be to the world as one already dead, and of whom no tidings shall ever come. Recognise me not, by word, by sign, by look! Breathe not the secret, above all, to the man thou wottest of. Shouldst thou fail me in this, beware! His fame, his position, his life will be in my hands. Beware!"

"I will keep thy secret, as I have his," said Hester.

"Swear it!" rejoined he.

And she took the oath.

"And now, Mistress Prynne," said old Roger Chillingworth, as he was hereafter to be named, "I leave thee alone: alone with thy infant and the scarlet letter! How is it, Hester? Doth thy sentence bind thee to wear the token in thy sleep? Art thou not afraid of nightmares and hideous dreams?"

"Why dost thou smile so at me?" inquired Hester, troubled at the expression of his eyes. "Art thou like the Black Man that haunts the forest round about us? Hast thou enticed me into a bond that will prove the ruin of my soul?"

"Not thy soul," he answered, with another smile. "No, not thine!"

V. Hester at Her Needle

Hester Prynne's term of confinement was now at an end. Her prison-door was thrown open, and she came forth into the sunshine, which, falling on all alike, seemed, to her sick and morbid heart, as if meant for no other purpose than to reveal the scarlet letter on her breast. Perhaps there was a more real torture in her first unattended footsteps from the threshold of the prison than even in the procession and spectacle that have been described, where she was made the common infamy, at which all mankind was summoned to point its finger. Then, she was supported by an unnatural tension of the nerves, and by all the combative energy of her character, which enabled her to convert the scene into a kind of lurid triumph. It was, moreover, a separate and insulated event, to occur but once in her lifetime, and to meet which, therefore, reckless of economy, she might call up the vital strength that would have sufficed for many quiet years. The very law that condemned her—a giant of stem featured but with vigour to support, as well as to annihilate, in his iron arm—had held her up through the terrible ordeal of her ignominy. But now, with this unattended walk from her prison door, began the daily custom; and she must either sustain and carry it forward by the ordinary resources of her nature, or sink beneath it. She could no longer borrow from the future to help her through the present grief. Tomorrow would bring its own trial with it; so would the next day, and so would the next: each its own trial, and yet the very same that was now so unutterably grievous to be borne. The days of the far-off future would toil onward, still with the same burden for her to take up, and bear along with her, but never to fling down; for the accumulating days and added years would pile up their misery upon the heap of shame. Throughout them all, giving up her individuality, she would become the general symbol at which the preacher and moralist might point, and in which they might vivify and embody their images of woman's frailty and sinful passion. Thus the young and pure would be taught to look at her, with the scarlet letter flaming on her breast—at her, the child of honourable parents—at her, the mother of a babe that would hereafter be a woman—at her, who had once been innocent—as the figure, the body, the reality of sin. And over her grave, the infamy that she must carry thither would be her only monument.

It may seem marvellous that, with the world before her—kept by no restrictive clause of her condemnation within the limits of the Puritan settlement, so remote and so obscure—free to return to her birth-place, or to any other European land, and there hide her character and identity under a new exterior, as completely as if emerging into another state of being—and having also the passes of the dark, inscrutable forest open to her, where the wildness of her nature might assimilate itself with a people whose customs and life were alien from the law that had condemned her—it may seem marvellous that this woman should still call that place her home, where, and where only, she must needs be the type of shame. But there is a fatality, a feeling so irresistible and inevitable that it has the force of doom, which almost invariably compels human beings to linger around and haunt, ghost-like, the spot where some great and marked event has given the colour to their lifetime; and, still the more irresistibly, the darker the tinge that saddens it. Her sin, her ignominy, were the roots which she had struck into the soil. It was as if a new birth, with stronger assimilations than the first, had converted the forest-land, still so uncongenial to every other pilgrim and wanderer, into Hester Prynne's wild and dreary, but life-long home. All other scenes of earth—even that village of rural England, where happy infancy and stainless maidenhood seemed yet to be in her mother's keeping, like garments put off long ago—were foreign to her, in comparison. The chain that bound her here was of iron links, and galling to her inmost soul, but could never be broken.

It might be, too—doubtless it was so, although she hid the secret from herself, and grew pale whenever it struggled out of her heart, like a serpent from its hole—it might be that another feeling kept her within the scene and pathway that had been so fatal. There dwelt, there trode, the feet of one with whom she deemed herself connected in a union that, unrecognised on earth, would bring them together before the bar of final judgment, and make that their marriage-altar, for a joint futurity of endless retribution. Over and over again, the tempter of souls had thrust this idea upon Hester's contemplation, and laughed at the passionate an desperate joy with which she seized, and then strove to cast it from her. She barely looked the idea in the face, and hastened to bar it in its dungeon. What she compelled herself to believe—what, finally, she reasoned upon as her motive for continuing a resident of New England—was half a truth, and half a self-delusion. Here, she said to herself had been the scene of her guilt, and here should be the scene of her earthly punishment; and so, perchance, the torture of her daily shame would at length purge her soul, and work out another purity than that which she had lost: more saint-like, because the result of martyrdom.

Hester Prynne, therefore, did not flee. On the outskirts of the town, within the verge of the peninsula, but not in close vicinity to any other habitation, there was a small thatched cottage. It had been built by an earlier settler, and abandoned, because the soil about it was too sterile for cultivation, while its comparative remoteness put it out of the sphere of that social activity which already marked the habits of the emigrants. It stood on the shore, looking across a basin of the sea at the forest-covered hills, towards the west. A clump of scrubby trees, such as alone grew on the peninsula, did not so much conceal the cottage from view, as seem to denote that here was some object which would fain have been, or at least ought to be, concealed. In this little lonesome dwelling, with some slender means that she possessed, and by the license of the magistrates, who still kept an inquisitorial watch over her, Hester established herself, with her infant child. A mystic shadow of suspicion immediately attached itself to the spot. Children, too young to comprehend wherefore this woman should be shut out from the sphere of human charities, would creep nigh enough to behold her plying her needle at the cottage-window, or standing in the doorway, or labouring in her little garden, or coming forth along the pathway that led townward, and, discerning the scarlet letter on her breast, would scamper off with a strange contagious fear.

Lonely as was Hester's situation, and without a friend on earth who dared to show himself, she, however, incurred no risk of want. She possessed an art that sufficed, even in a land that afforded comparatively little scope for its exercise, to supply food for her thriving infant and herself. It was the art, then, as now, almost the only one within a woman's grasp—of needle-work. She bore on her breast, in the curiously embroidered letter, a specimen of her delicate and imaginative skill, of which the dames of a court might gladly have availed themselves, to add the richer and more spiritual adornment of human ingenuity to their fabrics of silk and gold. Here, indeed, in the sable simplicity that generally characterised the Puritanic modes of dress, there might be an infrequent call for the finer productions of her handiwork. Yet the taste of the age, demanding whatever was elaborate in compositions of this kind, did not fail to extend its influence over our stern progenitors, who had cast behind them so many fashions which it might seem harder to dispense with.

Public ceremonies, such as ordinations, the installation of magistrates, and all that could give majesty to the forms in which a new government manifested itself to the people, were, as a matter of policy, marked by a stately and well-conducted ceremonial, and a sombre, but yet a studied magnificence. Deep ruffs, painfully wrought bands, and gorgeously embroidered gloves, were all deemed necessary to the official state of men assuming the reins of power, and were readily allowed to individuals dignified by rank or wealth, even while sumptuary laws forbade these and similar extravagances to the plebeian order. In the array of funerals, too—whether for the apparel of the dead body, or to typify, by manifold emblematic devices of sable cloth and snowy lawn, the sorrow of the survivors—there was a frequent and characteristic demand for such labour as Hester Prynne could supply. Baby-linen—for babies then wore robes of state—afforded still another possibility of toil and emolument.

By degrees, not very slowly, her handiwork became what would now be termed the fashion. Whether from commiseration for a woman of so miserable a destiny; or from the morbid curiosity that gives a fictitious value even to common or worthless things; or by whatever other intangible circumstance was then, as now, sufficient to bestow, on some persons, what others might seek in vain; or because Hester really filled a gap which must otherwise have remained vacant; it is certain that she had ready and fairly requited employment for as many hours as she saw fit to occupy with her needle. Vanity, it may be, chose to mortify itself, by putting on, for ceremonials of pomp and state, the garments that had been wrought by her sinful hands. Her needle-work was seen on the ruff of the Governor; military men wore it on their scarfs, and the minister on his band; it decked the baby's little cap; it was shut up, to be mildewed and moulder away, in the coffins of the dead. But it is not recorded that, in a single instance, her skill was called in to embroider the white veil which was to cover the pure blushes of a bride. The exception indicated the ever relentless vigour with which society frowned upon her sin.

Hester sought not to acquire anything beyond a subsistence, of the plainest and most ascetic description, for herself, and a simple abundance for her child. Her own dress was of the coarsest materials and the most sombre hue, with only that one ornament—the scarlet letter—which it was her doom to wear. The child's attire, on the other hand, was distinguished by a fanciful, or, we may rather say, a fantastic ingenuity, which served, indeed, to heighten the airy charm that early began to develop itself in the little girl, but which appeared to have also a deeper meaning. We may speak further of it hereafter. Except for that small expenditure in the decoration of her infant, Hester bestowed all her superfluous means in charity, on wretches less miserable than herself, and who not unfrequently insulted the hand that fed them. Much of the time, which she might readily have applied to the better efforts of her art, she employed in making coarse garments for the poor. It is probable that there was an idea of penance in this mode of occupation, and that she offered up a real sacrifice of enjoyment in devoting so many hours to such rude handiwork. She had in her nature a rich, voluptuous, Oriental characteristic—a taste for the gorgeously beautiful, which, save in the exquisite productions of her needle, found nothing else, in all the possibilities of her life, to exercise itself upon. Women derive a pleasure, incomprehensible to the other sex, from the delicate toil of the needle. To Hester Prynne it might have been a mode of expressing, and therefore soothing, the passion of her life. Like all other joys, she rejected it as sin. This morbid meddling of conscience with an immaterial matter betokened, it is to be feared, no genuine and steadfast penitence, but something doubtful, something that might be deeply wrong beneath.

In this matter, Hester Prynne came to have a part to perform in the world. With her native energy of character and rare capacity, it could not entirely cast her off, although it had set a mark upon her, more intolerable to a woman's heart than that which branded the brow of Cain. In all her intercourse with society, however, there was nothing that made her feel as if she belonged to it. Every gesture, every word, and even the silence of those with whom she came in contact, implied, and often expressed, that she was banished, and as much alone as if she inhabited another sphere, or communicated with the common nature by other organs and senses than the rest of human kind. She stood apart from moral interests, yet close beside them, like a ghost that revisits the familiar fireside, and can no longer make itself seen or felt; no more smile with the household joy, nor mourn with the kindred sorrow; or, should it succeed in manifesting its forbidden sympathy, awakening only terror and horrible repugnance. These emotions, in fact, and its bitterest scorn besides, seemed to be the sole portion that she retained in the universal heart. It was not an age of delicacy; and her position, although she understood it well, and was in little danger of forgetting it, was often brought before her vivid self-perception, like a new anguish, by the rudest touch upon the tenderest spot. The poor, as we have already said, whom she sought out to be the objects of her bounty, often reviled the hand that was stretched forth to succour them. Dames of elevated rank, likewise, whose doors she entered in the way of her occupation, were accustomed to distil drops of bitterness into her heart; sometimes through that alchemy of quiet malice, by which women can concoct a subtle poison from ordinary trifles; and sometimes, also, by a coarser expression, that fell upon the sufferer's defenceless breast like a rough blow upon an ulcerated wound. Hester had schooled herself long and well; and she never responded to these attacks, save by a flush of crimson that rose irrepressibly over her pale cheek, and again subsided into the depths of her bosom. She was patient—a martyr, indeed but she forebore to pray for enemies, lest, in spite of her forgiving aspirations, the words of the blessing should stubbornly twist themselves into a curse.

Continually, and in a thousand other ways, did she feel the innumerable throbs of anguish that had been so cunningly contrived for her by the undying, the ever-active sentence of the Puritan tribunal. Clergymen paused in the streets, to address words of exhortation, that brought a crowd, with its mingled grin and frown, around the poor, sinful woman. If she entered a church, trusting to share the Sabbath smile of the Universal Father, it was often her mishap to find herself the text of the discourse. She grew to have a dread of children; for they had imbibed from their parents a vague idea of something horrible in this dreary woman gliding silently through the town, with never any companion but one only child. Therefore, first allowing her to pass, they pursued her at a distance with shrill cries, and the utterances of a word that had no distinct purport to their own minds, but was none the less terrible to her, as proceeding from lips that babbled it unconsciously. It seemed to argue so wide a diffusion of her shame, that all nature knew of it; it could have caused her no deeper pang had the leaves of the trees whispered the dark story among themselves—had the summer breeze murmured about it—had the wintry blast shrieked it aloud! Another peculiar torture was felt in the gaze of a new eye. When strangers looked curiously at the scarlet letter and none ever failed to do so—they branded it afresh in Hester's soul; so that, oftentimes, she could scarcely refrain, yet always did refrain, from covering the symbol with her hand. But then, again, an accustomed eye had likewise its own anguish to inflict. Its cool stare of familiarity was intolerable. From first to last, in short, Hester Prynne had always this dreadful agony in feeling a human eye upon the token; the spot never grew callous; it seemed, on the contrary, to grow more sensitive with daily torture.

But sometimes, once in many days, or perchance in many months, she felt an eye—a human eye—upon the ignominious brand, that seemed to give a momentary relief, as if half of her agony were shared. The next instant, back it all rushed again, with still a deeper throb of pain; for, in that brief interval, she had sinned anew. (Had Hester sinned alone?)

Her imagination was somewhat affected, and, had she been of a softer moral and intellectual fibre would have been still more so, by the strange and solitary anguish of her life. Walking to and fro, with those lonely footsteps, in the little world with which she was outwardly connected, it now and then appeared to Hester—if altogether fancy, it was nevertheless too potent to be resisted—she felt or fancied, then, that the scarlet letter had endowed her with a new sense. She shuddered to believe, yet could not help believing, that it gave her a sympathetic knowledge of the hidden sin in other hearts. She was terror-stricken by the revelations that were thus made. What were they? Could they be other than the insidious whispers of the bad angel, who would fain have persuaded the struggling woman, as yet only half his victim, that the outward guise of purity was but a lie, and that, if truth were everywhere to be shown, a scarlet letter would blaze forth on many a bosom besides Hester Prynne's? Or, must she receive those intimations—so obscure, yet so distinct—as truth? In all her miserable experience, there was nothing else so awful and so loathsome as this sense. It perplexed, as well as shocked her, by the irreverent inopportuneness of the occasions that brought it into vivid action. Sometimes the red infamy upon her breast would give a sympathetic throb, as she passed near a venerable minister or magistrate, the model of piety and justice, to whom that age of antique reverence looked up, as to a mortal man in fellowship with angels. "What evil thing is at hand?" would Hester say to herself. Lifting her reluctant eyes, there would be nothing human within the scope of view, save the form of this earthly saint! Again a mystic sisterhood would contumaciously assert itself, as she met the sanctified frown of some matron, who, according to the rumour of all tongues, had kept cold snow within her bosom throughout life. That unsunned snow in the matron's bosom, and the burning shame on Hester Prynne's—what had the two in common? Or, once more, the electric thrill would give her warning—"Behold Hester, here is a companion!" and, looking up, she would detect the eyes of a young maiden glancing at the scarlet letter, shyly and aside, and quickly averted, with a faint, chill crimson in her cheeks as if her purity were somewhat sullied by that momentary glance. O Fiend, whose talisman was that fatal symbol, wouldst thou leave nothing, whether in youth or age, for this poor sinner to revere?—such loss of faith is ever one of the saddest results of sin. Be it accepted as a proof that all was not corrupt in this poor victim of her own frailty, and man's hard law, that Hester Prynne yet struggled to believe that no fellow-mortal was guilty like herself.

The vulgar, who, in those dreary old times, were always contributing a grotesque horror to what interested their imaginations, had a story about the scarlet letter which we might readily work up into a terrific legend. They averred that the symbol was not mere scarlet cloth, tinged in an earthly dye-pot, but was red-hot with infernal fire, and could be seen glowing all alight whenever Hester Prynne walked abroad in the night-time. And we must needs say it seared Hester's bosom so deeply, that perhaps there was more truth in the rumour than our modern incredulity may be inclined to admit.

VI. Pearl

We have as yet hardly spoken of the infant that little creature, whose innocent life had sprung, by the inscrutable decree of Providence, a lovely and immortal flower, out of the rank luxuriance of a guilty passion. How strange it seemed to the sad woman, as she watched the growth, and the beauty that became every day more brilliant, and the intelligence that threw its quivering sunshine over the tiny features of this child! Her Pearl—for so had Hester called her; not as a name expressive of her aspect, which had nothing of the calm, white, unimpassioned lustre that would be indicated by the comparison. But she named the infant "Pearl," as being of great price—purchased with all she had—her mother's only treasure! How strange, indeed! Man had marked this woman's sin by a scarlet letter, which had such potent and disastrous efficacy that no human sympathy could reach her, save it were sinful like herself. God, as a direct consequence of the sin which man thus punished, had given her a lovely child, whose place was on that same dishonoured bosom, to connect her parent for ever with the race and descent of mortals, and to be finally a blessed soul in heaven! Yet these thoughts affected Hester Prynne less with hope than apprehension. She knew that her deed had been evil; she could have no faith, therefore, that its result would be good. Day after day she looked fearfully into the child's expanding nature, ever dreading to detect some dark and wild peculiarity that should correspond with the guiltiness to which she owed her being.

Certainly there was no physical defect. By its perfect shape, its vigour, and its natural dexterity in the use of all its untried limbs, the infant was worthy to have been brought forth in Eden: worthy to have been left there to be the plaything of the angels after the world's first parents were driven out. The child had a native grace which does not invariably co-exist with faultless beauty; its attire, however simple, always impressed the beholder as if it were the very garb that precisely became it best. But little Pearl was not clad in rustic weeds. Her mother, with a morbid purpose that may be better understood hereafter, had bought the richest tissues that could be procured, and allowed her imaginative faculty its full play in the arrangement and decoration of the dresses which the child wore before the public eye. So magnificent was the small figure when thus arrayed, and such was the splendour of Pearl's own proper beauty, shining through the gorgeous robes which might have extinguished a paler loveliness, that there was an absolute circle of radiance around her on the darksome cottage floor. And yet a russet gown, torn and soiled with the child's rude play, made a picture of her just as perfect. Pearl's aspect was imbued with a spell of infinite variety; in this one child there were many children, comprehending the full scope between the wild-flower prettiness of a peasant-baby, and the pomp, in little, of an infant princess. Throughout all, however, there was a trait of passion, a certain depth of hue, which she never lost; and if in any of her changes, she had grown fainter or paler, she would have ceased to be herself—it would have been no longer Pearl!

This outward mutability indicated, and did not more than fairly express, the various properties of her inner life. Her nature appeared to possess depth, too, as well as variety; but—or else Hester's fears deceived her—it lacked reference and adaptation to the world into which she was born. The child could not be made amenable to rules. In giving her existence a great law had been broken; and the result was a being whose elements were perhaps beautiful and brilliant, but all in disorder, or with an order peculiar to themselves, amidst which the point of variety and arrangement was difficult or impossible to be discovered. Hester could only account for the child's character—and even then most vaguely and imperfectly—by recalling what she herself had been during that momentous period while Pearl was imbibing her soul from the spiritual world, and her bodily frame from its material of earth. The mother's impassioned state had been the medium through which were transmitted to the unborn infant the rays of its moral life; and, however white and clear originally, they had taken the deep stains of crimson and gold, the fiery lustre, the black shadow, and the untempered light of the intervening substance. Above all, the warfare of Hester's spirit at that epoch was perpetuated in Pearl. She could recognize her wild, desperate, defiant mood, the flightiness of her temper, and even some of the very cloud-shapes of gloom and despondency that had brooded in her heart. They were now illuminated by the morning radiance of a young child's disposition, but, later in the day of earthly existence, might be prolific of the storm and whirlwind.

The discipline of the family in those days was of a far more rigid kind than now. The frown, the harsh rebuke, the frequent application of the rod, enjoined by Scriptural authority, were used, not merely in the way of punishment for actual offences, but as a wholesome regimen for the growth and promotion of all childish virtues. Hester Prynne, nevertheless, the loving mother of this one child, ran little risk of erring on the side of undue severity. Mindful, however, of her own errors and misfortunes, she early sought to impose a tender but strict control over the infant immortality that was committed to her charge. But the task was beyond her skill. after testing both smiles and frowns, and proving that neither mode of treatment possessed any calculable influence, Hester was ultimately compelled to stand aside and permit the child to be swayed by her own impulses. Physical compulsion or restraint was effectual, of course, while it lasted. As to any other kind of discipline, whether addressed to her mind or heart, little Pearl might or might not be within its reach, in accordance with the caprice that ruled the moment. Her mother, while Pearl was yet an infant, grew acquainted with a certain peculiar look, that warned her when it would be labour thrown away to insist, persuade or plead.

It was a look so intelligent, yet inexplicable, perverse, sometimes so malicious, but generally accompanied by a wild flow of spirits, that Hester could not help questioning at such moments whether Pearl was a human child. She seemed rather an airy sprite, which, after playing its fantastic sports for a little while upon the cottage floor, would flit away with a mocking smile. Whenever that look appeared in her wild, bright, deeply black eyes, it invested her with a strange remoteness and intangibility: it was as if she were hovering in the air, and might vanish, like a glimmering light that comes we know not whence and goes we know not whither. Beholding it, Hester was constrained to rush towards the child—to pursue the little elf in the flight which she invariably began—to snatch her to her bosom with a close pressure and earnest kisses—not so much from overflowing love as to assure herself that Pearl was flesh and blood, and not utterly delusive. But Pearl's laugh, when she was caught, though full of merriment and music, made her mother more doubtful than before.

Heart-smitten at this bewildering and baffling spell, that so often came between herself and her sole treasure, whom she had bought so dear, and who was all her world, Hester sometimes burst into passionate tears. Then, perhaps—for there was no foreseeing how it might affect her—Pearl would frown, and clench her little fist, and harden her small features into a stern, unsympathising look of discontent. Not seldom she would laugh anew, and louder than before, like a thing incapable and unintelligent of human sorrow. Or—but this more rarely happened—she would be convulsed with rage of grief and sob out her love for her mother in broken words, and seem intent on proving that she had a heart by breaking it. Yet Hester was hardly safe in confiding herself to that gusty tenderness: it passed as suddenly as it came. Brooding over all these matters, the mother felt like one who has evoked a spirit, but, by some irregularity in the process of conjuration, has failed to win the master-word that should control this new and incomprehensible intelligence. Her only real comfort was when the child lay in the placidity of sleep. Then she was sure of her, and tasted hours of quiet, sad, delicious happiness; until—perhaps with that perverse expression glimmering from beneath her opening lids—little Pearl awoke!

How soon—with what strange rapidity, indeed did Pearl arrive at an age that was capable of social intercourse beyond the mother's ever-ready smile and nonsense-words! And then what a happiness would it have been could Hester Prynne have heard her clear, bird-like voice mingling with the uproar of other childish voices, and have distinguished and unravelled her own darling's tones, amid all the entangled outcry of a group of sportive children. But this could never be. Pearl was a born outcast of the infantile world. An imp of evil, emblem and product of sin, she had no right among christened infants.

Nothing was more remarkable than the instinct, as it seemed, with which the child comprehended her loneliness: the destiny that had drawn an inviolable circle round about her: the whole peculiarity, in short, of her position in respect to other children. Never since her release from prison had Hester met the public gaze without her. In all her walks about the town, Pearl, too, was there: first as the babe in arms, and afterwards as the little girl, small companion of her mother, holding a forefinger with her whole grasp, and tripping along at the rate of three or four footsteps to one of Hester's. She saw the children of the settlement on the grassy margin of the street, or at the domestic thresholds, disporting themselves in such grim fashions as the Puritanic nurture would permit! playing at going to church, perchance, or at scourging Quakers, or taking scalps in a sham fight with the Indians, or scaring one another with freaks of imitative witchcraft. Pearl saw, and gazed intently, but never sought to make acquaintance. If spoken to, she would not speak again. If the children gathered about her, as they sometimes did, Pearl would grow positively terrible in her puny wrath, snatching up stones to fling at them, with shrill, incoherent exclamations, that made her mother tremble, because they had so much the sound of a witch's anathemas in some unknown tongue.

The truth was, that the little Puritans, being of the most intolerant brood that ever lived, had got a vague idea of something outlandish, unearthly, or at variance with ordinary fashions, in the mother and child, and therefore scorned them in their hearts, and not unfrequently reviled them with their tongues. Pearl felt the sentiment, and requited it with the bitterest hatred that can be supposed to rankle in a childish bosom. These outbreaks of a fierce temper had a kind of value, and even comfort for the mother; because there was at least an intelligible earnestness in the mood, instead of the fitful caprice that so often thwarted her in the child's manifestations. It appalled her, nevertheless, to discern here, again, a shadowy reflection of the evil that had existed in herself. All this enmity and passion had Pearl inherited, by inalienable right, out of Hester's heart. Mother and daughter stood together in the same circle of seclusion from human society; and in the nature of the child seemed to be perpetuated those unquiet elements that had distracted Hester Prynne before Pearl's birth, but had since begun to be soothed away by the softening influences of maternity.

At home, within and around her mother's cottage, Pearl wanted not a wide and various circle of acquaintance. The spell of life went forth from her ever-creative spirit, and communicated itself to a thousand objects, as a torch kindles a flame wherever it may be applied. The unlikeliest materials—a stick, a bunch of rags, a flower—were the puppets of Pearl's witchcraft, and, without undergoing any outward change, became spiritually adapted to whatever drama occupied the stage of her inner world. Her one baby-voice served a multitude of imaginary personages, old and young, to talk withal. The pine-trees, aged, black, and solemn, and flinging groans and other melancholy utterances on the breeze, needed little transformation to figure as Puritan elders the ugliest weeds of the garden were their children, whom Pearl smote down and uprooted most unmercifully. It was wonderful, the vast variety of forms into which she threw her intellect, with no continuity, indeed, but darting up and dancing, always in a state of preternatural activity—soon sinking down, as if exhausted by so rapid and feverish a tide of life—and succeeded by other shapes of a similar wild energy. It was like nothing so much as the phantasmagoric play of the northern lights. In the mere exercise of the fancy, however, and the sportiveness of a growing mind, there might be a little more than was observable in other children of bright faculties; except as Pearl, in the dearth of human playmates, was thrown more upon the visionary throng which she created. The singularity lay in the hostile feelings with which the child regarded all these offsprings of her own heart and mind. She never created a friend, but seemed always to be sowing broadcast the dragon's teeth, whence sprung a harvest of armed enemies, against whom she rushed to battle. It was inexpressibly sad—then what depth of sorrow to a mother, who felt in her own heart the cause—to observe, in one so young, this constant recognition of an adverse world, and so fierce a training of the energies that were to make good her cause in the contest that must ensue.

Gazing at Pearl, Hester Prynne often dropped her work upon her knees, and cried out with an agony which she would fain have hidden, but which made utterance for itself betwixt speech and a groan—"O Father in Heaven—if Thou art still my Father—what is this being which I have brought into the world?" And Pearl, overhearing the ejaculation, or aware through some more subtle channel, of those throbs of anguish, would turn her vivid and beautiful little face upon her mother, smile with sprite-like intelligence, and resume her play.

One peculiarity of the child's deportment remains yet to be told. The very first thing which she had noticed in her life, was—what?—not the mother's smile, responding to it, as other babies do, by that faint, embryo smile of the little mouth, remembered so doubtfully afterwards, and with such fond discussion whether it were indeed a smile. By no means! But that first object of which Pearl seemed to become aware was—shall we say it?—the scarlet letter on Hester's bosom! One day, as her mother stooped over the cradle, the infant's eyes had been caught by the glimmering of the gold embroidery about the letter; and putting up her little hand she grasped at it, smiling, not doubtfully, but with a decided gleam, that gave her face the look of a much older child. Then, gasping for breath, did Hester Prynne clutch the fatal token, instinctively endeavouring to tear it away, so infinite was the torture inflicted by the intelligent touch of Pearl's baby-hand. Again, as if her mother's agonised gesture were meant only to make sport for her, did little Pearl look into her eyes, and smile. From that epoch, except when the child was asleep, Hester had never felt a moment's safety: not a moment's calm enjoyment of her. Weeks, it is true, would sometimes elapse, during which Pearl's gaze might never once be fixed upon the scarlet letter; but then, again, it would come at unawares, like the stroke of sudden death, and always with that peculiar smile and odd expression of the eyes.

Once this freakish, elvish cast came into the child's eyes while Hester was looking at her own image in them, as mothers are fond of doing; and suddenly for women in solitude, and with troubled hearts, are pestered with unaccountable delusions she fancied that she beheld, not her own miniature portrait, but another face in the small black mirror of Pearl's eye. It was a face, fiend-like, full of smiling malice, yet bearing the semblance of features that she had known full well, though seldom with a smile, and never with malice in them. It was as if an evil spirit possessed the child, and had just then peeped forth in mockery. Many a time afterwards had Hester been tortured, though less vividly, by the same illusion.

In the afternoon of a certain summer's day, after Pearl grew big enough to run about, she amused herself with gathering handfuls of wild flowers, and flinging them, one by one, at her mother's bosom; dancing up and down like a little elf whenever she hit the scarlet letter. Hester's first motion had been to cover her bosom with her clasped hands. But whether from pride or resignation, or a feeling that her penance might best be wrought out by this unutterable pain, she resisted the impulse, and sat erect, pale as death, looking sadly into little Pearl's wild eyes. Still came the battery of flowers, almost invariably hitting the mark, and covering the mother's breast with hurts for which she could find no balm in this world, nor knew how to seek it in another. At last, her shot being all expended, the child stood still and gazed at Hester, with that little laughing image of a fiend peeping out—or, whether it peeped or no, her mother so imagined it—from the unsearchable abyss of her black eyes.

"Child, what art thou?" cried the mother.

"Oh, I am your little Pearl!" answered the child.

But while she said it, Pearl laughed, and began to dance up and down with the humoursome gesticulation of a little imp, whose next freak might be to fly up the chimney.

"Art thou my child, in very truth?" asked Hester.

Nor did she put the question altogether idly, but, for the moment, with a portion of genuine earnestness; for, such was Pearl's wonderful intelligence, that her mother half doubted whether she were not acquainted with the secret spell of her existence, and might not now reveal herself.

"Yes; I am little Pearl!" repeated the child, continuing her antics.

"Thou art not my child! Thou art no Pearl of mine!" said the mother half playfully; for it was often the case that a sportive impulse came over her in the midst of her deepest suffering. "Tell me, then, what thou art, and who sent thee hither?"

"Tell me, mother!" said the child, seriously, coming up to Hester, and pressing herself close to her knees. "Do thou tell me!"

"Thy Heavenly Father sent thee!" answered Hester Prynne.

But she said it with a hesitation that did not escape the acuteness of the child. Whether moved only by her ordinary freakishness, or because an evil spirit prompted her, she put up her small forefinger and touched the scarlet letter.

"He did not send me!" cried she, positively. "I have no Heavenly Father!"

"Hush, Pearl, hush! Thou must not talk so!" answered the mother. suppressing a groan. "He sent us all into the world. He sent even me, thy mother. Then, much more thee! Or, if not, thou strange and elfish child, whence didst thou come?"

"Tell me! Tell me!" repeated Pearl, no longer seriously, but laughing and capering about the floor. "It is thou that must tell me!"

But Hester could not resolve the query, using herself in a dismal labyrinth of doubt. She remembered—betwixt a smile and a shudder—the talk of the neighbouring townspeople, who, seeking vainly elsewhere for the child's paternity, and observing some of her odd attributes, had given out that poor little Pearl was a demon offspring: such as, ever since old Catholic times, had occasionally been seen on earth, through the agency of their mother's sin, and to promote some foul and wicked purpose. Luther, according to the scandal of his monkish enemies, was a brat of that hellish breed; nor was Pearl the only child to whom this inauspicious origin was assigned among the New England Puritans.

VII. The Governor's Hall

Hester Prynne went one day to the mansion of Governor Bellingham, with a pair of gloves which she had fringed and embroidered to his order, and which were to be worn on some great occasion of state; for, though the chances of a popular election had caused this former ruler to descend a step or two from the highest rank, he still held an honourable and influential place among the colonial magistracy.

Another and far more important reason than the delivery of a pair of embroidered gloves, impelled Hester, at this time, to seek an interview with a personage of so much power and activity in the affairs of the settlement. It had reached her ears that there was a design on the part of some of the leading inhabitants, cherishing the more rigid order of principles in religion and government, to deprive her of her child. On the supposition that Pearl, as already hinted, was of demon origin, these good people not unreasonably argued that a Christian interest in the mother's soul required them to remove such a stumbling-block from her path. If the child, on the other hand, were really capable of moral and religious growth, and possessed the elements of ultimate salvation, then, surely, it would enjoy all the fairer prospect of these advantages by being transferred to wiser and better guardianship than Hester Prynne's. Among those who promoted the design, Governor Bellingham was said to be one of the most busy. It may appear singular, and, indeed, not a little ludicrous, that an affair of this kind, which in later days would have been referred to no higher jurisdiction than that of the select men of the town, should then have been a question publicly discussed, and on which statesmen of eminence took sides. At that epoch of pristine simplicity, however, matters of even slighter public interest, and of far less intrinsic weight than the welfare of Hester and her child, were strangely mixed up with the deliberations of legislators and acts of state. The period was hardly, if at all, earlier than that of our story, when a dispute concerning the right of property in a pig not only caused a fierce and bitter contest in the legislative body of the colony, but resulted in an important modification of the framework itself of the legislature.

Full of concern, therefore—but so conscious of her own right that it seemed scarcely an unequal match between the public on the one side, and a lonely woman, backed by the sympathies of nature, on the other—Hester Prynne set forth from her solitary cottage. Little Pearl, of course, was her companion. She was now of an age to run lightly along by her mother's side, and, constantly in motion from morn till sunset, could have accomplished a much longer journey than that before her. Often, nevertheless, more from caprice than necessity, she demanded to be taken up in arms; but was soon as imperious to be let down again, and frisked onward before Hester on the grassy pathway, with many a harmless trip and tumble. We have spoken of Pearl's rich and luxuriant beauty—a beauty that shone with deep and vivid tints, a bright complexion, eyes possessing intensity both of depth and glow, and hair already of a deep, glossy brown, and which, in after years, would be nearly akin to black. There was fire in her and throughout her: she seemed the unpremeditated offshoot of a passionate moment. Her mother, in contriving the child's garb, had allowed the gorgeous tendencies of her imagination their full play, arraying her in a crimson velvet tunic of a peculiar cut, abundantly embroidered in fantasies and flourishes of gold thread. So much strength of colouring, which must have given a wan and pallid aspect to cheeks of a fainter bloom, was admirably adapted to Pearl's beauty, and made her the very brightest little jet of flame that ever danced upon the earth.

But it was a remarkable attribute of this garb, and indeed, of the child's whole appearance, that it irresistibly and inevitably reminded the beholder of the token which Hester Prynne was doomed to wear upon her bosom. It was the scarlet letter in another form: the scarlet letter endowed with life! The mother herself—as if the red ignominy were so deeply scorched into her brain that all her conceptions assumed its form—had carefully wrought out the similitude, lavishing many hours of morbid ingenuity to create an analogy between the object of her affection and the emblem of her guilt and torture. But, in truth, Pearl was the one as well as the other; and only in consequence of that identity had Hester contrived so perfectly to represent the scarlet letter in her appearance.

As the two wayfarers came within the precincts of the town, the children of the Puritans looked up from their player what passed for play with those sombre little urchins—and spoke gravely one to another

"Behold, verily, there is the woman of the scarlet letter: and of a truth, moreover, there is the likeness of the scarlet letter running along by her side! Come, therefore, and let us fling mud at them!"

But Pearl, who was a dauntless child, after frowning, stamping her foot, and shaking her little hand with a variety of threatening gestures, suddenly made a rush at the knot of her enemies, and put them all to flight. She resembled, in her fierce pursuit of them, an infant pestilence—the scarlet fever, or some such half-fledged angel of judgment—whose mission was to punish the sins of the rising generation. She screamed and shouted, too, with a terrific volume of sound, which, doubtless, caused the hearts of the fugitives to quake within them. The victory accomplished, Pearl returned quietly to her mother, and looked up, smiling, into her face. Without further adventure, they reached the dwelling of Governor Bellingham. This was a large wooden house, built in a fashion of which there are specimens still extant in the streets of our older towns now moss—grown, crumbling to decay, and melancholy at heart with the many sorrowful or joyful occurrences, remembered or forgotten, that have happened and passed away within their dusky chambers. Then, however, there was the freshness of the passing year on its exterior, and the cheerfulness, gleaming forth from the sunny windows, of a human habitation, into which death had never entered. It had, indeed, a very cheery aspect, the walls being overspread with a kind of stucco, in which fragments of broken glass were plentifully intermixed; so that, when the sunshine fell aslant-wise over the front of the edifice, it glittered and sparkled as if diamonds had been flung against it by the double handful. The brilliancy might have be fitted Aladdin's palace rather than the mansion of a grave old Puritan ruler. It was further decorated with strange and seemingly cabalistic figures and diagrams, suitable to the quaint taste of the age which had been drawn in the stucco, when newly laid on, and had now grown hard and durable, for the admiration of after times.

Pearl, looking at this bright wonder of a house began to caper and dance, and imperatively required that the whole breadth of sunshine should be stripped off its front, and given her to play with.

"No, my little Pearl!" said her mother; "thou must gather thine own sunshine. I have none to give thee!"

They approached the door, which was of an arched form, and flanked on each side by a narrow tower or projection of the edifice, in both of which were lattice-windows, the wooden shutters to close over them at need. Lifting the iron hammer that hung at the portal, Hester Prynne gave a summons, which was answered by one of the Governor's bond servant—a free-born Englishman, but now a seven years' slave. During that term he was to be the property of his master, and as much a commodity of bargain and sale as an ox, or a joint-stool. The serf wore the customary garb of serving-men at that period, and long before, in the old hereditary halls of England.

"Is the worshipful Governor Bellingham within?" Inquired Hester.

"Yea, forsooth," replied the bond-servant, staring with wide-open eyes at the scarlet letter, which, being a new-comer in the country, he had never before seen. "Yea, his honourable worship is within. But he hath a godly minister or two with him, and likewise a leech. Ye may not see his worship now."

"Nevertheless, I will enter," answered Hester Prynne; and the bond-servant, perhaps judging from the decision of her air, and the glittering symbol in her bosom, that she was a great lady in the land, offered no opposition.

So the mother and little Pearl were admitted into the hall of entrance. With many variations, suggested by the nature of his building materials, diversity of climate, and a different mode of social life, Governor Bellingham had planned his new habitation after the residences of gentlemen of fair estate in his native land. Here, then, was a wide and reasonably lofty hall, extending through the whole depth of the house, and forming a medium of general communication, more or less directly, with all the other apartments. At one extremity, this spacious room was lighted by the windows of the two towers, which formed a small recess on either side of the portal. At the other end, though partly muffled by a curtain, it was more powerfully illuminated by one of those embowed hall windows which we read of in old books, and which was provided with a deep and cushion seat. Here, on the cushion, lay a folio tome, probably of the Chronicles of England, or other such substantial literature; even as, in our own days, we scatter gilded volumes on the centre table, to be turned over by the casual guest. The furniture of the hall consisted of some ponderous chairs, the backs of which were elaborately carved with wreaths of oaken flowers; and likewise a table in the same taste, the whole being of the Elizabethan age, or perhaps earlier, and heirlooms, transferred hither from the Governor's paternal home. On the table—in token that the sentiment of old English hospitality had not been left behind—stood a large pewter tankard, at the bottom of which, had Hester or Pearl peeped into it, they might have seen the frothy remnant of a recent draught of ale.

On the wall hung a row of portraits, representing the forefathers of the Bellingham lineage, some with armour on their breasts, and others with stately ruffs and robes of peace. All were characterised by the sternness and severity which old portraits so invariably put on, as if they were the ghosts, rather than the pictures, of departed worthies, and were gazing with harsh and intolerant criticism at the pursuits and enjoyments of living men.

At about the centre of the oaken panels that lined the hall was suspended a suit of mail, not, like the pictures, an ancestral relic, but of the most modern date; for it had been manufactured by a skilful armourer in London, the same year in which Governor Bellingham came over to New England. There was a steel head-piece, a cuirass, a gorget and greaves, with a pair of gauntlets and a sword hanging beneath; all, and especially the helmet and breastplate, so highly burnished as to glow with white radiance, and scatter an illumination everywhere about upon the floor. This bright panoply was not meant for mere idle show, but had been worn by the Governor on many a solemn muster and draining field, and had glittered, moreover, at the head of a regiment in the Pequod war. For, though bred a lawyer, and accustomed to speak of Bacon, Coke, Noye, and Finch, as his professional associates, the exigencies of this new country had transformed Governor Bellingham into a soldier, as well as a statesman and ruler.

Little Pearl, who was as greatly pleased with the gleaming armour as she had been with the glittering frontispiece of the house, spent some time looking into the polished mirror of the breastplate.

"Mother," cried she, "I see you here. Look! look!"

Hester looked by way of humouring the child; and she saw that, owing to the peculiar effect of this convex mirror, the scarlet letter was represented in exaggerated and gigantic proportions, so as to be greatly the most prominent feature of her appearance. In truth, she seemed absolutely hidden behind it. Pearl pointed upwards also, at a similar picture in the head-piece; smiling at her mother, with the elfish intelligence that was so familiar an expression on her small physiognomy. That look of naughty merriment was likewise reflected in the mirror, with so much breadth and intensity of effect, that it made Hester Prynne feel as if it could not be the image of her own child, but of an imp who was seeking to mould itself into Pearl's shape.

"Come along, Pearl," said she, drawing her away, "Come and look into this fair garden. It may be we shall see flowers there; more beautiful ones than we find in the woods."

Pearl accordingly ran to the bow-window, at the further end of the hall, and looked along the vista of a garden walk, carpeted with closely-shaven grass, and bordered with some rude and immature attempt at shrubbery. But the proprietor appeared already to have relinquished as hopeless, the effort to perpetuate on this side of the Atlantic, in a hard soil, and amid the close struggle for subsistence, the native English taste for ornamental gardening. Cabbages grew in plain sight; and a pumpkin-vine, rooted at some distance, had run across the intervening space, and deposited one of its gigantic products directly beneath the hall window, as if to warn the Governor that this great lump of vegetable gold was as rich an ornament as New England earth would offer him. There were a few rose-bushes, however, and a number of apple-trees, probably the descendants of those planted by the Reverend Mr. Blackstone, the first settler of the peninsula; that half mythological personage who rides through our early annals, seated on the back of a bull.

Pearl, seeing the rose-bushes, began to cry for a red rose, and would not be pacified.

"Hush, child—hush!" said her mother, earnestly. "Do not cry, dear little Pearl! I hear voices in the garden. The Governor is coming, and gentlemen along with him."

In fact, adown the vista of the garden avenue, a number of persons were seen approaching towards the house. Pearl, in utter scorn of her mother's attempt to quiet her, gave an eldritch scream, and then became silent, not from any motion of obedience, but because the quick and mobile curiosity of her disposition was excited by the appearance of those new personages.

VIII. The Elf-Child and the Minister

Governor Bellingham, in a loose gown and easy cap—such as elderly gentlemen loved to endue themselves with, in their domestic privacy—walked foremost, and appeared to be showing off his estate, and expatiating on his projected improvements. The wide circumference of an elaborate ruff, beneath his grey beard, in the antiquated fashion of King James's reign, caused his head to look not a little like that of John the Baptist in a charger. The impression made by his aspect, so rigid and severe, and frost-bitten with more than autumnal age, was hardly in keeping with the appliances of worldly enjoyment wherewith he had evidently done his utmost to surround himself. But it is an error to suppose that our great forefathers—though accustomed to speak and think of human existence as a state merely of trial and warfare, and though unfeignedly prepared to sacrifice goods and life at the behest of duty—made it a matter of conscience to reject such means of comfort, or even luxury, as lay fairly within their grasp. This creed was never taught, for instance, by the venerable pastor, John Wilson, whose beard, white as a snow-drift, was seen over Governor Bellingham's shoulders, while its wearer suggested that pears and peaches might yet be naturalised in the New England climate, and that purple grapes might possibly be compelled to flourish against the sunny garden-wall. The old clergyman, nurtured at the rich bosom of the English Church, had a long established and legitimate taste for all good and comfortable things, and however stern he might show himself in the pulpit, or in his public reproof of such transgressions as that of Hester Prynne, still, the genial benevolence of his private life had won him warmer affection than was accorded to any of his professional contemporaries.

Behind the Governor and Mr. Wilson came two other guests—one, the Reverend Arthur Dimmesdale, whom the reader may remember as having taken a brief and reluctant part in the scene of Hester Prynne's disgrace; and, in close companionship with him, old Roger Chillingworth, a person of great skill in physic, who for two or three years past had been settled in the town. It was understood that this learned man was the physician as well as friend of the young minister, whose health had severely suffered of late by his too unreserved self-sacrifice to the labours and duties of the pastoral relation.

The Governor, in advance of his visitors, ascended one or two steps, and, throwing open the leaves of the great hall window, found himself close to little Pearl. The shadow of the curtain fell on Hester Prynne, and partially concealed her.

"What have we here?" said Governor Bellingham, looking with surprise at the scarlet little figure before him. "I profess, I have never seen the like since my days of vanity, in old King James's time, when I was wont to esteem it a high favour to be admitted to a court mask! There used to be a swarm of these small apparitions in holiday time, and we called them children of the Lord of Misrule. But how gat such a guest into my hall?"

"Ay, indeed!" cried good old Mr. Wilson. "What little bird of scarlet plumage may this be? Methinks I have seen just such figures when the sun has been shining through a richly painted window, and tracing out the golden and crimson images across the floor. But that was in the old land. Prithee, young one, who art thou, and what has ailed thy mother to bedizen thee in this strange fashion? Art thou a Christian child—ha? Dost know thy catechism? Or art thou one of those naughty elfs or fairies whom we thought to have left behind us, with other relics of Papistry, in merry old England?"

"I am mother's child," answered the scarlet vision, "and my name is Pearl!"

"Pearl?—Ruby, rather—or Coral!—or Red Rose, at the very least, judging from thy hue!" responded the old minister, putting forth his hand in a vain attempt to pat little Pearl on the cheek. "But where is this mother of thine? Ah! I see," he added; and, turning to Governor Bellingham, whispered, "This is the selfsame child of whom we have held speech together; and behold here the unhappy woman, Hester Prynne, her mother!"

"Sayest thou so?" cried the Governor. "Nay, we might have judged that such a child's mother must needs be a scarlet woman, and a worthy type of her of Babylon! But she comes at a good time, and we will look into this matter forthwith."

Governor Bellingham stepped through the window into the hall, followed by his three guests.

"Hester Prynne," said he, fixing his naturally stern regard on the wearer of the scarlet letter, "there hath been much question concerning thee of late. The point hath been weightily discussed, whether we, that are of authority and influence, do well discharge our consciences by trusting an immortal soul, such as there is in yonder child, to the guidance of one who hath stumbled and fallen amid the pitfalls of this world. Speak thou, the child's own mother! Were it not, thinkest thou, for thy little one's temporal and eternal welfare that she be taken out of thy charge, and clad soberly, and disciplined strictly, and instructed in the truths of heaven and earth? What canst thou do for the child in this kind?"

"I can teach my little Pearl what I have learned from this!" answered Hester Prynne, laying her finger on the red token.

"Woman, it is thy badge of shame!" replied the stern magistrate. "It is because of the stain which that letter indicates that we would transfer thy child to other hands."

"Nevertheless," said the mother, calmly, though growing more pale, "this badge hath taught me—it daily teaches me—it is teaching me at this moment—lessons whereof my child may be the wiser and better, albeit they can profit nothing to myself."

"We will judge warily," said Bellingham, "and look well what we are about to do. Good Master Wilson, I pray you, examine this Pearl—since that is her name—and see whether she hath had such Christian nurture as befits a child of her age."

The old minister seated himself in an arm-chair and made an effort to draw Pearl betwixt his knees. But the child, unaccustomed to the touch or familiarity of any but her mother, escaped through the open window, and stood on the upper step, looking like a wild tropical bird of rich plumage, ready to take flight into the upper air. Mr. Wilson, not a little astonished at this outbreak—for he was a grandfatherly sort of personage, and usually a vast favourite with children—essayed, however, to proceed with the examination.

"Pearl," said he, with great solemnity, "thou must take heed to instruction, that so, in due season, thou mayest wear in thy bosom the pearl of great price. Canst thou tell me, my child, who made thee?"

Now Pearl knew well enough who made her, for Hester Prynne, the daughter of a pious home, very soon after her talk with the child about her Heavenly Father, had begun to inform her of those truths which the human spirit, at whatever stage of immaturity, imbibes with such eager interest. Pearl, therefore—so large were the attainments of her three years' lifetime—could have borne a fair examination in the New England Primer, or the first column of the Westminster Catechisms, although unacquainted with the outward form of either of those celebrated works. But that perversity, which all children have more or less of, and of which little Pearl had a tenfold portion, now, at the most inopportune moment, took thorough possession of her, and closed her lips, or impelled her to speak words amiss. After putting her finger in her mouth, with many ungracious refusals to answer good Mr. Wilson's question, the child finally announced that she had not been made at all, but had been plucked by her mother off the bush of wild roses that grew by the prison-door.

This fantasy was probably suggested by the near proximity of the Governor's red roses, as Pearl stood outside of the window, together with her recollection of the prison rose-bush, which she had passed in coming hither.

Old Roger Chillingworth, with a smile on his face, whispered something in the young clergyman's ear. Hester Prynne looked at the man of skill, and even then, with her fate hanging in the balance, was startled to perceive what a change had come over his features—how much uglier they were, how his dark complexion seemed to have grown duskier, and his figure more misshapen—since the days when she had familiarly known him. She met his eyes for an instant, but was immediately constrained to give all her attention to the scene now going forward.

"This is awful!" cried the Governor, slowly recovering from the astonishment into which Pearl's response had thrown him. "Here is a child of three years old, and she cannot tell who made her! Without question, she is equally in the dark as to her soul, its present depravity, and future destiny! Methinks, gentlemen, we need inquire no further."

Hester caught hold of Pearl, and drew her forcibly into her arms, confronting the old

Puritan magistrate with almost a fierce expression. Alone in the world, cast off by it, and with this sole treasure to keep her heart alive, she felt that she possessed indefeasible rights against the world, and was ready to defend them to the death.

"God gave me the child!" cried she. "He gave her in requital of all things else which ye had taken from me. She is my happiness—she is my torture, none the less! Pearl keeps me here in life! Pearl punishes me, too! See ye not, she is the scarlet letter, only capable of being loved, and so endowed with a million-fold the power of retribution for my sin? Ye shall not take her! I will die first!"

"My poor woman," said the not unkind old minister, "the child shall be well cared for—far better than thou canst do for it."

"God gave her into my keeping!" repeated Hester Prynne, raising her voice almost to a shriek. "I will not give her up!" And here by a sudden impulse, she turned to the young clergyman, Mr. Dimmesdale, at whom, up to this moment, she had seemed hardly so much as once to direct her eyes. "Speak thou for me!" cried she. "Thou wast my pastor, and hadst charge of my soul, and knowest me better than these men can. I will not lose the child! Speak for me! Thou knowest—for thou hast sympathies which these men lack—thou knowest what is in my heart, and what are a mother's rights, and how much the stronger they are when that mother has but her child and the scarlet letter! Look thou to it! I will not lose the child! Look to it!"

At this wild and singular appeal, which indicated that Hester Prynne's situation had provoked her to little less than madness, the young minister at once came forward, pale, and holding his hand over his heart, as was his custom whenever his peculiarly nervous temperament was thrown into agitation. He looked now more careworn and emaciated than as we described him at the scene of Hester's public ignominy; and whether it were his failing health, or whatever the cause might be, his large dark eyes had a world of pain in their troubled and melancholy depth.

"There is truth in what she says," began the minister, with a voice sweet, tremulous, but powerful, insomuch that the hall re-echoed and the hollow armour rang with it— "truth in what Hester says, and in the feeling which inspires her! God gave her the child, and gave her, too, an instinctive knowledge of its nature and requirements—both seemingly so peculiar—which no other mortal being can possess. And, moreover, is there not a quality of awful sacredness in the relation between this mother and this child?"

"Ay—how is that, good Master Dimmesdale?" interrupted the Governor. "Make that plain, I pray you!"

"It must be even so," resumed the minister. "For, if we deem it otherwise, do we not hereby say that the Heavenly Father, the creator of all flesh, hath lightly recognised a deed of sin, and made of no account the distinction between unhallowed lust and holy love? This child of its father's guilt and its mother's shame has come from the hand of God, to work in many ways upon her heart, who pleads so earnestly and with such bitterness of spirit the right to keep her. It was meant for a blessing—for the one blessing of her life! It was meant, doubtless, the mother herself hath told us, for a retribution, too; a torture to be felt at many an unthought-of moment; a pang, a sting, an ever-recurring agony, in the midst of a troubled joy! Hath she not expressed this thought in the garb of the poor child, so forcibly reminding us of that red symbol which sears her bosom?"

"Well said again!" cried good Mr. Wilson. "I feared the woman had no better thought than to make a mountebank of her child!"

"Oh, not so!—not so!" continued Mr. Dimmesdale. "She recognises, believe me, the solemn miracle which God hath wrought in the existence of that child. And may she feel, too—what, methinks, is the very truth—that this boon was meant, above all things else, to keep the mother's soul alive, and to preserve her from blacker depths of sin into which Satan might else have sought to plunge her! Therefore it is good for this poor, sinful woman, that she hath an infant immortality, a being capable of eternal joy or sorrow, confided to her care—to be trained up by her to righteousness, to remind her, at every moment, of her fall, but yet to teach her, as if it were by the Creator's sacred pledge, that, if she bring the child to heaven, the child also will bring its parents thither! Herein is the sinful mother happier than the sinful father. For Hester Prynne's sake, then, and no less for the poor child's sake, let us leave them as Providence hath seen fit to place them!"

"You speak, my friend, with a strange earnestness," said old Roger Chillingworth, smiling at him.

"And there is a weighty import in what my young brother hath spoken," added the Rev. Mr. Wilson.

"What say you, worshipful Master Bellingham? Hath he not pleaded well for the poor woman?"

"Indeed hath he," answered the magistrate; "and hath adduced such arguments, that we will even leave the matter as it now stands; so long, at least, as there shall be no further scandal in the woman. Care must be had nevertheless, to put the child to due and stated examination in the catechism, at thy hands or Master Dimmesdale's. Moreover, at a proper season, the tithing-men must take heed that she go both to school and to meeting."

The young minister, on ceasing to speak had withdrawn a few steps from the group, and stood with his face partially concealed in the heavy folds of the window-curtain; while the shadow of his figure, which the sunlight cast upon the floor, was tremulous with the vehemence of his appeal. Pearl, that wild and flighty little elf stole softly towards him, and taking his hand in the grasp of both her own, laid her cheek against it; a caress so tender, and withal so unobtrusive, that her mother, who was looking on, asked herself—"Is that my Pearl?" Yet she knew that there was love in the child's heart, although it mostly revealed itself in passion, and hardly twice in her lifetime had been softened by such gentleness as now. The minister—for, save the long-sought regards of woman, nothing is sweeter than these marks of childish preference, accorded spontaneously by a spiritual instinct, and therefore seeming to imply in us something truly worthy to be loved—the minister looked round, laid his hand on the child's head, hesitated an instant, and then kissed her brow. Little Pearl's unwonted mood of sentiment lasted no longer; she laughed, and went capering down the hall so airily, that old Mr. Wilson raised a question whether even her tiptoes touched the floor.

"The little baggage hath witchcraft in her, I profess," said he to Mr. Dimmesdale. "She needs no old woman's broomstick to fly withal!"

"A strange child!" remarked old Roger Chillingworth. "It is easy to see the mother's part in her. Would it be beyond a philosopher's research, think ye, gentlemen, to analyse that child's nature, and, from it make a mould, to give a shrewd guess at the father?"

"Nay; it would be sinful, in such a question, to follow the clue of profane philosophy," said Mr. Wilson. "Better to fast and pray upon it; and still better, it may be, to leave the mystery as we find it, unless Providence reveal it of its own accord Thereby, every good Christian man hath a title to show a father's kindness towards the poor, deserted babe."

The affair being so satisfactorily concluded, Hester Prynne, with Pearl, departed from the house. As they descended the steps, it is averred that the lattice of a chamber-window was thrown open, and forth into the sunny day was thrust the face of Mistress Hibbins, Governor Bellingham's bitter-tempered sister, and the same who, a few years later, was executed as a witch.

"Hist, hist!" said she, while her ill-omened physiognomy seemed to cast a shadow over the cheerful newness of the house. "Wilt thou go with us to-night? There will be a merry company in the forest; and I well-nigh promised the Black Man that comely Hester Prynne should make one."

"Make my excuse to him, so please you!" answered Hester, with a triumphant smile. "I must tarry at home, and keep watch over my little Pearl. Had they taken her from me, I would willingly have gone with thee into the forest, and signed my name in the Black Man's book too, and that with mine own blood!"

"We shall have thee there anon!" said the witch-lady, frowning, as she drew back her head.

But here—if we suppose this interview betwixt Mistress Hibbins and Hester Prynne to be authentic, and not a parable—was already an illustration of the young minister's argument against sundering the relation of a fallen mother to the offspring of her frailty. Even thus early had the child saved her from Satan's snare.

IX. The Leech

Under the appellation of Roger Chillingworth, the reader will remember, was hidden another name, which its former wearer had resolved should never more be spoken. It has been related, how, in the crowd that witnessed Hester Prynne's ignominious exposure, stood a man, elderly, travel-worn, who, just emerging from the perilous wilderness, beheld the woman, in whom he hoped to find embodied the warmth and cheerfulness of home, set up as a type of sin before the people. Her matronly fame was trodden under all men's feet. Infamy was babbling around her in the public market-place. For her kindred, should the tidings ever reach them, and for the companions of her unspotted life, there remained nothing but the contagion of her dishonour; which would not fail to be distributed in strict accordance arid proportion with the intimacy and sacredness of their previous relationship. Then why—since the choice was with himself—should the individual, whose connection with the fallen woman had been the most intimate and sacred of them all, come forward to vindicate his claim to an inheritance so little desirable? He resolved not to be pilloried beside her on her pedestal of shame. Unknown to all but Hester Prynne, and possessing the lock and key of her silence, he chose to withdraw his name from the roll of mankind, and, as regarded his former ties and interest, to vanish out of life as completely as if he indeed lay at the bottom of the ocean, whither rumour had long ago consigned him. This purpose once effected, new interests would immediately spring up, and likewise a new purpose; dark, it is true, if not guilty, but of force enough to engage the full strength of his faculties.

In pursuance of this resolve, he took up his residence in the Puritan town as Roger Chillingworth, without other introduction than the learning and intelligence of which he possessed more than a common measure. As his studies, at a previous period of his life, had made him extensively acquainted with the medical science of the day, it was as a physician that he presented himself and as such was cordially received. Skilful men, of the medical and chirurgical profession, were of rare occurrence in the colony. They seldom, it would appear, partook of the religious zeal that brought other emigrants across the Atlantic. In their researches into the human frame, it may be that the higher and more subtle faculties of such men were materialised, and that they lost the spiritual view of existence amid the intricacies of that wondrous mechanism, which seemed to involve art enough to comprise all of life within itself. At all events, the health of the good town of Boston, so far as medicine had aught to do with it, had hitherto lain in the guardianship of an aged deacon and apothecary, whose piety and godly deportment were stronger testimonials in his favour than any that he could have produced in the shape of a diploma. The only surgeon was one who combined the occasional exercise of that noble art with the daily and habitual flourish of a razor. To such a professional body Roger Chillingworth was a brilliant acquisition. He soon manifested his familiarity with the ponderous and imposing machinery of antique physic; in which every remedy contained a multitude of far-fetched and heterogeneous ingredients, as elaborately compounded as if the proposed result had been the Elixir of Life. In his Indian captivity, moreover, he had gained much knowledge of the properties of native herbs and roots; nor did he conceal from his patients that these simple medicines, Nature's boon to the untutored savage, had quite as large a share of his own confidence as the European Pharmacopoeia, which so many learned doctors had spent centuries in elaborating.

This learned stranger was exemplary as regarded at least the outward forms of a religious life; and early after his arrival, had chosen for his spiritual guide the Reverend Mr. Dimmesdale. The young divine, whose scholar-like renown still lived in Oxford, was considered by his more fervent admirers as little less than a heavenly ordained apostle, destined, should he live and labour for the ordinary term of life, to do as great deeds, for the now feeble New England Church, as the early Fathers had achieved for the infancy of the Christian faith. About this period, however, the health of Mr. Dimmesdale had evidently begun to fail. By those best acquainted with his habits, the paleness of the young minister's cheek was accounted for by his too earnest devotion to study, his scrupulous fulfilment of parochial duty, and more than all, to the fasts and vigils of which he made a frequent practice, in order to keep the grossness of this earthly state from clogging and obscuring his spiritual lamp. Some declared, that if Mr. Dimmesdale were really going to die, it was cause enough that the world was not worthy to be any longer trodden by his feet. He himself, on the other hand, with characteristic humility, avowed his belief that if Providence should see fit to remove him, it would be because of his own unworthiness to perform its humblest mission here on earth. With all this difference of opinion as to the cause of his decline, there could be no question of the fact. His form grew emaciated; his voice, though still rich and sweet, had a certain melancholy prophecy of decay in it; he was often observed, on any slight alarm or other sudden accident, to put his hand over his heart with first a flush and then a paleness, indicative of pain.

Such was the young clergyman's condition, and so imminent the prospect that his dawning light would be extinguished, all untimely, when Roger Chillingworth made his advent to the town. His first entry on the scene, few people could tell whence, dropping down as it were out of the sky or starting from the nether earth, had an aspect of mystery, which was easily heightened to the miraculous. He was now known to be a man of skill; it was observed that he gathered herbs and the blossoms of wild-flowers, and dug up roots and plucked off twigs from the forest-trees like one acquainted with hidden virtues in what was valueless to common eyes. He was heard to speak of Sir Kenelm Digby and other famous men—whose scientific attainments were esteemed hardly less than supernatural—as having been his correspondents or associates. Why, with such rank in the learned world, had he come hither? What, could he, whose sphere was in great cities, be seeking in the wilderness? In answer to this query, a rumour gained ground—and however absurd, was entertained by some very sensible people—that Heaven had wrought an absolute miracle, by transporting an eminent Doctor of Physic from a German university bodily through the air and setting him down at the door of Mr. Dimmesdale's study! Individuals of wiser faith, indeed, who knew that Heaven promotes its purposes without aiming at the stage-effect of what is called miraculous interposition, were inclined to see a providential hand in Roger Chillingworth's so opportune arrival.

This idea was countenanced by the strong interest which the physician ever manifested in the young clergyman; he attached himself to him as a parishioner, and sought to win a friendly regard and confidence from his naturally reserved sensibility. He expressed great alarm at his pastor's state of health, but was anxious to attempt the cure, and, if early undertaken, seemed not despondent of a favourable result. The elders, the deacons, the motherly dames, and the young and fair maidens of Mr. Dimmesdale's flock, were alike importunate that he should make trial of the physician's frankly offered skill. Mr. Dimmesdale gently repelled their entreaties.

"I need no medicine," said he.

But how could the young minister say so, when, with every successive Sabbath, his cheek was paler and thinner, and his voice more tremulous than before—when it had now become a constant habit, rather than a casual gesture, to press his hand over his heart? Was he weary of his labours? Did he wish to die? These questions were solemnly propounded to Mr. Dimmesdale by the elder ministers of Boston, and the deacons of his church, who, to use their own phrase, "dealt with him," on the sin of rejecting the aid which Providence so manifestly held out. He listened in silence, and finally promised to confer with the physician.

"Were it God's will," said the Reverend Mr. Dimmesdale, when, in fulfilment of this pledge, he requested old Roger Chillingworth's professional advice, "I could be well content that my labours, and my sorrows, and my sins, and my pains, should shortly end with me, and what is earthly of them be buried in my grave, and the spiritual go with me to my eternal state, rather than that you should put your skill to the proof in my behalf."

"Ah," replied Roger Chillingworth, with that quietness, which, whether imposed or natural, marked all his deportment, "it is thus that a young clergyman is apt to speak. Youthful men, not having taken a deep root, give up their hold of life so easily! And saintly men, who walk with God on earth, would fain be away, to walk with him on the golden pavements of the New Jerusalem."

"Nay," rejoined the young minister, putting his hand to his heart, with a flush of pain flitting over his brow, "were I worthier to walk there, I could be better content to toil here."

"Good men ever interpret themselves too meanly," said the physician.

In this manner, the mysterious old Roger Chillingworth became the medical adviser of the Reverend Mr. Dimmesdale. As not only the disease interested the physician, but he was strongly moved to look into the character and qualities of the patient, these two men, so different in age, came gradually to spend much time together. For the sake of the minister's health, and to enable the leech to gather plants with healing balm in them, they took long walks on the sea-shore, or in the forest; mingling various walks with the splash and murmur of the waves, and the solemn wind-anthem among the tree-tops. Often, likewise, one was the guest of the other in his place of study and retirement There was a fascination for the minister in the company of the man of science, in whom he recognised an intellectual cultivation of no moderate depth or scope; together with a range and freedom of ideas, that he would have vainly looked for among the members of his own profession. In truth, he was startled, if not shocked, to find this attribute in the physician. Mr. Dimmesdale was a true priest, a true religionist, with the reverential sentiment largely developed, and an order of mind that impelled itself powerfully along the track of a creed, and wore its passage continually deeper with the lapse of time. In no state of society would he have been what is called a man of liberal views; it would always be essential to his peace to feel the pressure of a faith about him, supporting, while it confined him within its iron framework. Not the less, however, though with a tremulous enjoyment, did he feel the occasional relief of looking at the universe through the medium of another kind of intellect than those with which he habitually held converse. It was as if a window were thrown open, admitting a freer atmosphere into the close and stifled study, where his life was wasting itself away, amid lamp-light, or obstructed day-beams, and the musty fragrance, be it sensual or moral, that exhales from books. But the air was too fresh and chill to be long breathed with comfort. So the minister, and the physician with him, withdrew again within the limits of what their Church defined as orthodox.

Thus Roger Chillingworth scrutinised his patient carefully, both as he saw him in his ordinary life, keeping an accustomed pathway in the range of thoughts familiar to him, and as he appeared when thrown amidst other moral scenery, the novelty of which might call out something new to the surface of his character. He deemed it essential, it would seem, to know the man, before attempting to do him good. Wherever there is a heart and an intellect, the diseases of the physical frame are tinged with the peculiarities of these. In Arthur Dimmesdale, thought and imagination were so active, and sensibility so intense, that the bodily infirmity would be likely to have its groundwork there. So Roger Chillingworth—the man of skill, the kind and friendly physician—strove to go deep into his patient's bosom, delving among his principles, prying into his recollections, and probing everything with a cautious touch, like a treasure-seeker in a dark cavern. Few secrets can escape an investigator, who has opportunity and license to undertake such a quest, and skill to follow it up. A man burdened with a secret should especially avoid the intimacy of his physician. If the latter possess native sagacity, and a nameless something more let us call it intuition; if he show no intrusive egotism, nor disagreeable prominent characteristics of his own; if he have the power, which must be born with him, to bring his mind into such affinity with his patient's, that this last shall unawares have spoken what he imagines himself only to have thought if such revelations be received without tumult, and acknowledged not so often by an uttered sympathy as by silence, an inarticulate breath, and here and there a word to indicate that all is understood; if to these qualifications of a confidant be joined the advantages afforded by his recognised character as a physician;—then, at some inevitable moment, will the soul of the sufferer be dissolved, and flow forth in a dark but transparent stream, bringing all its mysteries into the daylight.

Roger Chillingworth possessed all, or most, of the attributes above enumerated. Nevertheless, time went on; a kind of intimacy, as we have said, grew up between these two cultivated minds, which had as wide a field as the whole sphere of human thought and study to meet upon; they discussed every topic of ethics and religion, of public affairs, and private character; they talked much, on both sides, of matters that seemed personal to themselves; and yet no secret, such as the physician fancied must exist there, ever stole out of the minister's consciousness into his companion's ear. The latter had his suspicions, indeed, that even the nature of Mr. Dimmesdale's bodily disease had never fairly been revealed to him. It was a strange reserve!

After a time, at a hint from Roger Chillingworth, the friends of Mr. Dimmesdale effected an arrangement by which the two were lodged in the same house; so that every ebb and flow of the minister's life-tide might pass under the eye of his anxious and attached physician. There was much joy throughout the town when this greatly desirable object was attained. It was held to be the best possible measure for the young clergyman's welfare; unless, indeed, as often urged by such as felt authorised to do so, he had selected some one of the many blooming damsels, spiritually devoted to him, to become his devoted wife. This latter step, however, there was no present prospect that Arthur Dimmesdale would be prevailed upon to take; he rejected all suggestions of the kind, as if priestly celibacy were one of his articles of Church discipline. Doomed by his own choice, therefore, as Mr. Dimmesdale so evidently was, to eat his unsavoury morsel always at another's board, and endure the life-long chill which must be his lot who seeks to warm himself only at another's fireside, it truly seemed that this sagacious, experienced, benevolent old physician, with his concord of paternal and reverential love for the young pastor, was the very man, of all mankind, to be constantly within reach of his voice.

The new abode of the two friends was with a pious widow, of good social rank, who dwelt in a house covering pretty nearly the site on which the venerable structure of King's Chapel has since been built. It had the graveyard, originally Isaac Johnson's home-field, on one side, and so was well adapted to call up serious reflections, suited to their respective employments, in both minister and man of physic. The motherly care of the good widow assigned to Mr. Dimmesdale a front apartment, with a sunny exposure, and heavy window-curtains, to create a noontide shadow when desirable. The walls were hung round with tapestry, said to be from the Gobelin looms, and, at all events, representing the Scriptural story of David and Bathsheba, and Nathan the Prophet, in colours still unfaded, but which made the fair woman of the scene almost as grimly picturesque as the woe-denouncing seer. Here the pale clergyman piled up his library, rich with parchment-bound folios of the Fathers, and the lore of Rabbis, and monkish erudition, of which the Protestant divines, even while they vilified and decried that class of writers, were yet constrained often to avail themselves. On the other side of the house, old Roger Chillingworth arranged his study and laboratory: not such as a modern man of science would reckon even tolerably complete, but provided with a distilling apparatus and the means of compounding drugs and chemicals, which the practised alchemist knew well how to turn to purpose. With such commodiousness of situation, these two learned persons sat themselves down, each in his own domain, yet familiarly passing from one apartment to the other, and bestowing a mutual and not incurious inspection into one another's business.

And the Reverend Arthur Dimmesdale's best discerning friends, as we have intimated, very reasonably imagined that the hand of Providence had done all this for the purpose—besought in so many public and domestic and secret prayers—of restoring the young minister to health. But, it must now be said, another portion of the community had latterly begun to take its own view of the relation betwixt Mr. Dimmesdale and the mysterious old physician. When an uninstructed multitude attempts to see with its eyes, it is exceedingly apt to be deceived. When, however, it forms its judgment, as it usually does, on the intuitions of its great and warm heart, the conclusions thus attained are often so profound and so unerring as to possess the character of truth supernaturally revealed. The people, in the case of which we speak, could justify its prejudice against Roger Chillingworth by no fact or argument worthy of serious refutation. There was an aged handicraftsman, it is true, who had been a citizen of London at the period of Sir Thomas Overbury's murder, now some thirty years agone; he testified to having seen the physician, under some other name, which the narrator of the story had now forgotten, in company with Dr. Forman, the famous old conjurer, who was implicated in the affair of Overbury. Two or three individuals hinted that the man of skill, during his Indian captivity, had enlarged his medical attainments by joining in the incantations of the savage priests, who were universally acknowledged to be powerful enchanters, often performing seemingly miraculous cures by their skill in the black art. A large number— and many of these were persons of such sober sense and practical observation that their opinions would have been valuable in other matters—affirmed that Roger Chillingworth's aspect had undergone a remarkable change while he had dwelt in town, and especially since his abode with Mr. Dimmesdale. At first, his expression had been calm, meditative, scholar-like. Now there was something ugly and evil in his face, which they had not previously noticed, and which grew still the more obvious to sight the oftener they looked upon him. According to the vulgar idea, the fire in his laboratory had been brought from the lower regions, and was fed with infernal fuel; and so, as might be expected, his visage was getting sooty with the smoke.

To sum up the matter, it grew to be a widely diffused opinion that the Rev. Arthur Dimmesdale, like many other personages of special sanctity, in all ages of the Christian world, was haunted either by Satan himself or Satan's emissary, in the guise of old Roger Chillingworth. This diabolical agent had the Divine permission, for a season, to burrow into the clergyman's intimacy, and plot against his soul. No sensible man, it was confessed, could doubt on which side the victory would turn. The people looked, with an unshaken hope, to see the minister come forth out of the conflict transfigured with the glory which he would unquestionably win. Meanwhile, nevertheless, it was sad to think of the perchance mortal agony through which he must struggle towards his triumph.

Alas! to judge from the gloom and terror in the depth of the poor minister's eyes, the battle was a sore one, and the victory anything but secure.

X. The Leech and His Patient

Old Roger Chillingworth, throughout life, had been calm in temperament, kindly, though not of warm affections, but ever, and in all his relations with the world, a pure and upright man. He had begun an investigation, as he imagined, with the severe and equal integrity of a judge, desirous only of truth, even as if the question involved no more than the air-drawn lines and figures of a geometrical problem, instead of human passions, and wrongs inflicted on himself. But, as he proceeded, a terrible fascination, a kind of fierce, though still calm, necessity, seized the old man within its gripe, and never set him free again until he had done all its bidding. He now dug into the poor clergyman's heart, like a miner searching for gold; or, rather, like a sexton delving into a grave, possibly in quest of a jewel that had been buried on the dead man's bosom, but likely to find nothing save mortality and corruption. Alas, for his own soul, if these were what he sought!

Sometimes a light glimmered out of the physician's eyes, burning blue and ominous, like the reflection of a furnace, or, let us say, like one of those gleams of ghastly fire that darted from Bunyan's awful doorway in the hillside, and quivered on the pilgrim's face. The soil where this dark miner was working had perchance shown indications that encouraged him.

"This man," said he, at one such moment, to himself, "pure as they deem him—all spiritual as he seems—hath inherited a strong animal nature from his father or his mother. Let us dig a little further in the direction of this vein!"

Then after long search into the minister's dim interior, and turning over many precious materials, in the shape of high aspirations for the welfare of his race, warm love of souls, pure sentiments, natural piety, strengthened by thought and study, and illuminated by revelation—all of which invaluable gold was perhaps no better than rubbish to the seeker—he would turn back, discouraged, and begin his quest towards another point. He groped along as stealthily, with as cautious a tread, and as wary an outlook, as a thief entering a chamber where a man lies only half asleep—or, it may be, broad awake—with purpose to steal the very treasure which this man guards as the apple of his eye. In spite of his premeditated carefulness, the floor would now and then creak; his garments would rustle; the shadow of his presence, in a forbidden proximity, would be thrown across his victim. In other words, Mr. Dimmesdale, whose sensibility of nerve often produced the effect of spiritual intuition, would become vaguely aware that something inimical to his peace had thrust itself into relation with him. But Old Roger Chillingworth, too, had perceptions that were almost intuitive; and when the minister threw his startled eyes towards him, there the physician sat; his kind, watchful, sympathising, but never intrusive friend.

Yet Mr. Dimmesdale would perhaps have seen this individual's character more perfectly, if a certain morbidness, to which sick hearts are liable, had not rendered him suspicious of all mankind. Trusting no man as his friend, he could not recognize his enemy when the latter actually appeared. He therefore still kept up a familiar intercourse with him, daily receiving the old physician in his study, or visiting the laboratory, and, for recreation's sake, watching the processes by which weeds were converted into drugs of potency.

One day, leaning his forehead on his hand, and his elbow on the sill of the open window, that looked towards the grave-yard, he talked with Roger Chillingworth, while the old man was examining a bundle of unsightly plants.

"Where," asked he, with a look askance at them—for it was the clergyman's peculiarity that he seldom, now-a-days, looked straight forth at any object, whether human or inanimate, "where, my kind doctor, did you gather those herbs, with such a dark, flabby leaf?"

"Even in the graveyard here at hand," answered the physician, continuing his employment. "They are new to me. I found them growing on a grave, which bore no tombstone, no other memorial of the dead man, save these ugly weeds, that have taken upon themselves to keep him in remembrance. They grew out of his heart, and typify, it may be, some hideous secret that was buried with him, and which he had done better to confess during his lifetime."

"Perchance," said Mr. Dimmesdale, "he earnestly desired it, but could not."

"And wherefore?" rejoined the physician.

"Wherefore not; since all the powers of nature call so earnestly for the confession of sin, that these black weeds have sprung up out of a buried heart, to make manifest, an outspoken crime?"

"That, good sir, is but a fantasy of yours," replied the minister. "There can be, if I forbode aright, no power, short of the Divine mercy, to disclose, whether by uttered words, or by type or emblem, the secrets that may be buried in the human heart. The heart, making itself guilty of such secrets, must perforce hold them, until the day when all hidden things shall be revealed. Nor have I so read or interpreted Holy Writ, as to understand that the disclosure of human thoughts and deeds, then to be made, is intended as a part of the retribution. That, surely, were a shallow view of it. No; these revelations, unless I greatly err, are meant merely to promote the intellectual satisfaction of all intelligent beings, who will stand waiting, on that day, to see the dark problem of this life made plain. A knowledge of men's hearts will be needful to the completest solution of that problem. And, I conceive moreover, that the hearts holding such miserable secrets as you speak of, will yield them up, at that last day, not with reluctance, but with a joy unutterable."

"Then why not reveal it here?" asked Roger Chillingworth, glancing quietly aside at the minister. "Why should not the guilty ones sooner avail themselves of this unutterable solace?"

"They mostly do," said the clergyman, griping hard at his breast, as if afflicted with an importunate throb of pain. "Many, many a poor soul hath given its confidence to me, not only on the death-bed, but while strong in life, and fair in reputation. And ever, after such an outpouring, oh, what a relief have I witnessed in those sinful brethren! even as in one who at last draws free air, after a long stifling with his own polluted breath. How can it be otherwise? Why should a wretched man—guilty, we will say, of murder—prefer to keep the dead corpse buried in his own heart, rather than fling it forth at once, and let the universe take care of it!"

"Yet some men bury their secrets thus," observed the calm physician.

"True; there are such men," answered Mr. Dimmesdale. "But not to suggest more obvious reasons, it may be that they are kept silent by the very constitution of their nature. Or—can we not suppose it?—guilty as they may be, retaining, nevertheless, a zeal for God's glory and man's welfare, they shrink from displaying themselves black and filthy in the view of men; because, thenceforward, no good can be achieved by them; no evil of the past be redeemed by better service. So, to their own unutterable torment, they go about among their fellow-creatures, looking pure as new-fallen snow, while their hearts are all speckled and spotted with iniquity of which they cannot rid themselves."

"These men deceive themselves," said Roger Chillingworth, with somewhat more emphasis than usual, and making a slight gesture with his forefinger. "They fear to take up the shame that rightfully belongs to them. Their love for man, their zeal for God's service—these holy impulses may or may not coexist in their hearts with the evil inmates to which their guilt has unbarred the door, and which must needs propagate a hellish breed within them. But, if they seek to glorify God, let them not lift heavenward their unclean hands! If they would serve their fellowmen, let them do it by making manifest the power and reality of conscience, in constraining them to penitential self-abasement! Would thou have me to believe, O wise and pious friend, that a false show can be better—can be more for God's glory, or man' welfare—than God's own truth? Trust me, such men deceive themselves!"

"It may be so," said the young clergyman, indifferently, as waiving a discussion that he considered irrelevant or unseasonable. He had a ready faculty, indeed, of escaping from any topic that agitated his too sensitive and nervous temperament.—"But, now, I would ask of my well-skilled physician, whether, in good sooth, he deems me to have profited by his kindly care of this weak frame of mine?"

Before Roger Chillingworth could answer, they heard the clear, wild laughter of a young child's voice, proceeding from the adjacent burial-ground. Looking instinctively from the open window—for it was summer-time—the minister beheld Hester Prynne and little Pearl passing along the footpath that traversed the enclosure. Pearl looked as beautiful as the day, but was in one of those moods of perverse merriment which, whenever they occurred, seemed to remove her entirely out of the sphere of sympathy or human contact. She now skipped irreverently from one grave to another; until coming to the broad, flat, armorial tombstone of a departed worthy—perhaps of Isaac Johnson himself—she began to dance upon it. In reply to her mother's command and entreaty that she would behave more decorously, little Pearl paused to gather the prickly burrs from a tall burdock which grew beside the tomb. Taking a handful of these, she arranged them along the lines of the scarlet letter that decorated the maternal bosom, to which the burrs, as their nature was, tenaciously adhered. Hester did not pluck them off.

Roger Chillingworth had by this time approached the window and smiled grimly down.

"There is no law, nor reverence for authority, no regard for human ordinances or opinions, right or wrong, mixed up with that child's composition," remarked he, as much to himself as to his companion. "I saw her, the other day, bespatter the Governor himself with water at the cattle-trough in Spring Lane. What, in heaven's name, is she? Is the imp altogether evil? Hath she affections? Hath she any discoverable principle of being?"

"None, save the freedom of a broken law," answered Mr. Dimmesdale, in a quiet way, as if he had been discussing the point within himself, "Whether capable of good, I know not."

The child probably overheard their voices, for, looking up to the window with a bright, but naughty smile of mirth and intelligence, she threw one of the prickly burrs at the Rev. Mr. Dimmesdale. The sensitive clergyman shrank, with nervous dread, from the light missile. Detecting his emotion, Pearl clapped her little hands in the most extravagant ecstacy. Hester Prynne, likewise, had involuntarily looked up, and all these four persons, old and young, regarded one another in silence, till the child laughed aloud, and shouted—"Come away, mother! Come away, or yonder old black man will catch you! He hath got hold of the minister already. Come away, mother or he will catch you! But he cannot catch little Pearl!"

So she drew her mother away, skipping, dancing, and frisking fantastically among the hillocks of the dead people, like a creature that had nothing in common with a bygone and buried generation, nor owned herself akin to it. It was as if she had been made afresh out of new elements, and must perforce be permitted to live her own life, and be a law unto herself without her eccentricities being reckoned to her for a crime.

"There goes a woman," resumed Roger Chillingworth, after a pause, "who, be her demerits what they may, hath none of that mystery of hidden sinfulness which you deem so grievous to be borne. Is Hester Prynne the less miserable, think you, for that scarlet letter on her breast?"

"I do verily believe it," answered the clergyman. "Nevertheless, I cannot answer for her. There was a look of pain in her face which I would gladly have been spared the sight of. But still, methinks, it must needs be better for the sufferer to be free to show his pain, as this poor woman Hester is, than to cover it up in his heart."

There was another pause, and the physician began anew to examine and arrange the plants which he had gathered.

"You inquired of me, a little time agone," said he, at length, "my judgment as touching your health."

"I did," answered the clergyman, "and would gladly learn it. Speak frankly, I pray you, be it for life or death."

"Freely then, and plainly," said the physician, still busy with his plants, but keeping a wary eye on Mr. Dimmesdale, "the disorder is a strange one; not so much in itself nor as outwardly manifested,—in so far, at least as the symptoms have been laid open to my observation. Looking daily at you, my good sir, and watching the tokens of your aspect now for months gone by, I should deem you a man sore sick, it may be, yet not so sick but that an instructed and watchful physician might well hope to cure you. But I know not what to say, the disease is what I seem to know, yet know it not."

"You speak in riddles, learned sir," said the pale minister, glancing aside out of the window.

"Then, to speak more plainly," continued the physician, "and I crave pardon, sir, should it seem to require pardon, for this needful plainness of my speech. Let me ask as your friend, as one having charge, under Providence, of your life and physical well being, hath all the operations of this disorder been fairly laid open and recounted to me?"

"How can you question it?" asked the minister. "Surely it were child's play to call in a physician and then hide the sore!"

"You would tell me, then, that I know all?" said Roger Chillingworth, deliberately, and fixing an eye, bright with intense and concentrated intelligence, on the minister's face. "Be it so! But again! He to whom only the outward and physical evil is laid open, knoweth, oftentimes, but half the evil which he is called upon to cure. A bodily disease, which we look upon as whole and entire within itself, may, after all, be but a symptom of some ailment in the spiritual part. Your pardon once again, good sir, if my speech give the shadow of offence. You, sir, of all men whom I have known, are he whose body is the closest conjoined, and imbued, and identified, so to speak, with the spirit whereof it is the instrument."

"Then I need ask no further," said the clergyman, somewhat hastily rising from his chair. "You deal not, I take it, in medicine for the soul!"

"Thus, a sickness," continued Roger Chillingworth, going on, in an unaltered tone, without heeding the interruption, but standing up and confronting the emaciated and white-cheeked minister, with his low, dark, and misshapen figure,—"a sickness, a sore place, if we may so call it, in your spirit hath immediately its appropriate manifestation in your bodily frame. Would you, therefore, that your physician heal the bodily evil? How may this be unless you first lay open to him the wound or trouble in your soul?"

"No, not to thee! not to an earthly physician!" cried Mr. Dimmesdale, passionately, and turning his eyes, full and bright, and with a kind of fierceness, on old Roger Chillingworth. "Not to thee! But, if it be the soul's disease, then do I commit myself to the one Physician of the soul! He, if it stand with His good pleasure, can cure, or he can kill. Let Him do with me as, in His justice and wisdom, He shall see good. But who art thou, that meddlest in this matter? that dares thrust himself between the sufferer and his God?"

With a frantic gesture he rushed out of the room.

"It is as well to have made this step," said Roger Chillingworth to himself, looking after the minister, with a grave smile. "There is nothing lost. We shall be friends again anon. But see, now, how passion takes hold upon this man, and hurrieth him out of himself! As with one passion so with another. He hath done a wild thing ere now, this pious Master Dimmesdale, in the hot passion of his heart."

It proved not difficult to re-establish the intimacy of the two companions, on the same footing and in the same degree as heretofore. The young clergyman, after a few hours of privacy, was sensible that the disorder of his nerves had hurried him into an unseemly outbreak of temper, which there had been nothing in the physician's words to excuse or palliate. He marvelled, indeed, at the violence with which he had thrust back the kind old man, when merely proffering the advice which it was his duty to bestow, and which the minister himself had expressly sought. With these remorseful feelings, he lost no time in making the amplest apologies, and besought his friend still to continue the care which, if not successful in restoring him to health, had, in all probability, been the means of prolonging his feeble existence to that hour. Roger Chillingworth readily assented, and went on with his medical supervision of the minister; doing his best for him, in all good faith, but always quitting the patient's apartment, at the close of the professional interview, with a mysterious and puzzled smile upon his lips. This expression was invisible in Mr. Dimmesdale's presence, but grew strongly evident as the physician crossed the threshold.

"A rare case," he muttered. "I must needs look deeper into it. A strange sympathy betwixt soul and body! Were it only for the art's sake, I must search this matter to the bottom."

It came to pass, not long after the scene above recorded, that the Reverend Mr. Dimmesdale, noon-day, and entirely unawares, fell into a deep, deep slumber, sitting in his chair, with a large black-letter volume open before him on the table. It must have been a work of vast ability in the somniferous school of literature. The profound depth of the minister's repose was the more remarkable, inasmuch as he was one of those persons whose sleep ordinarily is as light as fitful, and as easily scared away, as a small bird hopping on a twig. To such an unwonted remoteness, however, had his spirit now withdrawn into itself that he stirred not in his chair when old Roger Chillingworth, without any extraordinary precaution, came into the room. The physician advanced directly in front of his patient, laid his hand upon his bosom, and thrust aside the vestment, that hitherto had always covered it even from the professional eye.

Then, indeed, Mr. Dimmesdale shuddered, and slightly stirred.

After a brief pause, the physician turned away.

But with what a wild look of wonder, joy, and honor! With what a ghastly rapture, as it were, too mighty to be expressed only by the eye and features, and therefore bursting forth through the whole ugliness of his figure, and making itself even riotously manifest by the extravagant gestures with which he threw up his arms towards the ceiling, and stamped his foot upon the floor! Had a man seen old Roger Chillingworth, at that moment of his ecstasy, he would have had no need to ask how Satan comports himself when a precious human soul is lost to heaven, and won into his kingdom.

But what distinguished the physician's ecstasy from Satan's was the trait of wonder in it!

XI. The Interior of a Heart

After the incident last described, the intercourse between the clergyman and the physician, though externally the same, was really of another character than it had previously been. The intellect of Roger Chillingworth had now a sufficiently plain path before it. It was not, indeed, precisely that which he had laid out for himself to tread. Calm, gentle, passionless, as he appeared, there was yet, we fear, a quiet depth of malice, hitherto latent, but active now, in this unfortunate old man, which led him to imagine a more intimate revenge than any mortal had ever wreaked upon an enemy. To make himself the one trusted friend, to whom should be confided all the fear, the remorse, the agony, the ineffectual repentance, the backward rush of sinful thoughts, expelled in vain!

All that guilty sorrow, hidden from the world, whose great heart would have pitied and forgiven, to be revealed to him, the Pitiless—to him, the Unforgiving! All that dark treasure to be lavished on the very man, to whom nothing else could so adequately pay the debt of vengeance!

The clergyman's shy and sensitive reserve had balked this scheme Roger Chillingworth, however, was inclined to be hardly, if at all, less satisfied with the aspect of affairs, which Providence—using the avenger and his victim for its own purposes, and, perchance, pardoning, where it seemed most to punish—had substituted for his black devices A revelation, he could almost say, had been granted to him. It mattered little for his object, whether celestial or from what other region. By its aid, in all the subsequent relations betwixt him and Mr. Dimmesdale, not merely the external presence, but the very inmost soul of the latter, seemed to be brought out before his eyes, so that he could see and comprehend its every movement. He became, thenceforth, not a spectator only, but a chief actor in the poor minister's interior world. He could play upon him as he chose. Would he arouse him with a throb of agony? The victim was for ever on the rack; it needed only to know the spring that controlled the engine: and the physician knew it well. Would he startle him with sudden fear? As at the waving of a magician's wand, up rose a grisly phantom—up rose a thousand phantoms—in many shapes, of death, or more awful shame, all flocking round about the clergyman, and pointing with their fingers at his breast!

All this was accomplished with a subtlety so perfect, that the minister, though he had constantly a dim perception of some evil influence watching over him, could never gain a knowledge of its actual nature. True, he looked doubtfully, fearfully—even, at times, with horror and the bitterness of hatred—at the deformed figure of the old physician. His gestures, his gait, his grizzled beard, his slightest and most indifferent acts, the very fashion of his garments, were odious in the clergyman's sight; a token implicitly to be relied on of a deeper antipathy in the breast of the latter than he was willing to acknowledge to himself. For, as it was impossible to assign a reason for such distrust and abhorrence, so Mr. Dimmesdale, conscious that the poison of one morbid spot was infecting his heart's entire substance, attributed all his presentiments to no other cause. He took himself to task for his bad sympathies in reference to Roger Chillingworth, disregarded the lesson that he should have drawn from them, and did his best to root them out. Unable to accomplish this, he nevertheless, as a matter of principle, continued his habits of social familiarity with the old man, and thus gave him constant opportunities for perfecting the purpose to which—poor forlorn creature that he was, and more wretched than his victim—the avenger had devoted himself.

While thus suffering under bodily disease, and gnawed and tortured by some black trouble of the soul, and given over to the machinations of his deadliest enemy, the Reverend Mr. Dimmesdale had achieved a brilliant popularity in his sacred office. He won it indeed, in great part, by his sorrows. His intellectual gifts, his moral perceptions, his power of experiencing and communicating emotion, were kept in a state of preternatural activity by the prick and anguish of his daily life. His fame, though still on its upward slope, already overshadowed the soberer reputations of his fellow-clergymen, eminent as several of them were. There are scholars among them, who had spent more years in acquiring abstruse lore, connected with the divine profession, than Mr. Dimmesdale had lived; and who might well, therefore, be more profoundly versed in such solid and valuable attainments than their youthful brother. There were men, too, of a sturdier texture of mind than his, and endowed with a far greater share of shrewd, hard iron, or granite understanding; which, duly mingled with a fair proportion of doctrinal ingredient, constitutes a highly respectable, efficacious, and unamiable variety of the clerical species. There were others again, true saintly fathers, whose faculties had been elaborated by weary toil among their books, and by patient thought, and etherealised, moreover, by spiritual communications with the better world, into which their purity of life had almost introduced these holy personages, with their garments of mortality still clinging to them. All that they lacked was, the gift that descended upon the chosen disciples at Pentecost, in tongues of flame; symbolising, it would seem, not the power of speech in foreign and unknown languages, but that of addressing the whole human brotherhood in the heart's native language. These fathers, otherwise so apostolic, lacked Heaven's last and rarest attestation of their office, the Tongue of Flame. They would have vainly sought—had they ever dreamed of seeking—to express the highest truths through the humblest medium of familiar words and images. Their voices came down, afar and indistinctly, from the upper heights where they habitually dwelt.

Not improbably, it was to this latter class of men that Mr. Dimmesdale, by many of his traits of character, naturally belonged. To the high mountain peaks of faith and sanctity he would have climbed, had not the tendency been thwarted by the burden, whatever it might be, of crime or anguish, beneath which it was his doom to totter. It kept him down on a level with the lowest; him, the man of ethereal attributes, whose voice the angels might else have listened to and answered! But this very burden it was that gave him sympathies so intimate with the sinful brotherhood of mankind; so that his heart vibrated in unison with theirs, and received their pain into itself and sent its own throb of pain through a thousand other hearts, in gushes of sad, persuasive eloquence. Oftenest persuasive, but sometimes terrible! The people knew not the power that moved them thus. They deemed the young clergyman a miracle of holiness. They fancied him the mouth-piece of Heaven's messages of wisdom, and rebuke, and love. In their eyes, the very ground on which he trod was sanctified. The virgins of his church grew pale around him, victims of a passion so imbued with religious sentiment, that they imagined it to be all religion, and brought it openly, in their white bosoms, as their most acceptable sacrifice before the altar. The aged members of his flock, beholding Mr. Dimmesdale's frame so feeble, while they were themselves so rugged in their infirmity, believed that he would go heavenward before them, and enjoined it upon their children that their old bones should be buried close to their young pastor's holy grave. And all this time, perchance, when poor Mr. Dimmesdale was thinking of his grave, he questioned with himself whether the grass would ever grow on it, because an accursed thing must there be buried!

It is inconceivable, the agony with which this public veneration tortured him. It was his genuine impulse to adore the truth, and to reckon all things shadow-like, and utterly devoid of weight or value, that had not its divine essence as the life within their life. Then what was he?—a substance?—or the dimmest of all shadows? He longed to speak out from his own pulpit at the full height of his voice, and tell the people what he was. "I, whom you behold in these black garments of the priesthood—I, who ascend the sacred desk, and turn my pale face heavenward, taking upon myself to hold communion in your behalf with the Most High Omniscience—I, in whose daily life you discern the sanctity of Enoch—I, whose footsteps, as you suppose, leave a gleam along my earthly track, whereby the Pilgrims that shall come after me may be guided to the regions of the blest— I, who have laid the hand of baptism upon your children—I, who have breathed the parting prayer over your dying friends, to whom the Amen sounded faintly from a world which they had quitted—I, your pastor, whom you so reverence and trust, am utterly a pollution and a lie!"

More than once, Mr. Dimmesdale had gone into the pulpit, with a purpose never to come down its steps until he should have spoken words like the above. More than once he had cleared his throat, and drawn in the long, deep, and tremulous breath, which, when sent forth again, would come burdened with the black secret of his soul. More than once—nay, more than a hundred times—he had actually spoken! Spoken! But how? He had told his hearers that he was altogether vile, a viler companion of the vilest, the worst of sinners, an abomination, a thing of unimaginable iniquity, and that the only wonder was that they did not see his wretched body shrivelled up before their eyes by the burning wrath of the Almighty! Could there be plainer speech than this? Would not the people start up in their seats, by a simultaneous impulse, and tear him down out of the pulpit which he defiled? Not so, indeed! They heard it all, and did but reverence him the more. They little guessed what deadly purport lurked in those self-condemning words. "The godly youth!" said they among themselves. "The saint on earth! Alas! if he discern such sinfulness in his own white soul, what horrid spectacle would he behold in thine or mine!" The minister well knew—subtle, but remorseful hypocrite that he was!—the light in which his vague confession would be viewed. He had striven to put a cheat upon himself by making the avowal of a guilty conscience, but had gained only one other sin, and a self-acknowledged shame, without the momentary relief of being self-deceived. He had spoken the very truth, and transformed it into the veriest falsehood. And yet, by the constitution of his nature, he loved the truth, and loathed the lie, as few men ever did. Therefore, above all things else, he loathed his miserable self!

His inward trouble drove him to practices more in accordance with the old, corrupted faith of Rome than with the better light of the church in which he had been born and bred. In Mr. Dimmesdale's secret closet, under lock and key, there was a bloody scourge. Oftentimes, this Protestant and Puritan divine had plied it on his own shoulders, laughing bitterly at himself the while, and smiting so much the more pitilessly because of that bitter laugh. It was his custom, too, as it has been that of many other pious Puritans, to fast—not however, like them, in order to purify the body, and render it the fitter medium of celestial illumination—but rigorously, and until his knees trembled beneath him, as an act of penance. He kept vigils, likewise, night after night, sometimes in utter darkness, sometimes with a glimmering lamp, and sometimes, viewing his own face in a looking-glass, by the most powerful light which he could throw upon it. He thus typified the constant introspection wherewith he tortured, but could not purify himself. In these lengthened vigils, his brain often reeled, and visions seemed to flit before him; perhaps seen doubtfully, and by a faint light of their own, in the remote dimness of the chamber, or more vividly and close beside him, within the looking-glass. Now it was a herd of diabolic shapes, that grinned and mocked at the pale minister, and beckoned him away with them; now a group of shining angels, who flew upward heavily, as sorrow-laden, but grew more ethereal as they rose. Now came the dead friends of his youth, and his white-bearded father, with a saint-like frown, and his mother turning her face away as she passed by Ghost of a mother—thinnest fantasy of a mother—methinks she might yet have thrown a pitying glance towards her son! And now, through the chamber which these spectral thoughts had made so ghastly, glided Hester Prynne leading along little Pearl, in her scarlet garb, and pointing her forefinger, first at the scarlet letter on her bosom, and then at the clergyman's own breast.

None of these visions ever quite deluded him. At any moment, by an effort of his will, he could discern substances through their misty lack of substance, and convince himself that they were not solid in their nature, like yonder table of carved oak, or that big, square, leather-bound and brazen-clasped volume of divinity. But, for all that, they were, in one sense, the truest and most substantial things which the poor minister now dealt with. It is the unspeakable misery of a life so false as his, that it steals the pith and substance out of whatever realities there are around us, and which were meant by Heaven to be the spirit's joy and nutriment. To the untrue man, the whole universe is false—it is impalpable—it shrinks to nothing within his grasp. And he himself in so far as he shows himself in a false light, becomes a shadow, or, indeed, ceases to exist. The only truth that continued to give Mr. Dimmesdale a real existence on this earth was the anguish in his inmost soul, and the undissembled expression of it in his aspect. Had he once found power to smile, and wear a face of gaiety, there would have been no such man!

On one of those ugly nights, which we have faintly hinted at, but forborne to picture forth, the minister started from his chair. A new thought had struck him. There might be a moment's peace in it. Attiring himself with as much care as if it had been for public worship, and precisely in the same manner, he stole softly down the staircase, undid the door, and issued forth.

XII. The Minister's Vigil

Walking in the shadow of a dream, as it were, and perhaps actually under the influence of a species of somnambulism, Mr. Dimmesdale reached the spot where, now so long since, Hester Prynne had lived through her first hours of public ignominy. The same platform or scaffold, black and weather-stained with the storm or sunshine of seven long years, and foot-worn, too, with the tread of many culprits who had since ascended it, remained standing beneath the balcony of the meeting-house. The minister went up the steps.

It was an obscure night in early May. An unwearied pall of cloud muffled the whole expanse of sky from zenith to horizon. If the same multitude which had stood as eye-witnesses while Hester Prynne sustained her punishment could now have been summoned forth, they would have discerned no face above the platform nor hardly the outline of a human shape, in the dark grey of the midnight. But the town was all asleep. There was no peril of discovery. The minister might stand there, if it so pleased him, until morning should redden in the east, without other risk than that the dank and chill night air would creep into his frame, and stiffen his joints with rheumatism, and clog his throat with catarrh and cough; thereby defrauding the expectant audience of to-morrow's prayer and sermon. No eye could see him, save that ever-wakeful one which had seen him in his closet, wielding the bloody scourge. Why, then, had he come hither? Was it but the mockery of penitence? A mockery, indeed, but in which his soul trifled with itself! A mockery at which angels blushed and wept, while fiends rejoiced with jeering laughter! He had been driven hither by the impulse of that Remorse which dogged him everywhere, and whose own sister and closely linked companion was that Cowardice which invariably drew him back, with her tremulous gripe, just when the other impulse had hurried him to the verge of a disclosure. Poor, miserable man! what right had infirmity like his to burden itself with crime? Crime is for the iron-nerved, who have their choice either to endure it, or, if it press too hard, to exert their fierce and savage strength for a good purpose, and fling it off at once! This feeble and most sensitive of spirits could do neither, yet continually did one thing or another, which intertwined, in the same inextricable knot, the agony of heaven-defying guilt and vain repentance.

And thus, while standing on the scaffold, in this vain show of expiation, Mr. Dimmesdale was overcome with a great horror of mind, as if the universe were gazing at a scarlet token on his naked breast, right over his heart. On that spot, in very truth, there was, and there had long been, the gnawing and poisonous tooth of bodily pain. Without any effort of his will, or power to restrain himself, he shrieked aloud: an outcry that went pealing through the night, and was beaten back from one house to another, and reverberated from the hills in the background; as if a company of devils, detecting so much misery and terror in it, had made a plaything of the sound, and were bandying it to and fro.

"It is done!" muttered the minister, covering his face with his hands. "The whole town will awake and hurry forth, and find me here!"

But it was not so. The shriek had perhaps sounded with a far greater power, to his own startled ears, than it actually possessed. The town did not awake; or, if it did, the drowsy slumberers mistook the cry either for something frightful in a dream, or for the noise of witches, whose voices, at that period, were often heard to pass over the settlements or lonely cottages, as they rode with Satan through the air. The clergyman, therefore, hearing no symptoms of disturbance, uncovered his eyes and looked about him. At one of the chamber-windows of Governor Bellingham's mansion, which stood at some distance, on the line of another street, he beheld the appearance of the old magistrate himself with a lamp in his hand a white night-cap on his head, and a long white gown enveloping his figure. He looked like a ghost evoked unseasonably from the grave. The cry had evidently startled him. At another window of the same house, moreover appeared old Mistress Hibbins, the Governor's sister, also with a lamp, which even thus far off revealed the expression of her sour and discontented face. She thrust forth her head from the lattice, and looked anxiously upward Beyond the shadow of a doubt, this venerable witch-lady had heard Mr. Dimmesdale's outcry, and interpreted it, with its multitudinous echoes and reverberations, as the clamour of the fiends and night-hags, with whom she was well known to make excursions in the forest.

Detecting the gleam of Governor Bellingham's lamp, the old lady quickly extinguished her own, and vanished. Possibly, she went up among the clouds. The minister saw nothing further of her motions. The magistrate, after a wary observation of the darkness—into which, nevertheless, he could see but little further than he might into a mill-stone—retired from the window.

The minister grew comparatively calm. His eyes, however, were soon greeted by a little glimmering light, which, at first a long way off was approaching up the street. It threw a gleam of recognition, on here a post, and there a garden fence, and here a latticed window-pane, and there a pump, with its full trough of water, and here again an arched door of oak, with an iron knocker, and a rough log for the door-step. The Reverend Mr. Dimmesdale noted all these minute particulars, even while firmly convinced that the doom of his existence was stealing onward, in the footsteps which he now heard; and that the gleam of the lantern would fall upon him in a few moments more, and reveal his long-hidden secret. As the light drew nearer, be beheld, within its illuminated circle, his brother clergyman—or, to speak more accurately, his professional father, as well as highly valued friend—the Reverend Mr. Wilson, who, as Mr. Dimmesdale now conjectured, had been praying at the bedside of some dying man. And so he had. The good old minister came freshly from the death-chamber of Governor Winthrop, who had passed from earth to heaven within that very hour. And now surrounded, like the saint-like personage of olden times, with a radiant halo, that glorified him amid this gloomy night of sin—as if the departed Governor had left him an inheritance of his glory, or as if he had caught upon himself the distant shine of the celestial city, while looking thitherward to see the triumphant pilgrim pass within its gates—now, in short, good Father Wilson was moving homeward, aiding his footsteps with a lighted lantern! The glimmer of this luminary suggested the above conceits to Mr. Dimmesdale, who smiled—nay, almost laughed at them—and then wondered if he was going mad.

As the Reverend Mr. Wilson passed beside the scaffold, closely muffling his Geneva cloak about him with one arm, and holding the lantern before his breast with the other, the minister could hardly restrain himself from speaking—

"A good evening to you, venerable Father Wilson. Come up hither, I pray you, and pass a pleasant hour with me!"

Good Heavens! Had Mr. Dimmesdale actually spoken? For one instant he believed that these words had passed his lips. But they were uttered only within his imagination. The venerable Father Wilson continued to step slowly onward, looking carefully at the muddy pathway before his feet, and never once turning his head towards the guilty platform. When the light of the glimmering lantern had faded quite away, the minister discovered, by the faintness which came over him, that the last few moments had been a crisis of terrible anxiety, although his mind had made an involuntary effort to relieve itself by a kind of lurid playfulness.

Shortly afterwards, the like grisly sense of the humorous again stole in among the solemn phantoms of his thought. He felt his limbs growing stiff with the unaccustomed chilliness of the night, and doubted whether he should be able to descend the steps of the scaffold. Morning would break and find him there The neighbourhood would begin to rouse itself. The earliest riser, coming forth in the dim twilight, would perceive a vaguely-defined figure aloft on the place of shame; and half-crazed betwixt alarm and curiosity, would go knocking from door to door, summoning all the people to behold the ghost—as he needs must think it—of some defunct transgressor. A dusky tumult would flap its wings from one house to another. Then—the morning light still waxing stronger—old patriarchs would rise up in great haste, each in his flannel gown, and matronly dames, without pausing to put off their night-gear. The whole tribe of decorous personages, who had never heretofore been seen with a single hair of their heads awry, would start into public view with the disorder of a nightmare in their aspects. Old Governor Bellingham would come grimly forth, with his King James' ruff fastened askew, and Mistress Hibbins, with some twigs of the forest clinging to her skirts, and looking sourer than ever, as having hardly got a wink of sleep after her night ride; and good Father Wilson too, after spending half the night at a death-bed, and liking ill to be disturbed, thus early, out of his dreams about the glorified saints. Hither, likewise, would come the elders and deacons of Mr. Dimmesdale's church, and the young virgins who so idolized their minister, and had made a shrine for him in their white bosoms, which now, by-the-bye, in their hurry and confusion, they would scantly have given themselves time to cover with their kerchiefs. All people, in a word, would come stumbling over their thresholds, and turning up their amazed and horror-stricken visages around the scaffold. Whom would they discern there, with the red eastern light upon his brow? Whom, but the Reverend Arthur Dimmesdale, half-frozen to death, overwhelmed with shame, and standing where Hester Prynne had stood!

Carried away by the grotesque horror of this picture, the minister, unawares, and to his own infinite alarm, burst into a great peal of laughter. It was immediately responded to by a light, airy, childish laugh, in which, with a thrill of the heart—but he knew not whether of exquisite pain, or pleasure as acute—he recognised the tones of little Pearl.

"Pearl! Little Pearl!" cried he, after a moment's pause; then, suppressing his voice—"Hester! Hester Prynne! Are you there?"

"Yes; it is Hester Prynne!" she replied, in a tone of surprise; and the minister heard her footsteps approaching from the side-walk, along which she had been passing. "It is I, and my little Pearl."

"Whence come you, Hester?" asked the minister. "What sent you hither?"

"I have been watching at a death-bed," answered Hester Prynne "at Governor Winthrop's death-bed, and have taken his measure for a robe, and am now going homeward to my dwelling."

"Come up hither, Hester, thou and Little Pearl," said the Reverend Mr. Dimmesdale. "Ye have both been here before, but I was not with you. Come up hither once again, and we will stand all three together."

She silently ascended the steps, and stood on the platform, holding little Pearl by the hand. The minister felt for the child's other hand, and took it. The moment that he did so, there came what seemed a tumultuous rush of new life, other life than his own pouring like a torrent into his heart, and hurrying through all his veins, as if the mother and the child were communicating their vital warmth to his half-torpid system. The three formed an electric chain.

"Minister!" whispered little Pearl.

"What wouldst thou say, child?" asked Mr. Dimmesdale.

"Wilt thou stand here with mother and me, to-morrow noontide?" inquired Pearl.

"Nay; not so, my little Pearl," answered the minister; for, with the new energy of the moment, all the dread of public exposure, that had so long been the anguish of his life, had returned upon him; and he was already trembling at the conjunction in which—with a strange joy, nevertheless—he now found himself—"not so, my child. I shall, indeed, stand with thy mother and thee one other day, but not to-morrow."

Pearl laughed, and attempted to pull away her hand. But the minister held it fast.

"A moment longer, my child!" said he.

"But wilt thou promise," asked Pearl, "to take my hand, and mother's hand, to-morrow noontide?"

"Not then, Pearl," said the minister; "but another time."

"And what other time?" persisted the child.

"At the great judgment day," whispered the minister; and, strangely enough, the sense that he was a professional teacher of the truth impelled him to answer the child so. "Then, and there, before the judgment-seat, thy mother, and thou, and I must stand together. But the daylight of this world shall not see our meeting!"

Pearl laughed again.

But before Mr. Dimmesdale had done speaking, a light gleamed far and wide over all the muffled sky. It was doubtless caused by one of those meteors, which the night-watcher may so often observe burning out to waste, in the vacant regions of the atmosphere. So powerful was its radiance, that it thoroughly illuminated the dense medium of cloud betwixt the sky and earth. The great vault brightened, like the dome of an immense lamp. It showed the familiar scene of the street with the distinctness of mid-day, but also with the awfulness that is always imparted to familiar objects by an unaccustomed light The wooden houses, with their jutting stories and quaint gable-peaks; the doorsteps and thresholds with the early grass springing up about them; the garden-plots, black with freshly-turned earth; the wheel-track, little worn, and even in the market-place margined with green on either side—all were visible, but with a singularity of aspect that seemed to give another moral interpretation to the things of this world than they had ever borne before. And there stood the minister, with his hand over his heart; and Hester Prynne, with the embroidered letter glimmering on her bosom; and little Pearl, herself a symbol, and the connecting link between those two. They stood in the noon of that strange and solemn splendour, as if it were the light that is to reveal all secrets, and the daybreak that shall unite all who belong to one another.

There was witchcraft in little Pearl's eyes; and her face, as she glanced upward at the minister, wore that naughty smile which made its expression frequently so elvish. She withdrew her hand from Mr. Dimmesdale's, and pointed across the street. But he clasped both his hands over his breast, and cast his eyes towards the zenith.

Nothing was more common, in those days, than to interpret all meteoric appearances, and other natural phenomena that occurred with less regularity than the rise and set of sun and moon, as so many revelations from a supernatural source. Thus, a blazing spear, a sword of flame, a bow, or a sheaf of arrows seen in the midnight sky, prefigured Indian warfare. Pestilence was known to have been foreboded by a shower of crimson light. We doubt whether any marked event, for good or evil, ever befell New England, from its settlement down to revolutionary times, of which the inhabitants had not been previously warned by some spectacle of its nature. Not seldom, it had been seen by multitudes. Oftener, however, its credibility rested on the faith of some lonely eye-witness, who beheld the wonder through the coloured, magnifying, and distorted medium of his imagination, and shaped it more distinctly in his after-thought. It was, indeed, a majestic idea that the destiny of nations should be revealed, in these awful hieroglyphics, on the cope of heaven. A scroll so wide might not be deemed too expensive for Providence to write a people's doom upon. The belief was a favourite one with our forefathers, as betokening that their infant commonwealth was under a celestial guardianship of peculiar intimacy and strictness. But what shall we say, when an individual discovers a revelation addressed to himself alone, on the same vast sheet of record. In such a case, it could only be the symptom of a highly disordered mental state, when a man, rendered morbidly self-contemplative by long, intense, and secret pain, had extended his egotism over the whole expanse of nature, until the firmament itself should appear no more than a fitting page for his soul's history and fate.

We impute it, therefore, solely to the disease in his own eye and heart that the minister, looking upward to the zenith, beheld there the appearance of an immense letter—the letter A—marked out in lines of dull red light. Not but the meteor may have shown itself at that point, burning duskily through a veil of cloud, but with no such shape as his guilty imagination gave it, or, at least, with so little definiteness, that another's guilt might have seen another symbol in it.

There was a singular circumstance that characterised Mr. Dimmesdale's psychological state at this moment. All the time that he gazed upward to the zenith, he was, nevertheless, perfectly aware that little Pearl was hinting her finger towards old Roger Chillingworth, who stood at no great distance from the scaffold. The minister appeared to see him, with the same glance that discerned the miraculous letter. To his feature as to all other objects, the meteoric light imparted a new expression; or it might well be that the physician was not careful then, as at all other times, to hide the malevolence with which he looked upon his victim. Certainly, if the meteor kindled up the sky, and disclosed the earth, with an awfulness that admonished Hester Prynne and the clergyman of the day of judgment, then might Roger Chillingworth have passed with them for the arch-fiend, standing there with a smile and scowl, to claim his own. So vivid was the expression, or so intense the minister's perception of it, that it seemed still to remain painted on the darkness after the meteor had vanished, with an effect as if the street and all things else were at once annihilated.

"Who is that man, Hester?" gasped Mr. Dimmesdale, overcome with terror. "I shiver at him! Dost thou know the man? I hate him, Hester!"

She remembered her oath, and was silent.

"I tell thee, my soul shivers at him!" muttered the minister again. "Who is he? Who is he? Canst thou do nothing for me? I have a nameless horror of the man!"

"Minister," said little Pearl, "I can tell thee who he is!"

"Quickly, then, child!" said the minister, bending his ear close to her lips. "Quickly, and as low as thou canst whisper."

Pearl mumbled something into his ear that sounded, indeed, like human language, but was only such gibberish as children may be heard amusing themselves with by the hour together. At all events, if it involved any secret information in regard to old Roger Chillingworth, it was in a tongue unknown to the erudite clergyman, and did but increase the bewilderment of his mind. The elvish child then laughed aloud.

"Dost thou mock me now?" said the minister.

"Thou wast not bold!—thou wast not true!" answered the child. "Thou wouldst not promise to take my hand, and mother's hand, to-morrow noon-tide!"

"Worthy sir," answered the physician, who had now advanced to the foot of the platform—"pious Master Dimmesdale! can this be you? Well, well, indeed! We men of study, whose heads are in our books, have need to be straightly looked after! We dream in our waking moments, and walk in our sleep. Come, good sir, and my dear friend, I pray you let me lead you home!"

"How knewest thou that I was here?" asked the minister, fearfully.

"Verily, and in good faith," answered Roger Chillingworth, "I knew nothing of the matter. I had spent the better part of the night at the bedside of the worshipful Governor Winthrop, doing what my poor skill might to give him ease. He, going home to a better world, I, likewise, was on my way homeward, when this light shone out. Come with me, I beseech you, Reverend sir, else you will be poorly able to do Sabbath duty to-morrow. Aha! see now how they trouble the brain—these books!—these books! You should study less, good sir, and take a little pastime, or these night whimsies will grow upon you."

"I will go home with you," said Mr. Dimmesdale.

With a chill despondency, like one awakening, all nerveless, from an ugly dream, he yielded himself to the physician, and was led away.

The next day, however, being the Sabbath, he preached a discourse which was held to be the richest and most powerful, and the most replete with heavenly influences, that had ever proceeded from his lips. Souls, it is said, more souls than one, were brought to the truth by the efficacy of that sermon, and vowed within themselves to cherish a holy gratitude towards Mr. Dimmesdale throughout the long hereafter. But as he came down the pulpit steps, the grey-bearded sexton met him, holding up a black glove, which the minister recognised as his own.

"It was found," said the Sexton, "this morning on the scaffold where evil-doers are set up to public shame. Satan dropped it there, I take it, intending a scurrilous jest against your reverence. But, indeed, he was blind and foolish, as he ever and always is. A pure hand needs no glove to cover it!"

"Thank you, my good friend," said the minister, gravely, but startled at heart; for so confused was his remembrance, that he had almost brought himself to look at the events of the past night as visionary.

"Yes, it seems to be my glove, indeed!"

"And, since Satan saw fit to steal it, your reverence must needs handle him without gloves henceforward," remarked the old sexton, grimly smiling. "But did your reverence hear of the portent that was seen last night? a great red letter in the sky—the letter A, which we interpret to stand for Angel. For, as our good Governor Winthrop was made an angel this past night, it was doubtless held fit that there should be some notice thereof!"

"No," answered the minister; "I had not heard of it."

XIII. Another View of Hester

In her late singular interview with Mr. Dimmesdale, Hester Prynne was shocked at the condition to which she found the clergyman reduced. His nerve seemed absolutely destroyed. His moral force was abased into more than childish weakness. It grovelled helpless on the ground, even while his intellectual faculties retained their pristine strength, or had perhaps acquired a morbid energy, which disease only could have given them. With her knowledge of a train of circumstances hidden from all others, she could readily infer that, besides the legitimate action of his own conscience, a terrible machinery had been brought to bear, and was still operating, on Mr. Dimmesdale's well-being and repose. Knowing what this poor fallen man had once been, her whole soul was moved by the shuddering terror with which he had appealed to her—the outcast woman—for support against his instinctively discovered enemy. She decided, moreover, that he had a right to her utmost aid. Little accustomed, in her long seclusion from society, to measure her ideas of right and wrong by any standard external to herself, Hester saw—or seemed to see—that there lay a responsibility upon her in reference to the clergyman, which she owned to no other, nor to the whole world besides. The links that united her to the rest of humankind—links of flowers, or silk, or gold, or whatever the material—had all been broken. Here was the iron link of mutual crime, which neither he nor she could break. Like all other ties, it brought along with it its obligations.

Hester Prynne did not now occupy precisely the same position in which we beheld her during the earlier periods of her ignominy. Years had come and gone. Pearl was now seven years old. Her mother, with the scarlet letter on her breast, glittering in its fantastic embroidery, had long been a familiar object to the townspeople. As is apt to be the case when a person stands out in any prominence before the community, and, at the same time, interferes neither with public nor individual interests and convenience, a species of general regard had ultimately grown up in reference to Hester Prynne. It is to the credit of human nature that, except where its selfishness is brought into play, it loves more readily than it hates. Hatred, by a gradual and quiet process, will even be transformed to love, unless the change be impeded by a continually new irritation of the original feeling of hostility. In this matter of Hester Prynne there was neither irritation nor irksomeness. She never battled with the public, but submitted uncomplainingly to its worst usage; she made no claim upon it in requital for what she suffered; she did not weigh upon its sympathies. Then, also, the blameless purity of her life during all these years in which she had been set apart to infamy was reckoned largely in her favour. With nothing now to lose, in the sight of mankind, and with no hope, and seemingly no wish, of gaining anything, it could only be a genuine regard for virtue that had brought back the poor wanderer to its paths.

It was perceived, too, that while Hester never put forward even the humblest title to share in the world's privileges—further than to breathe the common air and earn daily bread for little Pearl and herself by the faithful labour of her hands—she was quick to acknowledge her sisterhood with the race of man whenever benefits were to be conferred. None so ready as she to give of her little substance to every demand of poverty, even though the bitter-hearted pauper threw back a gibe in requital of the food brought regularly to his door, or the garments wrought for him by the fingers that could have embroidered a monarch's robe. None so self-devoted as Hester when pestilence stalked through the town. In all seasons of calamity, indeed, whether general or of individuals, the outcast of society at once found her place. She came, not as a guest, but as a rightful inmate, into the household that was darkened by trouble, as if its gloomy twilight were a medium in which she was entitled to hold intercourse with her fellow-creature There glimmered the embroidered letter, with comfort in its unearthly ray. Elsewhere the token of sin, it was the taper of the sick chamber. It had even thrown its gleam, in the sufferer's bard extremity, across the verge of time. It had shown him where to set his foot, while the light of earth was fast becoming dim, and ere the light of futurity could reach him. In such emergencies Hester's nature showed itself warm and rich—a well-spring of human tenderness, unfailing to every real demand, and inexhaustible by the largest. Her breast, with its badge of shame, was but the softer pillow for the head that needed one. She was self-ordained a Sister of Mercy, or, we may rather say, the world's heavy hand had so ordained her, when neither the world nor she looked forward to this result. The letter was the symbol of her calling. Such helpfulness was found in her—so much power to do, and power to sympathise—that many people refused to interpret the scarlet A by its original signification. They said that it meant Abel, so strong was Hester Prynne, with a woman's strength.

It was only the darkened house that could contain her. When sunshine came again, she was not there. Her shadow had faded across the threshold. The helpful inmate had departed, without one backward glance to gather up the meed of gratitude, if any were in the hearts of those whom she had served so zealously. Meeting them in the street, she never raised her head to receive their greeting. If they were resolute to accost her, she laid her finger on the scarlet letter, and passed on. This might be pride, but was so like humility, that it produced all the softening influence of the latter quality on the public mind. The public is despotic in its temper; it is capable of denying common justice when too strenuously demanded as a right; but quite as frequently it awards more than justice, when the appeal is made, as despots love to have it made, entirely to its generosity. Interpreting Hester Prynne's deportment as an appeal of this nature, society was inclined to show its former victim a more benign countenance than she cared to be favoured with, or, perchance, than she deserved.

The rulers, and the wise and learned men of the community, were longer in acknowledging the influence of Hester's good qualities than the people. The prejudices which they shared in common with the latter were fortified in themselves by an iron frame-work of reasoning, that made it a far tougher labour to expel them. Day by day, nevertheless, their sour and rigid wrinkles were relaxing into something which, in the due course of years, might grow to be an expression of almost benevolence. Thus it was with the men of rank, on whom their eminent position imposed the guardianship of the public morals. Individuals in private life, meanwhile, had quite forgiven Hester Prynne for her frailty; nay, more, they had begun to look upon the scarlet letter as the token, not of that one sin for which she had borne so long and dreary a penance, but of her many good deeds since. "Do you see that woman with the embroidered badge?" they would say to strangers. "It is our Hester—the town's own Hester—who is so kind to the poor, so helpful to the sick, so comfortable to the afflicted!" Then, it is true, the propensity of human nature to tell the very worst of itself, when embodied in the person of another, would constrain them to whisper the black scandal of bygone years. It was none the less a fact, however, that in the eyes of the very men who spoke thus, the scarlet letter had the effect of the cross on a nun's bosom. It imparted to the wearer a kind of sacredness, which enabled her to walk securely amid all peril. Had she fallen among thieves, it would have kept her safe. It was reported, and believed by many, that an Indian had drawn his arrow against the badge, and that the missile struck it, and fell harmless to the ground.

The effect of the symbol—or rather, of the position in respect to society that was indicated by it—on the mind of Hester Prynne herself was powerful and peculiar. All the light and graceful foliage of her character had been withered up by this red-hot brand, and had long ago fallen away, leaving a bare and harsh outline, which might have been repulsive had she possessed friends or companions to be repelled by it. Even the attractiveness of her person had undergone a similar change. It might be partly owing to the studied austerity of her dress, and partly to the lack of demonstration in her manners. It was a sad transformation, too, that her rich and luxuriant hair had either been cut off, or was so completely hidden by a cap, that not a shining lock of it ever once gushed into the sunshine. It was due in part to all these causes, but still more to something else, that there seemed to be no longer anything in Hester's face for Love to dwell upon; nothing in Hester's form, though majestic and statue like, that Passion would ever dream of clasping in its embrace; nothing in Hester's bosom to make it ever again the pillow of Affection. Some attribute had departed from her, the permanence of which had been essential to keep her a woman. Such is frequently the fate, and such the stern development, of the feminine character and person, when the woman has encountered, and lived through, an experience of peculiar severity. If she be all tenderness, she will die. If she survive, the tenderness will either be crushed out of her, or—and the outward semblance is the same—crushed so deeply into her heart that it can never show itself more. The latter is perhaps the truest theory. She who has once been a woman, and ceased to be so, might at any moment become a woman again, if there were only the magic touch to effect the transformation. We shall see whether Hester Prynne were ever afterwards so touched and so transfigured.

Much of the marble coldness of Hester's impression was to be attributed to the circumstance that her life had turned, in a great measure, from passion and feeling to thought. Standing alone in the world—alone, as to any dependence on society, and with little Pearl to be guided and protected—alone, and hopeless of retrieving her position, even had she not scorned to consider it desirable—she cast away the fragment a broken chain. The world's law was no law for her mind. It was an age in which the human intellect, newly emancipated, had taken a more active and a wider range than for many centuries before. Men of the sword had overthrown nobles and kings. Men bolder than these had overthrown and rearranged—not actually, but within the sphere of theory, which was their most real abode—the whole system of ancient prejudice, wherewith was linked much of ancient principle. Hester Prynne imbibed this spirit. She assumed a freedom of speculation, then common enough on the other side of the Atlantic, but which our forefathers, had they known it, would have held to be a deadlier crime than that stigmatised by the scarlet letter. In her lonesome cottage, by the seashore, thoughts visited her such as dared to enter no other dwelling in New England; shadowy guests, that would have been as perilous as demons to their entertainer, could they have been seen so much as knocking at her door.

It is remarkable that persons who speculate the most boldly often conform with the most perfect quietude to the external regulations of society. The thought suffices them, without investing itself in the flesh and blood of action. So it seemed to be with Hester. Yet, had little Pearl never come to her from the spiritual world, it might have been far otherwise. Then she might have come down to us in history, hand in hand with Ann Hutchinson, as the foundress of a religious sect. She might, in one of her phases, have been a prophetess. She might, and not improbably would, have suffered death from the stern tribunals of the period, for attempting to undermine the foundations of the Puritan establishment. But, in the education of her child, the mother's enthusiasm thought had something to wreak itself upon. Providence, in the person of this little girl, had assigned to Hester's charge, the germ and blossom of womanhood, to be cherished and developed amid a host of difficulties. Everything was against her. The world was hostile. The child's own nature had something wrong in it which continually betokened that she had been born amiss—the effluence of her mother's lawless passion—and often impelled Hester to ask, in bitterness of heart, whether it were for ill or good that the poor little creature had been born at all.

Indeed, the same dark question often rose into her mind with reference to the whole race of womanhood. Was existence worth accepting even to the happiest among them? As concerned her own individual existence, she had long ago decided in the negative, and dismissed the point as settled. A tendency to speculation, though it may keep women quiet, as it does man, yet makes her sad. She discerns, it may be, such a hopeless task before her. As a first step, the whole system of society is to be torn down and built up anew. Then the very nature of the opposite sex, or its long hereditary habit, which has become like nature, is to be essentially modified before woman can be allowed to assume what seems a fair and suitable position. Finally, all other difficulties being obviated, woman cannot take advantage of these preliminary reforms until she herself shall have undergone a still mightier change, in which, perhaps, the ethereal essence, wherein she has her truest life, will be found to have evaporated. A woman never overcomes these problems by any exercise of thought. They are not to be solved, or only in one way. If her heart chance to come uppermost, they vanish. Thus Hester Prynne, whose heart had lost its regular and healthy throb, wandered without a clue in the dark labyrinth of mind; now turned aside by an insurmountable precipice; now starting back from a deep chasm. There was wild and ghastly scenery all around her, and a home and comfort nowhere. At times a fearful doubt strove to possess her soul, whether it were not better to send Pearl at once to Heaven, and go herself to such futurity as Eternal Justice should provide.

The scarlet letter had not done its office. Now, however, her interview with the Reverend Mr. Dimmesdale, on the night of his vigil, had given her a new theme of reflection, and held up to her an object that appeared worthy of any exertion and sacrifice for its attainment. She had witnessed the intense misery beneath which the minister struggled, or, to speak more accurately, had ceased to struggle. She saw that he stood on the verge of lunacy, if he had not already stepped across it. It was impossible to doubt that, whatever painful efficacy there might be in the secret sting of remorse, a deadlier venom had been infused into it by the hand that proffered relief. A secret enemy had been continually by his side, under the semblance of a friend and helper, and had availed himself of the opportunities thus afforded for tampering with the delicate springs of Mr. Dimmesdale's nature. Hester could not but ask herself whether there had not originally been a defect of truth, courage, and loyalty on her own part, in allowing the minister to be thrown into position where so much evil was to be foreboded and nothing auspicious to be hoped. Her only justification lay in the fact that she had been able to discern no method of rescuing him from a blacker ruin than had overwhelmed herself except by acquiescing in Roger Chillingworth's scheme of disguise. Under that impulse she had made her choice, and had chosen, as it now appeared, the more wretched alternative of the two. She determined to redeem her error so far as it might yet be possible. Strengthened by years of hard and solemn trial, she felt herself no longer so inadequate to cope with Roger Chillingworth as on that night, abased by sin and half-maddened by the ignominy that was still new, when they had talked together in the prison-chamber. She had climbed her way since then to a higher point. The old man, on the other hand, had brought himself nearer to her level, or, perhaps, below it, by the revenge which he had stooped for.

In fine, Hester Prynne resolved to meet her former husband, and do what might be in her power for the rescue of the victim on whom he had so evidently set his gripe. The occasion was not long to seek. One afternoon, walking with Pearl in a retired part of the peninsula, she beheld the old physician with a basket on one arm and a staff in the other hand, stooping along the ground in quest of roots and herbs to concoct his medicine withal.

XIV. Hester and the Physician

Hester bade little Pearl run down to the margin of the water, and play with the shells and tangled sea-weed, until she should have talked awhile with yonder gatherer of herbs. So the child flew away like a bird, and, making bare her small white feet went pattering along the moist margin of the sea. Here and there she came to a full stop, ad peeped curiously into a pool, left by the retiring tide as a mirror for Pearl to see her face in. Forth peeped at her, out of the pool, with dark, glistening curls around her head, and an elf-smile in her eyes, the image of a little maid whom Pearl, having no other playmate, invited to take her hand and run a race with her. But the visionary little maid on her part, beckoned likewise, as if to say—"This is a better place; come thou into the pool." And Pearl, stepping in mid-leg deep, beheld her own white feet at the bottom; while, out of a still lower depth, came the gleam of a kind of fragmentary smile, floating to and fro in the agitated water.

Meanwhile her mother had accosted the physician. "I would speak a word with you," said she—"a word that concerns us much."

"Aha! and is it Mistress Hester that has a word for old Roger Chillingworth?" answered he, raising himself from his stooping posture. "With all my heart! Why, mistress, I hear good tidings of you on all hands! No longer ago than yester-eve, a magistrate, a wise and godly man, was discoursing of your affairs, Mistress Hester, and whispered me that there had been question concerning you in the council. It was debated whether or no, with safety to the commonweal, yonder scarlet letter might be taken off your bosom. On my life, Hester, I made my intreaty to the worshipful magistrate that it might be done forthwith."

"It lies not in the pleasure of the magistrates to take off the badge," calmly replied Hester. "Were I worthy to be quit of it, it would fall away of its own nature, or be transformed into something that should speak a different purport."

"Nay, then, wear it, if it suit you better," rejoined he, "A woman must needs follow her own fancy touching the adornment of her person. The letter is gaily embroidered, and shows right bravely on your bosom!"

All this while Hester had been looking steadily at the old man, and was shocked, as well as wonder-smitten, to discern what a change had been wrought upon him within the past seven years. It was not so much that he had grown older; for though the traces of advancing life were visible he bore his age well, and seemed to retain a wiry vigour and alertness. But the former aspect of an intellectual and studious man, calm and quiet, which was what she best remembered in him, had altogether vanished, and been succeeded by a eager, searching, almost fierce, yet carefully guarded look. It seemed to be his wish and purpose to mask this expression with a smile, but the latter played him false, and flickered over his visage so derisively that the spectator could see his blackness all the better for it. Ever and anon, too, there came a glare of red light out of his eyes, as if the old man's soul were on fire and kept on smouldering duskily within his breast, until by some casual puff of passion it was blown into a momentary flame. This he repressed as speedily as possible, and strove to look as if nothing of the kind had happened.

In a word, old Roger Chillingworth was a striking evidence of man's faculty of transforming himself into a devil, if he will only, for a reasonable space of time, undertake a devil's office. This unhappy person had effected such a transformation by devoting himself for seven years to the constant analysis of a heart full of torture, and deriving his enjoyment thence, and adding fuel to those fiery tortures which he analysed and gloated over.

The scarlet letter burned on Hester Prynne's bosom. Here was another ruin, the responsibility of which came partly home to her.

"What see you in my face," asked the physician, "that you look at it so earnestly?"

"Something that would make me weep, if there were any tears bitter enough for it," answered she. "But let it pass! It is of yonder miserable man that I would speak."

"And what of him?" cried Roger Chillingworth, eagerly, as if he loved the topic, and were glad of an opportunity to discuss it with the only person of whom he could make a confidant. "Not to hide the truth, Mistress Hester, my thoughts happen just now to be busy with the gentleman. So speak freely and I will make answer."

"When we last spake together," said Hester, "now seven years ago, it was your pleasure to extort a promise of secrecy as touching the former relation betwixt yourself and me. As the life and good fame of yonder man were in your hands there seemed no choice to me, save to be silent in accordance with your behest. Yet it was not without heavy misgivings that I thus bound myself, for, having cast off all duty towards other human beings, there remained a duty towards him, and something whispered me that I was betraying it in pledging myself to keep your counsel. Since that day no man is so near to him as you. You tread behind his every footstep. You are beside him, sleeping and waking. You search his thoughts. You burrow and rankle in his heart! Your clutch is on his life, and you cause him to die daily a living death, and still he knows you not. In permitting this I have surely acted a false part by the only man to whom the power was left me to be true!"

"What choice had you?" asked Roger Chillingworth. "My finger, pointed at this man, would have hurled him from his pulpit into a dungeon, thence, peradventure, to the gallows!"

"It had been better so!" said Hester Prynne.

"What evil have I done the man?" asked Roger Chillingworth again. "I tell thee, Hester Prynne, the richest fee that ever physician earned from monarch could not have bought such care as I have wasted on this miserable priest! But for my aid his life would have burned away in torments within the first two years after the perpetration of his crime and thine. For, Hester, his spirit lacked the strength that could have borne up, as thine has, beneath a burden like thy scarlet letter. Oh, I could reveal a goodly secret! But enough. What art can do, I have exhausted on him. That he now breathes and creeps about on earth is owing all to me!"

"Better he had died at once!" said Hester Prynne.

"Yea, woman, thou sayest truly!" cried old Roger Chillingworth, letting the lurid fire of his heart blaze out before her eyes. "Better had he died at once! Never did mortal suffer what this man has suffered. And all, all, in the sight of his worst enemy! He has been conscious of me. He has felt an influence dwelling always upon him like a curse. He knew, by some spiritual sense—for the Creator never made another being so sensitive as this—he knew that no friendly hand was pulling at his heartstrings, and that an eye was looking curiously into him, which sought only evil, and found it. But he knew not that the eye and hand were mine! With the superstition common to his brotherhood, he fancied himself given over to a fiend, to be tortured with frightful dreams and desperate thoughts, the sting of remorse and despair of pardon, as a foretaste of what awaits him beyond the grave. But it was the constant shadow of my presence, the closest propinquity of the man whom he had most vilely wronged, and who had grown to exist only by this perpetual poison of the direst revenge! Yea, indeed, he did not err, there was a fiend at his elbow! A mortal man, with once a human heart, has become a fiend for his especial torment."

The unfortunate physician, while uttering these words, lifted his hands with a look of horror, as if he had beheld some frightful shape, which he could not recognise, usurping the place of his own image in a glass. It was one of those moments—which sometimes occur only at the interval of years—when a man's moral aspect is faithfully revealed to his mind's eye. Not improbably he had never before viewed himself as he did now.

"Hast thou not tortured him enough?" said Hester, noticing the old man's look. "Has he not paid thee all?"

"No, no! He has but increased the debt!" answered the physician, and as he proceeded, his manner lost its fiercer characteristics, and subsided into gloom. "Dost thou remember me, Hester, as I was nine years agone? Even then I was in the autumn of my days, nor was it the early autumn. But all my life had been made up of earnest, studious, thoughtful, quiet years, bestowed faithfully for the increase of mine own knowledge, and faithfully, too, though this latter object was but casual to the other—faithfully for the advancement of human welfare. No life had been more peaceful and innocent than mine; few lives so rich with benefits conferred. Dost thou remember me? Was I not, though you might deem me cold, nevertheless a man thoughtful for others, craving little for himself—kind, true, just and of constant, if not warm affections? Was I not all this?"

"All this, and more," said Hester.

"And what am I now?" demanded he, looking into her face, and permitting the whole evil within him to be written on his features. "I have already told thee what I am—a fiend! Who made me so?"

"It was myself," cried Hester, shuddering. "It was I, not less than he. Why hast thou not avenged thyself on me?"

"I have left thee to the scarlet letter," replied Roger Chillingworth. "If that has not avenged me, I can do no more!"

He laid his finger on it with a smile.

"It has avenged thee," answered Hester Prynne.

"I judged no less," said the physician. "And now what wouldst thou with me touching this man?"

"I must reveal the secret," answered Hester, firmly. "He must discern thee in thy true character. What may be the result I know not. But this long debt of confidence, due from me to him, whose bane and ruin I have been, shall at length be paid. So far as concerns the overthrow or preservation of his fair fame and his earthly state, and perchance his life, he is in my hands. Nor do I—whom the scarlet letter has disciplined to truth, though it be the truth of red-hot iron entering into the soul—nor do I perceive such advantage in his living any longer a life of ghastly emptiness, that I shall stoop to implore thy mercy. Do with him as thou wilt! There is no good for him, no good for me, no good for thee. There is no good for little Pearl. There is no path to guide us out of this dismal maze."

"Woman, I could well-nigh pity thee," said Roger Chillingworth, unable to restrain a thrill of admiration too, for there was a quality almost majestic in the despair which she expressed. "Thou hadst great elements. Peradventure, hadst thou met earlier with a better love than mine, this evil had not been. I pity thee, for the good that has been wasted in thy nature."

"And I thee," answered Hester Prynne, "for the hatred that has transformed a wise and just man to a fiend! Wilt thou yet purge it out of thee, and be once more human? If not for his sake, then doubly for thine own! Forgive, and leave his further retribution to the Power that claims it! I said, but now, that there could be no good event for him, or thee, or me, who are here wandering together in this gloomy maze of evil, and stumbling at every step over the guilt wherewith we have strewn our path. It is not so! There might be good for thee, and thee alone, since thou hast been deeply wronged and hast it at thy will to pardon. Wilt thou give up that only privilege? Wilt thou reject that priceless benefit?"

"Peace, Hester—peace!" replied the old man, with gloomy sternness—"it is not granted me to pardon. I have no such power as thou tellest me of. My old faith, long forgotten, comes back to me, and explains all that we do, and all we suffer. By thy first step awry, thou didst plant the germ of evil; but since that moment it has all been a dark necessity. Ye that have wronged me are not sinful, save in a kind of typical illusion; neither am I fiend-like, who have snatched a fiend's office from his hands. It is our fate. Let the black flower blossom as it may! Now, go thy ways, and deal as thou wilt with yonder man."

He waved his hand, and betook himself again to his employment of gathering herbs.

XV. Hester and Pearl

So Roger Chillingworth—a deformed old figure with a face that haunted men's memories longer than they liked—took leave of Hester Prynne, and went stooping away along the earth. He gathered here and there a herb, or grubbed up a root and put it into the basket on his arm. His gray beard almost touched the ground as he crept onward. Hester gazed after him a little while, looking with a half fantastic curiosity to see whether the tender grass of early spring would not be blighted beneath him and show the wavering track of his footsteps, sere and brown, across its cheerful verdure. She wondered what sort of herbs they were which the old man was so sedulous to gather. Would not the earth, quickened to an evil purpose by the sympathy of his eye, greet him with poisonous shrubs of species hitherto unknown, that would start up under his fingers? Or might it suffice him that every wholesome growth should be converted into something deleterious and malignant at his touch? Did the sun, which shone so brightly everywhere else, really fall upon him? Or was there, as it rather seemed, a circle of ominous shadow moving along with his deformity whichever way he turned himself? And whither was he now going? Would he not suddenly sink into the earth, leaving a barren and blasted spot, where, in due course of time, would be seen deadly nightshade, dogwood, henbane, and whatever else of vegetable wickedness the climate could produce, all flourishing with hideous luxuriance? Or would he spread bat's wings and flee away, looking so much the uglier the higher he rose towards heaven?

"Be it sin or no," said Hester Prynne, bitterly, as still she gazed after him, "I hate the man!"

She upbraided herself for the sentiment, but could not overcome or lessen it. Attempting to do so, she thought of those long-past days in a distant land, when he used to emerge at eventide from the seclusion of his study and sit down in the firelight of their home, and in the light of her nuptial smile. He needed to bask himself in that smile, he said, in order that the chill of so many lonely hours among his books might be taken off the scholar's heart. Such scenes had once appeared not otherwise than happy, but now, as viewed through the dismal medium of her subsequent life, they classed themselves among her ugliest remembrances. She marvelled how such scenes could have been! She marvelled how she could ever have been wrought upon to marry him! She deemed in her crime most to be repented of, that she had ever endured and reciprocated the lukewarm grasp of his hand, and had suffered the smile of her lips and eyes to mingle and melt into his own. And it seemed a fouler offence committed by Roger Chillingworth than any which had since been done him, that, in the time when her heart knew no better, he had persuaded her to fancy herself happy by his side.

"Yes, I hate him!" repeated Hester more bitterly than before. "He betrayed me! He has done me worse wrong than I did him!"

Let men tremble to win the hand of woman, unless they win along with it the utmost passion of her heart! Else it may be their miserable fortune, as it was Roger Chillingworth's, when some mightier touch than their own may have awakened all her sensibilities, to be reproached even for the calm content, the marble image of happiness, which they will have imposed upon her as the warm reality. But Hester ought long ago to have done with this injustice. What did it betoken? Had seven long years, under the torture of the scarlet letter, inflicted so much of misery and wrought out no repentance?

The emotion of that brief space, while she stood gazing after the crooked figure of old Roger Chillingworth, threw a dark light on Hester's state of mind, revealing much that she might not otherwise have acknowledged to herself.

He being gone, she summoned back her child.

"Pearl! Little Pearl! Where are you?"

Pearl, whose activity of spirit never flagged, had been at no loss for amusement while her mother talked with the old gatherer of herbs. At first, as already told, she had flirted fancifully with her own image in a pool of water, beckoning the phantom forth, and—as it declined to venture—seeking a passage for herself into its sphere of impalpable earth and unattainable sky. Soon finding, however, that either she or the image was unreal, she turned elsewhere for better pastime. She made little boats out of birch-bark, and freighted them with snailshells, and sent out more ventures on the mighty deep than any merchant in New England; but the larger part of them foundered near the shore. She seized a live horse-shoe by the tail, and made prize of several five-fingers, and laid out a jelly-fish to melt in the warm sun. Then she took up the white foam that streaked the line of the advancing tide, and threw it upon the breeze, scampering after it with winged footsteps to catch the great snowflakes ere they fell. Perceiving a flock of beach-birds that fed and fluttered along the shore, the naughty child picked up her apron full of pebbles, and, creeping from rock to rock after these small sea-fowl, displayed remarkable dexterity in pelting them. One little gray bird, with a white breast, Pearl was almost sure had been hit by a pebble, and fluttered away with a broken wing. But then the elf-child sighed, and gave up her sport, because it grieved her to have done harm to a little being that was as wild as the sea-breeze, or as wild as Pearl herself.

Her final employment was to gather seaweed of various kinds, and make herself a scarf or mantle, and a head-dress, and thus assume the aspect of a little mermaid. She inherited her mother's gift for devising drapery and costume. As the last touch to her mermaid's garb, Pearl took some eel-grass and imitated, as best she could, on her own bosom the decoration with which she was so familiar on her mother's. A letter—the letter A—but freshly green instead of scarlet. The child bent her chin upon her breast, and contemplated this device with strange interest, even as if the one only thing for which she had been sent into the world was to make out its hidden import.

"I wonder if mother will ask me what it means?" thought Pearl.

Just then she heard her mother's voice, and, flitting along as lightly as one of the little sea-birds, appeared before Hester Prynne dancing, laughing, and pointing her finger to the ornament upon her bosom.

"My little Pearl," said Hester, after a moment's silence, "the green letter, and on thy childish bosom, has no purport. But dost thou know, my child, what this letter means which thy mother is doomed to wear?"

"Yes, mother," said the child. "It is the great letter A. Thou hast taught me in the horn-book."

Hester looked steadily into her little face; but though there was that singular expression which she had so often remarked in her black eyes, she could not satisfy herself whether Pearl really attached any meaning to the symbol. She felt a morbid desire to ascertain the point.

"Dost thou know, child, wherefore thy mother wears this letter?"

"Truly do I!" answered Pearl, looking brightly into her mother's face. "It is for the same reason that the minister keeps his hand over his heart!"

"And what reason is that?" asked Hester, half smiling at the absurd incongruity of the child's observation; but on second thoughts turning pale. "What has the letter to do with any heart save mine?"

"Nay, mother, I have told all I know," said Pearl, more seriously than she was wont to speak. "Ask yonder old man whom thou hast been talking with,—it may be he can tell. But in good earnest now, mother dear, what does this scarlet letter mean?—and why dost thou wear it on thy bosom?—and why does the minister keep his hand over his heart?"

She took her mother's hand in both her own, and gazed into her eyes with an earnestness that was seldom seen in her wild and capricious character. The thought occurred to Hester, that the child might really be seeking to approach her with childlike confidence, and doing what she could, and as intelligently as she knew how, to establish a meeting-point of sympathy. It showed Pearl in an unwonted aspect. Heretofore, the mother, while loving her child with the intensity of a sole affection, had schooled herself to hope for little other return than the waywardness of an April breeze, which spends its time in airy sport, and has its gusts of inexplicable passion, and is petulant in its best of moods, and chills oftener than caresses you, when you take it to your bosom; in requital of which misdemeanours it will sometimes, of its own vague purpose, kiss your cheek with a kind of doubtful tenderness, and play gently with your hair, and then be gone about its other idle business, leaving a dreamy pleasure at your heart. And this, moreover, was a mother's estimate of the child's disposition. Any other observer might have seen few but unamiable traits, and have given them a far darker colouring. But now the idea came strongly into Hester's mind, that Pearl, with her remarkable precocity and acuteness, might already have approached the age when she could have been made a friend, and intrusted with as much of her mother's sorrows as could be imparted, without irreverence either to the parent or the child. In the little chaos of Pearl's character there might be seen emerging and could have been from the very first—the steadfast principles of an unflinching courage—an uncontrollable will—sturdy pride, which might be disciplined into self-respect—and a bitter scorn of many things which, when examined, might be found to have the taint of falsehood in them. She possessed affections, too, though hitherto acrid and disagreeable, as are the richest flavours of unripe fruit. With all these sterling attributes, thought Hester, the evil which she inherited from her mother must be great indeed, if a noble woman do not grow out of this elfish child.

Pearl's inevitable tendency to hover about the enigma of the scarlet letter seemed an innate quality of her being. From the earliest epoch of her conscious life, she had entered upon this as her appointed mission. Hester had often fancied that Providence had a design of justice and retribution, in endowing the child with this marked propensity; but never, until now, had she bethought herself to ask, whether, linked with that design, there might not likewise be a purpose of mercy and beneficence. If little Pearl were entertained with faith and trust, as a spirit messenger no less than an earthly child, might it not be her errand to soothe away the sorrow that lay cold in her mother's heart, and converted it into a tomb?—and to help her to overcome the passion, once so wild, and even yet neither dead nor asleep, but only imprisoned within the same tomb-like heart?

Such were some of the thoughts that now stirred in Hester's mind, with as much vivacity of impression as if they had actually been whispered into her ear. And there was little Pearl, all this while, holding her mother's hand in both her own, and turning her face upward, while she put these searching questions, once and again, and still a third time.

"What does the letter mean, mother? and why dost thou wear it? and why does the minister keep his hand over his heart?"

"What shall I say?" thought Hester to herself. "No! if this be the price of the child's sympathy, I cannot pay it."

Then she spoke aloud—

"Silly Pearl," said she, "what questions are these? There are many things in this world that a child must not ask about. What know I of the minister's heart? And as for the scarlet letter, I wear it for the sake of its gold thread."

In all the seven bygone years, Hester Prynne had never before been false to the symbol on her bosom. It may be that it was the talisman of a stern and severe, but yet a guardian spirit, who now forsook her; as recognising that, in spite of his strict watch over her heart, some new evil had crept into it, or some old one had never been expelled. As for little Pearl, the earnestness soon passed out of her face.

But the child did not see fit to let the matter drop. Two or three times, as her mother and she went homeward, and as often at supper-time, and while Hester was putting her to bed, and once after she seemed to be fairly asleep, Pearl looked up, with mischief gleaming in her black eyes.

"Mother," said she, "what does the scarlet letter mean?"

And the next morning, the first indication the child gave of being awake was by popping up her head from the pillow, and making that other enquiry, which she had so unaccountably connected with her investigations about the scarlet letter—

"Mother!—Mother!—Why does the minister keep his hand over his heart?"

"Hold thy tongue, naughty child!" answered her mother, with an asperity that she had never permitted to herself before. "Do not tease me; else I shall put thee into the dark closet!"

XVI. A Forest Walk

Hester Prynne remained constant in her resolve to make known to Mr. Dimmesdale, at whatever risk of present pain or ulterior consequences, the true character of the man who had crept into his intimacy. For several days, however, she vainly sought an opportunity of addressing him in some of the meditative walks which she knew him to be in the habit of taking along the shores of the Peninsula, or on the wooded hills of the neighbouring country. There would have been no scandal, indeed, nor peril to the holy whiteness of the clergyman's good fame, had she visited him in his own study, where many a penitent, ere now, had confessed sins of perhaps as deep a dye as the one betokened by the scarlet letter. But, partly that she dreaded the secret or undisguised interference of old Roger Chillingworth, and partly that her conscious heart imparted suspicion where none could have been felt, and partly that both the minister and she would need the whole wide world to breathe in, while they talked together—for all these reasons Hester never thought of meeting him in any narrower privacy than beneath the open sky.

At last, while attending a sick chamber, whither the Rev. Mr. Dimmesdale had been summoned to make a prayer, she learnt that he had gone, the day before, to visit the Apostle Eliot, among his Indian converts. He would probably return by a certain hour in the afternoon of the morrow. Betimes, therefore, the next day, Hester took little Pearl—who was necessarily the companion of all her mother's expeditions, however inconvenient her presence—and set forth.

The road, after the two wayfarers had crossed from the Peninsula to the mainland, was no other than a foot-path. It straggled onward into the mystery of the primeval forest. This hemmed it in so narrowly, and stood so black and dense on either side, and disclosed such imperfect glimpses of the sky above, that, to Hester's mind, it imaged not amiss the moral wilderness in which she had so long been wandering. The day was chill and sombre. Overhead was a gray expanse of cloud, slightly stirred, however, by a breeze; so that a gleam of flickering sunshine might now and then be seen at its solitary play along the path. This flitting cheerfulness was always at the further extremity of some long vista through the forest. The sportive sunlight—feebly sportive, at best, in the predominant pensiveness of the day and scene—withdrew itself as they came nigh, and left the spots where it had danced the drearier, because they had hoped to find them bright.

"Mother," said little Pearl, "the sunshine does not love you. It runs away and hides itself, because it is afraid of something on your bosom. Now, see! There it is, playing a good way off. Stand you here, and let me run and catch it. I am but a child. It will not flee from me—for I wear nothing on my bosom yet!"

"Nor ever will, my child, I hope," said Hester.

"And why not, mother?" asked Pearl, stopping short, just at the beginning of her race. "Will not it come of its own accord when I am a woman grown?"

"Run away, child," answered her mother, "and catch the sunshine! It will soon be gone."

Pearl set forth at a great pace, and as Hester smiled to perceive, did actually catch the sunshine, and stood laughing in the midst of it, all brightened by its splendour, and scintillating with the vivacity excited by rapid motion. The light lingered about the lonely child, as if glad of such a playmate, until her mother had drawn almost nigh enough to step into the magic circle too.

"It will go now," said Pearl, shaking her head.

"See!" answered Hester, smiling; "now I can stretch out my hand and grasp some of it."

As she attempted to do so, the sunshine vanished; or, to judge from the bright expression that was dancing on Pearl's features, her mother could have fancied that the child had absorbed it into herself, and would give it forth again, with a gleam about her path, as they should plunge into some gloomier shade. There was no other attribute that so much impressed her with a sense of new and untransmitted vigour in Pearl's nature, as this never failing vivacity of spirits: she had not the disease of sadness, which almost all children, in these latter days, inherit, with the scrofula, from the troubles of their ancestors. Perhaps this, too, was a disease, and but the reflex of the wild energy with which Hester had fought against her sorrows before Pearl's birth. It was certainly a doubtful charm, imparting a hard, metallic lustre to the child's character. She wanted— what some people want throughout life—a grief that should deeply touch her, and thus humanise and make her capable of sympathy. But there was time enough yet for little Pearl.

"Come, my child!" said Hester, looking about her from the spot where Pearl had stood still in the sunshine—"we will sit down a little way within the wood, and rest ourselves."

"I am not aweary, mother," replied the little girl. "But you may sit down, if you will tell me a story meanwhile."

"A story, child!" said Hester. "And about what?"

"Oh, a story about the Black Man," answered Pearl, taking hold of her mother's gown, and looking up, half earnestly, half mischievously, into her face.

"How he haunts this forest, and carries a book with him a big, heavy book, with iron clasps; and how this ugly Black Man offers his book and an iron pen to everybody that meets him here among the trees; and they are to write their names with their own blood; and then he sets his mark on their bosoms. Didst thou ever meet the Black Man, mother?"

"And who told you this story, Pearl," asked her mother, recognising a common superstition of the period.

"It was the old dame in the chimney corner, at the house where you watched last night," said the child. "But she fancied me asleep while she was talking of it. She said that a thousand and a thousand people had met him here, and had written in his book, and have his mark on them. And that ugly tempered lady, old Mistress Hibbins, was one. And, mother, the old dame said that this scarlet letter was the Black Man's mark on thee, and that it glows like a red flame when thou meetest him at midnight, here in the dark wood. Is it true, mother? And dost thou go to meet him in the nighttime?"

"Didst thou ever awake and find thy mother gone?" asked Hester. "Not that I remember," said the child. "If thou fearest to leave me in our cottage, thou mightest take me along with thee. I would very gladly go! But, mother, tell me now! Is there such a Black Man? And didst thou ever meet him? And is this his mark?"

"Wilt thou let me be at peace, if I once tell thee?" asked her mother.

"Yes, if thou tellest me all," answered Pearl.

"Once in my life I met the Black Man!" said her mother. This scarlet letter is his mark!"

Thus conversing, they entered sufficiently deep into the wood to secure themselves from the observation of any casual passenger along the forest track. Here they sat down on a luxuriant heap of moss; which at some epoch of the preceding century, had been a gigantic pine, with its roots and trunk in the darksome shade, and its head aloft in the upper atmosphere It was a little dell where they had seated themselves, with a leaf-strewn bank rising gently on either side, and a brook flowing through the midst, over a bed of fallen and drowned leaves. The trees impending over it had flung down great branches from time to time, which choked up the current, and compelled it to form eddies and black depths at some points; while, in its swifter and livelier passages there appeared a channel-way of pebbles, and brown, sparkling sand. Letting the eyes follow along the course of the stream, they could catch the reflected light from its water, at some short distance within the forest, but soon lost all traces of it amid the bewilderment of tree-trunks and underbush, and here and there a huge rock covered over with gray lichens. All these giant trees and boulders of granite seemed intent on making a mystery of the course of this small brook; fearing, perhaps, that, with its never-ceasing loquacity, it should whisper tales out of the heart of the old forest whence it flowed, or mirror its revelations on the smooth surface of a pool. Continually, indeed, as it stole onward, the streamlet kept up a babble, kind, quiet, soothing, but melancholy, like the voice of a young child that was spending its infancy without playfulness, and knew not how to be merry among sad acquaintance and events of sombre hue.

"Oh, brook! Oh, foolish and tiresome little brook!" cried Pearl, after listening awhile to its talk, "Why art thou so sad? Pluck up a spirit, and do not be all the time sighing and murmuring!"

But the brook, in the course of its little lifetime among the forest trees, had gone through so solemn an experience that it could not help talking about it, and seemed to have nothing else to say. Pearl resembled the brook, inasmuch as the current of her life gushed from a well-spring as mysterious, and had flowed through scenes shadowed as heavily with gloom. But, unlike the little stream, she danced and sparkled, and prattled airily along her course.

"What does this sad little brook say, mother? inquired she.

"If thou hadst a sorrow of thine own, the brook might tell thee of it," answered her mother, "even as it is telling me of mine. But now, Pearl, I hear a footstep along the path, and the noise of one putting aside the branches. I would have thee betake thyself to play, and leave me to speak with him that comes yonder."

"Is it the Black Man?" asked Pearl.

"Wilt thou go and play, child?" repeated her mother, "But do not stray far into the wood. And take heed that thou come at my first call."

"Yes, mother," answered Pearl, "But if it be the Black Man, wilt thou not let me stay a moment, and look at him, with his big book under his arm?"

"Go, silly child!" said her mother impatiently. "It is no Black Man! Thou canst see him now, through the trees. It is the minister!"

"And so it is!" said the child. "And, mother, he has his hand over his heart! Is it because, when the minister wrote his name in the book, the Black Man set his mark in that place? But why does he not wear it outside his bosom, as thou dost, mother?"

"Go now, child, and thou shalt tease me as thou wilt another time," cried Hester Prynne. "But do not stray far. Keep where thou canst hear the babble of the brook."

The child went singing away, following up the current of the brook, and striving to mingle a more lightsome cadence with its melancholy voice. But the little stream would not be comforted, and still kept telling its unintelligible secret of some very mournful mystery that had happened—or making a prophetic lamentation about something that was yet to happen—within the verge of the dismal forest. So Pearl, who had enough of shadow in her own little life, chose to break off all acquaintance with this repining brook. She set herself, therefore, to gathering violets and wood-anemones, and some scarlet columbines that she found growing in the crevice of a high rock.

When her elf-child had departed, Hester Prynne made a step or two towards the track that led through the forest, but still remained under the deep shadow of the trees. She beheld the minister advancing along the path entirely alone, and leaning on a staff which he had cut by the wayside. He looked haggard and feeble, and betrayed a nerveless despondency in his air, which had never so remarkably characterised him in his walks about the settlement, nor in any other situation where he deemed himself liable to notice. Here it was woefully visible, in this intense seclusion of the forest, which of itself would have been a heavy trial to the spirits. There was a listlessness in his gait, as if he saw no reason for taking one step further, nor felt any desire to do so, but would have been glad, could he be glad of anything, to fling himself down at the root of the nearest tree, and lie there passive for evermore. The leaves might bestrew him, and the soil gradually accumulate and form a little hillock over his frame, no matter whether there were life in it or no. Death was too definite an object to be wished for or avoided.

To Hester's eye, the Reverend Mr. Dimmesdale exhibited no symptom of positive and vivacious suffering, except that, as little Pearl had remarked, he kept his hand over his heart.

XVII. The Pastor and His Parishioner

Slowly as the minister walked, he had almost gone by before Hester Prynne could gather voice enough to attract his observation. At length she succeeded.

"Arthur Dimmesdale!" she said, faintly at first, then louder, but hoarsely—"Arthur Dimmesdale!"

"Who speaks?" answered the minister. Gathering himself quickly up, he stood more erect, like a man taken by surprise in a mood to which he was reluctant to have witnesses. Throwing his eyes anxiously in the direction of the voice, he indistinctly beheld a form under the trees, clad in garments so sombre, and so little relieved from the gray twilight into which the clouded sky and the heavy foliage had darkened the noontide, that he knew not whether it were a woman or a shadow. It may be that his pathway through life was haunted thus by a spectre that had stolen out from among his thoughts.

He made a step nigher, and discovered the scarlet letter.

"Hester! Hester Prynne!', said he; "is it thou? Art thou in life?"

"Even so." she answered. "In such life as has been mine these seven years past! And thou, Arthur Dimmesdale, dost thou yet live?"

It was no wonder that they thus questioned one another's actual and bodily existence, and even doubted of their own. So strangely did they meet in the dim wood that it was like the first encounter in the world beyond the grave of two spirits who had been intimately connected in their former life, but now stood coldly shuddering in mutual dread, as not yet familiar with their state, nor wonted to the companionship of disembodied beings. Each a ghost, and awe-stricken at the other ghost. They were awe-stricken likewise at themselves, because the crisis flung back to them their consciousness, and revealed to each heart its history and experience, as life never does, except at such breathless epochs. The soul beheld its features in the mirror of the passing moment. It was with fear, and tremulously, and, as it were, by a slow, reluctant necessity, that Arthur Dimmesdale put forth his hand, chill as death, and touched the chill hand of Hester Prynne. The grasp, cold as it was, took away what was dreariest in the interview. They now felt themselves, at least, inhabitants of the same sphere.

Without a word more spoken—neither he nor she assuming the guidance, but with an unexpressed consent—they glided back into the shadow of the woods whence Hester had emerged, and sat down on the heap of moss where she and Pearl had before been sitting. When they found voice to speak, it was at first only to utter remarks and inquiries such as any two acquaintances might have made, about the gloomy sky, the threatening storm, and, next, the health of each. Thus they went onward, not boldly, but step by step, into the themes that were brooding deepest in their hearts. So long estranged by fate and circumstances, they needed something slight and casual to run before and throw open the doors of intercourse, so that their real thoughts might be led across the threshold.

After awhile, the minister fixed his eyes on Hester Prynne's.

"Hester," said he, "hast thou found peace?"

She smiled drearily, looking down upon her bosom.

"Hast thou?" she asked.

"None—nothing but despair!" he answered. "What else could I look for, being what I am, and leading such a life as mine? Were I an atheist—a man devoid of conscience—a wretch with coarse and brutal instincts—I might have found peace long ere now. Nay, I never should have lost it. But, as matters stand with my soul, whatever of good capacity there originally was in me, all of God's gifts that were the choicest have become the ministers of spiritual torment. Hester, I am most miserable!"

"The people reverence thee," said Hester. "And surely thou workest good among them! Doth this bring thee no comfort?"

"More misery, Hester!—Only the more misery!" answered the clergyman with a bitter smile. "As concerns the good which I may appear to do, I have no faith in it. It must needs be a delusion. What can a ruined soul like mine effect towards the redemption of other souls?—or a polluted soul towards their purification? And as for the people's reverence, would that it were turned to scorn and hatred! Canst thou deem it, Hester, a consolation that I must stand up in my pulpit, and meet so many eyes turned upward to my face, as if the light of heaven were beaming from it!—must see my flock hungry for the truth, and listening to my words as if a tongue of Pentecost were speaking!—and then look inward, and discern the black reality of what they idolise? I have laughed, in bitterness and agony of heart, at the contrast between what I seem and what I am! And Satan laughs at it!"

"You wrong yourself in this," said Hester gently.

"You have deeply and sorely repented. Your sin is left behind you in the days long past. Your present life is not less holy, in very truth, than it seems in people's eyes. Is there no reality in the penitence thus sealed and witnessed by good works? And wherefore should it not bring you peace?"

"No, Hester—no!" replied the clergyman. "There is no substance in it] It is cold and dead, and can do nothing for me! Of penance, I have had enough! Of penitence, there has been none! Else, I should long ago have thrown off these garments of mock holiness, and have shown myself to mankind as they will see me at the judgment-seat. Happy are you, Hester, that wear the scarlet letter openly upon your bosom! Mine burns in secret! Thou little knowest what a relief it is, after the torment of a seven years' cheat, to look into an eye that recognises me for what I am! Had I one friend—or were it my worst enemy!—to whom, when sickened with the praises of all other men, I could daily betake myself, and known as the vilest of all sinners, methinks my soul might keep itself alive thereby. Even thus much of truth would save me! But now, it is all falsehood!—all emptiness!—all death!"

Hester Prynne looked into his face, but hesitated to speak. Yet, uttering his long-restrained emotions so vehemently as he did, his words here offered her the very point of circumstances in which to interpose what she came to say. She conquered her fears, and spoke:

"Such a friend as thou hast even now wished for," said she, "with whom to weep over thy sin, thou hast in me, the partner of it!" Again she hesitated, but brought out the words with an effort "Thou hast long had such an enemy, and dwellest with him, under the same roof!"

The minister started to his feet, gasping for breath, and clutching at his heart, as if he would have torn it out of his bosom.

"Ha! What sayest thou?" cried he. "An enemy! And under mine own roof! What mean you?"

Hester Prynne was now fully sensible of the deep injury for which she was responsible to this unhappy man, in permitting him to lie for so many years, or, indeed, for a single moment, at the mercy of one whose purposes could not be other than malevolent. The very contiguity of his enemy, beneath whatever mask the latter might conceal himself, was enough to disturb the magnetic sphere of a being so sensitive as Arthur Dimmesdale. There had been a period when Hester was less alive to this consideration; or, perhaps, in the misanthropy of her own trouble, she left the minister to bear what she might picture to herself as a more tolerable doom. But of late, since the night of his vigil, all her sympathies towards him had been both softened and invigorated. She now read his heart more accurately. She doubted not that the continual presence of Roger Chillingworth—the secret poison of his malignity, infecting all the air about him—and his authorised interference, as a physician, with the minister's physical and spiritual infirmities—that these bad opportunities had been turned to a cruel purpose. By means of them, the sufferer's conscience had been kept in an irritated state, the tendency of which was, not to cure by wholesome pain, but to disorganize and corrupt his spiritual being. Its result, on earth, could hardly fail to be insanity, and hereafter, that eternal alienation from the Good and True, of which madness is perhaps the earthly type.

Such was the ruin to which she had brought the man, once—nay, why should we not speak it?—still so passionately loved! Hester felt that the sacrifice of the clergyman's good name, and death itself, as she had already told Roger Chillingworth, would have been infinitely preferable to the alternative which she had taken upon herself to choose. And now, rather than have had this grievous wrong to confess, she would gladly have laid down on the forest leaves, and died there, at Arthur Dimmesdale's feet.

"Oh, Arthur!" cried she, "forgive me! In all things else, I have striven to be true! Truth was the one virtue which I might have held fast, and did hold fast, through all extremity; save when thy good—thy life—thy fame—were put in question! Then I consented to a deception. But a lie is never good, even though death threaten on the other side! Dost thou not see what I would say? That old man!—the physician!—he whom they call Roger Chillingworth!—he was my husband!"

The minister looked at her for an instant, with all that violence of passion, which—intermixed in more shapes than one with his higher, purer, softer qualities—was, in fact, the portion of him which the devil claimed, and through which he sought to win the rest. Never was there a blacker or a fiercer frown than Hester now encountered. For the brief space that it lasted, it was a dark transfiguration. But his character had been so much enfeebled by suffering, that even its lower energies were incapable of more than a temporary struggle. He sank down on the ground, and buried his face in his hands.

"I might have known it," murmured he—"I did know it! Was not the secret told me, in the natural recoil of my heart at the first sight of him, and as often as I have seen him since? Why did I not understand? Oh, Hester Prynne, thou little, little knowest all the horror of this thing! And the shame!—the indelicacy!—the horrible ugliness of this exposure of a sick and guilty heart to the very eye that would gloat over it! Woman, woman, thou art accountable for this!—I cannot forgive thee!"

"Thou shalt forgive me!" cried Hester, flinging herself on the fallen leaves beside him. "Let God punish! Thou shalt forgive!"

With sudden and desperate tenderness she threw her arms around him, and pressed his head against her bosom, little caring though his cheek rested on the scarlet letter. He would have released himself, but strove in vain to do so. Hester would not set him free, lest he should look her sternly in the face. All the world had frowned on her—for seven long years had it frowned upon this lonely woman—and still she bore it all, nor ever once turned away her firm, sad eyes. Heaven, likewise, had frowned upon her, and she had not died. But the frown of this pale, weak, sinful, and sorrow-stricken man was what Hester could not bear, and live!

"Wilt thou yet forgive me?" she repeated, over and over again. "Wilt thou not frown? Wilt thou forgive?"

"I do forgive you, Hester," replied the minister at length, with a deep utterance, out of an abyss of sadness, but no anger. "I freely forgive you now. May God forgive us both. We are not, Hester, the worst sinners in the world. There is one worse than even the polluted priest! That old man's revenge has been blacker than my sin. He has violated, in cold blood, the sanctity of a human heart. Thou and I, Hester, never did so!"

"Never, never!" whispered she. "What we did had a consecration of its own. We felt it so! We said so to each other. Hast thou forgotten it?"

"Hush, Hester!" said Arthur Dimmesdale, rising from the ground. "No; I have not forgotten!"

They sat down again, side by side, and hand clasped in hand, on the mossy trunk of the fallen tree. Life had never brought them a gloomier hour; it was the point whither their pathway had so long been tending, and darkening ever, as it stole along—and yet it unclosed a charm that made them linger upon it, and claim another, and another, and, after all, another moment. The forest was obscure around them, and creaked with a blast that was passing through it. The boughs were tossing heavily above their heads; while one solemn old tree groaned dolefully to another, as if telling the sad story of the pair that sat beneath, or constrained to forbode evil to come.

And yet they lingered. How dreary looked the forest-track that led backward to the settlement, where Hester Prynne must take up again the burden of her ignominy and the minister the hollow mockery of his good name! So they lingered an instant longer. No golden light had ever been so precious as the gloom of this dark forest. Here seen only by his eyes, the scarlet letter need not burn into the bosom of the fallen woman! Here seen only by her eyes, Arthur Dimmesdale, false to God and man, might be, for one moment true!

He started at a thought that suddenly occurred to him.

"Hester!" cried he, "here is a new horror! Roger Chillingworth knows your purpose to reveal his true character. Will he continue, then, to keep our secret? What will now be the course of his revenge?"

"There is a strange secrecy in his nature," replied Hester, thoughtfully; "and it has grown upon him by the hidden practices of his revenge. I deem it not likely that he will betray the secret. He will doubtless seek other means of satiating his dark passion."

"And I!—how am I to live longer, breathing the same air with this deadly enemy?" exclaimed Arthur Dimmesdale, shrinking within himself, and pressing his hand nervously against his heart—a gesture that had grown involuntary with him. "Think for me, Hester! Thou art strong. Resolve for me!"

"Thou must dwell no longer with this man," said Hester, slowly and firmly. "Thy heart must be no longer under his evil eye!"

"It were far worse than death!" replied the minister. "But how to avoid it? What choice remains to me? Shall I lie down again on these withered leaves, where I cast myself when thou didst tell me what he was? Must I sink down there, and die at once?"

"Alas! what a ruin has befallen thee!" said Hester, with the tears gushing into her eyes. "Wilt thou die for very weakness? There is no other cause!"

"The judgment of God is on me," answered the conscience-stricken priest. "It is too mighty for me to struggle with!"

"Heaven would show mercy," rejoined Hester, "hadst thou but the strength to take advantage of it."

"Be thou strong for me!" answered he. "Advise me what to do."

"Is the world, then, so narrow?" exclaimed Hester Prynne, fixing her deep eyes on the minister's, and instinctively exercising a magnetic power over a spirit so shattered and subdued that it could hardly hold itself erect. "Doth the universe lie within the compass of yonder town, which only a little time ago was but a leaf-strewn desert, as lonely as this around us? Whither leads yonder forest-track? Backward to the settlement, thou sayest! Yes; but, onward, too! Deeper it goes, and deeper into the wilderness, less plainly to be seen at every step; until some few miles hence the yellow leaves will show no vestige of the white man's tread. There thou art free! So brief a journey would bring thee from a world where thou hast been most wretched, to one where thou mayest still be happy! Is there not shade enough in all this boundless forest to hide thy heart from the gaze of Roger Chillingworth?"

"Yes, Hester; but only under the fallen leaves!" replied the minister, with a sad smile.

"Then there is the broad pathway of the sea!" continued Hester. "It brought thee hither. If thou so choose, it will bear thee back again. In our native land, whether in some remote rural village, or in vast London—or, surely, in Germany, in France, in pleasant Italy—thou wouldst be beyond his power and knowledge! And what hast thou to do with all these iron men, and their opinions? They have kept thy better part in bondage too long already!"

"It cannot be!" answered the minister, listening as if he were called upon to realise a dream. "I am powerless to go. Wretched and sinful as I am, I have had no other thought than to drag on my earthly existence in the sphere where Providence hath placed me. Lost as my own soul is, I would still do what I may for other human souls! I dare not quit my post, though an unfaithful sentinel, whose sure reward is death and dishonour, when his dreary watch shall come to an end!"

"Thou art crushed under this seven years' weight of misery," replied Hester, fervently resolved to buoy him up with her own energy. "But thou shalt leave it all behind thee! It shall not cumber thy steps, as thou treadest along the forest-path: neither shalt thou freight the ship with it, if thou prefer to cross the sea. Leave this wreck and ruin here where it hath happened. Meddle no more with it! Begin all anew! Hast thou exhausted possibility in the failure of this one trial? Not so! The future is yet full of trial and success. There is happiness to be enjoyed! There is good to be done! Exchange this false life of thine for a true one. Be, if thy spirit summon thee to such a mission, the teacher and apostle of the red men. Or, as is more thy nature, be a scholar and a sage among the wisest and the most renowned of the cultivated world. Preach! Write! Act! Do anything, save to lie down and die! Give up this name of Arthur Dimmesdale, and make thyself another, and a high one, such as thou canst wear without fear or shame. Why shouldst thou tarry so much as one other day in the torments that have so gnawed into thy life? that have made thee feeble to will and to do? that will leave thee powerless even to repent? Up, and away!"

"Oh, Hester!" cried Arthur Dimmesdale, in whose eyes a fitful light, kindled by her enthusiasm, flashed up and died away, "thou tellest of running a race to a man whose knees are tottering beneath him! I must die here! There is not the strength or courage left me to venture into the wide, strange, difficult world alone!"

It was the last expression of the despondency of a broken spirit. He lacked energy to grasp the better fortune that seemed within his reach.

He repeated the word—"Alone, Hester!"

"Thou shall not go alone!" answered she, in a deep whisper. Then, all was spoken!

XVIII. A Flood of Sunshine

Arthur Dimmesdale gazed into Hester's face with a look in which hope and joy shone out, indeed, but with fear betwixt them, and a kind of horror at her boldness, who had spoken what he vaguely hinted at, but dared not speak.

But Hester Prynne, with a mind of native courage and activity, and for so long a period not merely estranged, but outlawed from society, had habituated herself to such latitude of speculation as was altogether foreign to the clergyman. She had wandered, without rule or guidance, in a moral wilderness, as vast, as intricate, and shadowy as the untamed forest, amid the gloom of which they were now holding a colloquy that was to decide their fate. Her intellect and heart had their home, as it were, in desert places, where she roamed as freely as the wild Indian in his woods. For years past she had looked from this estranged point of view at human institutions, and whatever priests or legislators had established; criticising all with hardly more reverence than the Indian would feel for the clerical band, the judicial robe, the pillory, the gallows, the fireside, or the church. The tendency of her fate and fortunes had been to set her free. The scarlet letter was her passport into regions where other women dared not tread. Shame, Despair, Solitude! These had been her teachers—stern and wild ones—and they had made her strong, but taught her much amiss.

The minister, on the other hand, had never gone through an experience calculated to lead him beyond the scope of generally received laws; although, in a single instance, he had so fearfully transgressed one of the most sacred of them. But this had been a sin of passion, not of principle, nor even purpose. Since that wretched epoch, he had watched with morbid zeal and minuteness, not his acts—for those it was easy to arrange—but each breath of emotion, and his every thought. At the head of the social system, as the clergymen of that day stood, he was only the more trammelled by its regulations, its principles, and even its prejudices. As a priest, the framework of his order inevitably hemmed him in. As a man who had once sinned, but who kept his conscience all alive and painfully sensitive by the fretting of an unhealed wound, he might have been supposed safer within the line of virtue than if he had never sinned at all.

Thus we seem to see that, as regarded Hester Prynne, the whole seven years of outlaw and ignominy had been little other than a preparation for this very hour. But Arthur Dimmesdale! Were such a man once more to fall, what plea could be urged in extenuation of his crime? None; unless it avail him somewhat that he was broker, down by long and exquisite suffering; that his mind was darkened and confused by the very remorse which harrowed it; that, between fleeing as an avowed criminal, and remaining as a hypocrite, conscience might find it hard to strike the balance; that it was human to avoid the peril of death and infamy, and the inscrutable machinations of an enemy; that, finally, to this poor pilgrim, on his dreary and desert path, faint, sick, miserable, there appeared a glimpse of human affection and sympathy, a new life, and a true one, in exchange for the heavy doom which he was now expiating. And be the stern and sad truth spoken, that the breach which guilt has once made into the human soul is never, in this mortal state, repaired. It may be watched and guarded, so that the enemy shall not force his way again into the citadel, and might even in his subsequent assaults, select some other avenue, in preference to that where he had formerly succeeded. But there is still the ruined wall, and near it the stealthy tread of the foe that would win over again his unforgotten triumph.

The struggle, if there were one, need not be described. Let it suffice that the clergyman resolved to flee, and not alone.

"If in all these past seven years," thought he, "I could recall one instant of peace or hope, I would yet endure, for the sake of that earnest of Heaven's mercy. But now—since I am irrevocably doomed—wherefore should I not snatch the solace allowed to the condemned culprit before his execution? Or, if this be the path to a better life, as Hester would persuade me, I surely give up no fairer prospect by pursuing it! Neither can I any longer live without her companionship; so powerful is she to sustain—so tender to soothe! O Thou to whom I dare not lift mine eyes, wilt Thou yet pardon me?"

"Thou wilt go!" said Hester calmly, as he met her glance.

The decision once made, a glow of strange enjoyment threw its flickering brightness over the trouble of his breast. It was the exhilarating effect—upon a prisoner just escaped from the dungeon of his own heart—of breathing the wild, free atmosphere of an unredeemed, unchristianised, lawless region His spirit rose, as it were, with a bound, and attained a nearer prospect of the sky, than throughout all the misery which had kept him grovelling on the earth. Of a deeply religious temperament, there was inevitably a tinge of the devotional in his mood.

"Do I feel joy again?" cried he, wondering at himself. "Methought the germ of it was dead in me! Oh, Hester, thou art my better angel! I seem to have flung myself—sick, sin-stained, and sorrow-blackened—down upon these forest leaves, and to have risen up all made anew, and with new powers to glorify Him that hath been merciful! This is already the better life! Why did we not find it sooner?"

"Let us not look back," answered Hester Prynne. "The past is gone! Wherefore should we linger upon it now? See! With this symbol I undo it all, and make it as if it had never been!"

So speaking, she undid the clasp that fastened the scarlet letter, and, taking it from her bosom, threw it to a distance among the withered leaves. The mystic token alighted on the hither verge of the stream. With a hand's-breadth further flight, it would have fallen into the water, and have give, the little brook another woe to carry onward, besides the unintelligible tale which it still kept murmuring about. But there lay the embroidered letter, glittering like a lost jewel, which some ill-fated wanderer might pick up, and thenceforth be haunted by strange phantoms of guilt, sinkings of the heart, and unaccountable misfortune.

The stigma gone, Hester heaved a long, deep sigh, in which the burden of shame and anguish departed from her spirit. O exquisite relief! She had not known the weight until she felt the freedom! By another impulse, she took off the formal cap that confined her hair, and down it fell upon her shoulders, dark and rich, with at once a shadow and a light in its abundance, and imparting the charm of softness to her features. There played around her mouth, and beamed out of her eyes, a radiant and tender smile, that seemed gushing from the very heart of womanhood. A crimson flush was glowing on her cheek, that had been long so pale. Her sex, her youth, and the whole richness of her beauty, came back from what men call the irrevocable past, and clustered themselves with her maiden hope, and a happiness before unknown, within the magic circle of this hour. And, as if the gloom of the earth and sky had been but the effluence of these two mortal hearts, it vanished with their sorrow. All at once, as with a sudden smile of heaven, forth burst the sunshine, pouring a very flood into the obscure forest, gladdening each green leaf, transmuting the yellow fallen ones to gold, and gleaming adown the gray trunks of the solemn trees. The objects that had made a shadow hitherto, embodied the brightness now. The course of the little brook might be traced by its merry gleam afar into the wood's heart of mystery, which had become a mystery of joy.

Such was the sympathy of Nature—that wild, heathen Nature of the forest, never subjugated by human law, nor illumined by higher truth—with the bliss of these two spirits! Love, whether newly-born, or aroused from a death-like slumber, must always create a sunshine, filling the heart so full of radiance, that it overflows upon the outward world. Had the forest still kept its gloom, it would have been bright in Hester's eyes, and bright in Arthur Dimmesdale's!

Hester looked at him with a thrill of another joy.

"Thou must know Pearl!" said she. "Our little Pearl! Thou hast seen her—yes, I know it!—but thou wilt see her now with other eyes. She is a strange child! I hardly comprehend her! But thou wilt love her dearly, as I do, and wilt advise me how to deal with her!"

"Dost thou think the child will be glad to know me?" asked the minister, somewhat uneasily. "I have long shrunk from children, because they often show a distrust—a backwardness to be familiar with me. I have even been afraid of little Pearl!"

"Ah, that was sad!" answered the mother. "But she will love thee dearly, and thou her. She is not far off. I will call her. Pearl! Pearl!"

"I see the child," observed the minister. "Yonder she is, standing in a streak of sunshine, a good way off, on the other side of the brook. So thou thinkest the child will love me?"

Hester smiled, and again called to Pearl, who was visible at some distance, as the minister had described her, like a bright-apparelled vision in a sunbeam, which fell down upon her through an arch of boughs. The ray quivered to and fro, making her figure dim or distinct—now like a real child, now like a child's spirit—as the splendour went and came again. She heard her mother's voice, and approached slowly through the forest.

Pearl had not found the hour pass wearisomely while her mother sat talking with the clergyman. The great black forest—stern as it showed itself to those who brought the guilt and troubles of the world into its bosom—became the playmate of the lonely infant, as well as it knew how. Sombre as it was, it put on the kindest of its moods to welcome her. It offered her the partridge-berries, the growth of the preceding autumn, but ripening only in the spring, and now red as drops of blood upon the withered leaves. These Pearl gathered, and was pleased with their wild flavour. The small denizens of the wilderness hardly took pains to move out of her path. A partridge, indeed, with a brood of ten behind her, ran forward threateningly, but soon repented of her fierceness, and clucked to her young ones not to be afraid. A pigeon, alone on a low branch, allowed Pearl to come beneath, and uttered a sound as much of greeting as alarm. A squirrel, from the lofty depths of his domestic tree, chattered either in anger or merriment—for the squirrel is such a choleric and humorous little personage, that it is hard to distinguish between his moods—so he chattered at the child, and flung down a nut upon her head. It was a last year's nut, and already gnawed by his sharp tooth. A fox, startled from his sleep by her light footstep on the leaves, looked inquisitively at Pearl, as doubting whether it were better to steal off, or renew his nap on the same spot. A wolf, it is said—but here the tale has surely lapsed into the improbable—came up and smelt of Pearl's robe, and offered his savage head to be patted by her hand. The truth seems to be, however, that the mother-forest, and these wild things which it nourished, all recognised a kindred wilderness in the human child.

And she was gentler here than in the grassy-margined streets of the settlement, or in her mother's cottage. The flowers appeared to know it, and one and another whispered as she passed, "Adorn thyself with me, thou beautiful child, adorn thyself with me!"—and, to please them, Pearl gathered the violets, and anemones, and columbines, and some twigs of the freshest green, which the old trees held down before her eyes. With these she decorated her hair and her young waist, and became a nymph child, or an infant dryad, or whatever else was in closest sympathy with the antique wood. In such guise had Pearl adorned herself, when she heard her mother's voice, and came slowly back.

Slowly—for she saw the clergyman!

XIX. The Child at the Brookside

"Thou will love her dearly," repeated Hester Prynne, as she and the minister sat watching little Pearl. "Dost thou not think her beautiful? And see with what natural skill she has made those simple flowers adorn her! Had she gathered pearls, and diamonds, and rubies in the wood, they could not have become her better! She is a splendid child! But I know whose brow she has!"

"Dost thou know, Hester," said Arthur Dimmesdale, with an unquiet smile, "that this dear child, tripping about always at thy side, hath caused me many an alarm? Methought—oh, Hester, what a thought is that, and how terrible to dread it!—that my own features were partly repeated in her face, and so strikingly that the world might see them! But she is mostly thine!"

"No, no! Not mostly!" answered the mother, with a tender smile. "A little longer, and thou needest not to be afraid to trace whose child she is. But how strangely beautiful she looks with those wild flowers in her hair! It is as if one of the fairies, whom we left in dear old England, had decked her out to meet us."

It was with a feeling which neither of them had ever before experienced, that they sat and watched Pearl's slow advance. In her was visible the tie that united them. She had been offered to the world, these seven past years, as the living hieroglyphic, in which was revealed the secret they so darkly sought to hide—all written in this symbol—all plainly manifest—had there been a prophet or magician skilled to read the character of flame! And Pearl was the oneness of their being. Be the foregone evil what it might, how could they doubt that their earthly lives and future destinies were conjoined when they beheld at once the material union, and the spiritual idea, in whom they met, and were to dwell immortally together; thoughts like these—and perhaps other thoughts, which they did not acknowledge or define—threw an awe about the child as she came onward.

"Let her see nothing strange—no passion or eagerness—in thy way of accosting her," whispered Hester. "Our Pearl is a fitful and fantastic little elf sometimes. Especially she is generally intolerant of emotion, when she does not fully comprehend the why and wherefore. But the child hath strong affections! She loves me, and will love thee!"

"Thou canst not think," said the minister, glancing aside at Hester Prynne, "how my heart dreads this interview, and yearns for it! But, in truth, as I already told thee, children are not readily won to be familiar with me. They will not climb my knee, nor prattle in my ear, nor answer to my smile, but stand apart, and eye me strangely. Even little babes, when I take them in my arms, weep bitterly. Yet Pearl, twice in her little lifetime, hath been kind to me! The first time—thou knowest it well! The last was when thou ledst her with thee to the house of yonder stern old Governor."

"And thou didst plead so bravely in her behalf and mine!" answered the mother. "I remember it; and so shall little Pearl. Fear nothing. She may be strange and shy at first, but will soon learn to love thee!"

By this time Pearl had reached the margin of the brook, and stood on the further side, gazing silently at Hester and the clergyman, who still sat together on the mossy tree-trunk waiting to receive her. Just where she had paused, the brook chanced to form a pool so smooth and quiet that it reflected a perfect image of her little figure, with all the brilliant picturesqueness of her beauty, in its adornment of flowers and wreathed foliage, but more refined and spiritualized than the reality. This image, so nearly identical with the living Pearl, seemed to communicate somewhat of its own shadowy and intangible quality to the child herself. It was strange, the way in which Pearl stood, looking so steadfastly at them through the dim medium of the forest gloom, herself, meanwhile, all glorified with a ray of sunshine, that was attracted thitherward as by a certain sympathy. In the brook beneath stood another child—another and the same—with likewise its ray of golden light. Hester felt herself, in some indistinct and tantalizing manner, estranged from Pearl, as if the child, in her lonely ramble through the forest, had strayed out of the sphere in which she and her mother dwelt together, and was now vainly seeking to return to it.

There were both truth and error in the impression; the child and mother were estranged, but through Hester's fault, not Pearl's. Since the latter rambled from her side, another inmate had been admitted within the circle of the mother's feelings, and so modified the aspect of them all, that Pearl, the returning wanderer, could not find her wonted place, and hardly knew where she was.

"I have a strange fancy," observed the sensitive minister, "that this brook is the boundary between two worlds, and that thou canst never meet thy Pearl again. Or is she an elfish spirit, who, as the legends of our childhood taught us, is forbidden to cross a running stream? Pray hasten her, for this delay has already imparted a tremor to my nerves."

"Come, dearest child!" said Hester encouragingly, and stretching out both her arms. "How slow thou art! When hast thou been so sluggish before now? Here is a friend of mine, who must be thy friend also. Thou wilt have twice as much love henceforward as thy mother alone could give thee! Leap across the brook and come to us. Thou canst leap like a young deer!"

Pearl, without responding in any manner to these honey-sweet expressions, remained on the other side of the brook. Now she fixed her bright wild eyes on her mother, now on the minister, and now included them both in the same glance, as if to detect and explain to herself the relation which they bore to one another. For some unaccountable reason, as Arthur Dimmesdale felt the child's eyes upon himself, his hand—with that gesture so habitual as to have become involuntary—stole over his heart. At length, assuming a singular air of authority, Pearl stretched out her hand, with the small forefinger extended, and pointing evidently towards her mother's breast. And beneath, in the mirror of the brook, there was the flower-girdled and sunny image of little Pearl, pointing her small forefinger too.

"Thou strange child! why dost thou not come to me?" exclaimed Hester.

Pearl still pointed with her forefinger, and a frown gathered on her brow—the more impressive from the childish, the almost baby-like aspect of the features that conveyed it. As her mother still kept beckoning to her, and arraying her face in a holiday suit of unaccustomed smiles, the child stamped her foot with a yet more imperious look and gesture. In the brook, again, was the fantastic beauty of the image, with its reflected frown, its pointed finger, and imperious gesture, giving emphasis to the aspect of little Pearl.

"Hasten, Pearl, or I shall be angry with thee!" cried Hester Prynne, who, however, inured to such behaviour on the elf-child's part at other seasons, was naturally anxious for a more seemly deportment now. "Leap across the brook, naughty child, and run hither! Else I must come to thee!"

But Pearl, not a whit startled at her mother's threats any more than mollified by her entreaties, now suddenly burst into a fit of passion, gesticulating violently, and throwing her small figure into the most extravagant contortions She accompanied this wild outbreak with piercing shrieks, which the woods reverberated on all sides, so that, alone as she was in her childish and unreasonable wrath, it seemed as if a hidden multitude were lending her their sympathy and encouragement. Seen in the brook once more was the shadowy wrath of Pearl's image, crowned and girdled with flowers, but stamping its foot, wildly gesticulating, and, in the midst of all, still pointing its small forefinger at Hester's bosom.

"I see what ails the child," whispered Hester to the clergyman, and turning pale in spite of a strong effort to conceal her trouble and annoyance, "Children will not abide any, the slightest, change in the accustomed aspect of things that are daily before their eyes. Pearl misses something that she has always seen me wear!"

"I pray you," answered the minister, "if thou hast any means of pacifying the child, do it forthwith! Save it were the cankered wrath of an old witch like Mistress Hibbins," added he, attempting to smile, "I know nothing that I would not sooner encounter than this passion in a child. In Pearl's young beauty, as in the wrinkled witch, it has a preternatural effect. Pacify her if thou lovest me!"

Hester turned again towards Pearl with a crimson blush upon her cheek, a conscious glance aside clergyman, and then a heavy sigh, while, even before she had time to speak, the blush yielded to a deadly pallor.

"Pearl," said she sadly, "look down at thy feet! There!—before thee!—on the hither side of the brook!"

The child turned her eyes to the point indicated, and there lay the scarlet letter so close upon the margin of the stream that the gold embroidery was reflected in it.

"Bring it hither!" said Hester.

"Come thou and take it up!" answered Pearl.

"Was ever such a child!" observed Hester aside to the minister. "Oh, I have much to tell thee about her! But, in very truth, she is right as regards this hateful token. I must bear its torture yet a little longer—only a few days longer—until we shall have left this region, and look back hither as to a land which we have dreamed of. The forest cannot hide it! The mid-ocean shall take it from my hand, and swallow it up for ever!"

With these words she advanced to the margin of the brook, took up the scarlet letter, and fastened it again into her bosom. Hopefully, but a moment ago, as Hester had spoken of drowning it in the deep sea, there was a sense of inevitable doom upon her as she thus received back this deadly symbol from the hand of fate. She had flung it into infinite space! she had drawn an hour's free breath! and here again was the scarlet misery glittering on the old spot! So it ever is, whether thus typified or no, that an evil deed invests itself with the character of doom. Hester next gathered up the heavy tresses of her hair and confined them beneath her cap. As if there were a withering spell in the sad letter, her beauty, the warmth and richness of her womanhood, departed like fading sunshine, and a gray shadow seemed to fall across her.

When the dreary change was wrought, she extended her hand to Pearl.

"Dost thou know thy mother now, child?", asked she, reproachfully, but with a subdued tone. "Wilt thou come across the brook, and own thy mother, now that she has her shame upon her—now that she is sad?"

"Yes; now I will!" answered the child, bounding across the brook, and clasping Hester in her arms "Now thou art my mother indeed! and I am thy little Pearl!"

In a mood of tenderness that was not usual with her, she drew down her mother's head, and kissed her brow and both her cheeks. But then—by a kind of necessity that always impelled this child to alloy whatever comfort she might chance to give with a throb of anguish—Pearl put up her mouth and kissed the scarlet letter, too

"That was not kind!" said Hester. "When thou hast shown me a little love, thou mockest me!"

"Why doth the minister sit yonder?" asked Pearl.

"He waits to welcome thee," replied her mother. "Come thou, and entreat his blessing! He loves thee, my little Pearl, and loves thy mother, too. Wilt thou not love him? Come he longs to greet thee!"

"Doth he love us?" said Pearl, looking up with acute intelligence into her mother's face. "Will he go back with us, hand in hand, we three together, into the town?"

"Not now, my child," answered Hester. "But in days to come he will walk hand in hand with us. We will have a home and fireside of our own; and thou shalt sit upon his knee; and he will teach thee many things, and love thee dearly. Thou wilt love him—wilt thou not?"

"And will he always keep his hand over his heart?" inquired Pearl.

"Foolish child, what a question is that!" exclaimed her mother. "Come, and ask his blessing!"

But, whether influenced by the jealousy that seems instinctive with every petted child towards a dangerous rival, or from whatever caprice of her freakish nature, Pearl would show no favour to the clergyman. It was only by an exertion of force that her mother brought her up to him, hanging back, and manifesting her reluctance by odd grimaces; of which, ever since her babyhood, she had possessed a singular variety, and could transform her mobile physiognomy into a series of different aspects, with a new mischief in them, each and all. The minister—painfully embarrassed, but hoping that a kiss might prove a talisman to admit him into the child's kindlier regards—bent forward, and impressed one on her brow. Hereupon, Pearl broke away from her mother, and, running to the brook, stooped over it, and bathed her forehead, until the unwelcome kiss was quite washed off and diffused through a long lapse of the gliding water. She then remained apart, silently watching Hester and the clergyman; while they talked together and made such arrangements as were suggested by their new position and the purposes soon to be fulfilled.

And now this fateful interview had come to a close. The dell was to be left in solitude among its dark, old trees, which, with their multitudinous tongues, would whisper long of what had passed there, and no mortal be the wiser. And the melancholy brook would add this other tale to the mystery with which its little heart was already overburdened, and whereof it still kept up a murmuring babble, with not a whit more cheerfulness of tone than for ages heretofore.

XX. The Minister in a Maze

As the minister departed, in advance of Hester Prynne and little Pearl, he threw a backward glance, half expecting that he should discover only some faintly traced features or outline of the mother and the child, slowly fading into the twilight of the woods. So great a vicissitude in his life could not at once be received as real. But there was Hester, clad in her gray robe, still standing beside the tree-trunk, which some blast had overthrown a long antiquity ago, and which time had ever since been covering with moss, so that these two fated ones, with earth's heaviest burden on them, might there sit down together, and find a single hour's rest and solace. And there was Pearl, too, lightly dancing from the margin of the brook—now that the intrusive third person was gone—and taking her old place by her mother's side. So the minister had not fallen asleep and dreamed!

In order to free his mind from this indistinctness and duplicity of impression, which vexed it with a strange disquietude, he recalled and more thoroughly defined the plans which Hester and himself had sketched for their departure. It had been determined between them that the Old World, with its crowds and cities, offered them a more eligible shelter and concealment than the wilds of New England or all America, with its alternatives of an Indian wigwam, or the few settlements of Europeans scattered thinly along the sea-board. Not to speak of the clergyman's health, so inadequate to sustain the hardships of a forest life, his native gifts, his culture, and his entire development would secure him a home only in the midst of civilization and refinement; the higher the state the more delicately adapted to it the man. In futherance of this choice, it so happened that a ship lay in the harbour; one of those unquestionable cruisers, frequent at that day, which, without being absolutely outlaws of the deep, yet roamed over its surface with a remarkable irresponsibility of character. This vessel had recently arrived from the

Spanish Main, and within three days' time would sail for Bristol. Hester Prynne—whose vocation, as a self-enlisted Sister of Charity, had brought her acquainted with the captain and crew—could take upon herself to secure the passage of two individuals and a child with all the secrecy which circumstances rendered more than desirable.

The minister had inquired of Hester, with no little interest, the precise time at which the vessel might be expected to depart. It would probably be on the fourth day from the present. "This is most fortunate!" he had then said to himself. Now, why the Reverend Mr. Dimmesdale considered it so very fortunate we hesitate to reveal. Nevertheless—to hold nothing back from the reader—it was because, on the third day from the present, he was to preach the Election Sermon; and, as such an occasion formed an honourable epoch in the life of a New England Clergyman, he could not have chanced upon a more suitable mode and time of terminating his professional career. "At least, they shall say of me," thought this exemplary man, "that I leave no public duty unperformed or ill-performed!" Sad, indeed, that an introspection so profound and acute as this poor minister's should be so miserably deceived! We have had, and may still have, worse things to tell of him; but none, we apprehend, so pitiably weak; no evidence, at once so slight and irrefragable, of a subtle disease that had long since begun to eat into the real substance of his character. No man, for any considerable period, can wear one face to himself and another to the multitude, without finally getting bewildered as to which may be the true.

The excitement of Mr. Dimmesdale's feelings as he returned from his interview with Hester, lent him unaccustomed physical energy, and hurried him townward at a rapid pace. The pathway among the woods seemed wilder, more uncouth with its rude natural obstacles, and less trodden by the foot of man, than he remembered it on his outward journey. But he leaped across the plashy places, thrust himself through the clinging underbush, climbed the ascent, plunged into the hollow, and overcame, in short, all the difficulties of the track, with an unweariable activity that astonished him. He could not but recall how feebly, and with what frequent pauses for breath he had toiled over the same ground, only two days before. As he drew near the town, he took an impression of change from the series of familiar objects that presented themselves. It seemed not yesterday, not one, not two, but many days, or even years ago, since he had quitted them. There, indeed, was each former trace of the street, as he remembered it, and all the peculiarities of the houses, with the due multitude of gable-peaks, and a weather-cock at every point where his memory suggested one. Not the less, however, came this importunately obtrusive sense of change. The same was true as regarded the acquaintances whom he met, and all the well-known shapes of human life, about the little town. They looked neither older nor younger now; the beards of the aged were no whiter, nor could the creeping babe of yesterday walk on his feet to-day; it was impossible to describe in what respect they differed from the individuals on whom he had so recently bestowed a parting glance; and yet the minister's deepest sense seemed to inform him of their mutability. A similar impression struck him most remarkably a he passed under the walls of his own church. The edifice had so very strange, and yet so familiar an aspect, that Mr. Dimmesdale's mind vibrated between two ideas; either that he had seen it only in a dream hitherto, or that he was merely dreaming about it now.

This phenomenon, in the various shapes which it assumed, indicated no external change, but so sudden and important a change in the spectator of the familiar scene, that the intervening space of a single day had operated on his consciousness like the lapse of years. The minister's own will, and Hester's will, and the fate that grew between them, had wrought this transformation. It was the same town as heretofore, but the same minister returned not from the forest. He might have said to the friends who greeted him—"I am not the man for whom you take me! I left him yonder in the forest, withdrawn into a secret dell, by a mossy tree trunk, and near a melancholy brook! Go, seek your minister, and see if his emaciated figure, his thin cheek, his white, heavy, pain-wrinkled brow, be not flung down there, like a cast-off garment!" His friends, no doubt, would still have insisted with him—"Thou art thyself the man!" but the error would have been their own, not his. Before Mr. Dimmesdale reached home, his inner man gave him other evidences of a revolution in the sphere of thought and feeling. In truth, nothing short of a total change of dynasty and moral code, in that interior kingdom, was adequate to account for the impulses now communicated to the unfortunate and startled minister. At every step he was incited to do some strange, wild, wicked thing or other, with a sense that it would be at once involuntary and intentional, in spite of himself, yet growing out of a profounder self than that which opposed the impulse. For instance, he met one of his own deacons. The good old man addressed him with the paternal affection and patriarchal privilege which his venerable age, his upright and holy character, and his station in the church, entitled him to use and, conjoined with this, the deep, almost worshipping respect, which the minister's professional and private claims alike demanded. Never was there a more beautiful example of how the majesty of age and wisdom may comport with the obeisance and respect enjoined upon it, as from a lower social rank, and inferior order of endowment, towards a higher. Now, during a conversation of some two or three moments between the Reverend Mr. Dimmesdale and this excellent and hoary-bearded deacon, it was only by the most careful self-control that the former could refrain from uttering certain blasphemous suggestions that rose into his mind, respecting the communion-supper. He absolutely trembled and turned pale as ashes, lest his tongue should wag itself in utterance of these horrible matters, and plead his own consent for so doing, without his having fairly given it. And, even with this terror in his heart, he could hardly avoid laughing, to imagine how the sanctified old patriarchal deacon would have been petrified by his minister's impiety.

Again, another incident of the same nature. Hurrying along the street, the Reverend Mr. Dimmesdale encountered the eldest female member of his church, a most pious and exemplary old dame, poor, widowed, lonely, and with a heart as full of reminiscences about her dead husband and children, and her dead friends of long ago, as a burial-ground is full of storied gravestones. Yet all this, which would else have been such heavy sorrow, was made almost a solemn joy to her devout old soul, by religious consolations and the truths of Scripture, wherewith she had fed herself continually for more than thirty years. And since Mr. Dimmesdale had taken her in charge, the good grandam's chief earthly comfort—which, unless it had been likewise a heavenly comfort, could have been none at all—was to meet her pastor, whether casually, or of set purpose, and be refreshed with a word of warm, fragrant, heaven-breathing Gospel truth, from his beloved lips, into her dulled, but rapturously attentive ear. But, on this occasion, up to the moment of putting his lips to the old woman's ear, Mr. Dimmesdale, as the great enemy of souls would have it, could recall no text of Scripture, nor aught else, except a brief, pithy, and, as it then appeared to him, unanswerable argument against the immortality of the human soul. The instilment thereof into her mind would probably have caused this aged sister to drop down dead, at once, as by the effect of an intensely poisonous infusion. What he really did whisper, the minister could never afterwards recollect. There was, perhaps, a fortunate disorder in his utterance, which failed to impart any distinct idea to the good widows comprehension, or which Providence interpreted after a method of its own.

Assuredly, as the minister looked back, he beheld an expression of divine gratitude and ecstasy that seemed like the shine of the celestial city on her face, so wrinkled and ashy pale.

Again, a third instance. After parting from the old church member, he met the youngest sister of them all. It was a maiden newly-won—and won by the Reverend Mr. Dimmesdale's own sermon, on the Sabbath after his vigil—to barter the transitory pleasures of the world for the heavenly hope that was to assume brighter substance as life grew dark around her, and which would gild the utter gloom with final glory. She was fair and pure as a lily that had bloomed in Paradise. The minister knew well that he was himself enshrined within the stainless sanctity of her heart, which hung its snowy curtains about his image, imparting to religion the warmth of love, and to love a religious purity. Satan, that afternoon, had surely led the poor young girl away from her mother's side, and thrown her into the pathway of this sorely tempted, or—shall we not rather say?—this lost and desperate man. As she drew nigh, the arch-fiend whispered him to condense into small compass, and drop into her tender bosom a germ of evil that would be sure to blossom darkly soon, and bear black fruit betimes. Such was his sense of power over this virgin soul, trusting him as she did, that the minister felt potent to blight all the field of innocence with but one wicked look, and develop all its opposite with but a word. So—with a mightier struggle than he had yet sustained—he held his Geneva cloak before his face, and hurried onward, making no sign of recognition, and leaving the young sister to digest his rudeness as she might. She ransacked her conscience—which was full of harmless little matters, like her pocket or her work-bag—and took herself to task, poor thing! for a thousand imaginary faults, and went about her household duties with swollen eyelids the next morning.

Before the minister had time to celebrate his victory over this last temptation, he was conscious of another impulse, more ludicrous, and almost as horrible. It was—we blush to tell it—it was to stop short in the road, and teach some very wicked words to a knot of little Puritan children who were playing there, and had but just begun to talk. Denying himself this freak, as unworthy of his cloth, he met a drunken seaman, one of the ship's crew from the Spanish Main. And here, since he had so valiantly forborne all other wickedness, poor Mr. Dimmesdale longed at least to shake hands with the tarry black-guard, and recreate himself with a few improper jests, such as dissolute sailors so abound with, and a volley of good, round, solid, satisfactory, and heaven-defying oaths! It was not so much a better principle, as partly his natural good taste, and still more his buckramed habit of clerical decorum, that carried him safely through the latter crisis.

"What is it that haunts and tempts me thus?" cried the minister to himself, at length, pausing in the street, and striking his hand against his forehead.

"Am I mad? or am I given over utterly to the fiend? Did I make a contract with him in the forest, and sign it with my blood? And does he now summon me to its fulfilment, by suggesting the performance of every wickedness which his most foul imagination can conceive?"

At the moment when the Reverend Mr. Dimmesdale thus communed with himself, and struck his forehead with his hand, old Mistress Hibbins, the reputed witch-lady, is said to have been passing by. She made a very grand appearance, having on a high head-dress, a rich gown of velvet, and a ruff done up with the famous yellow starch, of which Anne Turner, her especial friend, had taught her the secret, before this last good lady had been hanged for Sir Thomas Overbury's murder. Whether the witch had read the minister's thoughts or no, she came to a full stop, looked shrewdly into his face, smiled craftily, and—though little given to converse with clergymen—began a conversation.

"So, reverend sir, you have made a visit into the forest," observed the witch-lady, nodding her high head-dress at him. "The next time I pray you to allow me only a fair warning, and I shall be proud to bear you company. Without taking overmuch upon myself my good word will go far towards gaining any strange gentleman a fair reception from yonder potentate you wot of."

"I profess, madam," answered the clergyman, with a grave obeisance, such as the lady's rank demanded, and his own good breeding made imperative—"I profess, on my conscience and character, that I am utterly bewildered as touching the purport of your words! I went not into the forest to seek a potentate, neither do I, at any future time, design a visit thither, with a view to gaining the favour of such personage. My one sufficient object was to greet that pious friend of mine, the Apostle Eliot, and rejoice with him over the many precious souls he hath won from heathendom!"

"Ha, ha, ha!" cackled the old witch-lady, still nodding her high head-dress at the minister. "Well, well! we must needs talk thus in the daytime! You carry it off like an old hand! But at midnight, and in the forest, we shall have other talk together!"

She passed on with her aged stateliness, but often turning back her head and smiling at him, like one willing to recognise a secret intimacy of connection.

"Have I then sold myself," thought the minister, "to the fiend whom, if men say true, this yellow-starched and velveted old hag has chosen for her prince and master?"

The wretched minister! He had made a bargain very like it! Tempted by a dream of happiness, he had yielded himself with deliberate choice, as he had never done before, to what he knew was deadly sin. And the infectious poison of that sin had been thus rapidly diffused throughout his moral system. It had stupefied all blessed impulses, and awakened into vivid life the whole brotherhood of bad ones. Scorn, bitterness, unprovoked malignity, gratuitous desire of ill, ridicule of whatever was good and holy, all awoke to tempt, even while they frightened him. And his encounter with old Mistress Hibbins, if it were a real incident, did but show its sympathy and fellowship with wicked mortals, and the world of perverted spirits.

He had by this time reached his dwelling on the edge of the burial ground, and, hastening up the stairs, took refuge in his study. The minister was glad to have reached this shelter, without first betraying himself to the world by any of those strange and wicked eccentricities to which he had been continually impelled while passing through the streets. He entered the accustomed room, and looked around him on its books, its windows, its fireplace, and the tapestried comfort of the walls, with the same perception of strangeness that had haunted him throughout his walk from the forest dell into the town and thitherward. Here he had studied and written; here gone through fast and vigil, and come forth half alive; here striven to pray; here borne a hundred thousand agonies! There was the Bible, in its rich old Hebrew, with Moses and the Prophets speaking to him, and God's voice through all.

There on the table, with the inky pen beside it, was an unfinished sermon, with a sentence broken in the midst, where his thoughts had ceased to gush out upon the page two days before. He knew that it was himself, the thin and white-cheeked minister, who had done and suffered these things, and written thus far into the Election Sermon! But he seemed to stand apart, and eye this former self with scornful pitying, but half-envious curiosity. That self was gone. Another man had returned out of the forest—a wiser one— with a knowledge of hidden mysteries which the simplicity of the former never could have reached. A bitter kind of knowledge that!

While occupied with these reflections, a knock came at the door of the study, and the minister said, "Come in!"—not wholly devoid of an idea that he might behold an evil spirit. And so he did! It was old Roger Chillingworth that entered. The minister stood white and speechless, with one hand on the Hebrew Scriptures, and the other spread upon his breast.

"Welcome home, reverend sir," said the physician "And how found you that godly man, the Apostle Eliot? But methinks, dear sir, you look pale, as if the travel through the wilderness had been too sore for you. Will not my aid be requisite to put you in heart and strength to preach your Election Sermon?"

"Nay, I think not so," rejoined the Reverend Mr. Dimmesdale. "My journey, and the sight of the holy Apostle yonder, and the free air which I have breathed have done me good, after so long confinement in my study. I think to need no more of your drugs, my kind physician, good though they be, and administered by a friendly hand."

All this time Roger Chillingworth was looking at the minister with the grave and intent regard of a physician towards his patient. But, in spite of this outward show, the latter was almost convinced of the old man's knowledge, or, at least, his confident suspicion, with respect to his own interview with Hester Prynne. The physician knew then that in the minister's regard he was no longer a trusted friend, but his bitterest enemy. So much being known, it would appear natural that a part of it should he expressed. It is singular, however, how long a time often passes before words embody things; and with what security two persons, who choose to avoid a certain subject, may approach its very verge, and retire without disturbing it. Thus the minister felt no apprehension that Roger Chillingworth would touch, in express words, upon the real position which they sustained towards one another. Yet did the physician, in his dark way, creep frightfully near the secret.

"Were it not better," said he, "that you use my poor skill tonight? Verily, dear sir, we must take pains to make you strong and vigorous for this occasion of the Election discourse. The people look for great things from you, apprehending that another year may come about and find their pastor gone."

"Yes, to another world," replied the minister with pious resignation. "Heaven grant it be a better one; for, in good sooth, I hardly think to tarry with my flock through the flitting seasons of another year! But touching your medicine, kind sir, in my present frame of body I need it not."

"I joy to hear it," answered the physician. "It may be that my remedies, so long administered in vain, begin now to take due effect. Happy man were I, and well deserving of New England's gratitude, could I achieve this cure!"

"I thank you from my heart, most watchful friend," said the Reverend Mr. Dimmesdale with a solemn smile. "I thank you, and can but requite your good deeds with my prayers."

"A good man's prayers are golden recompense!" rejoined old Roger Chillingworth, as he took his leave. "Yea, they are the current gold coin of the New Jerusalem, with the King's own mint mark on them!"

Left alone, the minister summoned a servant of the house, and requested food, which, being set before him, he ate with ravenous appetite. Then flinging the already written pages of the Election Sermon into the fire, he forthwith began another, which he wrote with such an impulsive flow of thought and emotion, that he fancied himself inspired; and only wondered that Heaven should see fit to transmit the grand and solemn music of its oracles through so foul an organ pipe as he. However, leaving that mystery to solve itself, or go unsolved for ever, he drove his task onward with earnest haste and ecstasy.

Thus the night fled away, as if it were a winged steed, and he careering on it; morning came, and peeped, blushing, through the curtains; and at last sunrise threw a golden beam into the study, and laid it right across the minister's bedazzled eyes. There he was, with the pen still between his fingers, and a vast, immeasurable tract of written space behind him!

XXI. The New England Holiday

Betimes in the morning of the day on which the new Governor was to receive his office at the hands of the people, Hester Prynne and little Pearl came into the market-place. It was already thronged with the craftsmen and other plebeian inhabitants of the town, in considerable numbers, among whom, likewise, were many rough figures, whose attire of deer-skins marked them as belonging to some of the forest settlements, which surrounded the little metropolis of the colony.

On this public holiday, as on all other occasions for seven years past, Hester was clad in a garment of coarse gray cloth. Not more by its hue than by some indescribable peculiarity in its fashion, it had the effect of making her fade personally out of sight and outline; while again the scarlet letter brought her back from this twilight indistinctness, and revealed her under the moral aspect of its own illumination. Her face, so long familiar to the townspeople, showed the marble quietude which they were accustomed to behold there. It was like a mask; or, rather like the frozen calmness of a dead woman's features; owing this dreary resemblance to the fact that Hester was actually dead, in respect to any claim of sympathy, and had departed out of the world with which she still seemed to mingle.

It might be, on this one day, that there was an expression unseen before, nor, indeed, vivid enough to be detected now; unless some preternaturally gifted observer should have first read the heart, and have afterwards sought a corresponding development in the countenance and mien. Such a spiritual sneer might have conceived, that, after sustaining the gaze of the multitude through several miserable years as a necessity, a penance, and something which it was a stern religion to endure, she now, for one last time more, encountered it freely and voluntarily, in order to convert what had so long been agony into a kind of triumph. "Look your last on the scarlet letter and its wearer!"—the people's victim and lifelong bond-slave, as they fancied her, might say to them. "Yet a little while, and she will be beyond your reach! A few hours longer and the deep, mysterious ocean will quench and hide for ever the symbol which ye have caused to burn on her bosom!" Nor were it an inconsistency too improbable to be assigned to human nature, should we suppose a feeling of regret in Hester's mind, at the moment when she was about to win her freedom from the pain which had been thus deeply incorporated with her being. Might there not be an irresistible desire to quaff a last, long, breathless draught of the cup of wormwood and aloes, with which nearly all her years of womanhood had been perpetually flavoured. The wine of life, henceforth to be presented to her lips, must be indeed rich, delicious, and exhilarating, in its chased and golden beaker, or else leave an inevitable and weary languor, after the lees of bitterness wherewith she had been drugged, as with a cordial of intensest potency.

Pearl was decked out with airy gaiety. It would have been impossible to guess that this bright and sunny apparition owed its existence to the shape of gloomy gray; or that a fancy, at once so gorgeous and so delicate as must have been requisite to contrive the child's apparel, was the same that had achieved a task perhaps more difficult, in imparting so distinct a peculiarity to Hester's simple robe. The dress, so proper was it to little Pearl, seemed an effluence, or inevitable development and outward manifestation of her character, no more to be separated from her than the many-hued brilliancy from a butterfly's wing, or the painted glory from the leaf of a bright flower. As with these, so with the child; her garb was all of one idea with her nature. On this eventful day, moreover, there was a certain singular inquietude and excitement in her mood, resembling nothing so much as the shimmer of a diamond, that sparkles and flashes with the varied throbbings of the breast on which it is displayed. Children have always a sympathy in the agitations of those connected with them: always, especially, a sense of any trouble or impending revolution, of whatever kind, in domestic circumstances; and therefore Pearl, who was the gem on her mother's unquiet bosom, betrayed, by the very dance of her spirits, the emotions which none could detect in the marble passiveness of Hester's brow.

This effervescence made her flit with a bird-like movement, rather than walk by her mother's side.

She broke continually into shouts of a wild, inarticulate, and sometimes piercing music. When they reached the market-place, she became still more restless, on perceiving the stir and bustle that enlivened the spot; for it was usually more like the broad and lonesome green before a village meeting-house, than the centre of a town's business

"Why, what is this, mother?" cried she. "Wherefore have all the people left their work to-day? Is it a play-day for the whole world? See, there is the blacksmith! He has washed his sooty face, and put on his Sabbath-day clothes, and looks as if he would gladly be merry, if any kind body would only teach him how! And there is Master Brackett, the old jailer, nodding and smiling at me. Why does he do so, mother?"

"He remembers thee a little babe, my child," answered Hester.

"He should not nod and smile at me, for all that—the black, grim, ugly-eyed old man!" said Pearl.

"He may nod at thee, if he will; for thou art clad in gray, and wearest the scarlet letter. But see, mother, how many faces of strange people, and Indians among them, and sailors! What have they all come to do, here in the market-place?"

"They wait to see the procession pass," said Hester. "For the Governor and the magistrates are to go by, and the ministers, and all the great people and good people, with the music and the soldiers marching before them."

"And will the minister be there?" asked Pearl. "And will he hold out both his hands to me, as when thou led'st me to him from the brook-side?"

"He will be there, child," answered her mother, "but he will not greet thee to-day, nor must thou greet him."

"What a strange, sad man is he!" said the child, as if speaking partly to herself. "In the dark nighttime he calls us to him, and holds thy hand and mine, as when we stood with him on the scaffold yonder! And in the deep forest, where only the old trees can hear, and the strip of sky see it, he talks with thee, sitting on a heap of moss! And he kisses my forehead, too, so that the little brook would hardly wash it off! But, here, in the sunny day, and among all the people, he knows us not; nor must we know him! A strange, sad man is he, with his hand always over his heart!"

"Be quiet, Pearl—thou understandest not these things," said her mother. "Think not now of the minister, but look about thee, and see how cheery is everybody's face to-day.

The children have come from their schools, and the grown people from their workshops and their fields, on purpose to be happy, for, to-day, a new man is beginning to rule over them; and so—as has been the custom of mankind ever since a nation was first gathered—they make merry and rejoice: as if a good and golden year were at length to pass over the poor old world!"

It was as Hester said, in regard to the unwonted jollity that brightened the faces of the people. Into this festal season of the year—as it already was, and continued to be during the greater part of two centuries—the Puritans compressed whatever mirth and public joy they deemed allowable to human infirmity; thereby so far dispelling the customary cloud, that, for the space of a single holiday, they appeared scarcely more grave than most other communities at a period of general affliction.

But we perhaps exaggerate the gray or sable tinge, which undoubtedly characterized the mood and manners of the age. The persons now in the market-place of Boston had not been born to an inheritance of Puritanic gloom. They were native Englishmen, whose fathers had lived in the sunny richness of the Elizabethan epoch; a time when the life of England, viewed as one great mass, would appear to have been as stately, magnificent, and joyous, as the world has ever witnessed. Had they followed their hereditary taste, the New England settlers would have illustrated all events of public importance by bonfires, banquets, pageantries, and processions. Nor would it have been impracticable, in the observance of majestic ceremonies, to combine mirthful recreation with solemnity, and give, as it were, a grotesque and brilliant embroidery to the great robe of state, which a nation, at such festivals, puts on. There was some shadow of an attempt of this kind in the mode of celebrating the day on which the political year of the colony commenced. The dim reflection of a remembered splendour, a colourless and manifold diluted repetition of what they had beheld in proud old London—we will not say at a royal coronation, but at a Lord Mayor's show—might be traced in the customs which our forefathers instituted, with reference to the annual installation of magistrates. The fathers and founders of the commonwealth—the statesman, the priest, and the soldier—seemed it a duty then to assume the outward state and majesty, which, in accordance with antique style, was looked upon as the proper garb of public and social eminence. All came forth to move in procession before the people's eye, and thus impart a needed dignity to the simple framework of a government so newly constructed.

Then, too, the people were countenanced, if not encouraged, in relaxing the severe and close application to their various modes of rugged industry, which at all other times, seemed of the same piece and material with their religion. Here, it is true, were none of the appliances which popular merriment would so readily have found in the England of Elizabeth's time, or that of James—no rude shows of a theatrical kind; no minstrel, with his harp and legendary ballad, nor gleeman with an ape dancing to his music; no juggler, with his tricks of mimic witchcraft; no Merry Andrew, to stir up the multitude with jests, perhaps a hundred years old, but still effective, by their appeals to the very broadest sources of mirthful sympathy. All such professors of the several branches of jocularity would have been sternly repressed, not only by the rigid discipline of law, but by the general sentiment which give law its vitality. Not the less, however, the great, honest face of the people smiled—grimly, perhaps, but widely too. Nor were sports wanting, such as the colonists had witnessed, and shared in, long ago, at the country fairs and on the village-greens of England; and which it was thought well to keep alive on this new soil, for the sake of the courage and manliness that were essential in them. Wrestling matches, in the different fashions of Cornwall and Devonshire, were seen here and there about the market-place; in one corner, there was a friendly bout at quarterstaff; and—what attracted most interest of all—on the platform of the pillory, already so noted in our pages, two masters of defence were commencing an exhibition with the buckler and broadsword. But, much to the disappointment of the crowd, this latter business was broken off by the interposition of the town beadle, who had no idea of permitting the majesty of the law to be violated by such an abuse of one of its consecrated places.

It may not be too much to affirm, on the whole, (the people being then in the first stages of joyless deportment, and the offspring of sires who had known how to be merry, in their day), that they would compare favourably, in point of holiday keeping, with their descendants, even at so long an interval as ourselves. Their immediate posterity, the generation next to the early emigrants, wore the blackest shade of Puritanism, and so darkened the national visage with it, that all the subsequent years have not sufficed to clear it up. We have yet to learn again the forgotten art of gaiety.

The picture of human life in the market-place, though its general tint was the sad gray, brown, or black of the English emigrants, was yet enlivened by some diversity of hue. A party of Indians—in their savage finery of curiously embroidered deerskin robes, wampum-belts, red and yellow ochre, and feathers, and armed with the bow and arrow and stone-headed spear—stood apart with countenances of inflexible gravity, beyond what even the Puritan aspect could attain. Nor, wild as were these painted barbarians, were they the wildest feature of the scene. This distinction could more justly be claimed by some mariners—a part of the crew of the vessel from the Spanish Main—who had come ashore to see the humours of Election Day. They were rough-looking desperadoes, with sun-blackened faces, and an immensity of beard; their wide short trousers were confined about the waist by belts, often clasped with a rough plate of gold, and sustaining always a long knife, and in some instances, a sword. From beneath their broad-brimmed hats of palm-leaf, gleamed eyes which, even in good-nature and merriment, had a kind of animal ferocity. They transgressed without fear or scruple, the rules of behaviour that were binding on all others: smoking tobacco under the beadle's very nose, although each whiff would have cost a townsman a shilling; and quaffing at their pleasure, draughts of wine or aqua-vitae from pocket flasks, which they freely tendered to the gaping crowd around them. It remarkably characterised the incomplete morality of the age, rigid as we call it, that a license was allowed the seafaring class, not merely for their freaks on shore, but for far more desperate deeds on their proper element. The sailor of that day would go near to be arraigned as a pirate in our own. There could be little doubt, for instance, that this very ship's crew, though no unfavourable specimens of the nautical brotherhood, had been guilty, as we should phrase it, of depredations on the Spanish commerce, such as would have perilled all their necks in a modern court of justice.

But the sea in those old times heaved, swelled, and foamed very much at its own will, or subject only to the tempestuous wind, with hardly any attempts at regulation by human law. The buccaneer on the wave might relinquish his calling and become at once if he chose, a man of probity and piety on land; nor, even in the full career of his reckless life, was he regarded as a personage with whom it was disreputable to traffic or casually associate. Thus the Puritan elders in their black cloaks, starched bands, and steeple-crowned hats, smiled not unbenignantly at the clamour and rude deportment of these jolly seafaring men; and it excited neither surprise nor animadversion when so reputable a citizen as old Roger Chillingworth, the physician, was seen to enter the market-place in close and familiar talk with the commander of the questionable vessel.

The latter was by far the most showy and gallant figure, so far as apparel went, anywhere to be seen among the multitude. He wore a profusion of ribbons on his garment, and gold lace on his hat, which was also encircled by a gold chain, and surmounted with a feather. There was a sword at his side and a sword-cut on his forehead, which, by the arrangement of his hair, he seemed anxious rather to display than hide. A landsman could hardly have worn this garb and shown this face, and worn and shown them both with such a galliard air, without undergoing stern question before a magistrate, and probably incurring a fine or imprisonment, or perhaps an exhibition in the stocks. As regarded the shipmaster, however, all was looked upon as pertaining to the character, as to a fish his glistening scales.

After parting from the physician, the commander of the Bristol ship strolled idly through the market-place; until happening to approach the spot where Hester Prynne was standing, he appeared to recognise, and did not hesitate to address her. As was usually the case wherever Hester stood, a small vacant area—a sort of magic circle—had formed itself about her, into which, though the people were elbowing one another at a little distance, none ventured or felt disposed to intrude. It was a forcible type of the moral solitude in which the scarlet letter enveloped its fated wearer; partly by her own reserve, and partly by the instinctive, though no longer so unkindly, withdrawal of her fellow-creatures. Now, if never before, it answered a good purpose by enabling Hester and the seaman to speak together without risk of being overheard; and so changed was Hester Prynne's repute before the public, that the matron in town, most eminent for rigid morality, could not have held such intercourse with less result of scandal than herself.

"So, mistress," said the mariner, "I must bid the steward make ready one more berth than you bargained for! No fear of scurvy or ship fever this voyage. What with the ship's surgeon and this other doctor, our only danger will be from drug or pill; more by token, as there is a lot of apothecary's stuff aboard, which I traded for with a Spanish vessel."

"What mean you?" inquired Hester, startled more than she permitted to appear. "Have you another passenger?"

"Why, know you not," cried the shipmaster, "that this physician here—Chillingworth he calls himself—is minded to try my cabin-fare with you? Ay, ay, you must have known it; for he tells me he is of your party, and a close friend to the gentleman you spoke of— he that is in peril from these sour old Puritan rulers."

"They know each other well, indeed," replied Hester, with a mien of calmness, though in the utmost consternation. "They have long dwelt together."

Nothing further passed between the mariner and Hester Prynne. But at that instant she beheld old Roger Chillingworth himself, standing in the remotest corner of the market-place and smiling on her; a smile which—across the wide and bustling square, and through all the talk and laughter, and various thoughts, moods, and interests of the crowd—conveyed secret and fearful meaning.

XXII. The Procession

Before Hester Prynne could call together her thoughts, and consider what was practicable to be done in this new and startling aspect of affairs, the sound of military music was heard approaching along a contiguous street. It denoted the advance of the procession of magistrates and citizens on its way towards the meeting-house: where, in compliance with a custom thus early established, and ever since observed, the Reverend Mr. Dimmesdale was to deliver an Election Sermon.

Soon the head of the procession showed itself, with a slow and stately march, turning a corner, and making its way across the market-place. First came the music. It comprised a variety of instruments, perhaps imperfectly adapted to one another, and played with no great skill; but yet attaining the great object for which the harmony of drum and clarion addresses itself to the multitude—that of imparting a higher and more heroic air to the scene of life that passes before the eye. Little Pearl at first clapped her hands, but then lost for an instant the restless agitation that had kept her in a continual effervescence throughout the morning; she gazed silently, and seemed to be borne upward like a floating sea-bird on the long heaves and swells of sound. But she was brought back to her former mood by the shimmer of the sunshine on the weapons and bright armour of the military company, which followed after the music, and formed the honorary escort of the procession. This body of soldiery—which still sustains a corporate existence, and marches down from past ages with an ancient and honourable fame—was composed of no mercenary materials. Its ranks were filled with gentlemen who felt the stirrings of martial impulse, and sought to establish a kind of College of Arms, where, as in an association of Knights Templars, they might learn the science, and, so far as peaceful exercise would teach them, the practices of war. The high estimation then placed upon the military character might be seen in the lofty port of each individual member of the company. Some of them, indeed, by their services in the Low Countries and on other fields of European warfare, had fairly won their title to assume the name and pomp of soldiership. The entire array, moreover, clad in burnished steel, and with plumage nodding over their bright morions, had a brilliancy of effect which no modern display can aspire to equal.

And yet the men of civil eminence, who came immediately behind the military escort, were better worth a thoughtful observer's eye. Even in outward demeanour they showed a stamp of majesty that made the warrior's haughty stride look vulgar, if not absurd. It was an age when what we call talent had far less consideration than now, but the massive materials which produce stability and dignity of character a great deal more. The people possessed by hereditary right the quality of reverence, which, in their descendants, if it survive at all, exists in smaller proportion, and with a vastly diminished force in the selection and estimate of public men. The change may be for good or ill, and is partly, perhaps, for both. In that old day the English settler on these rude shores—having left king, nobles, and all degrees of awful rank behind, while still the faculty and necessity of reverence was strong in him—bestowed it on the white hair and venerable brow of age—on long-tried integrity—on solid wisdom and sad-coloured experience—on endowments of that grave and weighty order which gave the idea of permanence, and comes under the general definition of respectability. These primitive statesmen, therefore—Bradstreet, Endicott, Dudley, Bellingham, and their compeers—who were elevated to power by the early choice of the people, seem to have been not often brilliant, but distinguished by a ponderous sobriety, rather than activity of intellect. They had fortitude and self-reliance, and in time of difficulty or peril stood up for the welfare of the state like a line of cliffs against a tempestuous tide. The traits of character here indicated were well represented in the square cast of countenance and large physical development of the new colonial magistrates. So far as a demeanour of natural authority was concerned, the mother country need not have been ashamed to see these foremost men of an actual democracy adopted into the House of Peers, or make the Privy Council of the Sovereign.

Next in order to the magistrates came the young and eminently distinguished divine, from whose lips the religious discourse of the anniversary was expected. His was the profession at that era in which intellectual ability displayed itself far more than in political life; for—leaving a higher motive out of the question it offered inducements powerful enough in the almost worshipping respect of the community, to win the most aspiring ambition into its service. Even political power—as in the case of Increase Mather—was within the grasp of a successful priest.

It was the observation of those who beheld him now, that never, since Mr. Dimmesdale first set his foot on the New England shore, had he exhibited such energy as was seen in the gait and air with which he kept his pace in the procession. There was no feebleness of step as at other times; his frame was not bent, nor did his hand rest ominously upon his heart. Yet, if the clergyman were rightly viewed, his strength seemed not of the body. It might be spiritual and imparted to him by angelical ministrations. It might be the exhilaration of that potent cordial which is distilled only in the furnace-glow of earnest and long-continued thought. Or perchance his sensitive temperament was invigorated by the loud and piercing music that swelled heaven-ward, and uplifted him on its ascending wave. Nevertheless, so abstracted was his look, it might be questioned whether Mr. Dimmesdale ever heard the music. There was his body, moving onward, and with an unaccustomed force. But where was his mind? Far and deep in its own region, busying itself, with preternatural activity, to marshal a procession of stately thoughts that were soon to issue thence; and so he saw nothing, heard nothing, knew nothing of what was around him; but the spiritual element took up the feeble frame and carried it along, unconscious of the burden, and converting it to spirit like itself. Men of uncommon intellect, who have grown morbid, possess this occasional power of mighty effort, into which they throw the life of many days and then are lifeless for as many more.

Hester Prynne, gazing steadfastly at the clergyman, felt a dreary influence come over her, but wherefore or whence she knew not, unless that he seemed so remote from her own sphere, and utterly beyond her reach. One glance of recognition she had imagined must needs pass between them. She thought of the dim forest, with its little dell of solitude, and love, and anguish, and the mossy tree-trunk, where, sitting hand-in-hand, they had mingled their sad and passionate talk with the melancholy murmur of the brook. How deeply had they known each other then! And was this the man? She hardly knew him now! He, moving proudly past, enveloped as it were, in the rich music, with the procession of majestic and venerable fathers; he, so unattainable in his worldly position, and still more so in that far vista of his unsympathizing thoughts, through which she now beheld him! Her spirit sank with the idea that all must have been a delusion, and that, vividly as she had dreamed it, there could be no real bond betwixt the clergyman and herself. And thus much of woman was there in Hester, that she could scarcely forgive him—least of all now, when the heavy footstep of their approaching Fate might be heard, nearer, nearer, nearer!—for being able so completely to withdraw himself from their mutual world—while she groped darkly, and stretched forth her cold hands, and found him not.

Pearl either saw and responded to her mother's feelings, or herself felt the remoteness and intangibility that had fallen around the minister. While the procession passed, the child was uneasy, fluttering up and down, like a bird on the point of taking flight. When the whole had gone by, she looked up into Hester's face—

"Mother," said she, "was that the same minister that kissed me by the brook?"

"Hold thy peace, dear little Pearl!" whispered her mother. "We must not always talk in the marketplace of what happens to us in the forest."

"I could not be sure that it was he—so strange he looked," continued the child. "Else

I would have run to him, and bid him kiss me now, before all the people, even as he did yonder among the dark old trees. What would the minister have said, mother? Would he have clapped his hand over his heart, and scowled on me, and bid me begone?"

"What should he say, Pearl," answered Hester, "save that it was no time to kiss, and that kisses are not to be given in the market-place? Well for thee, foolish child, that thou didst not speak to him!"

Another shade of the same sentiment, in reference to Mr. Dimmesdale, was expressed by a person whose eccentricities—insanity, as we should term it—led her to do what few of the townspeople would have ventured on—to begin a conversation with the wearer of the scarlet letter in public. It was Mistress Hibbins, who, arrayed in great magnificence, with a triple ruff, a broidered stomacher, a gown of rich velvet, and a gold-headed cane, had come forth to see the procession. As this ancient lady had the renown (which subsequently cost her no less a price than her life) of being a principal actor in all the works of necromancy that were continually going forward, the crowd gave way before her, and seemed to fear the touch of her garment, as if it carried the plague among its gorgeous folds. Seen in conjunction with Hester Prynne—kindly as so many now felt towards the latter—the dread inspired by Mistress Hibbins had doubled, and caused a general movement from that part of the market-place in which the two women stood.

"Now, what mortal imagination could conceive it?" whispered the old lady confidentially to Hester. "Yonder divine man! That saint on earth, as the people uphold him to be, and as—I must needs say—he really looks! Who, now, that saw him pass in the procession, would think how little while it is since he went forth out of his study—chewing a Hebrew text of Scripture in his mouth, I warrant—to take an airing in the forest! Aha! we know what that means, Hester Prynne! But truly, forsooth, I find it hard to believe him the same man. Many a church member saw I, walking behind the music, that has danced in the same measure with me, when Somebody was fiddler, and, it might be, an Indian powwow or a Lapland wizard changing hands with us! That is but a trifle, when a woman knows the world. But this minister. Couldst thou surely tell, Hester, whether he was the same man that encountered thee on the forest path?"

"Madam, I know not of what you speak," answered Hester Prynne, feeling Mistress Hibbins to be of infirm mind; yet strangely startled and awe-stricken by the confidence with which she affirmed a personal connection between so many persons (herself among them) and the Evil One. "It is not for me to talk lightly of a learned and pious minister of the Word, like the Reverend Mr. Dimmesdale."

"Fie, woman—fie!" cried the old lady, shaking her finger at Hester. "Dost thou think I have been to the forest so many times, and have yet no skill to judge who else has been there? Yea, though no leaf of the wild garlands which they wore while they danced be left in their hair! I know thee, Hester, for I behold the token. We may all see it in the sunshine! and it glows like a red flame in the dark. Thou wearest it openly, so there need be no question about that. But this minister! Let me tell thee in thine ear! When the Black Man sees one of his own servants, signed and sealed, so shy of owning to the bond as is the Reverend Mr. Dimmesdale, he hath a way of ordering matters so that the mark shall be disclosed, in open daylight, to the eyes of all the world! What is that the minister seeks to hide, with his hand always over his heart? Ha, Hester Prynne?"

"What is it, good Mistress Hibbins?" eagerly asked little Pearl. "Hast thou seen it?"

"No matter, darling!" responded Mistress Hibbins, making Pearl a profound reverence. "Thou thyself wilt see it, one time or another. They say, child, thou art of the lineage of the Prince of Air! Wilt thou ride with me some fine night to see thy father?

Then thou shalt know wherefore the minister keeps his hand over his heart!"

Laughing so shrilly that all the market-place could hear her, the weird old gentlewoman took her departure.

By this time the preliminary prayer had been offered in the meeting-house, and the accents of the Reverend Mr. Dimmesdale were heard commencing his discourse. An irresistible feeling kept Hester near the spot. As the sacred edifice was too much thronged to admit another auditor, she took up her position close beside the scaffold of the pillory. It was in sufficient proximity to bring the whole sermon to her ears, in the shape of an indistinct but varied murmur and flow of the minister's very peculiar voice.

This vocal organ was in itself a rich endowment, insomuch that a listener, comprehending nothing of the language in which the preacher spoke, might still have been swayed to and fro by the mere tone and cadence. Like all other music, it breathed passion and pathos, and emotions high or tender, in a tongue native to the human heart, wherever educated. Muffled as the sound was by its passage through the church walls, Hester Prynne listened with such intenseness, and sympathized so intimately, that the sermon had throughout a meaning for her, entirely apart from its indistinguishable words. These, perhaps, if more distinctly heard, might have been only a grosser medium, and have clogged the spiritual sense. Now she caught the low undertone, as of the wind sinking down to repose itself; then ascended with it, as it rose through progressive gradations of sweetness and power, until its volume seemed to envelop her with an atmosphere of awe and solemn grandeur. And yet, majestic as the voice sometimes became, there was for ever in it an essential character of plaintiveness. A loud or low expression of anguish—the whisper, or the shriek, as it might be conceived, of suffering humanity, that touched a sensibility in every bosom! At times this deep strain of pathos was all that could be heard, and scarcely heard sighing amid a desolate silence. But even when the minister's voice grew high and commanding—when it gushed irrepressibly upward—when it assumed its utmost breadth and power, so overfilling the church as to burst its way through the solid walls, and diffuse itself in the open air—still, if the auditor listened intently, and for the purpose, he could detect the same cry of pain. What was it? The complaint of a human heart, sorrow-laden, perchance guilty, telling its secret, whether of guilt or sorrow, to the great heart of mankind; beseeching its sympathy or forgiveness,—at every moment,—in each accent,—and never in vain! It was this profound and continual undertone that gave the clergyman his most appropriate power.

During all this time, Hester stood, statue-like, at the foot of the scaffold. If the minister's voice had not kept her there, there would, nevertheless, have been an inevitable magnetism in that spot, whence she dated the first hour of her life of ignominy. There was a sense within her—too ill-defined to be made a thought, but weighing heavily on her mind—that her whole orb of life, both before and after, was connected with this spot, as with the one point that gave it unity.

Little Pearl, meanwhile, had quitted her mother's side, and was playing at her own will about the market-place. She made the sombre crowd cheerful by her erratic and glistening ray, even as a bird of bright plumage illuminates a whole tree of dusky foliage by darting to and fro, half seen and half concealed amid the twilight of the clustering leaves. She had an undulating, but oftentimes a sharp and irregular movement. It indicated the restless vivacity of her spirit, which to-day was doubly indefatigable in its tip-toe dance, because it was played upon and vibrated with her mother's disquietude. Whenever Pearl saw anything to excite her ever active and wandering curiosity, she flew thitherward, and, as we might say, seized upon that man or thing as her own property, so far as she desired it, but without yielding the minutest degree of control over her motions in requital. The Puritans looked on, and, if they smiled, were none the less inclined to pronounce the child a demon offspring, from the indescribable charm of beauty and eccentricity that shone through her little figure, and sparkled with its activity. She ran and looked the wild Indian in the face, and he grew conscious of a nature wilder than his own. Thence, with native audacity, but still with a reserve as characteristic, she flew into the midst of a group of mariners, the swarthy-cheeked wild men of the ocean, as the Indians were of the land; and they gazed wonderingly and admiringly at Pearl, as if a flake of the sea-foam had taken the shape of a little maid, and were gifted with a soul of the sea-fire, that flashes beneath the prow in the night-time.

One of these seafaring men the shipmaster, indeed, who had spoken to Hester Prynne was so smitten with Pearl's aspect, that he attempted to lay hands upon her, with purpose to snatch a kiss. Finding it as impossible to touch her as to catch a humming-bird in the air, he took from his hat the gold chain that was twisted about it, and threw it to the child. Pearl immediately twined it around her neck and waist with such happy skill, that, once seen there, it became a part of her, and it was difficult to imagine her without it.

"Thy mother is yonder woman with the scarlet letter," said the seaman, "Wilt thou carry her a message from me?"

"If the message pleases me, I will," answered Pearl.

"Then tell her," rejoined he, "that I spake again with the black-a-visaged, hump shouldered old doctor, and he engages to bring his friend, the gentleman she wots of, aboard with him. So let thy mother take no thought, save for herself and thee. Wilt thou tell her this, thou witch-baby?"

"Mistress Hibbins says my father is the Prince of the Air!" cried Pearl, with a naughty smile. "If thou callest me that ill-name, I shall tell him of thee, and he will chase thy ship with a tempest!"

Pursuing a zigzag course across the marketplace, the child returned to her mother, and communicated what the mariner had said. Hester's strong, calm steadfastly-enduring spirit almost sank, at last, on beholding this dark and grim countenance of an inevitable doom, which at the moment when a passage seemed to open for the minister and herself out of their labyrinth of misery—showed itself with an unrelenting smile, right in the midst of their path.

With her mind harassed by the terrible perplexity in which the shipmaster's intelligence involved her, she was also subjected to another trial. There were many people present from the country round about, who had often heard of the scarlet letter, and to whom it had been made terrific by a hundred false or exaggerated rumours, but who had never beheld it with their own bodily eyes. These, after exhausting other modes of amusement, now thronged about Hester Prynne with rude and boorish intrusiveness. Unscrupulous as it was, however, it could not bring them nearer than a circuit of several yards. At that distance they accordingly stood, fixed there by the centrifugal force of the repugnance which the mystic symbol inspired. The whole gang of sailors, likewise, observing the press of spectators, and learning the purport of the scarlet letter, came and thrust their sunburnt and desperado-looking faces into the ring. Even the Indians were affected by a sort of cold shadow of the white man's curiosity and, gliding through the crowd, fastened their snake-like black eyes on Hester's bosom, conceiving, perhaps, that the wearer of this brilliantly embroidered badge must needs be a personage of high dignity among her people. Lastly, the inhabitants of the town (their own interest in this worn-out subject languidly reviving itself, by sympathy with what they saw others feel) lounged idly to the same quarter, and tormented Hester Prynne, perhaps more than all the rest, with their cool, well-acquainted gaze at her familiar shame. Hester saw and recognized the selfsame faces of that group of matrons, who had awaited her forthcoming from the prison-door seven years ago; all save one, the youngest and only compassionate among them, whose burial-robe she had since made. At the final hour, when she was so soon to fling aside the burning letter, it had strangely become the centre of more remark and excitement, and was thus made to sear her breast more painfully, than at any time since the first day she put it on.

While Hester stood in that magic circle of ignominy, where the cunning cruelty of her sentence seemed to have fixed her for ever, the admirable preacher was looking down from the sacred pulpit upon an audience whose very inmost spirits had yielded to his control. The sainted minister in the church! The woman of the scarlet letter in the marketplace! What imagination would have been irreverent enough to surmise that the same scorching stigma was on them both!

XXIII. The Revelation of the Scarlet Letter

The eloquent voice, on which the souls of the listening audience had been borne aloft as on the swelling waves of the sea, at length came to a pause. There was a momentary silence, profound as what should follow the utterance of oracles. Then ensued a murmur and half-hushed tumult, as if the auditors, released from the high spell that had transported them into the region of another's mind, were returning into themselves, with all their awe and wonder still heavy on them. In a moment more the crowd began to gush forth from the doors of the church. Now that there was an end, they needed more breath, more fit to support the gross and earthly life into which they relapsed, than that atmosphere which the preacher had converted into words of flame, and had burdened with the rich fragrance of his thought.

In the open air their rapture broke into speech. The street and the market-place absolutely babbled, from side to side, with applauses of the minister. His hearers could not rest until they had told one another of what each knew better than he could tell or hear.

According to their united testimony, never had man spoken in so wise, so high, and so holy a spirit, as he that spake this day; nor had inspiration ever breathed through mortal lips more evidently than it did through his. Its influence could be seen, as it were, descending upon him, and possessing him, and continually lifting him out of the written discourse that lay before him, and filling him with ideas that must have been as marvellous to himself as to his audience. His subject, it appeared, had been the relation between the Deity and the communities of mankind, with a special reference to the New England which they were here planting in the wilderness. And, as he drew towards the close, a spirit as of prophecy had come upon him, constraining him to its purpose as mightily as the old prophets of Israel were constrained, only with this difference, that, whereas the Jewish seers had denounced judgments and ruin on their country, it was his mission to foretell a high and glorious destiny for the newly gathered people of the Lord. But, throughout it all, and through the whole discourse, there had been a certain deep, sad undertone of pathos, which could not be interpreted otherwise than as the natural regret of one soon to pass away. Yes; their minister whom they so loved—and who so loved them all, that he could not depart heavenward without a sigh—had the foreboding of untimely death upon him, and would soon leave them in their tears. This idea of his transitory stay on earth gave the last emphasis to the effect which the preacher had produced; it was if an angel, in his passage to the skies, had shaken his bright wings over the people for an instant—at once a shadow and a splendour—and had shed down a shower of golden truths upon them.

Thus, there had come to the Reverend Mr. Dimmesdale—as to most men, in their various spheres, though seldom recognised until they see it far behind them—an epoch of life more brilliant and full of triumph than any previous one, or than any which could hereafter be. He stood, at this moment, on the very proudest eminence of superiority, to which the gifts or intellect, rich lore, prevailing eloquence, and a reputation of whitest sanctity, could exalt a clergyman in New England's earliest days, when the professional character was of itself a lofty pedestal. Such was the position which the minister occupied, as he bowed his head forward on the cushions of the pulpit at the close of his Election Sermon. Meanwhile Hester Prynne was standing beside the scaffold of the pillory, with the scarlet letter still burning on her breast!

Now was heard again the clamour of the music, and the measured tramp of the military escort issuing from the church door. The procession was to be marshalled thence to the town hall, where a solemn banquet would complete the ceremonies of the day.

Once more, therefore, the train of venerable and majestic fathers were seen moving through a broad pathway of the people, who drew back reverently, on either side, as the Governor and magistrates, the old and wise men, the holy ministers, and all that were eminent and renowned, advanced into the midst of them. When they were fairly in the marketplace, their presence was greeted by a shout. This—though doubtless it might acquire additional force and volume from the child-like loyalty which the age awarded to its rulers—was felt to be an irrepressible outburst of enthusiasm kindled in the auditors by that high strain of eloquence which was yet reverberating in their ears. Each felt the impulse in himself, and in the same breath, caught it from his neighbour. Within the church, it had hardly been kept down; beneath the sky it pealed upward to the zenith. There were human beings enough, and enough of highly wrought and symphonious feeling to produce that more impressive sound than the organ tones of the blast, or the thunder, or the roar of the sea; even that mighty swell of many voices, blended into one great voice by the universal impulse which makes likewise one vast heart out of the many. Never, from the soil of New England had gone up such a shout! Never, on New England soil had stood the man so honoured by his mortal brethren as the preacher!

How fared it with him, then? Were there not the brilliant particles of a halo in the air about his head? So etherealised by spirit as he was, and so apotheosised by worshipping admirers, did his footsteps, in the procession, really tread upon the dust of earth?

As the ranks of military men and civil fathers moved onward, all eyes were turned towards the point where the minister was seen to approach among them. The shout died into a murmur, as one portion of the crowd after another obtained a glimpse of him. How feeble and pale he looked, amid all his triumph! The energy—or say, rather, the inspiration which had held him up, until he should have delivered the sacred message that had brought its own strength along with it from heaven—was withdrawn, now that it had so faithfully performed its office. The glow, which they had just before beheld burning on his cheek, was extinguished, like a flame that sinks down hopelessly among the late decaying embers. It seemed hardly the face of a man alive, with such a death-like hue: it was hardly a man with life in him, that tottered on his path so nervously, yet tottered, and did not fall!

One of his clerical brethren—it was the venerable John Wilson—observing the state in which Mr. Dimmesdale was left by the retiring wave of intellect and sensibility, stepped forward hastily to offer his support. The minister tremulously, but decidedly, repelled the old man's arm. He still walked onward, if that movement could be so described, which rather resembled the wavering effort of an infant, with its mother's arms in view, outstretched to tempt him forward. And now, almost imperceptible as were the latter steps of his progress, he had come opposite the well-remembered and weather-darkened scaffold, where, long since, with all that dreary lapse of time between, Hester Prynne had encountered the world's ignominious stare. There stood Hester, holding little Pearl by the hand! And there was the scarlet letter on her breast! The minister here made a pause; although the music still played the stately and rejoicing march to which the procession moved. It summoned him onward—inward to the festival!—but here he made a pause.

Bellingham, for the last few moments, had kept an anxious eye upon him. He now left his own place in the procession, and advanced to give assistance judging, from Mr. Dimmesdale's aspect that he must otherwise inevitably fall. But there was something in the latter's expression that warned back the magistrate, although a man not readily obeying the vague intimations that pass from one spirit to another. The crowd, meanwhile, looked on with awe and wonder. This earthly faintness, was, in their view, only another phase of the minister's celestial strength; nor would it have seemed a miracle too high to be wrought for one so holy, had he ascended before their eyes, waxing dimmer and brighter, and fading at last into the light of heaven!

He turned towards the scaffold, and stretched forth his arms.

"Hester," said he, "come hither! Come, my little Pearl!"

It was a ghastly look with which he regarded them; but there was something at once tender and strangely triumphant in it. The child, with the bird-like motion, which was one of her characteristics, flew to him, and clasped her arms about his knees. Hester Prynne—slowly, as if impelled by inevitable fate, and against her strongest will—likewise drew near, but paused before she reached him. At this instant old Roger Chillingworth thrust himself through the crowd—or, perhaps, so dark, disturbed, and evil was his look, he rose up out of some nether region—to snatch back his victim from what he sought to do! Be that as it might, the old man rushed forward, and caught the minister by the arm.

"Madman, hold! what is your purpose?" whispered he. "Wave back that woman! Cast off this child All shall be well! Do not blacken your fame, and perish in dishonour! I can yet save you! Would you bring infamy on your sacred profession?"

"Ha, tempter! Methinks thou art too late!" answered the minister, encountering his eye, fearfully, but firmly. "Thy power is not what it was! With God's help, I shall escape thee now!"

He again extended his hand to the woman of the scarlet letter.

"Hester Prynne," cried he, with a piercing earnestness, "in the name of Him, so terrible and so merciful, who gives me grace, at this last moment, to do what—for my own heavy sin and miserable agony—I withheld myself from doing seven years ago, come hither now, and twine thy strength about me! Thy strength, Hester; but let it be guided by the will which God hath granted me! This wretched and wronged old man is opposing it with all his might!—with all his own might, and the fiend's! Come, Hester—come! Support me up yonder scaffold."

The crowd was in a tumult. The men of rank and dignity, who stood more immediately around the clergyman, were so taken by surprise, and so perplexed as to the purport of what they saw—unable to receive the explanation which most readily presented itself, or to imagine any other—that they remained silent and inactive spectators of the judgement which Providence seemed about to work. They beheld the minister, leaning on Hester's shoulder, and supported by her arm around him, approach the scaffold, and ascend its steps; while still the little hand of the sin-born child was clasped in his. Old Roger Chillingworth followed, as one intimately connected with the drama of guilt and sorrow in which they had all been actors, and well entitled, therefore to be present at its closing scene.

"Hadst thou sought the whole earth over," said he looking darkly at the clergyman, "there was no one place so secret—no high place nor lowly place, where thou couldst have escaped me—save on this very scaffold!"

"Thanks be to Him who hath led me hither!" answered the minister.

Yet he trembled, and turned to Hester, with an expression of doubt and anxiety in his eyes, not the less evidently betrayed, that there was a feeble smile upon his lips.

"Is not this better," murmured he, "than what we dreamed of in the forest?"

"I know not! I know not!" she hurriedly replied "Better? Yea; so we may both die, and little Pearl die with us!"

"For thee and Pearl, be it as God shall order," said the minister; "and God is merciful! Let me now do the will which He hath made plain before my sight. For, Hester, I am a dying man. So let me make haste to take my shame upon me!"

Partly supported by Hester Prynne, and holding one hand of little Pearl's, the Reverend Mr. Dimmesdale turned to the dignified and venerable rulers; to the holy ministers, who were his brethren; to the people, whose great heart was thoroughly appalled yet overflowing with tearful sympathy, as knowing that some deep life-matter—which, if full of sin, was full of anguish and repentance likewise—was now to be laid open to them. The sun, but little past its meridian, shone down upon the clergyman, and gave a distinctness to his figure, as he stood out from all the earth, to put in his plea of guilty at the bar of Eternal Justice.

"People of New England!" cried he, with a voice that rose over them, high, solemn, and majestic—yet had always a tremor through it, and sometimes a shriek, struggling up out of a fathomless depth of remorse and woe—"ye, that have loved me!—ye, that have deemed me holy!—behold me here, the one sinner of the world! At last—at last!—I stand upon the spot where, seven years since, I should have stood, here, with this woman, whose arm, more than the little strength wherewith I have crept hitherward, sustains me at this dreadful moment, from grovelling down upon my face! Lo, the scarlet letter which Hester wears! Ye have all shuddered at it! Wherever her walk hath been—wherever, so miserably burdened, she may have hoped to find repose—it hath cast a lurid gleam of awe and horrible repugnance round about her. But there stood one in the midst of you, at whose brand of sin and infamy ye have not shuddered!"

It seemed, at this point, as if the minister must leave the remainder of his secret undisclosed. But he fought back the bodily weakness—and, still more, the faintness of heart—that was striving for the mastery with him. He threw off all assistance, and stepped passionately forward a pace before the woman and the children.

"It was on him!" he continued, with a kind of fierceness; so determined was he to speak out tile whole. "God's eye beheld it! The angels were for ever pointing at it! (The Devil knew it well, and fretted it continually with the touch of his burning finger!) But he hid it cunningly from men, and walked among you with the mien of a spirit, mournful, because so pure in a sinful world!—and sad, because he missed his heavenly kindred! Now, at the death-hour, he stands up before you! He bids you look again at Hester's scarlet letter! He tells you, that, with all its mysterious horror, it is but the shadow of what he bears on his own breast, and that even this, his own red stigma, is no more than the type of what has seared his inmost heart! Stand any here that question God's judgment on a sinner! Behold! Behold, a dreadful witness of it!"

With a convulsive motion, he tore away the ministerial band from before his breast. It was revealed! But it were irreverent to describe that revelation. For an instant, the gaze of the horror-stricken multitude was concentrated on the ghastly miracle; while the minister stood, with a flush of triumph in his face, as one who, in the crisis of acutest pain, had won a victory. Then, down he sank upon the scaffold! Hester partly raised him, and supported his head against her bosom. Old Roger Chillingworth knelt down beside him, with a blank, dull countenance, out of which the life seemed to have departed,

"Thou hast escaped me!" he repeated more than once. "Thou hast escaped me!"

"May God forgive thee!" said the minister. "Thou, too, hast deeply sinned!"

He withdrew his dying eyes from the old man, and fixed them on the woman and the child.

"My little Pearl," said he, feebly and there was a sweet and gentle smile over his face, as of a spirit sinking into deep repose; nay, now that the burden was removed, it seemed almost as if he would be sportive with the child—"dear little Pearl, wilt thou kiss me now? Thou wouldst not, yonder, in the forest! But now thou wilt?"

Pearl kissed his lips. A spell was broken. The great scene of grief, in which the wild infant bore a part had developed all her sympathies; and as her tears fell upon her father's cheek, they were the pledge that she would grow up amid human joy and sorrow, nor forever do battle with the world, but be a woman in it. Towards her mother, too, Pearl's errand as a messenger of anguish was fulfilled.

"Hester," said the clergyman, "farewell!"

"Shall we not meet again?" whispered she, bending her face down close to his. "Shall we not spend our immortal life together? Surely, surely, we have ransomed one another, with all this woe! Thou lookest far into eternity, with those bright dying eyes! Then tell me what thou seest!"

"Hush, Hester—hush!" said he, with tremulous solemnity. "The law we broke I—the sin here awfully revealed!—let these alone be in thy thoughts! I fear! I fear! It may be, that, when we forgot our God—when we violated our reverence each for the other's soul—it was thenceforth vain to hope that we could meet hereafter, in an everlasting and pure reunion. God knows; and He is merciful! He hath proved his mercy, most of all, in my afflictions. By giving me this burning torture to bear upon my breast! By sending yonder dark and terrible old man, to keep the torture always at red-heat! By bringing me hither, to die this death of triumphant ignominy before the people! Had either of these agonies been wanting, I had been lost for ever! Praised be His name! His will be done! Farewell!"

That final word came forth with the minister's expiring breath. The multitude, silent till then, broke out in a strange, deep voice of awe and wonder, which could not as yet find utterance, save in this murmur that rolled so heavily after the departed spirit.

XXIV. Conclusion

After many days, when time sufficed for the people to arrange their thoughts in reference to the foregoing scene, there was more than one account of what had been witnessed on the scaffold.

Most of the spectators testified to having seen, on the breast of the unhappy minister, a SCARLET LETTER—the very semblance of that worn by Hester Prynne—imprinted in the flesh. As regarded its origin there were various explanations, all of which must necessarily have been conjectural. Some affirmed that the Reverend Mr. Dimmesdale, on the very day when Hester Prynne first wore her ignominious badge, had begun a course of penance—which he afterwards, in so many futile methods, followed out—by inflicting a hideous torture on himself. Others contended that the stigma had not been produced until a long time subsequent, when old Roger Chillingworth, being a potent necromancer, had caused it to appear, through the agency of magic and poisonous drugs. Others, again and those best able to appreciate the minister's peculiar sensibility, and the wonderful operation of his spirit upon the body—whispered their belief, that the awful symbol was the effect of the ever-active tooth of remorse, gnawing from the inmost heart outwardly, and at last manifesting Heaven's dreadful judgment by the visible presence of the letter. The reader may choose among these theories. We have thrown all the light we could acquire upon the portent, and would gladly, now that it has done its office, erase its deep print out of our own brain, where long meditation has fixed it in very undesirable distinctness.

It is singular, nevertheless, that certain persons, who were spectators of the whole scene, and professed never once to have removed their eyes from the Reverend Mr. Dimmesdale, denied that there was any mark whatever on his breast, more than on a new-born infant's. Neither, by their report, had his dying words acknowledged, nor even remotely implied, any—the slightest—connection on his part, with the guilt for which Hester Prynne had so long worn the scarlet letter. According to these highly-respectable witnesses, the minister, conscious that he was dying—conscious, also, that the reverence of the multitude placed him already among saints and angels—had desired, by yielding up his breath in the arms of that fallen woman, to express to the world how utterly nugatory is the choicest of man's own righteousness. After exhausting life in his efforts for mankind's spiritual good, he had made the manner of his death a parable, in order to impress on his admirers the mighty and mournful lesson, that, in the view of Infinite Purity, we are sinners all alike. It was to teach them, that the holiest amongst us has but attained so far above his fellows as to discern more clearly the Mercy which looks down, and repudiate more utterly the phantom of human merit, which would look aspiringly upward. Without disputing a truth so momentous, we must be allowed to consider this version of Mr. Dimmesdale's story as only an instance of that stubborn fidelity with which a man's friends—and especially a clergyman's—will sometimes uphold his character, when proofs, clear as the mid-day sunshine on the scarlet letter, establish him a false and sin-stained creature of the dust.

The authority which we have chiefly followed—a manuscript of old date, drawn up from the verbal testimony of individuals, some of whom had known Hester Prynne, while others had heard the tale from contemporary witnesses fully confirms the view taken in the foregoing pages. Among many morals which press upon us from the poor minister's miserable experience, we put only this into a sentence:—"Be true! Be true! Be true!

Show freely to the world, if not your worst, yet some trait whereby the worst may be inferred!"

Nothing was more remarkable than the change which took place, almost immediately after Mr. Dimmesdale's death, in the appearance and demeanour of the old man known as Roger Chillingworth. All his strength and energy—all his vital and intellectual force—seemed at once to desert him, insomuch that he positively withered up, shrivelled away and almost vanished from mortal sight, like an uprooted weed that lies wilting in the sun. This unhappy man had made the very principle of his life to consist in the pursuit and systematic exercise revenge; and when, by its completest triumph consummation that evil principle was left with no further material to support it—when, in short, there was no more Devil's work on earth for him to do, it only remained for the unhumanised mortal to betake himself whither his master would find him tasks enough, and pay him his wages duly. But, to all these shadowy beings, so long our near acquaintances—as well Roger Chillingworth as his companions we would fain be merciful. It is a curious subject of observation and inquiry, whether hatred and love be not the same thing at bottom. Each, in its utmost development, supposes a high degree of intimacy and heart-knowledge; each renders one individual dependent for the food of his affections and spiritual fife upon another: each leaves the passionate lover, or the no less passionate hater, forlorn and desolate by the withdrawal of his subject. Philosophically considered, therefore, the two passions seem essentially the same, except that one happens to be seen in a celestial radiance, and the other in a dusky and lurid glow. In the spiritual world, the old physician and the minister—mutual victims as they have been—may, unawares, have found their earthly stock of hatred and antipathy transmuted into golden love.

Leaving this discussion apart, we have a matter of business to communicate to the reader. At old Roger Chillingworth's decease, (which took place within the year), and by his last will and testament, of which Governor Bellingham and the Reverend Mr. Wilson were executors, he bequeathed a very considerable amount of property, both here and in England to little Pearl, the daughter of Hester Prynne.

So Pearl—the elf child—the demon offspring, as some people up to that epoch persisted in considering her—became the richest heiress of her day in the New World. Not improbably this circumstance wrought a very material change in the public estimation; and had the mother and child remained here, little Pearl at a marriageable period of life might have mingled her wild blood with the lineage of the devoutest Puritan among them all. But, in no long time after the physician's death, the wearer of the scarlet letter disappeared, and Pearl along with her. For many years, though a vague report would now and then find its way across the sea—like a shapeless piece of driftwood tossed ashore with the initials of a name upon it—yet no tidings of them unquestionably authentic were received. The story of the scarlet letter grew into a legend. Its spell, however, was still potent, and kept the scaffold awful where the poor minister had died, and likewise the cottage by the sea-shore where Hester Prynne had dwelt. Near this latter spot, one afternoon some children were at play, when they beheld a tall woman in a gray robe approach the cottage-door. In all those years it had never once been opened; but either she unlocked it or the decaying wood and iron yielded to her hand, or she glided shadow-like through these impediments—and, at all events, went in.

On the threshold she paused—turned partly round—for perchance the idea of entering alone and all so changed, the home of so intense a former life, was more dreary and desolate than even she could bear. But her hesitation was only for an instant, though long enough to display a scarlet letter on her breast.

And Hester Prynne had returned, and taken up her long-forsaken shame! But where was little Pearl? If still alive she must now have been in the flush and bloom of early womanhood. None knew—nor ever learned with the fulness of perfect certainty—whether the elf-child had gone thus untimely to a maiden grave; or whether her wild, rich nature had been softened and subdued and made capable of a woman's gentle happiness. But through the remainder of Hester's life there were indications that the recluse of the scarlet letter was the object of love and interest with some inhabitant of another land. Letters came, with armorial seals upon them, though of bearings unknown to English heraldry. In the cottage there were articles of comfort and luxury such as Hester never cared to use, but which only wealth could have purchased and affection have imagined for her. There were trifles too, little ornaments, beautiful tokens of a continual remembrance, that must have been wrought by delicate fingers at the impulse of a fond heart. And once Hester was seen embroidering a baby-garment with such a lavish richness of golden fancy as would have raised a public tumult had any infant thus apparelled, been shown to our sober-hued community.

In fine, the gossips of that day believed—and Mr. Surveyor Pue, who made investigations a century later, believed—and one of his recent successors in office, moreover, faithfully believes—that Pearl was not only alive, but married, and happy, and mindful of her mother; and that she would most joyfully have entertained that sad and lonely mother at her fireside.

But there was a more real life for Hester Prynne, here, in New England, that in that unknown region where Pearl had found a home. Here had been her sin; here, her sorrow; and here was yet to be her penitence. She had returned, therefore, and resumed of her own free will, for not the sternest magistrate of that iron period would have imposed it—resumed the symbol of which we have related so dark a tale. Never afterwards did it quit her bosom. But, in the lapse of the toilsome, thoughtful, and self-devoted years that made up Hester's life, the scarlet letter ceased to be a stigma which attracted the world's scorn and bitterness, and became a type of something to be sorrowed over, and looked upon with awe, yet with reverence too. And, as Hester Prynne had no selfish ends, nor lived in any measure for her own profit and enjoyment, people brought all their sorrows and perplexities, and besought her counsel, as one who had herself gone through a mighty trouble. Women, more especially—in the continually recurring trials of wounded, wasted, wronged, misplaced, or erring and sinful passion—or with the dreary burden of a heart unyielded, because unvalued and unsought came to Hester's cottage, demanding why they were so wretched, and what the remedy! Hester comforted and counselled them, as best she might. She assured them, too, of her firm belief that, at some brighter period, when the world should have grown ripe for it, in Heaven's own time, a new truth would be revealed, in order to establish the whole relation between man and woman on a surer ground of mutual happiness. Earlier in life, Hester had vainly imagined that she herself might be the destined prophetess, but had long since recognised the impossibility that any mission of divine and mysterious truth should be confided to a woman stained with sin, bowed down with shame, or even burdened with a life-long sorrow. The angel and apostle of the coming revelation must be a woman, indeed, but lofty, pure, and beautiful, and wise; moreover, not through dusky grief, but the ethereal medium of joy; and showing how sacred love should make us happy, by the truest test of a life successful to such an end.

So said Hester Prynne, and glanced her sad eyes downward at the scarlet letter. And, after many, many years, a new grave was delved, near an old and sunken one, in that burial-ground beside which King's Chapel has since been built. It was near that old and sunken grave, yet with a space between, as if the dust of the two sleepers had no right to mingle. Yet one tomb-stone served for both. All around, there were monuments carved with armorial bearings; and on this simple slab of slate—as the curious investigator may still discern, and perplex himself with the purport—there appeared the semblance of an engraved escutcheon. It bore a device, a herald's wording of which may serve for a motto and brief description of our now concluded legend; so sombre is it, and relieved only by one ever-glowing point of light gloomier than the shadow:—

"ON A FIELD, SABLE, THE LETTER A, GULES"

THE END

CPSIA information can be obtained
at www.ICGtesting.com
Printed in the USA
BVHW032220160821
614594BV00006B/116

9 781420 974508